POLICE, CRIMINAL JUSTICE, AND THE COMMUNITY

POLICE, CRIMINAL JUSTICE, AND THE COMMUNITY

ALAN E. BENT
RALPH A. ROSSUM

HARPER & ROW, PUBLISHERS
New York   Hagerstown   San Francisco   London

Sponsoring Editor: Ronald K. Taylor
Project Editor: Richard T. Viggiano
Designer: Andrea Clark
Production Supervisor: Will C. Jomarrón

Photo Researcher: Myra Schachne
Compositor: American Book–Stratford Press, Inc.
Printer and Binder: Halliday Lithograph Corporation
Art Studio: Eric G. Hieber Associates Inc.

POLICE, CRIMINAL JUSTICE, AND THE COMMUNITY

Library of Congress Cataloging in Publication Data

Bent, Alan Edward.
    Police, criminal justice, and the community.
    Includes bibliographical references and index.
    1. Public relations—Police. 2. Police—United States. 3. Criminal justice, Administration of—United States. I. Rossum, Ralph Arthur, 1946-joint author. II. Title.
HV7936.P8B44   363.2'0973   75-26715
ISBN 0-06-040637-2

Contents

3.   **The Police and Enforcement of the Law**   66

4.   **The Courts and the Protection of Individual Rights**   96

5.   **Corrections: Success Through Failure**   143

Preface

The need to strengthen the relationship between police and community is critical. However, merely acknowledging the need for mutual cooperation in no way ensures that this need will be met. *Police, Criminal Justice, and the Community* has been written to help meet this need. In an effort to encourage an effective working relationship between police and community, this book goes beyond most literature written on the subject and focuses on the relations of the community not only with the police but also with the other components of the criminal justice system; advances a sustained, theoretical (as well as practical) justification for police-community relations; and introduces into this area of public concern a much needed dosage of political and social realism. Each of these three themes deserves additional comment.

While the police may be organizationally separate from courts and corrections, all three components of the criminal justice system are functionally interrelated. For example, the release of an otherwise guilty suspect because a court found the evidence necessary for conviction unlawfully seized or the failure of correctional personnel to reform an inmate prior to release has a direct effect upon the manner and conditions in which the police perform their tasks. This text explores the full range of consequences these interrelationship or "interface" problems have on police-community relations. The police are the component of the criminal justice system in closest contact with the community, and as a result they are often blamed for failures in the other parts of the system. For police-community relations to be improved, not only must problems within the criminal justice system be kept to a minimum, but both courts and corrections must also become increasingly concerned with improving their relations with the community.

Police-community relations programs can be justified in very pragmatic terms. For example, the President's Commission on Law Enforcement and Administration of Justice points out that "the police department's capacity to deal with crime depends to a large extent on its relationship with the citizenry. Indeed, no lasting improvement in law enforcement is likely in this country unless police-community relations are substantially improved." However compelling these pragmatic arguments may be, a coherent and significant theoretical argument on behalf of police-community relations also exists and is spelled out in this book. This theoretical argument centers on the American constitutional commitment to the preservation of a tension or balance between majority rule and minority rights. Alexander Hamilton gave expression to this constitutional principle when he declared at the Constitutional Convention in Philadelphia in 1787: "Give all power to the many, they will oppress the few. Give all power to the few, they will oppress the many. Both therefore ought to have power that each may defend itself against the other." This tension between the power of the majority and the power of the minority is also found in the criminal justice system. For the most part, the police are recruited from, reflect the values of, and express the apprehensions of the law-abiding majority; and for the most part, courts and corrections promote and represent the rights and interests of the minority and individuals. However, courts and corrections, as this book indicates, have fundamentally failed to provide sufficient protection for the minority and hence have been unable by themselves to preserve the proper balance between majority rule and minority rights. Thus, this text argues that police departments themselves must internalize this tension through a genuine commitment to practices that will improve relations with all segments of the community, including society's minorities, that is, persons outside the dominant ruling coalition.

In addition to its focus on the entire criminal justice system and its sustained justification of police-community relations on the basis of the political principles of majority rule and minority rights, this book also emphasizes the need for political and social realism. It presents police-community relations as essentially problematic; and it does not regard police-community relations as a cure-all for the ills of society. Rather, it stresses that police-community relations are in fact two-way communication, and that even when the police (and courts and corrections as well) fully appreciate the need for improved relations with the community, all of their insights and efforts may well be for naught if there is not a reciprocal and equal response and commitment to police-community relations on the part of the community.

These three themes are, of course, explored throughout the entire book. Nevertheless, the order in which they are mentioned in this preface also reflects the rough outline of the text. After an introductory examination of the practical and theoretical issues involved in police-community relations, Part I explores at length the entire criminal justice system, its components, and its problems. Part II then takes up the problem that the police (as representatives of the majority and as enforcers of its laws) have when they must deal with various minorities. Part III concludes by examining particular police-community relations programs and assessing institutional and organizational ways by which they can be improved and made more successful. Fundamentally, Part III argues for a substantial commitment to improved police professionalism and presents various reforms necessary for the achievement of this goal.

Police, Criminal Justice, and the Community is written for a variety of readers. It is written as a primary textbook for college students in "Criminal Justice and the Community" or "Police-Community Relations" courses; and because of its interdisciplinary nature it can be used in a number of other courses concerned with similar subject matters. Finally, because of the importance of improving law enforcement in this country, this text is also directed at criminal justice practitioners and the general public. We hope that the book is sufficiently provocative to cause discussions among friends and foes of law enforcement that could lead to improvements in both police-community relations and street-level justice.

A book cannot be written without considerable assistance. The authors owe a special debt of gratitude to Constance Rossum for editing the entire manuscript; to Kathleen Mulligan for furnishing helpful suggestions; to Larry L. Wade, J. D. Williams, and Dwight T. Moore—all graduate students in the Department of Political Science at Memphis State University—for providing much appreciated research assistance; and to Laura Ingram and Cathy Collier for diligently and good-naturedly typing the manuscript.

ALAN E. BENT
RALPH A. ROSSUM

INTRODUCTION

1

||||||||||||||||||||||||||||||||||||||||||||||||||||||||||||||||||||||||||||||||||||||||||||||||||||||||

ROLES OF POLICE
IN URBAN SOCIETY

This is a time when to be a police officer is to be the focus of a great deal of public attention. On practically any night of the week media supercops perform in
exciting adventures on millions of television screens across America. Police have
been shown rescuing a girl from her kidnaper after a shoot-out on the "Streets
of San Francisco," breaking up a black-market selling of babies on "Police Story,"
busting the narcotics kingpin after years of diligent effort on "Kojak," preventing international conspirators from flooding the American economy with bogus
money on "Hawaii Five-O," and so on. Not to be outdone, the movie industry has
done its best to capitalize on the public's interest by producing a large number of
films that either glamorize or vilify policemen and police work. Books and
articles are being written about police with rewarding commercial success. Indeed, it is becoming rare not to have at least one book about police or police work
on the current list of best sellers. The action end of policing is receiving widespread glamour treatment. But, as any real policeman knows, most of the
glamour and adventure in police work is confined to television, the movies, and
novels. As one police officer in New Orleans recently said: "Those guys on 'Adam
Twelve' have more action on a half-hour show than I do in one month patrolling
my beat."

One side of the police story is the phenomenon of the policeman's arrival
as a pop-culture hero. But in the real world of the streets, the attitude toward
police by the public is mixed. As the most visible arm of government, the policeman symbolizes security in some segments of the community and a threat in
others. To some he is a champion, to others he is either brutal and bigoted or
too soft. Some desire strict law enforcement, while others want limited enforcement or no enforcement at all. The policeman is charged with bringing all
lawbreakers to justice, but while doing so he is compelled to observe their constitutional rights. In quiet times he is ignored; in turbulent times he is belittled.

Operating from prescribed laws and statutes, he is made to enforce popular and unpopular laws. He is subjected to pressure by the legal-political structure on the one hand and the myriad vocal and angry groups in our society on the other. The policeman lives and works in an environment of cross-fires in a highly charged environment.[1]

The variations of urban life and the needs of some members of the urban community have imposed on the police a whole range of tasks. This has made the policeman's role a most difficult and versatile one. With this in mind, Ramsey Clark writes that the modern policeman must be

> law enforcer and lawyer, scientist in a whole range of physical sciences— chemistry, physics, electronics—medic, psychologist, social worker, human relations and race relations expert, marriage counsellor, youth advisor, athlete, public servant—these are but a few of the many skills a major police department must exercise daily. Individual policemen must personally possess many of them—and perform them with excellence. Safety, life and property, equal justice, liberty, confidence in government and in the purpose of our laws will depend on it.[2]

It will be seen that the working life of the policeman is not that of the super-cop. His functions are neither limited nor so filled with glory as they are portrayed on the screen and in the pages of popular books; his environment is far more confusing, fast changing, and turbulent than the world of make-believe would have us see, for policing in a real urban America consists of work that is usually routine if occasionally dangerous and even explosive, both for the policeman and for society.

Police Roles

Formally and officially the duties of a police officer are prescribed by legislative or administrative mandate. A conventional list of duties would include:

1. protection of life and property,
2. preservation of the peace,
3. prevention of crime,
4. detection and arrest of violators of law,
5. enforcement of laws and ordinances,
6. safeguarding the rights of individuals.[3]

However, the formal outlining of police duties shows only the tip of the iceberg of the police officer's occupational concerns. No amount of cataloguing of duties can fully encompass the wide dimensions of an urban policeman's responsibilities. These responsibilities may include the apprehension of felons, the serving of warrants, the issuance of tickets for traffic violations, the inspection of buildings for signs of burglary, routine patrolling to observe violations, intervention in domestic disputes, the checking of licensed establishments for orderly conduct, follow-up investigations, writing accident reports, providing emergency assistance of all types, investigating suspicious behavior and complaints, and many more.[4]

Cataloguing of police tasks is an attempt to standardize their bureaucratic functions, as all bureaucratic functions are standardized. The conventional listing of duties has invariably stressed the crime-prevention and peace-keeping aspects of police tasks. This has not altogether been in keeping with the intentions of progressive police administrators. David Couper, chief of police in Madison, Wisconsin, speaks to the unconventional breadth of police roles when he includes among police responsibilities such things as the creation and maintenance of a feeling of security in the community, the resolution of conflict, the protection of constitutional guarantees and the helping of those who cannot care for themselves.[5] The wide-ranging and unusual tasks of the police make it difficult, if not impossible, to develop a consistent, packaged description of their duties. While the standardization of bureaucratic tasks is not unusual, and is in fact organizationally efficient, the attempt to apply this method to the police is wholly unrealistic.

However, the police officer has become so accustomed to a static enumeration of his tasks that his reply to a query about his duties is likely to result in the mechanical statement: "Protection of life and property and the preservation of peace." This is the dogma that is often taught in police training academies.[6] But this simple tenet is largely inaccurate and does not begin to explain the various job-related roles that the policeman must play. The police are set apart from their bureaucratic counterparts not just because of the breadth and nature of these roles, but for their social implications as well, for the roles played by individual officers not only shape the nature of law enforcement in a community, but also provide the sources of tension within the community. Additionally, they lead to a self-identity crisis for the policeman as he tries to perform the various, often contradictory roles.

The roles that a policeman may be expected to fulfill include those that are somewhat conventional and others that are not widely identified as police-related. Nonetheless, they are real and are sources of conflict vis-à-vis the community and the officer internally. First are the traditional roles: peace-keeping—or order maintenance—crime fighting, and community service, the last one only belatedly recognized as an inherent police function. Next are the less historically defined roles fulfilled by the police: paramilitary, quasi-judicial, establishment protective capabilities,[7] and the personification of the "ideal man." Each of these roles and the difficulties they pose for the police will be examined.

Peace-Keeping and Community Service

Although both the public and the police consider crime fighting as the principal police activity, this role is a relatively new one for police forces. In many U.S. cities it was not until well into the twentieth century that the police became responsible for the apprehension of thieves, robbers, and murderers.[8] The first legally sanctioned role, following the example of policing in Britain, was peace-keeping or preservation of the peace. The preservation of the peace is another way of saying "maintaining public safety" and provides the police with a broad mandate to protect lives and property with functions that range from controlling a full-scale riot to getting kittens out of trees. In a more practical sense, a great deal of the patrolman's time in this role involves the settlement of violent family disputes, handling drunk and disorderly persons and street-corner brawls, and attending to such charges as trespassing, vagrancy, and related offenses.[9]

Some of the peace-keeping activities may be more properly termed service functions, especially when they concern such activities as rescuing cats, providing first aid, working with dependent and neglected children, rendering emergency medical or rescue services, and helping those who are under the influence of alcohol or drugs. Not least among these responsibilities is intervention in domestic quarrels, a task that is as common as it is volatile and dangerous; for it is not uncommon for a marriage partner to turn violently on the police officer called to intervene in a domestic quarrel. With the stresses of urban living and the breakdown of primary social control institutions—such as the family, the church, schools—government agencies are now expected to fulfill a number of social service functions. The police, as the most visible symbols of governmental authority, have been "generally acting as a social agency of last resort—particularly after 5 P.M. and on week-ends—for the impoverished, the sick, the old, and the lower socio-economic classes."[10]

The conflicting demands on the police function have created tensions, and these are described by James S. Campbell:

> Perhaps the most important source of police frustration and the most severe limitation under which they operate, is the conflicting rules and demands involved in the order-maintenance, community-service and crime-fighting responsibilities of the police. Here both the individual police officer and the police community as a whole find not only inconsistent public expectations and public reactions, but also inner conflict growing out of the interaction of the policeman's values, customs, and traditions with his intimate experience with the criminal element of the population. The policeman lives on the grinding edge of social conflict, without a well-defined, well-understood notion of what he is supposed to be doing there.[11]

Crime Fighting

Although there is ample evidence to support the contention that the police's primary duty is that of peace-keeping, most policemen articulate a preoccupation with crime fighting. This is because the apprehension and conviction of the felon is the most prestigious and rewarding job task in the minds of the police and the public. The "good pinch" is the avenue for a policeman's career progression and the way the police are able to project a positive public image. Conversely, peace-keeping and service tasks are not rewarded by superiors, esteemed by peers, or, the police feel, appreciated by the public.

The "lure of crime fighting," as Jesse Ruben describes it, is so irresistible that policemen will go to great lengths to fulfill it. This is evidenced in the way policemen will respond to broadcasts of a holdup or a prowler call. On busy nights a police dispatcher may have to delay such calls as complaints, accidents, or disturbances because of a shortage of available patrol cars. Yet the broadcast of a holdup, prowler, or shooting call will usually result in the arrival of more patrol cars on the scene than are needed. These crimes-in-progress calls provide exciting interludes in the general boredom of patrolling. However, even in crime-fighting categories the majority of arrests do not consist of felony arrests—the "good pinch"—but rather the arrests of drunks, vagrants, individuals causing disturbances, shoplifters, and so on.

Despite the gratification that a policeman receives from his duties as a crime fighter, most of his time is nonetheless spent in peace-keeping activities. James Q. Wilson reported that service—noncriminal—calls were the largest single category of calls (37.5 percent) in the Syracuse Police Department. Next in order of frequency of calls was order-maintenance (30.1 percent), while law enforcement (crime fighting) made up only 10.3 percent of all calls.[12] A similar study of a Baltimore police district also showed that the vast majority of resident requests for police services were for maintenance of order, the settling of interpersonal disputes, and the need for advice and emergency assistance. Meanwhile, crime-related calls accounted for less than one-fourth of the police service calls.[13]

A recent survey of police service calls in the Memphis Police Department (Table 1.1) demonstrates a consistency in the pattern of police service categories requested by citizens. In the Memphis study, law-enforcement calls constituted approximately one-fifth of the police service calls, while service and order-maintenance calls represented over 70 percent of the calls.

As Table 1.1 shows, crime-fighting or crime-prevention activities make up only a small part of the police role. However, because a police officer has been popularized as a crime fighter, additional attention must be paid to the realities of this function. Crime prevention provides most of the statistics by which the efforts and efficiency of police departments are measured by police administrators and by the public. In truth, the police are seriously handicapped in their role as crime fighters by factors beyond their control.

First, it is physically impossible to "control crime" effectively because of the large geographical area in which crime takes place and because of the limited number of personnel resources available to each police department. Memphis, Tennessee, for instance, with a population of approximately 620,000, has only some 1,060 police officers on its police force. On an average day there are about 90 policemen in some 45 patrol cars on the streets to cover the 230-square-mile area of this city. According to the Uniform Crime Report of 1972, Memphis crime statistics in the seven major crime categories were as follows: criminal homicide, 165; forcible rape, 373; robbery, 1,676; aggravated assault, 1,539; burglary, 12,913; larceny, 15,735; auto theft, 3,219. It is apparent from these crime figures that an urban police force, limited numerically and held respon-

TABLE 1.1   Citizen complaints radioed to patrol vehicles, Memphis Police Department, April 7–13, 1974

(Based on a one-fifth sample of a week's calls)

Calls		Number in sample	Full count (sample multiplied by 5)	Percent
Information gathering		51	255	9.1
Getting a report	51			
Service		239	1195	42.9
Accidents, illnesses, ambulance calls	128			
Animals	4			
Drunk person	19			
Fire, power line or tree down	7			
Lost or found property or person	4			
Property damage	13			
General complaint	64			
Order maintenance		153	765	27.5
Gang disturbance	10			
Assault, fight	27			
Neighbor trouble	20			
General disturbance	81			
Armed person	15			
Law enforcement		114	570	20.5
Burglary-in-progress alarms	24			
Prowler	16			
Holding prisoner	22			
Check a car or person	46			
Robbery	6			
TOTALS:		557	2785	100.0

sible for a large variety of tasks, would be hard pressed to fulfill the crime fighting role even if it were to devote full time to this function. The sheer limitation of the size of each city's police force makes it impractical to expect the kind of protection of life and property that would make American cities safe from crime.

Memphis shares with other cities the problem of insufficient police manpower for adequate coverage of physical territory. This problem is largely attributable to the fact that most cities do not have the financial resources to afford large enough police forces. Table 1.2 provides a sample of cities from 300,000 to a million in population and illustrates their fiscal commitment to police protection with the corresponding police personnel resources that this commitment purchases. The data show that while the cost factor is critical in maintaining large police forces, sheer size of the police force alone does not always correspond with reduced crime rates. The most significant statistic is

TABLE 1.2 Police patrol and crime rates in major American cities

	Police budget per capita		Police per 1000 population		Patrolmen per 1000 population		Major crimes per patrolman	
1.	Washington	$124.85	Washington	6.66	Washington	5.55	Denver[a]	55.6
2.	Baltimore	75.11	Boston	4.20	Boston	3.11	San Jose[a]	52.6
3.	San Francisco	68.98	Baltimore	3.80	St. Louis	3.05	Memphis[a]	50.3
4.	Boston	63.93	St. Louis	3.59	Baltimore	2.79	Jacksonville	40.9
5.	St. Louis	54.70	Pittsburgh	3.14	Cleveland	2.67	Minneapolis[a]	39.4
6.	Kansas City	47.24	Cleveland	3.13	Pittsburgh	2.37	Atlanta[a]	37.9
7.	Seattle	46.59	Buffalo	2.96	San Francisco	2.08	San Antonio[a]	37.4
8.	Buffalo	44.63	San Francisco	2.73	Kansas City	2.00	Phoenix[a]	33.7
9.	Cleveland	43.90	Kansas City	2.55	Seattle	1.83	San Diego[a]	33.6
10.	Pittsburgh	40.83	Denver[a]	2.36	New Orleans	1.83	Dallas	33.0
11.	Denver[a]	39.00	New Orleans	2.35	Buffalo	1.64	Cincinnati	32.6
12.	Honolulu	34.99	Indianapolis	2.29	Dallas	1.56	San Francisco	32.0
13.	Phoenix[a]	34.39	Seattle	2.24	Columbus	1.54	Nashville	29.5
14.	Indianapolis	34.20	Honolulu	2.18	Honolulu	1.51	Indianapolis	29.2
15.	Dallas	31.64	Cincinnati	2.16	Phoenix[a]	1.47	Fort Worth	28.1
16.	Minneapolis[a]	30.23	Dallas	2.12	Atlanta[a]	1.46	New Orleans	27.8
17.	Cincinnati	28.75	Atlanta[a]	2.04	Cincinnati	1.42	Seattle	27.5
18.	Memphis[a]	28.47	Minneapolis[a]	1.88	Minneapolis[a]	1.42	Columbus	27.3
19.	New Orleans	28.12	Columbus	1.86	Denver[a]	1.33	Buffalo	24.9
20.	Atlanta[a]	26.54	Phoenix[a]	1.74	Indianapolis	1.29	Kansas City	23.9
21.	Columbus	25.16	Memphis[a]	1.69	Nashville	1.28	St. Louis	22.7
22.	San Jose[a]	23.24	Fort Worth	1.59	Fort Worth	1.15	Honolulu	21.3
23.	Fort Worth	22.72	Nashville	1.50	San Diego[a]	1.11	Cleveland	20.8
24.	Jacksonville	22.00	Jacksonville	1.46	San Antonio[a]	1.05	Baltimore	20.2
25.	San Diego[a]	21.79	San Antonio[a]	1.40	Jacksonville	1.03	Boston	19.5
26.	Nashville	20.37	San Diego	1.36	Memphis[a]	0.92	Pittsburgh	19.5
27.	San Antonio[a]	20.31	San Jose[a]	1.29	San Jose[a]	0.74	Washington	8.9

Source: *Memphis Press-Scimitar*, May 16, 1973, p. 4.

[a]Cities with crime rate increases during 1972.

that a reduction in crime is attributable not to the sheer size of the police force, but rather to the number of patrolmen actually on the streets. Thus the utilization of patrolmen has stronger correlation with crime-rate increases than indices of department size. Cities that employ fewer front-line patrolmen show increases in major crimes per patrolman and subsequent increases in the crime rate. While this would suggest that crime prevention may be optimized by making fundamentally sound administrative decisions in the proper allocation and utilization of personnel resources, this, of itself, will not eradicate crime: it mainly indicates that the crime rate will be reduced to the extent that police management is improved.[14]

A second deterrent to effective crime prevention is that most crimes "are not subject to prevention or control of the police."[15] In the case of violent crimes, such as homicide, the act is usually committed before the police are even called. This effectively precludes prevention and involves the police only in after-the-act investigatory duties and the subsequent arrest of the criminal. Then there are the white-collar crimes, or the victimless crimes such as prostitution and gambling, which are "invisible"—done in private—and therefore immune to prevention. It can thus be seen that although crime prevention receives a great deal of attention, the police role in this connection is a vexing one. In view of this condition the following assertion is especially noteworthy: "[Police] agencies may sometimes hamper potential criminal conduct, hinder its progress, or impede its momentum. They cannot deal meaningfully with the deep-rooted social problems found in close association with crime. Crime prevention efforts can be realistically expected of law enforcement; the prevention of crime cannot!"[16] It is apparent that the war on crime "is an on-going phenomenon which the police have no hope of ending; they can only hope to reduce the rise of crimes."[17]

Another aspect of the crime-prevention role is that no police department can be realistically expected to carry out the task of detection and arrest alone. The heavy burden of other roles and the invisibility of many crimes act as major obstacles to police effectiveness. Additionally, police are impeded by the public's lack of support and cooperation. The citizen who does not want to get involved or did not see anything or does not want to prosecute or testify means that crimes will go undetected or that felons will be freed for lack of evidence. In the execution of their crime-prevention function the police need all the help they can get from the public, the judicial system, the legislatures, and correctional institutions. Citizen support can be obtained by their willingness to provide the police with information and to perform their civic duty by testifying against wrongdoers whose crimes they observe. They can also aid the police through an appreciation of effective law enforcement, and by making demands of their elected officials and their legislatures for adequate funding and salaries for police forces. The latter type of support appears to have the professed backing of a majority of American citizens. A 1970 Gallup poll asked respondents if they believed that Congress should provide more money to help local police deal with crime, and an overwhelming 91 percent said that they thought that Congress should.[18]

The judiciary can aid the police by providing definitive guidelines in such matters as arrest, search and seizure, confessions, and rights of individuals arrested. Courts can also be helpful by streamlining their procedures so that arrested individuals can be assured of speedy trials. This is an especially crucial consideration if the arrested person is indeed guilty of the act for which he was apprehended. Delaying a trial may mean that a felon is free to roam the streets at will, posing the potential hazard that he may resort to further criminal acts while awaiting trial for the preceding one. This is not an uncommon occurrence in cities where overcrowded court dockets have enabled felons to continue to practice their "occupation" between the time of arrest and the eventual trial.

Legislatures and elected officials can help, too, not only by providing adequate finances for police departments, but also by thoroughly considering their expectations of police roles, and whether existing agencies or new agencies might not better handle some functions now allocated to the police. Finally, the correctional institutions can aid immeasurably in the reduction of the crime rate. Unfortunately, all too often our penal institutions have served to improve the criminal skills of incarcerated felons rather than to rehabilitate them. The felon the policeman deals with on the street is often a recidivist, and if the correctional institutions are to play a positive part in the criminal justice process, then they must improve their methods, as well as obtain the necessary financial and public support so that the vicious cycle of criminality can be broken.

The tension between the police role of law enforcement and the roles of peace-keeping and community service has been debilitating psychologically and intellectually to individual police officers as well as an impediment to the provision of the best possible police service. Both the police and the public perceive the crime-fighting role as the essence of real police work. But in reality the police officer is occupied with many other tasks and spends a minimum of his time in crime prevention. Furthermore, the police can do nothing about the causes of crime and are often confined to reacting to occurrences that have already taken place. It has been seen that with the proper utilization of police manpower in their patrol capacities, the occurrence of crime can be reduced by the visible presence of police officers on the street. But the social, economic, and psychological factors that spawn criminality cannot be eradicated by policemen; they can be handled only by the whole of society and the myriad institutions—created or yet to be created—that are better equipped to handle these conditions.

On the one hand society expects the police to be efficient crime fighters, while on the other they are expected to be adroit and skilled peace-keepers and social servants of the community. There is a sufficient blurring of the tasks that go into peace keeping and that relate to community service. After all, at which point is the intervention into domestic quarrels, dealing with those who are under the influence of alcohol or drugs, quelling barking dogs and rescuing cats from trees and so on, a function of peace-keeping or community service? At any rate, these are tasks that society now expects of the police and expects them to be performed well. Yet so sharply do the roles of crime fighting and community service conflict, as do the skills and temperament required to perform them, that it may be unreasonable to expect a person to adjust to both roles with ease and to be able to leap from one to the other at any given moment. When police officers are called upon to perform both roles, they often appear to be improperly trained or equipped to do justice to either one.[19]

The demands of the various police roles have necessitated a whole range of capabilities for individual policemen that may not be humanly attainable. Professor George L. Kirkham of Florida State University's School of Criminology provides some useful insights into the matter. Professor Kirkham found himself "troubled by the fact that most of us who write books and articles on the police have never been policemen ourselves." He decided to take up the challenge. He took a leave of absence, attended a police academy, and became, temporarily, a patrolman on the 800-man police force of Jacksonville-Duval County, Florida.

Among Kirkham's instructive observations about the working conditions of a policeman was this comment about the pressures on police officers that society has created:

> As a police officer myself, I found that society demands too much of its policemen: not only are they expected to enforce the law, but to be curbside psychiatrists, marriage counselors, social workers, and even ministers and doctors. I found that a good officer combines in his daily work splinters of each of these complex professions and many more. Certainly it is unreasonable for us to ask so much of the men in blue; yet we must, for there is simply no one else to whom we can turn for help in the kind of crisis and problems policemen deal with. No one else wants to counsel a family with problems at 3 A.M. on Sunday; no one else wants to enter a darkened building after a burglary; no one else wants to confront a robber or madman with a gun. No one else wants to stare poverty, mental illness, and human tragedy in the face day after day, to pick up the pieces of shattered lives.[20]

Paramilitary Role

The roles already considered are enough to confound police agencies and police officers, as well as provide a schism between police and the community. But there are other tension-inducing roles, and the next one to consider is the paramilitary role performed by the police. Police forces have all the appearances and the symbols of a paramilitary and authoritarian organization. Policemen wear uniforms, carry military ranks, and possess weapons. Implicit, too, in police hierarchical structures is a commitment to a chain of command, submission to authority, and the functioning of individual police officers in a well-integrated and well-disciplined unit. In actual practice, this is not the case. Police on patrol generally operate in pairs or alone, without the benefit of direct supervision or control. Individual officers are assigned territories under their policing jurisdiction and are given a great deal of discretionary authority in taking action against perceived or observed lawbreaking activities. In effect, each policeman is granted the autonomy to make an on-the-spot decision about whether an activity violates one of 30,000 existing laws and statutes and almost instantaneously to initiate the criminal justice process. This discretionary authority is not to be taken lightly, for with it is carried the capability to take a person's life or deprive him of his liberty.

The ambivalence in the paramilitary role occurs with command authority. While police commanders stress that they must have command control over their men and over situations in which their men are involved, they are appreciative of the inescapable discretionary authority that a police officer must have when he is assigned a territory in which he is expected to maintain law and order. Furthermore, in order to gain or retain favor with their men, commanders are known to back up their subordinates no matter what they did. This means that there is an unwillingness to challenge individual autonomy on police forces despite the rhetoric about command authority.[21] The lack of organizational control over its members makes standardized police practice difficult on the street level. In effect, this allows the policeman to behave pretty much as he wants to. Some want to behave well, some do not. This kind of discretionary behavior has obvious repercussions for police-community relations, especially in neighborhoods where the police are perceived as symbols of oppression.

Quasi-Judicial and Establishment Protective Roles

The next two roles—the quasi-judicial and the establishment protective capacities—are somewhat interlocked. Because it is practicably impossible to enforce all the laws all the time, the police are allowed a great deal of discretion in their selection of violations to be enforced. This is especially the case when there is no social consensus about whether such laws as those concerning gambling, adult sexual behavior, alcoholism, drug use, and minor traffic offenses should be enforced.

The police have used their discretionary or quasi-judicial authority to stop and investigate citizens they consider suspicious. The lack of precise guidelines on how and when policemen should check out suspects has raised questions among some citizens about the possible motives behind this practice. Some members of the community consider this type of police behavior to be harassment and feel that the criterion for attracting the attention of the police is not a possible wrongdoing but the color of one's skin, the quality of one's clothes, the model of one's automobile, or one's apparent social class membership. Here again the police officer is faced with a dilemma. His job calls for him to perform a discretionary, quasi-judicial role, "but this role is not even ill-defined—it is not defined at all."[22]

In the matter of police involvement in an "establishment protective" role, it has become speculative as to whether police are disinterested enforcement agents of an impartial judicial system or are there "to support and enforce the interest of the dominant, political, social, and economic interests of the town and only incidentally to enforce the law."[23] For those who hold the latter view, the police are not interested in either community service or law enforcement, but in the maintenance of the status quo. This leads to the contention that the police do not enforce the laws of a community impartially; the laws chosen for enforcement "are those which the power structure of the community wants enforced."[24] The supposed selective or unequal enforcement of the law has come increasingly under attack from the black civil-rights movement. Blacks and other minority groups argue that the police are unwilling or unable to cope within their environment and with the social changes of the past two decades.

In the "establishment protective" context, the system of law enforcement and order maintenance is regarded as a process of socialization of the community in order to "maintain the ascendancy of the dominant social norms."[25] The police are used as a moral force in support of the interests of the dominant group. The police act out their support for the dominant social and political group by arresting those who fail to adhere to prevailing norms. In this manner, deviant behavior is not only stigmatized but criminalized. Harlan Hahn addresses this phenomenon when he writes: "As a public agency that has developed more contact with citizens than nearly any other government bureau, perhaps the police have had greater direct impact upon the association between personal conduct and abstract social standards than many other political leaders."[26]

However, Brian Chapman argues that the police serve more as regulators of conflict between social classes than as enforcers of the dominant mores.[27] Policemen, often from working-class or lower middle-class backgrounds, are expected to enforce the laws and the mores enacted for the community by the upper class in a lower-class environment. In fact, a policeman may sympathetically believe that these laws are inappropriate for this milieu. Consequently he uses his judgment and discretionary flexibility to try to strike a balance among the divergent norms and values of the various community subgroups.[28] Sociologist William Whyte observes:

> Under these circumstances the smoothest course for the officer is to conform to the social organization with which he is in direct contact and at the same time to try to give the impression to the outside world that he is enforcing the law. He must play an elaborate role of make-believe, and, in so doing, he serves as a buffer between divergent social organizations with their conflicting standards of conduct. . . .[29]

The role of moral mediator and interpreter of social norms leads to the final and correlative role performed by police: serving as a model for the ideal man.

Policeman as the "Ideal Man"

Joseph Lohman claims that the police officer "stands as the symbol of the impartial authority of society."[30] Michael Banton refers to the policeman as a kind of professional citizen,—a good policeman and a good citizen respected by the community in either case.[31] It is from this image that the authority of the police, as opposed to their power, is acquired, in that authority includes a moral element that power does not. That the police possess power as well as authority is an inescapable fact. They have power as the legitimate enforcers of the state's legal system as well as the paramilitary counterpart of the nation's armed forces. In addition, they are empowered to use force in the pursuit of their tasks with a monopoly over the legitimate use of force and violence. But the moral source of police authority is the positive factor in police-community relations and in the public's compliance with the law. As Banton states: "If someone has power over you he can force you to do his will, but if he has authority over you, you accept his right to command you and you obey him voluntarily."[32]

As the most visible symbol of the political system, a moral force in society, and because of an intensive interaction with all elements of the community in his myriad roles, the police officer is in a key position to exert influence on society. J. E. Curry, former police chief of Dallas, writes: "The police themselves are a tremendous force for molding public opinion. The activities and attitudes of individual policemen can influence citizens to respect the rights of others, or can give the impression that they can attack some group without fear of punishment."[33] David Bayley contends that "social change may be brought about by government instrumentalities, among them the police, just as these instrumentalities are in turn influenced in their activity by the surrounding environment."[34] This implies that the police, by their behavior and role playing, have a direct effect on the shaping of the character and behavior in society. For example, John Bellamy argues that misdoers "are often influenced in their criminal behavior by methods used to maintain public order in their country."[35]

Police historian Sir Charles Reith stated that English society was fundamentally reshaped after the introduction of Sir Robert Peel's police system in London in 1829.[36] Geoffrey Gorer supports this contention by stating that

> increasingly during the past century the English policeman has been for his peers not only an object of respect but also a model of the ideal male character, self-controlled, possessing more strength than he ever has to call into use except in the greatest emergency, fair and impartial, serving the abstractions of Peace and Justice rather than any personal allegiance or sectional advantage.[37]

In effect, these arguments suggest that the mores and norms of a society will reflect to an undetermined extent the mores and norms of its police agencies. Bayley provides us with the British example:

> The model behavior of British police, a by-word around the world, is not a

reflection of a deep-rooted, primordial love of order among the British people. In fact, before 1829 such qualities were distinctive by their absence. The British love of order and respect for law is a result of model behavior on the part of the British police in spite of appalling conditions of crime, vice, public insecurity, and individual apathy, hostility, and indifference to law enforcement.[38]

If the British example is transferrable, it has obvious implications for American police and American society. Sir Charles Reith takes issue with those who argue that America is a violent, corrupt, bestial country because of inherent defects in the American character, and thus excuse police malpractices as reflections of this kind of environment. Instead he asserts that violence and corruption in the United States continue to exist principally because America's "ideal men" —the police—are models of violence and corruption.[39] Unfortunately, there is some historic evidence to support Reith's contention. Bruce Smith, Jr., described the police of early America as shiftless, incompetent, and ignorant, and frequently the source of various types of community scandals.[40] Asher Byrnes offers this account of American police of the Civil War period:

> . . . bribery seems to have been universal; there was more lawlessness inside the departments than anywhere else. Assaulting superior officers, refusing to go on patrol, releasing prisoners from the custody of other policemen, drunkenness, extorting money from prisoners—these were offenses of daily occurrence, committed often with impunity under the protection of a political overlord. They were little respected, not at all feared, and frequently beaten up by gangsters.[41]

What is even more disturbing is that some of these conditions continue to exist in today's departments. For example, former New York policeman Frank Serpico testified before the Knapp Commission that ". . . the problem is that the atmosphere does not yet exist in which an honest police officer can act without fear of ridicule or reprisal from fellow officers. . . ."[42] In this connection, Michael Armstrong, an investigator for the Knapp Commission, made this alarming statement: "It is not a question of a few rotten apples in the barrel. It is a question of finding a few good apples in the barrel."[43] Availability of data supporting contentions of police malpractice and corruption in varying degrees in many American cities has profound consequences. If Bayley and Reith are correct in their assertions that the police exert a formative effect on society's mores, then in some cases, the influences exerted by our urban police forces on the communities they serve have been both negative and undesirable. The importance of this analysis for contemporary police administration is momentous.

Influences on Police Roles

Police roles are primarily determined by three factors: societal norms, mores, and influences; the individual policeman's discretion; and the level of urbanization of society. Society's norms and mores are consequential for police roles because a particular society or culture will incorporate into its legal structure what it views as proper police jurisdiction. Pre-occupation Japan delegated duties to its police agencies that can be classified as administrative, legislative, judicial, and quasi-judicial.[44] Among the Japanese policeman's prescribed duties were such things as trade licensing, fire protection, and public health.[45] Today's Danish policeman performs a very diversified set of functions that include responsibilities over fire brigades, health authorities, certain matters of trade, conscription, approval of divorces, custody of children and alimony payments, paternity cases, adoptions, changes of names, registration and taxation of motor vehicles, and the control of public amusement.[46]

It is difficult to envision these concerns as being within the province of either the American or the British policeman. As Chapman says: ". . . Americans have shared with the English an extreme suspicion of policemen and police activities. . . ."[47] The result of this suspicion is that both cultures are very cautious about assigning duties to their police and prefer to keep their police agencies as decentralized as possible.[48] It is interesting to note, however, that whereas the prescribed activities of American policemen are far more limited than those of their Japanese or Danish counterparts, the roles that the exigencies of modern society have pressed upon them are nevertheless multivarious, complex, and all too often conflicting.

The local political climate may also exert an influence on police roles and activities, at least in terms of setting priorities for enforcement. Herbert Jacob argues that elected public officials, especially mayors, are influential in determining priorities among the multiple police roles. He states:

> The degree of direct control a mayor may exercise depends on his power to appoint the police chief, on the existence of a special police commission which serves as a buffer between the mayor and the police, on the degree to which the police are under civil service regulations, and on the extent to which police are unionized.[49]

Presumably, to the extent that enforcement priorities are determined by the mayor, an elected public official, police roles and activities are more responsive to the community will. Of course, this holds up only insofar as the public official is responsive and accountable to his constituents.

James Q. Wilson advances the view that a community's political culture is a prime determinant of policing styles. However, he notes that police discretion limits the potential considerably for administrative or political control. He argues that ". . . the prevailing police style is not explicitly determined by community decisions, though a few of its elements may be shaped by those decisions. Put another way, the police are, in all cases, keenly sensitive to their political environment without in all cases being governed by it."[50] In his study of police departments in eight communities, Wilson identified three distinctive styles of police behavior: watchman, legalistic, and service.[51] Basically, these styles differ in their philosophy of police work because each emphasizes particular duties and activities. In each of these styles the patrolman plays a different role in the community, and the role played is largely influenced by the political culture in the environment.

In the "watchman" style the police exercise a great deal of discretion in their major concern: maintaining order. Here, the police "judge the requirements of order differently depending on the character of the group in which the infraction occurs."[52] In essence, unless the offense is a serious one, police discretion to initiate the criminal justice process is based for the most part on who the violator is. In the watchman style of policing, the police act as caretakers whose purpose is not to rock the boat and to act only when necessary.

In the "legalistic" style, police behave on the assumption that there is a universal standard of community conduct. Here the law is enforced to the hilt. Departments performing the legalistic style of policing will tend to have high arrest rates, will issue a large number of traffic tickets, and will act as though the law is a punitive instrument. Finally, the "service" style is one in which "police take seriously all requests for either law enforcement or order maintenance (unlike police with the watchman style) but are less likely to respond by making an arrest or otherwise imposing formal sanctions (unlike police with the legalistic style)."[53]

Whether one argues that police tasks and roles are influenced more by custom or by political conditions, it is evident that both play an influential part and account for some of the variance in the way cities are policed. Another determinant of police roles is the policeman himself through his discretionary authority. As noted earlier, the policeman is free to exercise his own judgment at the street level within broad administrative, statutory, and constitutional guidelines. William A. Westley argues that . . . because "the application of the law depends to a large degree on the definition of the situation and the decision reached by the patrolman, he, in effect, makes the law; it is his decision that establishes the boundary between legal and illegal."[54]

The third determinant, urbanization, is extremely important because of its influence on deviant behavior and the nature of crimes committed. The rapid increase in urbanization of the United States has led to ever higher population concentrations in urban areas.[55] Some research indicates that high population density—crowding—produces abnormal and deviant behavior, commonly referred to as "crime" in human society.[56] In his famous experiments involving colonies of rats, John Calhoun discovered the conditions of stress under which a "behavioral sink" emerges.[57] He found that when rat populations were crowded together in close proximity, incidents of viciousness, sexual perversion, and apathy increased among them. From this, Calhoun argued that a behavioral sink, his term for gross distortion of behavior, is the inevitable outcome "of any behavioral process that collects animals together in unusually great numbers."[58]

There are strong indications that urbanization aids in the development of a behavioral sink in human behavior as well. The President's Commission on Law Enforcement and Administration of Justice noted:

> Crime flourishes, and always has flourished, in city slums, those neighbor-
> hoods where overcrowding, economic deprivation, social disruption and
> racial discrimination are endemic. Crime flourishes in conditions of
> affluence, when there is much desire for material goods and many
> opportunities to acquire them illegally. Crime flourishes when there are
> many restless, relatively foot-loose young people in the population. Crime
> flourishes when standards of morality are changing rapidly.[59]

The implication for these conditions is that the police have obviously more responsibilities in an urban environment, and these responsibilities have given rise to a multiplicity of police roles and tasks.

The pressure that the effects of urbanization have placed on police agencies has led to some specialization of police activities, a traditional bureaucratic response when improvements in efficiency are required. Specialization as a bureaucratic response to environmental needs is not unique to the police. Urbanization, from practically its very beginning, has made changes in police service. Byrnes found that the onset of the Industrial Revolution, with its creation of a mobile and unstable proletariat, led to new crime problems for the police, who responded by gradually specializing their activities. Examples of these early specialized functions included the formation of patrol divisions, traffic divisions, criminal investigation departments, homicide divisions, vice squads, and so on.[60]

The diversity of police roles and responsibilities is also a direct result of a failure of society and its specialized agencies to solve its problems exacerbated by urbanization. Lohman cites racial tension as a case in point:

> Race problems may be associated with the movement and re-distribution of
> population throughout the nation, the fact that houses are in short supply,
> the presence in the community of excessive numbers of unemployed or
> disadvantaged workers, or the failure to provide adequate public facilities
> for all elements of the community. Because these failures have occurred
> . . . the consequences of these failures become responsibilities of the police
> department.[61]

Urbanization, the product of industrialization and population concentration—of too many people in too few spaces with all the attendant problems—has had a far-reaching impact on the number and kinds of duties that a contemporary policeman must perform. This has led to new police task specialization in an effort to achieve greater efficiency in police service.

Whether greater efficiency has been achieved is a debatable point and certainly one that is arguable from a different perspective, depending on which group is doing the arguing—whether it is the police administrator, the police practitioner on the street, or the clientele group served. In any case, the multiplicity of roles performed by the policeman has been conflict-inducing and psychologically wearing on the man who must assume these roles. Furthermore, tensions that exist in urban America are proving to be resiliently impervious to the various efforts that public agencies, and especially the police, have attempted. Ultimately, the policeman, as the most visible symbol of the American system and society, appears to be the one who must bear the brunt of the frustration that enrages some urban communities.

Our urban environment faces a number of crucial social issues, and many of them can be linked to the rising crime rates and other major concerns of police agencies. Racial tensions, inadequate housing, vast income differentials, radical changes in population and population distribution, lack of education or educational opportunities, the revolution of rising expectations for the poor, technology, the accelerated tempo of urban life, and many other concerns provide the scenario of urban America. And the people who are victims of many of these problems, as well as the people who like to rationalize their unlawful behavior on what they consider to be the ills of American life, are the ones with whom the police are very likely to deal. As George Edwards points out, it is the city's complexity and congestion, anonymity, affluence and poverty, and abundance of opportunity that are all conducive to our growing crime rates and the explosive potential of our urban scene.[62] Although the police officer operates in an environment he did not create, it is essential that he understand the conditions that exist there. He must be aware that the manner in which he executes his daily functions can possibly mean the difference between a relatively quiet city and one that is riot-torn; between urban peace and urban war.

Problems of an Urban Society

The city is the best and the worst of places. Art, music, literature, education, science, and organizational skills are all found in the nutrient mix of wealth, population diversity, and divisions of labor that characterize the essence of the city. But the essence of the city also includes vice, crime, poverty, violence, cruelty, and despair. Until this century most of the citizens of this nation lived in towns or villages or in the open countryside, their lives relatively untouched by the ways of the city, both the good and the bad.

In the years since 1900 this country has been transformed from a predominantly rural and small-town society to one where nearly two-thirds of the people now live in metropolitan areas comprised essentially of central cities and their suburbs. The way in which these metropolitan areas have developed recently has significance for urban population characteristics and, concomitantly, for urban policing. Urban America is fast becoming two societies: one almost all white, located in the suburbs, and one that is almost wholly black, in the central cities. The growth of the suburbs, public policy, and racial attitudes have all contributed to the divided society. While each of these factors has played a discrete role in contemporary urban development, the process has been made more meaningful and devastating by the interrelatedness of these causalities.

The city grew in a period of active industrialization requiring economies of scale, large numbers of unskilled and semiskilled workers, and proximity to transportation arteries. Cities were physically fashioned to accommodate clustered production techniques near railway lines, and housing for the workers within walking distance of their jobs. Earlier restrictions upon communications and transportation led to concentrations of industries, warehouses, wholesale outlets, and related services in central business districts. Growth led to further growth as capital and labor were attracted by advantages of flourishing development. This city was the product of industrialization.

New technology, new production techniques, and new means of transportation and communication have created conditions of postindustrialization. Machines have displaced low-skilled labor. Modern mass-production techniques now require large tracts of land to house extensive one-story manufacturing layouts instead of the traditional several-story factories in clustered surroundings. Trucking, "piggy-backing," and other new freight-moving techniques have made unnecessary the need for centralized locations; and the economies in warehousing and freight handling for retail industries located in the city's environs are substantial. The emerging commercial pattern in urban areas is that the central business district is losing its manufacturing, retailing, household services, and wholesaling to the suburbs, while gaining service industries—banks, law firms, advertising agencies, financial brokerages, management consultants, government agencies, and the like.

The automobile, freeways, and post–World War II public policies[63] stimulating single-home ownership have aided and abetted the centrifugal development of urban areas. Racial fears, too, have contributed to the demographic pattern in the metropolis. The mechanization of farming and the attraction of higher paid jobs in the cities created a steady stream of immigrants displaced from rural communities. Most of these immigrants settled in the decaying centers of cities vacated by the prospering earlier generation of new arrivals. Unfortunately, the newcomers moved to the city at a time when their labor, usually low-skilled and overpriced, was no longer essential, and many of them became permanently unemployed. A large majority of the new immigrants are black, and their added numbers hasten the departure of middle-class whites to the suburbs. Events have evidenced a "tipping point"[64] for cities as well as for neighborhoods. Not least among the reasons for the wholesale departure of middle-class whites from the cities has been court-ordered school desegregation and the busing of schoolchildren for purposes of school integration. Census figures project that an increasing number of metropolitan areas will soon have cities with heavy black majorities encircled by predominantly white suburbs. Blacks have already become the majority in several cities—Washington, Atlanta, Newark, and Gary, Indiana—and it is expected that by the 1980s they will attain an ethnic plurality in a number of other major cities: Chicago, Cleveland, Detroit, Philadelphia, St. Louis, Richmond, New Orleans, and Oakland, among others.

The continued exodus of tax-paying middle and upper classes to the suburbs has created a fiscal crisis for most American cities. Cities are faced with a deteriorating tax base at a time when demands and costs for services are highest. The new immigrants have contributed to the expansion of needs for police, firemen, housing, welfare, sanitation, and education. To counteract their incipient demise, cities have sought ways to retain taxpayers and businesses and to attract new ones. Public authorities strive to influence market decisions in favor of their communities by instituting urban renewal projects, rejuvenation of mass transit systems, planning and zoning, and capital improvement programs.

The suburbs have become havens for those in search of middle-class amenities, homogeneous communities, and professionalized government. Escaping from heavy tax burdens, deteriorating neighborhoods, and rising crime rates in the city, suburban residents jealously guard their newly found life style from possible encroachments. A distinct barrier is drawn between the cities and their suburbs resulting from the unhappy past experiences of suburbanites when they were city dwellers.

The demographic characteristics of metropolitan areas are significant for police work, especially when they concern policing of central cities. Cities will tend, more and more, to be the homes of young singles, for whom the city is a life style; of older citizens, for whom suburban life is impractical; of whites at the lower end of the socioeconomic spectrum, for whom suburban life is financially unattainable; of blacks, largely unskilled or semiskilled, for whom escape is unforeseeable. This poses great difficulties for the men and women who choose police work as their occupation and who must maintain law and order, while retaining the confidence and support of the citizens in this environment.[65]

The demographic changes in cities may also induce substantial changes in the makeup of police personnel. If the police are indeed representative of the dominant group in a community, then the forthcoming demographic changes should give rise to substantial changes not only in the composition of police forces, but also in their styles of policing. As central city governance begins to move into the hands of ethnic minorities, who in effect will become majorities in these cities, it is not unlikely that recruitment standards will be altered to benefit the new dominant group, and expectations of police service will reflect the emergent norms and values. As it is now, minority groups are highly critical of police. Spokesmen for these groups believe that city police operate more or less unfeelingly toward the lower classes and especially toward members of minority groups. There exists, too, the conviction that this behavior is at the behest of the present-day dominant white classes and is encouraged by them. It is unquestionable that there is intense resentment against the police by minority groups. Blacks and other minority citizens often accuse the police of brutality and harassment on the basis of race. This is a most serious problem in police-community relations.

Police Image

In the 1960s many of our cities—Newark, Los Angeles, Detroit, Memphis, to name a few—suffered riots that resulted in the loss of life and property damage in the hundreds of millions of dollars. In the aftermath of these disorders a number of studies were conducted into the nature, causes, and participants of riots, and the behavior of the police in connection with community tensions. From these studies has come valuable information, which can aid the police in their contact with the various segments of the urban population.

Riots have been defined as "a spontaneous outburst of group violence characterized by excitement mixed with rage. The riot is usually directed against alleged perpetrators of injustice or gross misuses of political power."[66] While the actual outbreak of violence is often sparked by a specific incident that causes a spontaneous outburst leading to a riot, the conditions leading to the outbreak are usually of long standing. The National Advisory Commission on Civil Disorders compiled a list of grievances as expressed by riot participants. The following grievances are in the order of importance as mentioned by rioters:

Police practices
Unemployment
Inadequate housing
Inadequate education
Poor recreational facilities
Political structure and grievance mechanisms
White attitudes
Administration of justice
Federal programs
Municipal services
Consumer and credit practices
Welfare[67]

It is instructive to note that police practices headed the list of grievances. Complaints about police practices focused on their use of insulting language, stop-and-search techniques, and brutality, and on the lack of law enforcement in black neighborhoods.

Ironically, many black citizens have expressed repeated concern over the lack of police protection and law enforcement in their neighborhoods. Although it is true, according to crime report statistics, that blacks are most likely to be offenders in crimes of violence and burglaries among others, it is also true that most of the victims of these crimes are other blacks. Consequently, in the black community it is felt that there is no contradiction between "widespread hostility toward police and widespread desire for more and better police protection."[68] Many critics of the police practices support the contention that the most telling discrimination inflicted in black ghettos is the lax enforcement of the law.[69] The late Martin Luther King, Jr., shared this view. He once said that brutality "was not the most serious charge against the police, rather it was the fact that they allowed organized crime to flourish in the ghetto."[70]

In the 1960s it was popularly thought that the typical rioter was a young black racist, possibly Communist-inspired, whose avowed aim was to butcher whites and to destroy this country. However, studies of the profile of a rioter showed this conventional depiction to be patently false. Instead, these studies found that those who participated in riots were "not preponderantly wild adolescents, hoodlums, racial extremists, and radical agitators . . ." Indeed, the profile that emerged showed that rioters were pretty much representative of a cross-section of the black community, especially of its youthful residents. They also tended to be lifelong residents of the city, of average education, and were steadily employed. Perhaps the most significant difference betwen the rioters and those who did not riot was the depth of feeling about job discrimination, white attitudes, the political system, and black civil rights.[71]

With the conditions precipitating a riot still generally prevalent, urban police departments must be prepared to deal with this kind of contingency. The task of a police department faced with large-scale civil disturbance is all the more difficult if it must be confronted alone. The police response as well as the department's ability to mobilize appropriate community resources may mean the difference between a heavy loss of life and property and confinement of the disturbance to a relatively small area and to manageable proportions.

It is possible for the police to avoid a major calamity by a precipitous mobilization of its own resources and by calling on assistance available in the community. It happened in Detroit in 1966. On August 9, 1966, in Detroit's east side—a lower-class black neighborhood—a routine arrest quickly turned into a potentially ugly situation when a large crowd, too large for the officers on the scene to handle, formed in an angry, spontaneous resistance to the arrest. A call for help by the officers on the scene resulted in a swift and positive reaction from the department. Within an hour some two hundred men, trained in riot prevention duty, were dispatched to the area. Simultaneously the police department called on the help of community leaders, whose early arrival on the scene helped to quiet tensions. This case helps to indicate that when police, dealing with possible riotous situations, are able to mobilize sufficient manpower and equipment, and because of their previous contacts are able to obtain outside assistance from recognized community leaders, they can maintain the upper hand in this kind of volatile peace-keeping situation. Police show of force, coupled with positive contacts in the community, kept a skirmish in the urban war from becoming a full-blown battle that day in Detroit. By their actions, the police were able to convince the hostile crowd that they "can and will maintain law and order—if necessary by force."[72]

Public attitudes about police play an important part in the support a police officer can expect in the performance of his duties. That there are segments of the public who are highly critical of the police can be supported by results of a number of studies and by the everyday evidence that is obvious even to the casual observer. As recently as the 1960s, overt demonstrations of hostility directed toward policemen were commonplace and even considered chic in some circles. The recurring confrontations between police and college students on campuses across the country, and similar confrontations in black neighborhoods, can be vividly recalled by most Americans.

A study for the Kerner Commission regarding attitudes toward police found that race and age were the most important characteristics in identifying those who were critical of the police. This confirmed what the media had focused on in the late sixties—the reciprocating antagonism between police and the young and the nonwhite. The report found that the young, black and white, were more likely to feel that the police used insulting language, that they used improper frisk or search procedures, and that they were brutal. However, it is important to qualify the antagonism that the young hold against the police. Realistically, the police and the young man—black or white, rich or poor—are natural adversaries. From all available evidence, most crimes are perpetrated by young men, who are known to be the principal actors in such transgressions as brawls, riots, and other disturbances. But, crucially, the Kerner Commission also learned that despite a general sense of hostility by the young toward the police, young black males evidenced more hostility than their white counterparts.

Table 1.3 shows that in all categories tested and at all age levels, blacks hold more negative attitudes toward police than whites. The data also show that although critical beliefs about the police decline in direct proportion to the age of the respondent, the decline is greater for the whites. The youngest age group of blacks (16–19) is approximately twice as negative about the police as whites; but in the older age groups, the disparity grows to three or four times the critical feelings of the whites. In other words, negative feelings toward the police by black citizens pervade all age groups. Even blacks in the oldest age group (60–69) feel as negative about the police as the most negative of the white group, the youngest age group. The data also indicate that there is a large number of people who, although never having experienced actual mistreatment from the police, still believe that police use insulting language, practice illegal searches, and rough up people. This manifestation of antipolice bias indicates that there exist fear and mistrust of the police, which impede effective law enforcement.

Importance of Police-Community Relations

An ideal state for law enforcement is one in which the citizens voluntarily comply with the law, thereby making enforcement innocuous or even unnecessary. But this would require a society far more perfect than any that is known in recorded history. The best that police can expect is an environment where social conditions do not encourage crime and disorder. Unfortunately, this has not proved to be the case in urban America. Here, perhaps more than anywhere else among Western societies, divisions among classes and races as well as socioeconomic inequities, both real and perceived, have bred a climate of despair, frustration, and anger and a lawlessness that has imposed a burden on the urban police forces of this country.

Although police forces are charged by government to be the agencies of social control, in real terms they may be social control agencies of last resort, in view of the breakdown of the traditional agencies of control: the family, the church, the schools. To be effective in their task, the police must gain the sup-

TABLE 1.3 Attitudes toward the police

Based on a survey of 6000 persons, black and white, in fifteen cities

I. "Police use insulting language"

Age Group (both sexes)	Believe it has happened		Happened to them	
	White	Black	White	Black
16–19	24%	55%	14%	24%
20–29	24	45	11	19
30–39	14	37	7	14
40–49	13	36	3	15
50–59	9	26	6	7
60–69	8	24	3	5

II. "Police frisk and search without good reason"

Age Group (both sexes)	Believe it has happened		Happened to them	
	White	Black	White	Black
16–19	25%	51%	12%	22%
20–29	15	43	5	18
30–39	7	33	2	11
40–49	9	32	2	9
50–59	7	28	1	4
60–69	4	24	1	8

III. "Police rough people up unnecessarily"

Age Group (both sexes)	Believe it has happened		Happened to them	
	White	Black	White	Black
16–19	25%	49%	3%	8%
20–29	13	43	1	7
30–39	7	33	3	3
40–49	5	30	0	2
50–59	6	26	1	4
60–69	3	20	0	1

Source: Angus Campbell and Howard Schuman, "Racial Attitudes in Fifteen American Cities," in *Supplemental Studies for the National Advisory Commission on Civil Disorders* (Washington, D.C.: U.S. Government Printing Office, 1968), p. 44.

port and the cooperation of the public. The role of citizen participation in law enforcement is crucial. It is the citizens who are the major reporters of crime, witnesses of crime, and accusers of wrongdoers; they are the information sources that set in motion the criminal justice process.

Citizens, by their participation in law-enforcement activities, markedly influence the decision to invoke the criminal justice process. Citizens are expected to call upon the police when they witness the violation of the law, to testify before the court, and to serve as jurors. The criminal justice process can be subverted if citizens withhold their participation. They can do so by denying the police the vital information needed in making an arrest, by refusing to testify, or by falsifying their testimony before the courts. In addition to the possibility of denying the police support in their law-enforcement activities by a refusal to participate, citizens can also be major obstacles to police officers who are trying to perform their duties. That these kinds of impediments to law enforcement occur all too frequently indicates a breakdown in the application of the police as a social control mechanism.

It may be expedient to fault the American sociopolitical system for having alienated so many citizens to this extent. However, the police too must share the blame, for they have not provided adequate mechanisms that would allow citizens to be major contributors to the maintenance of social control. And, it should be added, there have occurred a sufficient number of instances of either improper or inadequate law-enforcement practices to suggest that at times the police have exacerbated relations with the community. This is especially true in police-community relations with racial minority groups and minority culture groups, such as young people. The slighting of these groups cannot be rationalized on the grounds that their life styles are alien to conventional norms and mores and therefore have no place in American society. Like the majority of Americans, these minority groups have a right to law, safety, order, and police protection. In the latter case, it has been found that because of the failings of the myriad designated social agencies, the police are often called upon to provide more than just protection to these citizens. It is with these groups that the police service role is the most energized. But it is also by these groups that the police are the least appreciated.

Members of the minority community have had a lengthy history of dealing with impersonal bureaucratic agencies like the police. One of the causes of the lack of cooperation that the police have received from these citizens is that their experience with the police has not changed their minds about the coldness and impersonality of governmental institutions. Furthermore, the probability is very high that contacts a minority citizen has had with police have been disagreeable ones. As things now stand in minority neighborhoods, the tension between the police and the citizens is almost a way of life. The expectation that a majority of minority citizens will take a positive role in police activities is unrealistic, at least for the foreseeable future.

In addition to the essential need for citizen involvement in crime prevention is the importance of community relationships in the police peace-keeping role. There is evidence that a police department's reputation among the dwellers in those central city neighborhoods where peace-keeping duties are most often required is very much affected by the manner in which they are carried out. Pride and dignity are often involved in these volatile operations, which require delicate handling by policemen, who should refrain from using blunt and provocative approaches such as abusive language and threats of arrest, let alone unnecessary violence.

For instance, family disturbances constitute the largest single category of police calls.[73] In some cities more police calls involve family conflict than calls for all criminal incidents, including murders, rape, nonfamily assaults, robberies, and muggings. For this reason violence in the home deserves at least as much public concern as crime in the streets. The police dislike and fear family-conflict calls for several reasons. First, this type of call lacks the glamour, prestige, and public appreciation of a crime-fighting summons. Most important, such calls are extremely dangerous. Many a policeman coming to the aid of a wife who is being beaten by her husband has had a chair or a bottle thrown at him or has even been stabbed or shot by a wife who suddenly becomes fearful of what is going to happen to her husband and who abruptly transfers her rage from her husband to the policeman. Twenty-two percent of all police fatalities occur during investigations of altercations between husband and wife or parent and child.

In recognition of the importance of family disturbance calls, the New York City Police Academy has introduced sessions into its curriculum wherein trainees of both sexes take turns playing the roles of battling spouses and summoned policemen. This provides rookie policemen and policewomen with insights into the subtle dynamics at work in such situations and demonstrates practical techniques for dealing constructively with them.[74]

The isolation of police officials from some segments of society adversely affects law enforcement. This condition is especially prevalent in the urban areas where the need for law enforcement is the greatest and where police community services are the most needed. It is not contradictory that this should be the case. Where behavior and values are most contrary to the prevailing majoritarian standards is where much of the police presence is likely to be. Deviation from the norms of the dominant group may be found to be criminal, in a legal sense, or at least intolerable from a moral viewpoint. If laws and moral standards condemn certain types of behavior, then the police, as instruments of the law, are forced to prevent or eradicate the offending behavior. Realistically, it must be expected, then, that the police and citizens whose behavior brings them into negative contact with police will be natural adversaries. But it is important that the police be able to distinguish between individuals whose behavior is unlawful and the groups with which these individuals are associated. Stated another way, police officials should not attribute criminality to the black race or to young people of any race just because much of their law-enforcement activities concern blacks and young men.

If a police officer is to be effective in every neighborhood, he must understand the habits and the culture of the people in the area he patrols. Without this knowledge his ability to detect *truly* suspicious behavior is impaired; he deprives himself of important sources of information; and he fails to identify the decent people in the community, those who have a stake in society just like every other law-abiding American citizen—the homeowners, small businessmen, professional men, citizens who are anxious to support proper law enforcement. By failing to recognize these potential sources of support, the policeman sacrifices the contributions they can make to the maintenance of order in the community. The way a policeman handles day-to-day relationships with citizens will, to a large extent, shape the attitudes of the community toward the police. These contacts involve considerable discretion on the part of each individual officer. Improper exercise of such discretion can needlessly create tension and contribute to community grievances.

Community relations programs are important to improve communication and decrease hostilities between the police and groups antagonistic to them. One way to bridge the communications gap between citizens and the police is through community relations programs that try to explain police efforts to reduce crime such as new patrol practices and other law-enforcement programs. Another is to provide needed services to a community, and to act on the needs of citizens. While community relations should be an integral part of all law enforcement, the police have a right to expect reciprocity on the part of the citizens, such as having community leaders working responsibly to reduce crime.

The arguments presented thus far stressing the importance of police-community relations have tended to be of a rather practical nature. These pragmatic arguments are, however, directly linked and wholly consistent with a deeper, more theoretical defense of police-community relations. David Bayley and Harold Mendelsohn provide a convenient springboard to this theoretical argument when they write:

> In sum, the position the police occupy in the minority world is only partly a result of what the police do in that world; more importantly, their position is a function of fundamental emotional judgments made by people subjected to pervasive deprivation and inequality. This being the case, substantial improvements in police-minority relations cannot be expected solely as a result of changes in police policy and behavior. It will be necessary to change their symbolic status as well, and that is a function of a total system of majority-minority relationships.[75]

Bayley and Mendelsohn see police-community relations in terms of "the total system of majority-minority relationships"; this provides a useful introduction, as it shows at once both the limitations and the extreme importance of police-community relations. Police-community relations are limited, for the American regime is fundamentally based on a certain relationship between the majority and the minority. They are important, for they can and must contribute vitally to this relationship.

The American regime is fundamentally based on a tension or balance between the majority and the minority. Alexander Hamilton provided the classic defense for this arrangement when he declared at the Federal Convention in 1787:

> In every community where industry is encouraged, there will be a division of it into the few and the many. Hence, separate interests will arise . . . Give all power to the many, they will oppress the few. Give all power to the few, they will oppress the many. Both, therefore, ought to have power, that each may defend itself against the other.[76]

According to Hamilton and other members of the founding generation, divisions among men are inevitable.

The latent causes of faction are thus sown in the nature of man; and we see them every where brought into different degrees of activity, according to the different circumstances of civil society. A zeal for different opinions concerning religion, concerning Government and many other points, as well of speculation as of practice; an attachment to different leaders ambitiously contending for pre-eminence and power; or to persons of other descriptions whose fortunes have been interesting to the human passions, have in turn divided mankind into parties, inflamed them with mutual animosity, and rendered them much more disposed to vex and oppose each other, than to cooperate for their common good. So strong is this propensity of mankind to fall into mutual animosities, that where no substantial occasion presents itself, the most frivolous and fanciful distinctions have been sufficient to kindle their unfriendly passions, and excite their most violent conflicts.[77]

Any attempt by government to eradicate those divisions that exist among men and which lead them to "vex and oppress each other" could be accomplished only by "destroying the liberty which is essential to . . . [their] existence." Yet, as *Federalist No. 10* is quick to note:

It could never be more truly said of . . . [this] remedy, that it is worse than the disease. Liberty is to faction, what air is to fire, an aliment without which it instantly expires. But it could not be a less folly to abolish liberty, which is essential to political life, because it nourishes faction, than it would be to wish the annihilation of air, which is essential to animal life, because it imparts to fire its destructive agency.[78]

Thus, the only way in a free society to deal with the natural division that arises among men into the few and the many is to control its effects—and this, Hamilton and other members of the founding generation believed, could best be achieved by giving power both to the majority and to the minority, "that each may defend itself against the other."

This balance of power, this tension between the majority and the minority, between the many and the few, constitutes one of the principal ways by which the United States government is prevented from becoming an engine of tyranny and oppression. This balance or tension is also present in many of the subsystems of this government, including the criminal justice system. Thus, tensions exist between the police on the one hand and courts and corrections on the other. As the ensuing chapters will unfold, the police are representatives of the majority. Most policemen are recruited from the working and lower-middle classes and reflect the values and express the apprehensions of the law-abiding majority. Moreover, they enforce the laws enacted by that majority. In contrast, courts and corrections have come to represent the rights and interests of minorities and individuals. Thus the courts are often more concerned with due process for defendants than with due process for victims. Instead of promoting the interests of the majority, they are far more likely to strive to provide blacks, the poor, and the young with an equal opportunity to share in those interests that the majority already enjoys.

Similarly, corrections are far more inclined to emphasize rehabilitation of the offender than restitution to the victim upon whom the offender has preyed. Their concern is with the individual and with his successful reintegration into society, not with society and the excision and isolation of threats to it. Yet this is as it should be. Both majority and minority sentiment thereby have access to, and institutional support in, the criminal justice system. Both the majority and the minority are represented and have power, and, as a result, neither can be simply tyrannized or oppressed by the other. However, useful as this balance or tension between majority rule and minority rights may be, it does impose rather serious limitations on the prospects for police-community relations. As Bayley and Mendelsohn point out:

> [T]hose who would ameliorate the relations between police and minorities must also realize that it may not be within the power of the police to do much more than palliate the situation, no matter how heroic their efforts to change. In order to produce better police-community relations changes in police behavior and practices must be one part of a program touching all those aspects of human interaction which create minority status. For the police will continue to function as a lightning rod for minority discontent as long as they must enforce laws created by a community with which minority people only imperfectly identify.[79]

Bayley and Mendelsohn's comments are realistic; there are obvious and inevitable limitations on what police-community relations can hope to accomplish, especially given the American commitment to a balance between majority rule and minority rights. Yet this balance, this tension, is extremely valuable; on it rests the liberty and ultimately the political salvation of the United States. And, although police-community relations are limited by the tension between the majority and the minority, this very limitation makes police-community relations all the more important: police-community relations are and must be regarded as a way of preserving this balance within the criminal justice system.

After all, the police are by far the most significant component in the criminal justice system. Simply in terms of personnel, there are over 420,000 policemen in the United States; in contrast, there are fewer than 30,000 judges and approximately 125,000 correctional officers.[80] The policemen are the gatekeepers of the criminal justice system. It is their discretion—their decision and their actions—that brings defendants into the system or screens them from it. Moreover, they are the most visible. They perform their functions "where all eyes are upon them and where the going is the roughest, on the street."[81]

Courts and corrections, on the other hand, deal only with those individuals already brought by the police into the criminal justice system. In their efforts to promote the rights and interests of these individuals, they have failed abysmally. Thus, in the lower courts, over 90 percent of all criminal cases end in plea bargaining, with the defendant in effect waiving all of those constitutional rights the Supreme Court has been striving to protect; and in corrections, over 65 percent of all offenders treated are later rearrested. For these and many other reasons that will be explored throughout this book, the check placed on the police by the courts and corrections has been insufficient—the balance between majority rule and minority rights is tilted in favor of majority rule. Police-community relations programs can be understood as a response to this concern. They represent an attempt to banish the prospect of a tyranny by the majority, as much to be feared in the criminal justice system as it is in the overall government itself.

This understanding of the need for police-community relations programs is at once both realistic and positive. It sees police-community relations as problematic and perhaps ultimately impossible so long as the division and tension between the majority and minority exists. Yet it also sees police-community relations as ultimately indispensable in preserving this tension and preventing either the majority or the minority from dominating. Police-community relations do not provide simple relief; they will not make everyone a member of one big urban (or bigger still, American) family. Rather, they constitute a realistic appreciation that divisions between free men are inevitable and that every measure consistent with this freedom should be taken which militates against the antisocial consequences of these divisions.

There is no easy solution to police-community relations and there is no single procedure or program that has all the answers and that can solve all the problems. Improving community relations is a full-time assignment for every commander and every officer. Since police relations with the community are an interactional process, additional knowledge about the police roles and the way police perceive various segments of the community needs to be matched by considerably more information about the way the community perceives the police roles, the police in action, and law-enforcement efforts in general.

Police departments across the country are doing many different kinds of things relating to police-community relations, some worthwhile and some meaningless.

The inability of the police to remedy their problems with the nonwhite, the young, and the deviant generally parallels similar failures of other public agencies such as those in welfare, education, and housing. In fairness, the entire fault cannot and should not be placed on the police. Other actors and institutions must play active roles in this urban dilemma in which the police are caught up. Local governments must be willing to pay for the higher salaries that will attract better police officers and to provide funds and support for the kind of training programs that a contemporary urban police force must undertake. The majority public must not make demands of "law and order" with an indifference to the methods that may be used to accomplish this goal; methods that may prove to be prejudicial to democratic practice by way of depriving the civil liberties of the persons affected—both the guilty and the innocent. Minority leaders must be willing to be judicious in their criticisms against the police; to criticize the police responsibly but to withhold allegations until all the facts are known, and to preclude having their criticism lead to violence. Community organizations should be willing to criticize the police when criticism is called for, but they should also rally support for the police so that they can carry out their essential functions.

Ultimately, with or without the help of other interested parties, the primary responsibility for improving police-community relations must rest with the police. If the police do not take the initiative in making good police-community relations a reality, the environment of law enforcement in some urban communities or neighborhoods will become untenable; realistically, this may already be the case in some communities. Understandably, there are numerous causes of community unrest; many of the causes are beyond the scope of law enforcement or criminal justice. There is, nonetheless, a significant relationship between law enforcement and certain aspects of unrest. Symptoms of unrest frequently foreshadow direct intervention by law enforcement. Moreover, law enforcement may become involved in various causal aspects of community tension. At the very least, police must produce efforts that will prevent them from being the prime sources of community tension, even if these efforts or programs can do little to alleviate all the grievances that some citizens hold against this country and its representative institutions. If this is not done, or cannot be done, then the police may indeed gain a new role for themselves: that of an occupying army in a hostile territory fighting an urban guerrilla war. This is not as farfetched as it may seem. Were the events in the 1960s acts of urban guerrilla theater or dress rehearsals for greater drama?

NOTES

1. Howard H. Earle, *Police-Community Relations: Crisis in Our Time,* 2nd ed. (Springfield, Ill.: C. C Thomas, 1972), p. 114.

2. Ramsey Clark, *Crime in America: Observations on Its Nature, Causes, Prevention, and Control* (New York: Simon & Schuster, 1971), p. 139.

3. J. Edgar Hoover, *Should You Go into Law Enforcement?* (New York: New York Life Insurance Co., 1961), p. 7.

4. For an account of a policeman's tour of duty, see Albert J. Reiss, Jr., *The Police and the Public* (New Haven: Yale University Press, 1971), pp. 20–45.

5. Jesse Rubin, "Police Identity and the Police Role," in *The Police and the Community,* ed. Robert E. Steadman; a supplementary paper of the Committee for Economic Development (Baltimore: Johns Hopkins University Press, 1972).

6. David Couper, "A New Breed of Cop: Today's Police Professional," speech at Southwestern University, Memphis, Tennessee, January 30, 1974.

7. Rubin, "Police Identity," p. 23.

8. Ibid., p. 24.

9. The International City Managers Association, *Municipal Police Administration* (Chicago: International City Managers Assn., 1961), p. 236.

10. Bernard I. Garmire, "The Police Role in an Urban Society," in *Police and the Community,* ed. Steadman, p. 4.

11. James S. Campbell et al., *Law and Order Reconsidered: Report of the Task Force on Law*

and Law Enforcement to the National Commission on the Causes and Prevention of Violence (New York: Bantam Books, 1970), p. 286.

12. James Q. Wilson, *Varieties of Police Behavior: The Management of Law and Order in Eight Communities* (New York: Atheneum, 1972), p. 18.

13. Irving A. Wallach, *Police Functions in a Negro Community* (McLean, Va.: Search Analysis Corp., 1970), vol. 1, p. 6.

14. For a more extensive examination of the effect of police management practices on public crime rates, see Alan Edward Bent, *The Politics of Law Enforcement: Conflict and Power in Urban Communities* (Lexington, Mass.: Heath, 1974), pp. 149–154.

15. Clarence H. Patrick, *The Police, Crime, and Society* (Springfield, Ill.: C. C Thomas, 1972), p. 27.

16. Harry Caldwell, *Basic Law Enforcement* (Pacific Palisades, Calif.: Goodyear, 1972), p. 6.

17. Ibid.

18. George H. Gallup, *The Gallup Poll: Public Opinion from 1935 to 1971* (New York: Random House, 1972), p. 2271.

19. Bernard I. Garmire, "The Police Role in an Urban Society," in *Police and the Community,* ed. Steadman, pp. 4–5.

20. George L. Kirkham, "A Professor's 'Street Lessons'," *FBI Law Enforcement Bulletin,* March 1974, pp. 8–9.

21. Rubin, "Police Identity," pp. 33–35.

22. Ibid., p. 36.

23. William A. Westley, *Violence and the Police: A Sociological Study of Law, Custom, and Morality* (Cambridge: M.I.T. Press, 1970), p. 18.

24. Asher Byrnes, *Government Against the People* (New York: Dodd, Mead, 1946), p. 15.

25. Herbert Jacob, *Urban Justice: Law and Order in American Cities* (Englewood Cliffs, N.J.: Prentice-Hall, 1973), p. 135.

26. Harlan Hahn, "The Public and the Police," in *Police in Urban Society,* ed. H. Hahn (Beverly Hills, Calif.: Sage, 1971), pp. 10–11.

27. Brian Chapman, *Police State* (New York: Praeger, 1970), pp. 96–97.

28. Ibid.

29. William Whyte, *Street Corner Society* (Chicago: University of Chicago Press, 1963), pp. 138–139. Chapman notes that this rule of moral mediation may be reduced in a legalistic style police operation. Indeed, the actual implication of the adoption of a legalistically oriented style of policing may be that the dominant group of the community wants the assurance that their mores are being enforced across the board. In the legalistic style of policing, one might imagine there were a single standard of community conduct. For a complete description of the legalistic and other politically induced styles of policing, see Wilson, *Varieties of Police Behavior,* p. 172.

30. Joseph Lohman, "New Dimensions in Race, Tension, and Conflict," in *Police and the Changing Community,* ed. Nelson A. Watson (Washington, D.C.: International Association of Chiefs of Police, 1965), p. 42.

31. Michael Banton, "Social Integration and Police Authority," in *Police and the Changing Community,* ed. Watson, p. 30.

32. Ibid., p. 31.

34 Introduction

33. J. E. Curry and Glen D. King, *Race Tensions and the Police* (Springfield, Ill.: C. C Thomas, 1962), p. 13.

34. David H. Bayley, *The Police and Political Development in India* (Princeton: Princeton University Press, 1969), p. 15.

35. John Bellamy, *Crime and Public Order in England in the Later Middle Ages* (London: Routledge & Kegan Paul, 1973), p. 67.

36. Bayley, *Police and Political Development*, p. 13.

37. Geoffrey Gorer, *Exploring English Character* (London: Cresset Press, 1955), pp. 310–311.

38. Bayley, *Police and Political Development*, p. 13. For additional discussion of this issue, refer to two books by Sir Charles Reith, *A Short History of the British Police* (London: Oxford University Press, 1948) and *The Blind Eye of History: A Study of the Origins of the Present Era* (London: Faber & Faber, 1952), as well as Bellamy's study of crime and police in medieval England, cited earlier.

39. As reviewed in Bayley, *Police and Political Development*, p. 14.

40. Bruce Smith, Jr., *Police Systems in the United States*, 2nd ed., rev. (New York: Harper & Row, 1960), pp. 104–105.

41. Byrnes, *Government Against the People*, p. 213.

42. As quoted in Leonard Ruchelman, ed., *Who Rules the Police?* (New York: New York University Press, 1973), p. 189.

43. Fred J. Cook, "The Pusher Cop: The Institutionalizing of Police Corruption," *New York*, August 16, 1971, p. 22.

44. Shuichi Sugai, "The Japanese Police System," in *Five Studies in Japanese Politics*, ed. Robert Ward (Ann Arbor: University of Michigan Press, 1968), p. 3.

45. Ibid., pp. 3–5.

46. Thomas A. Aaron, *The Control of Police Discretion* (Springfield, Ill., C. C Thomas, 1966), pp. 12–14.

47. Chapman, *Police State*, p. 52.

48. Ibid.

49. Jacob, *Urban Justice*, p. 25. Jacob cites the example of Chicago as a city where the mayor has very strong authority over the police department; Los Angeles, with a fragmented political structure and a weak mayor, represents the other extreme.

50. Wilson, *Varieties of Police Behavior*, p. 230.

51. Ibid. See pp. 140–226 for a complete description.

52. Ibid., p. 140.

53. Ibid., p. 200.

54. William A. Westley, "The Police: A Sociological Study of Law, Custom, and Morality," unpublished Ph.D. dissertation, University of Chicago, 1951, pp. 60–61.

55. See Neil W. Chamberlain, *Beyond Malthus: Population and Power* (New York: Basic Books, 1970).

56. "A crime is behavior labeled deviant and considered so dangerous that perpetrators are threatened with punishment legitimately imposed by the government" (Herbert Jacob in *Urban Justice*, p. 16).

57. Based on the account in Edward T. Hall, *The Hidden Dimension* (Garden City, N.Y.: Doubleday, 1969), pp. 23–32.

58. Ibid., p. 26.

59. The President's Commission on Law Enforcement and the Administration of Justice, *The Challenge of Crime in a Free Society* (New York: Avon, 1968), pp. 88–89. Refer also to John Kaplan, *Criminal Justice: Introductory Cases and Materials* (Mineola, N.Y.: Foundation Press, 1973), pp. 602–606.

60. See Byrnes, *Government Against the People*, p. 164.

61. Lohman, "New Dimensions," p. 42.

62. George Edwards, *The Police on the Urban Frontier* (New York: Institute of Human Relations Press, 1968), pp. 7–8.

63. The creation of the Federal Housing Administration (FHA) encouraged middle-income, single-family dwelling construction in the outlying areas of a city. The FHA was established for the purpose of insuring home loans made by insurance companies and savings and commercial banks. However, it also provided guidelines that restricted insuring of home loans to new construction—preferably suburban construction—and to low-risk home buyers. Although the act was passed in 1934, its impact on urban development was not fully felt until after World War II. It was then that the growing affluence of white Americans, coupled with the severe postwar housing shortage, led to wide-scale development of suburban bedroom communities. Minority citizens were not able to take advantage of the FHA because private lending institutions and the federal government regarded them as financial bad risks, nor was there then a sufficient number of minority citizens affluent enough to attain the middle-class status of homeownership. Furthermore, residential segregation in these new suburban developments was encouraged by the FHA, whose initial guidelines called for "homogeneity" in developed communities. See Alan Edward Bent, *Escape from Anarchy: A Strategy for Urban Survival* (Memphis: Memphis State University Press, 1972).

64. A tipping point is reached when an area's black-to-white population ratio has reached an unacceptable level to the white residents and a wholesale white exodus ensues, turning the area into a black ghetto.

65. Also, there will be the wealthy few who remain in the city, and some of them may feel that their privileges extend to the law. The consequences of this attitude will be an added burden to law-enforcement officers if those who are privileged choose to flaunt the law and, while doing so, can call on their political "connections" in order to try to obtain immunity even in cases when their activity is criminal.

66. Harry W. More, Jr., *Critical Issues in Law Enforcement* (Cincinnati: W. H. Anderson, 1972), p. 346.

67. Alan R. Coffey, Edward Eldefonso, and Walter Hartinger, *Police-Community Relations* (Englewood Cliffs, N.J.: Prentice-Hall, 1971), p. 23.

68. Edwards, *Police on the Urban Frontier*, p. 33.

69. George E. Berkley, *The Democratic Policeman* (Boston: Beacon, 1969), p. 147.

70. Ibid.

71. Ibid., p. 21–22.

72. Edwards, *Police on the Urban Frontier*, pp. 60, 67.

73. Suzanne K. Steinmetz, "The Family Is Cradle of Violence," *Social Science and Modern Society* (September/October, 1973), vol. 10, no. 6, p. 51.

74. Edwards, *Police on the Urban Frontier*, pp. 60 and 67; also see Ralph W. English, Jr.,

"The Police in Our Changing Cities," *Current History: A World Affairs Monthly* (Nov., 1970), pp. 273–277 and 307–308.

75. David H. Bayley and Harold Mendelsohn, *Minorities and the Police: Confrontation in America* (New York: Free Press, 1969), pp. 141–142. Copyright © 1969 by The Free Press, a division of the Macmillan Company.

76. Max Farrand, ed., *The Records of the Federal Convention of 1787*, Vol. 1 (New Haven: Yale University Press, 1937), p. 288.

77. Alexander Hamilton, James Madison, and John Jay, *The Federalist*, ed. Jacob E. Cooke (New York: Meridian Books, 1961), pp. 58–59.

78. Ibid., p. 58.

79. Bayley and Mendelsohn, *Minorities and the Police*, p. 142.

80. Data obtained from President's Commission on Law Enforcement and Administration of Justice, *Task Force Report: The Police* (Washington, D.C.: U.S. Government Printing Office, 1967), p. 95: and National Advisory Commission on Criminal Justice Standards and Goals, *Report on Courts* (Washington, D.C.: U.S. Government Printing Office, 1973), p. 161.

81. President's Commission on Law Enforcement and Administration of Justice, *Task Force Report: The Police*, p. 1.

BIBLIOGRAPHY

AARON, THOMAS A. *The Control of Police Discretion*. Springfield, Ill.: C. C Thomas, 1966.

BAYLEY, DAVID H. *The Police and Political Development in India*. Princeton: Princeton University Press, 1969.

———— and MENDELSOHN, HAROLD. *Minorities and the Police: Confrontation in America*. New York: Free Press, 1969.

BELLAMY, JOHN. *Crime and Public Order in England in the Later Middle Ages*. London: Routledge & Kegan Paul, 1973.

BENT, ALAN EDWARD. *Escape from Anarchy: A Strategy for Urban Survival*. Memphis: Memphis State University Press, 1972.

————. *The Politics of Law Enforcement: Conflict and Power in Urban Communities*. Lexington, Mass.: Heath, 1974.

BERKLEY, GEORGE E. *The Democratic Policeman*. Boston: Beacon, 1969.

BYRNES, ASHER. *Government Against the People*. New York: Dodd, Mead, 1946.

CALDWELL, HARRY. *Basic Law Enforcement*. Pacific Palisades, Calif.: Goodyear, 1972.

CAMPBELL, JAMES S. et al. *Law and Order Reconsidered: Report of the Task Force on Law and Law Enforcement to the National Commission on the Causes and Prevention of Violence*. New York: Bantam Books, 1970.

CHAMBERLAIN, NEIL W. *Beyond Malthus: Population and Power*. New York: Basic Books, 1970.

CHAPMAN, BRIAN. *Police State*. New York: Praeger, 1970.

CLARK, RAMSEY. *Crime in America: Observations on Its Nature, Causes, Prevention, and Control*. New York: Simon & Schuster, 1971.

COFFEY, ALAN R.; ELDEFONSO, EDWARD; and HARTINGER, WALTER. *Police-Community Relations*. Englewood Cliffs, N.J.: Prentice-Hall, 1971.

CURRY, J. E., and KING, GLEN D. *Race Tensions and the Police.* Springfield, Ill.: C. C Thomas, 1962.

EARLE, HOWARD H. *Police-Community Relations: Crisis in Our Time,* 2nd ed. Springfield, Ill.: C. C Thomas, 1972.

EDWARDS, GEORGE. *The Police on the Urban Frontier.* New York: Institute of Human Relations Press, 1968.

GALLUP, GEORGE H. *The Gallup Poll: Public Opinion from 1935 to 1971.* New York: Random House, 1972.

GORER, GEOFFREY. *Exploring English Character.* London: Cresset Press, 1955.

HAHN, HARLAN, ed. *Police in Urban Society.* Beverly Hills, Calif.: Sage, 1971.

HALL, EDWARD T. *The Hidden Dimension.* Garden City, N.Y.: Doubleday, 1969.

HOOVER, J. EDGAR. *Should You Go Into Law Enforcement?* New York: New York Life Insurance Co., 1961.

INTERNATIONAL CITY MANAGERS' ASSOCIATION. *Municipal Police Administration.* Chicago, 1961.

JACOB, HERBERT. *Urban Justice: Law and Order in American Cities.* Englewood Cliffs, N.J.: Prentice-Hall, 1973.

KAPLAN, JOHN. *Criminal Justice: Introductory Cases and Materials.* Mineola, N.Y.: Foundation Press, 1973.

MORE, HARRY W., JR. *Critical Issues in Law Enforcement.* Cincinnati: W. H. Anderson, 1972.

PATRICK, CLARENCE H. *The Police, Crime, and Society.* Springfield, Ill.: C. C Thomas, 1972.

PRESIDENT'S COMMISSION ON LAW ENFORCEMENT AND THE ADMINISTRATION OF JUSTICE. *The Challenge of Crime in a Free Society.* New York: Avon, 1968.

REISS, ALBERT J., JR. *The Police and the Public.* New Haven: Yale University Press, 1971.

REITH, SIR CHARLES. *The Blind Eye of History: A Study of the Origins of the Present Police Era.* London: Faber & Faber, 1952.

————. *A Short History of the British Police.* London: Oxford University Press, 1948.

RUCHELMAN, LEONARD, ed. *Who Rules the Police?* New York: New York University Press, 1973.

SMITH, BRUCE, JR. *Police Systems in the United States,* 2nd ed., rev. New York: Harper & Row, 1960.

WALLACH, IRVING A. *Police Function in a Negro Community.* McLean, Va.: Search Analysis Corp., 1970.

WARD, ROBERT, ed. *Five Studies in Japanese Politics.* Ann Arbor: University of Michigan Press, 1968.

WATSON, NELSON A., ed. *Police and the Changing Community.* Washington, D.C.: International Association of Chiefs of Police, 1965.

WESTLEY, WILLIAM A. *Violence and the Police: A Sociological Study of Law, Custom, and Morality.* Cambridge: M.I.T. Press, 1970.

WILSON, JAMES Q. *Varieties of Police Behavior: The Management of Law and Order in Eight Communities.* New York: Atheneum, 1972.

THE CRIMINAL JUSTICE SYSTEM AND COMMUNITY RELATIONS

III

THE CRIMINAL JUSTICE SYSTEM: THE POLICE AND THEIR RELATION TO COURTS AND CORRECTIONS

In order to appreciate better the role of the police in the criminal justice system and their centrality to the question of majority rule versus minority rights, a basic understanding of the formal procedural framework within which the police operate is necessary. Every village, town, city, county, and state has its own criminal justice system; so does the federal government. While no two of these systems operate precisely alike, they all serve basically the same purpose. They are used by the society to enforce the standards of conduct necessary to protect all the members of the community. They operate by apprehending, prosecuting, convicting, and sentencing those members of the community who violate the society's basic rules. These actions taken against lawbreakers are designed to serve three purposes beyond the immediately punitive one: they remove dangerous people from the community; they deter others from criminal behavior; and they give society an opportunity to attempt to transform lawbreakers into law-abiding citizens. All of these actions, however, are marked by their solicitude for the worth and dignity of the defendant. As the President's Commission on Law Enforcement and Administration of Justice said in its general report, *The Challenge of Crime in a Free Society*, what most significantly distinguishes the criminal justice system of one country from that of another is "the extent and the form of the protections it offers individuals in the process of determining guilt and imposing punishment."[1] In other words, what distinguishes one country's criminal justice system from that of another is the way it resolves the question of majority rule versus minority rights. Our system of justice deliberately frustrates the majority and sacrifices much in efficiency and even in effectiveness in order to protect individuals and minorities.

The criminal justice system has three separately organized components: the police, the courts, and corrections. Each has distinct tasks and, as will become apparent, each is affected differently by the way in which our country has chosen to deal with the question of majority rule versus minority rights. However distinct these components may be, they are by no means independent of each other. What each one does and the way it does it have a direct effect on the operations of the others. For example, in most cases, the police act before the other elements of the system. The subsequent release from custody of an otherwise guilty person because a court found the evidence necessary for his conviction to be unlawfully seized, because a prosecutor was reluctant to present a case for court determination, or because a correctional agency failed to reform a convict prior to his release, has a direct impact on the manner in which the police will perform their tasks.[2] These interrelationships are often characterized by conflict and even hostility. In part, this is the result of competition for attention and funds from outside the system. The following illustration highlights this issue: Consider a large city that has $250,000 in additional funds for law-enforcement and crime-prevention purposes. How should these funds be spent? The $250,000 could provide for ten policemen for a year's time, including salaries, uniforms, training, equipment, overhead, and fringe benefits. The same money, however, could provide for eight new prosecutors together with their necessary support services. It could also buy three months of special training in prerelease centers for each of 120 offenders or pay for an entire year of noninstitutional aftercare for 70 people in the system. The same money could greatly aid narcotic treatment centers, or maintain for a year's time three or four prearrest youth service bureaus.[3] The competition for these funds inevitably leads to a deterioration in relationships among the components of the criminal justice system. But such competition is not the only source of conflict and hostility. As has also been suggested, these tensions can result from viewing the common task of prosecuting accused persons from different perspectives. These conflict-prone interrelationships among the three components of the criminal justice system will become more apparent by following a criminal case through the system.

The Arrest

Figure 2.1 sets forth in simplified form the process of criminal administration and shows the many decision points along its course where friction and hostility among the components of the criminal justice system can arise. Typically, the first formal contact of an accused with the criminal justice system will be his arrest by a police officer. In most cases, the arrest will be made upon the police officer's own evaluation that there is sufficient basis for believing that a crime has been committed by the accused. However, it must be remembered that policemen cannot and do not arrest all the offenders they encounter. As the President's Commission was quick to point out, "a criminal code, in practice, is not a set of specific instructions to policemen but a more or less rough map of the territory in which policemen work. How an individual policeman moves around that territory depends largely on his personal discretion."[4]

A variety of reasons accounts for this need for personal discretion. To begin

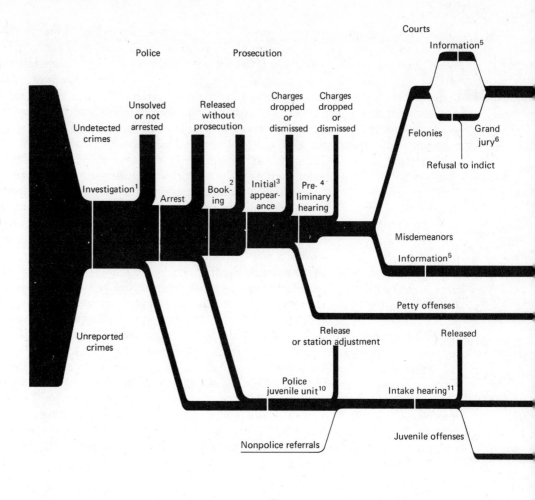

Police Prosecution Courts

Undetected crimes

Unsolved or not arrested

Released without prosecution

Charges dropped or dismissed

Charges dropped or dismissed

Information[5]

Felonies Grand jury[6]

Refusal to indict

Investigation[1] Arrest Book-ing[2] Initial[3] appear-ance Pre-[4] liminary hearing

Misdemeanors

Information[5]

Petty offenses

Unreported crimes

Release or station adjustment

Released

Police juvenile unit[10] Intake hearing[11]

Nonpolice referrals Juvenile offenses

[1] May continue until trial.

[2] Administrative record of arrest. First step at which temporary release on bail may be available.

[3] Before magistrate, commissioner, or justice of peace. Formal notice of charge, advice of rights. Bail set. Summary trials for petty offenses usually conducted here without further processing.

[4] Preliminary testing of evidence against defendant. Charge may be reduced. No separate preliminary hearing for mis-demeanors in some systems.

[5] Charge filed by prosecutor on basis of information submitted by police or citizens. Alternative to grand jury indictment; often used in felonies, almost always in misdemeanors.

[6] Reviews whether government evidence sufficient to justify trial. Some states have no grand jury system; others seldom use it.

FIGURE 2.1 A General View of the Criminal Justice System. This chart seeks to present a simple yet comprehensive view of the movement of cases through the criminal justice system. Procedures in individual jurisdictions may vary from the pattern shown here. The differing weights of line indicate the relative volumes of cases disposed of at various points in the system, but this is only suggestive since no nationwide data of this sort exist. From: *The Challenge of Crime in a Free Society:* Report by the President's Commission on Law Enforcement and Admin-istration of Justice (Government Printing Office, 1967), pp. 8-9.

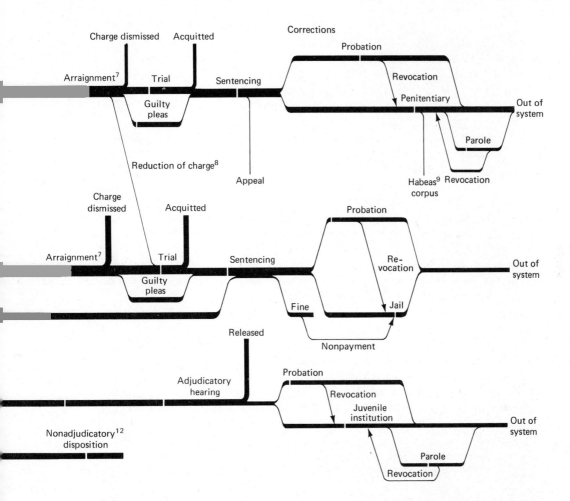

Charge dismissed   Acquitted   Corrections
                                                      Probation

Arraignment[7]   Trial   Sentencing   Revocation
                                                                                      Penitentiary   Out of
                      Guilty   system
                      pleas

                                                                                                   Parole

              Reduction of charge[8]   Revocation
                                        Appeal   Habeas[9]
                                                                                 corpus

              Charge
              dismissed   Acquitted   Probation

Arraignment[7]   Trial   Sentencing   Re-
                                                                                 vocation   Out of
                      Guilty   system
                      pleas   Fine   Jail

                             Released   Nonpayment

                      Adjudicatory   Probation
                      hearing   Revocation
                                                          Juvenile
                                                          institution   Out of
                                                                                                   system
Nonadjudicatory[12]
disposition   Parole

                                                              Revocation

[7] Appearance for plea; defendant elects trial by judge or jury (if available); counsel for indigent usually appointed here in felonies. Often not at all in other cases.

[8] Charge may be reduced at any time prior to trial in return for plea of guilty or for other reasons.

[9] Challenge on constitutional grounds to legality of detention. May be sought at any point in process.

[10] Police often hold informal hearings, dismiss or adjust many cases without further processing.

[11] Probation officer decides desirability of further court action.

[12] Welfare agency, social services, counselling, medical care, etc., for cases where adjudicatory handling not needed.

with, there are definitional problems. For example, how much noise or profanity make conduct "disorderly" within the meaning of the law? What makes a brawl a criminal assault: the first threat, the first shove, the first blow, after blood is drawn, or when serious injury is inflicted? What behavior is suspicious enough to constitute "probable cause," the constitutional basis for an arrest? Clearly, crime often does not appear the same on the streets as it does in the legislative chamber.

A second reason for the exercise of police discretion stems from the fact that in situation after situation, invoking criminal sanctions is a questionable line of action. This is especially true when dealing with juveniles. Thus, although it is obvious that a boy throwing rocks at a school's windows is committing the statutory offense of vandalism, it is often not altogether obvious whether a policeman would better serve the interests of the community and of the boy by taking the boy home to his parents or by arresting him. Only the answers to another set of questions can assure the proper disposition of such a matter: Who are the boy's parents? Can they control him? Is he a frequent offender who has responded badly to leniency? Is vandalism so epidemic in the neighborhood that he should be made a cautionary example?

Finally, a third reason for the exercise of personal discretion arises from the extent to which police work is influenced by practical matters. For example, what is the legal strength of the available evidence? Are the victims willing to press charges, and are witnesses willing to testify? What is the temper of the community? How much time and information are at the policeman's disposal? Obviously, much is at stake in the way the policeman exercises this discretion. If he judges conduct not suspicious enough to justify intervention, the chance to prevent a robbery, rape, or murder may be lost. On the other hand, if he overestimates the seriousness of a situation, tensions within the criminal justice system may be heightened through court action favorable to the accused and critical of the police. Worse still, his intervention may hurt or kill someone or even set off a riot.

Not all arrests are the result of a policeman's exercise of personal discretion. An arrest may be made pursuant to a warrant. In this case, evidence against the accused will have been submitted to a judicial officer who determines whether the evidence is sufficient to justify an arrest. Moreover, in some situations, the accused may have no formal contact with the law until he has been indicted by a grand jury. Following such an indictment, a court order may be issued authorizing the police to take the accused into custody. However, these are exceptional situations. For the most part, arrests are made without any court order, and the court's contact with the accused comes only after the arrest.

Even if there has been no court involvement in the initial decision to arrest the defendant, courts may still have been involved in the case at an earlier stage. The Fourth Amendment to the United States Constitution requires that all searches be reasonable. This requirement has been interpreted to mean that a warrant must be obtained from a judicial officer before all searches, unless there are specific reasons for not doing so. Thus, prearrest investigations sometimes involve searches made pursuant to a search warrant issued by a court. The court role in criminal investigation is broadening in other areas as well, and procedures are being developed whereby suspects may be compelled to submit to photographing, fingerprinting, voice printing, and similar processes by court order. Thus, court involvement in the criminal procedural system in the early phases of the police investigatory stage is becoming an increasing reality.

The Initial Judicial Appearance

In all jurisdictions, a police officer or other person making an arrest must bring the arrested person before a judge within a short period of time. It is at this initial appearance that most accused have their first contact with the courts. This initial appearance is usually before a lower court—a justice of the peace or a magistrate. As a consequence, in prosecutions for serious cases the initial appearance occurs in a court that does not have jurisdiction to determine the guilt or innocence of the accused. By the time of the initial appearance, the prosecution will have typically prepared a formal document called a complaint, which charges the defendant with a specific crime.

Several things occur at the initial appearance. First, the defendant is informed of the charges against him, usually by means of the complaint. Second, he is informed of his constitutional rights, including the protection against self-incrimination. Third, if the accused is indigent and wishes court-appointed counsel, the mechanical process of assigning counsel may begin at this stage. Fourth, unless the defendant is convicted of an offense at this point, arrangements may be made concerning the release of the defendant as he awaits further proceedings. This may take the traditional form of setting bail. Bail is a procedure for releasing arrested persons on financial or other conditions to ensure their return for trial. Typically, this involves the establishment of an amount of security the defendant himself or a professional bondsman whom he may hire must deposit with the court to assure that the defendant will appear for later proceedings. In some jurisdictions, pretrial release may take the form of being released on one's own recognizance; that is, release simply upon the defendant's promise to appear at a later time.

While all of these matters are collateral to the issue of guilt, the initial appearance also begins judicial inquiry into the merits of the case. Thus, if the charge is minor and is one the lower court has authority to try, the defendant may be asked how he pleads. If he pleads guilty, he may be convicted at this point. If he pleads not guilty, a trial date may be set and trial held later in the same court. However, if the charge is more serious, the defendant must be given the opportunity for a judicial evaluation to determine whether there is enough evidence to justify putting him to trial in the higher court. In such a case, the judge at the initial appearance will typically ask the defendant if he wants a preliminary hearing. If he does, the matter is usually continued or postponed to give both the prosecution and the defense time to prepare their cases.

The Preliminary Hearing

The preliminary hearing typically occurs in the same lower court before which the defendant has had his initial appearance. At this proceeding, the prosecutor introduces evidence showing probable cause to warrant holding the defendant for trial. He does not have to convince the court of the defendant's guilt beyond a reasonable doubt; he has only to establish that he has enough evidence for an average person to conclude that the defendant is guilty of the crime charged.

At this preliminary hearing, the defendant, through his attorney, may cross-examine witnesses produced by the presecution and present evidence himself. If the court finds at the end of the preliminary hearing that probable cause does not exist, it dismisses the complaint. Typically, however, this does not prevent the prosecution from bringing another charge. On the other hand, if the court finds that probable cause does exist, it orders that the defendant be bound over to the next step in the prosecution.

In addition to establishing probable cause, the preliminary hearing serves another very valuable function for the defendant: it gives him and his attorney a look at the case the prosecution will produce at trial. It gives a defense attorney the opportunity to cross-examine witnesses he will later have to confront. As the National Advisory Commission on Criminal Justice Standards and Goals points out, "This informal previewing function may be more valuable to defendants than the theoretical function of the preliminary hearing."[5]

The Formal Criminal Charge

Following the decision of the lower court that probable cause exists to bind over the defendant, a formal criminal charge is made in the court that will hear the case if it goes to formal trial. If no grand jury action is necessary, this is a relatively simple procedure. The prosecutor merely files with the court a document called an information, which specifies the formal charges against the defendant. In many jurisdictions, however, use of the grand jury is necessary, and this complicates the process considerably. In these jurisdictions, if it is the determination of the preliminary hearing that probable cause exists, the defendant is bound over for consideration by the grand jury. The prosecutor must then go before the grand jury and present his evidence again. Only if the grand jury likewise determines that there is probable cause does it act against the defendant. Its action, consisting of issuing a document called an indictment, constitutes the formal charging of the defendant. If the grand jury determines that there is no probable cause, it takes no action and the prosecution is dismissed. Unlike the case in the preliminary hearing, the defendant has no right to be heard or to present evidence before the grand jury.

Following the formal charge, by either information or indictment, a whole range of legal questions may arise which require resolution. For example, an issue may arise concerning the defendant's competency to stand trial. The court may have to resolve the question of whether the defendant is too ill mentally or otherwise impaired to participate meaningfully in his trial. If he is adjudged to be sufficiently impaired, trial must be postponed until he regains his competency. The defendant may also challenge the validity of the formal charge itself. If he has been indicted, he may, for instance, assert that the grand jury was selected in a manner contrary to state or federal law and that the indictment is therefore invalid. Or he may assert that the acts with which he is charged do not constitute a crime under the laws of the jurisdiction. The defendant may also challenge the admissibility of certain evidence, claiming violation of the United States Constitution's Fourth Amendment protections against unreasonable searches and seizures and its Fifth Amendment protection against self-incrimination. Still another issue that may have to be resolved is the disclosure by the prosecution of evidence to the defendant. Increasingly the courts are abandoning the traditional approach that neither side is entitled to know what evidence the other side is going to produce until it is actually presented at trial. Rather, defendants are now routinely granted greater access to witnesses' statements and physical evidence (e.g., fingerprints) that will be used against them. Some jurisdictions even compel defendants to grant limited disclosure to the prosecution.

Arraignment

In view of the time-consuming complexity of these pretrial matters, much activity in the criminal prosecution may have already occurred prior to the defendant's first formal appearance before the court that is to try him. This first appearance is called the arraignment. It is the point at which the defendant is asked to plead to the charge. The defendant can respond in one of four ways. He can decline to plead, in which case a plea of not guilty is automatically entered for him. He can plead not guilty, in which case the full adversary process is put in motion. If the defendant pleads not guilty, he may make several pretrial motions, typically seeking dismissal of the charges for want of probable cause, suppression of evidence, or disclosure of evidence—all issues that may have been the subject of previous discussion. He can plead guilty; however, if he does, the law requires that certain precautions be taken to assure that this plea is made validly. Generally, the trial judge accepting the plea must inquire of the defendant whether he is knowingly, willingly, and intelligently waiving such constitutional protections as the right to trial by jury, the right to confrontation of witnesses, and the protection against self-incrimination, and whether he understands the charges against him and the penalties that can be imposed. The judge may also wish to assure himself that there is in fact some reasonable basis for the plea by requiring the prosecution to present some of its evidence. Finally, the defendant can plead *nolo contendere,* or no contest. This plea has the same legal effect as a plea of guilty so far as regards all proceedings on the individual and on which the defendant may be sentenced. However, it is not to be used as an admission elsewhere, as in a subsequent civil suit for damages.

The Trial

If the defendant pleads not guilty at his arraignment, it is then up to the prosecution in full trial to establish to a jury or a judge the guilt of the defendant beyond a reasonable doubt. Unless both the defendant and the prosecution voluntarily waive a jury trial, a jury is selected. The jury selection process is frequently time-consuming and arduous. Prospective jurors are questioned and their views on numerous matters are explored in an effort to determine whether they might be biased. Both sides have the right to reject potential jurors on the grounds that they might be biased. In addition, both sides have a limited number of preemptory challenges that they can use to reject potential jurors without having to state any reason. When the jury has been impaneled, both sides may make opening statements explaining what they intend to prove or disprove in the course of the trial.

Since the burden of proof rests with the prosecution, it presents its evidence first. After all the evidence is in, the defendant will typically move to dismiss, asserting that the prosecution's case is so weak that no jury could conclude beyond a reasonable doubt that the defendant is guilty. If the judge grants the motion, he is, in effect, agreeing with the defendant. This not only results in a dismissal of the prosecution, but also prevents the prosecution from bringing another charge for the same crime.[6] If the judge rejects the motion, the defendant still has two options: He can make no case and rely on the prosecution's inability to establish in the minds of the jurors guilt beyond a reasonable doubt, or he can present evidence tending to disprove the prosecution's case or tending to prove additional facts constituting a defense under applicable law.

Once the evidence is in and all defense motions have been disposed of, the judge instructs the jury on the applicable law. After these instructions are read, both sides present formal arguments to the jury.[7] Armed with the evidence and now applicable law, the jury retires for its deliberations.

Typically, the jury may return only one of two verdicts: not guilty or guilty. A verdict of not guilty may be misleading; while it may mean that the jury does not believe that the defendant is guilty of the charge against him, it may also mean that the jury does not believe that the prosecution has established guilt by the criterion that the law imposes—guilt beyond a reasonable doubt. If a verdict of guilty is returned, the court formally enters a judgment of conviction unless there is a legally sufficient reason for not doing so. Generally, the guilty verdict will be for the offense charged, although juries may find the defendant guilty of a lesser included offense. On occasion, a jury may become hopelessly deadlocked and unable to render a verdict. When this occurs and is reported to the judge, the judge may insist that the jury continue its efforts to reach a verdict, or he may dismiss it and call for a new trial.[8]

The court's judgment of conviction may be attacked by the defendant, usually through a motion to set aside the verdict and order a new trial. In his attack, the defendant may contend that tainted evidence—that is, evidence unconstitutionally seized—was improperly admitted during the trial; that the evidence was so weak that no reasonable jury could find that it established guilt beyond a reasonable doubt; or that new evidence has been discovered that, had it been available at the time of the trial, would have led to an acquittal. If the court grants a motion raising one of these arguments, the common practice is not to acquit the defendant, but rather to require the holding of a new trial.

Sentencing

The next stage in the criminal justice system is sentencing. (If a court has accepted the defendant's plea of guilty, this stage immediately follows acceptance of the plea.) The President's Commission on Law Enforcement and Administration of Justice was well aware of the significance of this stage:

> There is no decision in the criminal process that is as complicated and difficult as the one made by the sentencing judge. A sentence prescribes punishment, but it also should be the foundation of an attempt to rehabilitate the offender, to insure that he does not endanger the community, and to deter others from similar crimes in the future. Often these objectives are mutually inconsistent, and the sentencing judge must choose one at the expense of the others.[9]

To assist the judge in fashioning appropriate sentences, an increasing number of jurisdictions require the preparation of a presentence report by professional probation officers. This includes an investigation of the offense, the offender, and his background, and any other matters of potential value to the sentencing judge. Armed with this report, the judge is then in a better position to impose the sentencing alternative most fitting to the offender: imprisonment, probation, or fine.

Appeal

With the conclusion of these proceedings in the trial court, the matter shifts to the appellate courts. In most jurisdictions, a defendant convicted of a minor offense in a lower court has the right to a new trial (trial de nova) in a higher court. However, in most situations and in all cases involving serious offenses, the right of appeal is limited to an appellate court examination of the record of the trial proceedings for error. If error is found, the appellate court may order that the prosecution be dismissed. It may also set aside the conviction and remand the case for a new trial, thereby giving the prosecution the opportunity to obtain a valid conviction. Generally, a time limit is placed upon the period during which an appeal may be made.

Collateral Attack

Once a convicted defendant has exhausted his appeals rights or has declined to exercise them within the appropriate time limits, his conviction is said to become final. Even then, however, further relief is available to the defendant by means of a collateral attack upon his conviction. For the most part, such collateral relief is sought by applying either in the federal or state courts for a writ of habeas corpus on the grounds that the conviction under which the applicant is held is invalid. These collateral attacks, although a source of considerable relief to defendants, have become increasingly a point of friction in state-federal relations. Defendants convicted in state courts apparently have concluded, and with some justification, that federal courts offer a more sympathetic forum for assertions that federal constitutional rights have been violated during state court prosecutions. State judges and prosecutors have come to resent these federal court actions, which have typically reversed the convictions for reasons the state courts either considered of no legal merit or refused to consider for what they felt were valid reasons.

Correctional Measures

Those defendants whose convictions have not been overturned on appeal or through collateral attack and who have been sentenced to imprisonment or probation enter the last and perhaps least well-known stage of the criminal justice system. Imprisonment is, of course, incarceration in a penal institution, either a jail or a prison. Probation, on the other hand, has been defined by the American Bar Association Project on Standards for Criminal Justice as follows:

> A sentence not involving confinement which imposes conditions and retains authority in the sentencing court to modify the conditions of sentence or to resentence the offender if he violates the conditions. Such a sentence should not involve or require suspension of the imposition or execution of any other sentence. . . .
> A sentence to probation should be treated as a final judgment for purposes of appeal and similar procedural purposes.[10]

Probation and parole are often confused. They are in fact quite similar in that both provide the defendant with a degree of liberty in the community, under supervision, and both involve a threat of incarceration by a summary proceeding, far short of a trial, for violation of the conditions of liberty. Parole, however, involves the release of one who has already served a portion of his sentence in a correctional or penal institution and is understood to be a part of his prison term. In contrast, probation is granted prior to incarceration and is understood to be an alternative to imprisonment.

Interrelationships Within the Criminal Justice System

The criminal justice system is obviously complex and interdependent. Although the components of the criminal justice system are organizationally separate, they are functionally interrelated. Neither the police, the courts, nor correctional agencies can perform their tasks without directly affecting the efforts of the others. Although they are in general agreement that the major goal of the criminal justice system is the reduction of crime through the use of procedures consistent with protection of individual liberties, they are in frequent disagreement on the specific means for achieving that goal and on what to do when one set of means conflicts with another.

The courts' heavy reliance on the plea-bargaining process—negotiation of a plea of guilty in exchange for a lesser sentence—is a good example. It shows the conflict and hostility that can characterize the interrelationships among the components of the criminal justice system. In many courts across the land, plea bargaining accounts for over 90 percent of all criminal convictions obtained. This practice can be defended on a number of grounds. As the President's Commission on Law Enforcement and Administration of Justice has pointed out:

> There are good reasons for this. The most readily apparent is the enormous number of cases that come into the process, especially in the nation's metropolitan areas. If a substantial percentage of them were not dropped or carried to negotiated conclusions administratively, justice would not be merely slowed down; it would be stopped. A second reason is that the facts in most cases are not in dispute. The suspect either clearly did or clearly did not do what he is accused of having done. In these cases a trial, which is a careful and expensive procedure for determining disputed facts, should not be needed.[11]

However, neither the police nor correctional agencies share the courts' enthusiasm for plea bargaining. The police often view the results of such bargains as unjustified leniency. They condemn them as indicative of the prosecution's permissiveness or inefficiency in not being able to try all the cases brought to it by the police. Correctional officials, on the other hand, fear that plea bargaining may reinforce an offender's belief that he can manipulate the criminal justice system, thus minimizing his motivation to participate in correctional programs. Thus the administration of justice is not the "continuous and coordinated process" it may at first appear to be. Rather, it suffers from "serious gaps and barriers."

> Inconsistencies inhibit cooperation; chasms cut communications. The process of criminal justice becomes a series of segments, separated from each other by differences in philosophy, purpose, and practice. Moreover, the segments themselves are often characterized by internal conflicts and confusion. The blanket of the administration of justice, when seen at close range, becomes a patchwork quilt.[12]

With such a "patchwork quilt," a "coordinated and consistent response to crime" becomes impossible.[13] Since the police are that component of the criminal justice system in closest contact with the public, they are often blamed for the failures of the courts and corrections as well. Thus, the need for an understanding of those interrelationships within the criminal justice system wherein hostility and conflict frequently result becomes increasingly important. With this understanding, two consequences are possible: (1) the conflict and hostility may be minimized, thereby improving the overall performance of the criminal justice system and increasing the public confidence in the police, its most visible component; and (2) the relations of the police, the courts, and corrections to the general theoretical problem of majority rule versus minority rights may be better appreciated.

The Police and Correctional Agencies

The police and corrections are those two components of the criminal justice system that are the most separated both in the sequence of their operations and in the tasks they perform. Yet conflict and hostility can arise even in their interrelationships. Thus, the police, because of their law-enforcement and order-maintenance orientation, often consider confinement of an offender as an excellent if temporary answer to a police problem.[14] The police regard the community at large as their responsibility and seek to discharge that responsibility by ridding it of known offenders.

The police are much more intimately involved than correctional personnel with the specific criminal offense. They see the victim and have to deal with the havoc the offender has caused. "They are subjected to and influenced by the emotional reactions of the community."[15] Like the community, they are likely to regard retribution and incapacitation rather than rehabilitation and reintegration as the proper objectives of corrections. In contrast, correctional personnel seldom are confronted with the victim and the emotions surrounding him. George L. Kirkham, the Florida State University professor of criminology who joined the Jacksonville, Florida, police department, provides some useful insights on this matter. He relates how his experiences as a policeman altered some of his ideas about the police, criminals, and the victims of crime. Among other things, Professor Kirkham reveals the following:

I found that there was a world of difference between encountering individuals, as I had, in mental health or correctional settings and facing them as a policeman must: when they are violent, hysterical, desperate. When I put the uniform of a police officer on, I lost the luxury of sitting in an air conditioned office with my pipe and books, calmly discussing with a rapist or armed robber the past problems which had led him into trouble with the law.

Such offenders had seemed so innocent, so harmless in the sterile setting of prison. The often terrible crimes which they had committed were long since past, reduced, like their victims, to so many printed words on a page.[16]

Correctional personnel, unlike the police, get to deal with sanitized defendants. However, correctional personnel, again unlike the police, must also take a longer view. Since over 98 percent of all inmates eventually return to the community, the short-range objective of the police—the arrest of the criminal—must be replaced in the criminal justice system by the long-range view of the correctional staff: the successful reintegration of the offender into the community. This long-range correctional goal frequently necessitates the taking of short-run risks. The release of an offender into the community, either at the completion of his sentence or on parole, always involves some risks. These risks, however, are often unacceptable to the police.

For the most part, those released offenders with whom the police have contact are those who have turned out to be bad risks. As a consequence, the police acquire a distorted and inaccurate view of the risks correctional officers take. Nonetheless, each correctional failure, each parole or probation violator, each individual who fails to return from a furlough, adds a burden to already overtaxed police resources, thereby increasing misunderstanding and mistrust between police and corrections.

The impact of correctional risk-taking on the police is often great. However, the effects of various police practices on corrections, though not so dramatic and tangible, are nonetheless important and often critical to the correctional system's ability to perform its functions properly. The arresting officer is the first contact most offenders have with the law. He is the initiator of the relationship between the offender and the criminal justice system. He is also the ambassador and representative of the society that system serves. As the National Advisory Commission on Criminal Justice and Goals declares, "To the extent that the offender's attitude towards society and its institutions will affect his willingness to respect society's laws, the police in their initial and continued contact with the offender may have substantial influence on his future behavior."[17]

The influence of the police is not limited to their contact with the offender at the time of arrest. The success of such community-based correctional programs as probation and parole often are fundamentally dependent upon police understanding and cooperation. Offenders in these programs are likely to come in contact with the police. The nature of this contact may directly affect an offender's adjustment. For example, police understandably keep close surveillance on released felons, since they are a more identifiable risk than the average citizen. However, when police make a practice of checking ex-offenders first whenever a crime is committed, the ex-offender may begin to feel that the presumption of innocence has been altered to a presumption of guilt. This may have significant disadvantages for correctional programs. In short, "the police should recognize that the nature of their contact with ex-offenders, as with citizens in general, is critically important in developing respect for the law and legal institutions."[18]

The Police and the Courts

If conflict is evident in the interrelationships between the police and corrections, it is all the more pronounced in the interrelationships between the police and the courts. The courts play a dual role in the criminal justice system. They are both participants in the criminal justice process and the supervisors of its practice. As participants, they determine the guilt or innocence of those accused of crime and impose sanctions. As supervisors, they act as guardians of the requirements of the Constitution and statutory law. Both roles have generated conflict and hostility between the police and the courts. Each role will be considered in turn.

Hostility and conflict certainly attend the interrelationships between the police and the courts as the courts function as participants in the criminal justice process. This is true both in the formal and informal aspects of court procedure. Thus, for example, formal trials frequently result in delay. This delay is a source of some irritation to police, who see offenders with pending trials free on bail and engaged in further illegal activity. In practically every criminal case, testimony is needed from police officers, who are subpoenaed like other prosecution witnesses. But cases often are postponed or are disposed of by the entering of a plea, and there is a substantial waste of police resources as officers must wait hours to testify—if at all.[19] During the trial itself, police officers often observe and are subjected to procedural arrangements that they consider useless—or worse, detrimental to a determination of guilt. Police may also be critical of the quality of the prosecution. They may conclude that their efforts are rendered useless by the lack of skill or effort on the part of prosecution attorneys. The disposition of the offender following formal conviction may also be a point of friction. The police may feel that the sentence was too lenient.

Several informal aspects of court processing also cause conflict between the police and the courts. One of these, plea bargaining, has already been mentioned. Two others are also significant: screening and pretrial diversion. Screening typically refers to a discretionary decision to stop, prior to trial or plea, all formal proceedings against a person who has become involved in the criminal justice system. It is often resented by the police as unjustifiably negating their efforts. It is also of concern to correctional personnel because it screens the individual from the system and thereby deprives correctional agencies of the opportunity to provide him with services they can offer. Yet, despite these strains, screening is widely used. The President's Commission on Law Enforcement and Administration of Justice reports that of the adults apprehended for major crimes in 1965, only about 40 percent were formally charged.[20] Much the same is true of diversion. Diversion involves a decision to encourage an individual to partici- pate in a noncriminal rehabilitative program by suspending or dismissing for- mal proceedings. Police are likely to view such action as unreasonable leniency. Correctional agencies may also resent diversion as an attempt to pressure a per- son into participating in a program he may feel is not appropriate for him.

Conflict and hostility have thus resulted when the courts have played the role of participants in the criminal justice system. This same conflict and hos- tility have been all the more intensified when the courts have assumed a super- visory role. When practices of the criminal justice system come into conflict with other values in the society, the courts in their supervisory capacity must deter- mine which take precedence over the other. In recent years, the courts have determined that those values reflected in the Constitution must take precedence over the efficient administration of criminal justice. For purposes of this discus- sion, two examples must suffice.

The first example is the exclusionary rule of evidence. Stated in its broadest form, the rule declares: "Upon appropriate motion by the defendant in a crimi- nal prosecution, evidence obtained from the defendant in violation of his con- stitutional rights to be free from unreasonable searches and seizures will be suppressed by order of the court."[21] In *Boyd* v. *United States*[22] and *Weeks* v. *United States*,[23] decided in 1886 and 1914 respectively, the United States Su- preme Court limited this interpretation of the Fourth Amendment simply to the federal courts. However, in *Mapp* v. *Ohio*[24] in 1961, it applied this same rule to the states through the due process clause of the Fourteenth Amendment. The rea- son for the Court's decision was simple: It was to deprive the police of any incen- tive to violate constitutional rights in their efforts to obtain criminal convictions. As California Chief Justice Roger J. Traynor has pointed out:

> Granted that the adoption of the exclusionary rule will not prevent all illegal searches and seizures, it will discourage them. Police officers and prosecuting officials are primarily interested in convicting criminals. Given the exclusionary rule and a choice between securing evidence by legal rather than illegal means, officers will be impelled to obey the law themselves since not to do so will jeopardize their objectives.[25]

The second example of how conflict and hostility have emerged in the inter- relationships between the police and the courts in their supervisory role deals with police interrogation and confessions. As law professors Jerold H. Israel and Wayne R. La Fave have pointed out: "No area of constitutional criminal proce- dure has provoked more debate over the years than that dealing with police interrogation."[26] This has certainly been the case with respect to *Miranda* v. *Arizona*.[27] The Supreme Court in *Miranda* expressed considerable suspicion of police interrogation. It found the salient features of such practice to be "incommunicado interrogation of individuals in a police-dominated atmosphere, resulting in self-incriminating statements without forewarnings of Constitutional rights." The Court reviewed representative samples of interrogation techniques found in various police manuals and texts. It concluded that such interrogation techniques were employed

> for no other purpose than to subjugate the individual to the will of his examiner. This atmosphere carries its own badge of intimidation. To be sure, this is not physical intimidation, but is equally destructive of human dignity. The current practice of incommunicado interrogation is at odds with one of our nation's most cherished principles—that the individual may not be compelled to incriminate himself. Unless adequate protective devices are employed to dispel the compulsions inherent in custodial surroundings, no statement obtained from the defendant can truly be the product of his free choice.

To ensure that all statements made to police interrogators are the product of the defendant's free choice, the Court suggested the following safeguards:

> Prior to any questioning, the person must be warned that he has a right to remain silent, that any statement he does make may be used as evidence against him, that he has a right to the presence of an attorney, either retained or appointed. The defendant may waive effectuation of these rights, provided the waiver is made voluntarily, knowingly, and intelligently. If, however, he indicates in any manner at any stage of the process that he wishes to consult with an attorney before speaking, there can be no questioning. Likewise, if the individual is alone and indicates in any manner that he does not wish to be interrogated, the police may not question him. The mere fact that he may have answered some questions or volunteered some statements on his own does not deprive him of the right to refrain from answering other inquiries until he has consulted with an attorney and thereafter consents to be questioned.

The response of the police to this supervision by the courts has been predictable. Policemen are often led to question the reasonableness or intelligence of judges and to express wonderment that such wrong-headed men have risen to such high positions of authority.[28] There is also a police attitude toward judges somewhat akin to that of George Bernard Shaw's quip, "Those who can, do; those who cannot, teach." Like other doers, the police tend to be resentful of those critics who measure their value by abstract principles rather than the reality of the world that they know, live in, and see.[29] Jerome Skolnick has noted that the police view criminal procedure with the "administrative bias of a craftsman."[30] They tend to emphasize their own expertise and specialized abilities to make judgments concerning what is necessary to apprehend criminals and to estimate accurately the guilt or innocence of suspects. They see themselves as craftsmen, as masters of their trade; they feel no need for supervision, and certainly not by the courts. They believe that they ought to be free to employ the techniques of their trade; and yet the criminal justice system, in large part because of the supervisory role of the courts, has constricted rather than expanded this freedom.

The Courts and Corrections

Similar conflict and tension exist in the interrelationships between the courts and corrections. As with the police, problems arise for corrections when the courts act either as participants or supervisors. As participants, the courts cause correctional agencies four types of problems. First, repeated court delay may eliminate any specific deterrent effect that the threat of immediate punishment may provide. Second, the technicalities of litigation, like plea negotiations, may discourage an offender from attempting to change his life style by reinforcing his belief that he can manipulate the system. Third, court sentencing may have an adverse effect. Lack of sentencing uniformity is often cited as a source of offender resentment that makes the correctional task all the more difficult. On the other hand, individualizing of sentences—that is, making the punishment fit the crime—is often also a desirable correctional objective. Fourth, the lengthy and intricate review process of the courts is also a cause of friction. Frequent delays during appeal often mean that incarceration is delayed, during which time the offender is given the opportunity to commit additional crimes. Moreover, many correctional officials believe that offenders who spend all of their time and effort seeking means of invalidating their convictions are unlikely to develop new patterns of behavior and are consequently less susceptible to correctional programs.[31]

Interrelationship problems between the courts and corrections also occur as a result of the court's supervisory role. Until recently, an offender upon conviction was deemed to have forfeited virtually all rights. He retained only such rights as were expressly granted to him by statute or correctional authority. It was commonly believed that, short of extreme physical abuse, virtually anything could be done with an offender in the name of "correction" or, in some instances, "punishment."[32] However, since *Coffin* v. *Reichard*,[33] courts have come to accept the premise that a "prisoner retains all the rights of an ordinary citizen except those expressly or by necessary implication taken from him by law." No longer will courts accept administrative convenience as sufficient justification for deprivation of offenders' rights. When rights are limited, correctional authorities must now bear the burden of proof justifying this action. Additionally, courts have subjected correctional administrators to due process standards. They require that all agencies and programs be administered with clearly enunciated policies and established, fair procedures for the resolution of grievances. This increased willingness of the courts to evaluate correctional practices has resulted in such Supreme Court decisions as *Morrissey* v. *Brewer*,[34] which held that formal procedures are required in order to revoke a person's parole; *Jackson* v. *Indiana*,[35] which held that indefinite commitment of a person who is not mentally competent to stand trial for a criminal offense violates due process of law; and *Procunier* v. *Martinez,*[36] which held invalid California's prison mail censorship regulations as burdening the First and Fourteenth Amendment rights of prisoners to send and outsiders to receive correspondence to an extent greater than necessary to protect the substantial and legitimate state interests of prison security, order, and rehabilitation. Various lower federal courts have been even more willing to abandon the Court's traditional hands-off policy toward problems of correctional administration. Thus, in *Holt* v. *Sarver,*[37] the Federal District Court for the Eastern District of Arkansas held that imprisonment in the Arkansas state prison system constituted "cruel and unusual punishment" and gave the state two years to correct the situation or release all prisoners then incarcerated in the state facilities. More recently, in the 1974 decision of *Rehm* v. *Malcolm,*[38] the U.S. District Court for Southern New York found mass violations of untried inmates' constitutional rights in the then Manhattan House of Detention, better known as the Tombs, and ordered sweeping changes. It was extremely critical of the Tombs' practice of treating the entire population as maximum security prisoners and ordered the establishment of a prisoner classification system. It also declared that untried detainees have rights that can be invaded only to the extent necessary to assure presence at the trial and to preserve the security of the jail. Clearly, these supervisory actions by the courts have added to the tension and conflict already present in the criminal justice system.

The Criminal Justice System and Majority Rule Versus Minority Rights

Although conflict and hostility continue to characterize the interrelationships among all components of the criminal justice system—police and the courts, police and corrections, courts and corrections—the tensions present in the interrelationships between the courts and corrections have been eased considerably. Increasingly, correctional personnel are adapting the courts' "least restrictive alternative" test; when some restriction of an offender's rights is necessary, they are selecting the least restrictive alternative sufficient to satisfy the state's interest. Even the National Advisory Commission on Criminal Justice Standards and Goals has accepted this premise. "The entire tenor" of its *Report on Corrections* is that "incarceration is not an effective answer for most criminal offenders. It is neither effective in reducing criminal behavior nor efficient in the utilization of scarce resources."[39] The commission was of the opinion that

> there has been a growing realization that prison commitment for most offenders can be avoided or at least abbreviated without significant loss of public protection. If the committed offender eventually returns to the community, it is best that his commitment removes him for as short a time as possible. The principle has evolved: Incarcerate only when nothing less will do, and then incarcerate as briefly as possible.[40]

Likewise with respect to the rights of offenders, correctional officials and the courts are in fundamental agreement. As the Task Force Report on Corrections of the President's Commission on Law Enforcement and Administration of Justice advanced:

> Correctional administrators should develop guidelines defining prisoners' rights with respect to such issues as access to legal materials, correspondence, visitors, religious practice, medical care, and disciplinary sanctions. Many correctional systems have taken important steps in this direction, but there is a long way to go.
>
> Such actions on the part of correctional administrators will enable the courts to act in a reviewing rather than a directly supervisory capacity. Where administrative procedures are adequate, courts are not likely to intervene in the merits of correctional decisions. And where well-thought-out policies regarding prisoners' procedural and substantive rights have been established, courts are likely to defer to administrative expertise.[41]

Efforts have also been made to reduce the tension between the police and the courts and the police and corrections. Thus, to encourage cooperation and improved communication among the system's components, New York City established in 1967 the first Criminal Justice Coordinating Council. It was charged with the responsibility of developing "an overall coordinated approach to criminal justice problems."[42] Following the successful example of New York and the requirements established in the 1968 Omnibus Crime Control and Safe Streets Act, some thirty of the nation's major cities have established their own criminal justice coordinating councils. Membership of these councils typically includes the mayor, police chief, sheriff, chairman of the County Board of Supervisors, district attorney, chief executive of the local public defender's office, administrative and presiding judges, local directors of probation and parole, and executives of other local criminal justice agencies. They are charged generally with the development of local policies and priorities, the preparation of local comprehensive criminal justice plans, review of proposals for Safe Streets Act funding, the development and implementation of specific projects, and the monitoring and evaluation of such programs.

Another program designed to improve the relations between the police and the other elements of the criminal justice system is unified interdisciplinary training. Such consolidated training is believed to improve communications and effectiveness within the system and to reduce interagency conflict. The Southeast Florida Institute of Criminal Justice in Miami–Dade County, Florida, provides such consolidated criminal justice training in policing, adjudication, rehabilitation, and prevention. Currently it is responsible for the training of all police recruits in Dade County and for personnel of the Dade County Department of Rehabilitation and Corrections. The Modesto, California, Regional Criminal Justice Training Center provides a similar service for eight California counties, offering comprehensive preservice and in-service programs in the fields of law enforcement, judicial process, and corrections.

Despite these programs, however, conflict remains and is likely to remain between the police and the other elements of the criminal justice system. As Albert Reiss sees this conflict, it is the result of a "classic case of dispute over jurisdiction; indeed, of professional jurisdiction."[43] With one set of professionals (lawyers, judges, and to a certain extent psychiatric social workers) attempting to restrict the powers of "would-be professionals" (the police), conflict is inevitable. As Reiss summarizes the problem:

> Whenever a number of roles are involved in making decisions about the same case, problems of overlapping jurisdiction and rights to make the decision arise. Where professionals are involved, there will be competing claims to professional competence to make the decision. The role of the patrol officer, occurring as it does at the lowest rank order in the decision-making system, makes his role most vulnerable to counter-claims to competence, and least defensible. Paradoxically, however, it is the officer's original decision that controls whether law enforcement and criminal justice agents can process the decision at all. He has the broadest potential range of discretion and jurisdiction and therefore of possibilities for the exercise of "professional" judgment, but the most vulnerable position in the system of law enforcement and criminal justice for restricting his jurisdiction.[44]

Reiss is aware, however, that the conflict between the police and the other elements of the criminal justice system is more fundamental than merely a dispute of "professional jurisdiction." As he goes on to elaborate:

> Regarding their position as the more professional one, providing the greater amount of discretion . . . the public prosecutor will insist upon his right of "choice" among the charges that the police will bring against an individual, and the court will insist upon their view of "justice." Yet the police, in the nature of the case, insist upon broader jurisdiction, greater discretion, and they are engaged in the doing of justice.[45]

Ultimately, Reiss implicitly concludes, the conflict is caused by differing understandings of justice. Thus, justice for the courts, and increasingly for corrections, consists of the safeguarding of the civil liberties of the individual, in opposition to the majority and even at the cost of increased crime. The civil liberties and rights of the individual are spelled out in the Bill of Rights in the United States Constitution, and, as Justice Robert Jackson of the United States Supreme Court has noted:

> The very purpose of the Bill of Rights was to withdraw certain subjects from the vicissitudes of political controversy, to place them beyond the reach of majorities and officials and to establish them as legal principles to be applied by the courts. One's right to life, liberty, and to property, to free speech, a free press, freedom of worship and assembly, and other fundamental rights may not be submitted to a vote; they depend on the outcome of no elections.[46]

Justice for the police is something quite different. It includes the assurance of a secure and peaceful society through a reduction, if not an elimination, of crime. The *Report on Police* of the National Advisory Commission on Criminal Justice Standards and Goals underscores the importance of this view of justice:

The fact remains that the fear of crime has limited the personal movement, and therefore the freedom, of Americans. Every decision to limit freedom in order to protect against crime is an acknowledgement that crime continues to erode the human spirit and the quality of peoples' lives.[47]

Crime must be stamped out, even at the cost of the civil liberties of criminal defendants, so that the freedom of the vast majority of law-abiding citizens can be enhanced. This, for the most part, is the view of justice of the majority—and the police.

Clearly, these two views of justice are in conflict with each other. The courts and corrections are emphasizing law, while the police are emphasizing order; and as Jerome Skolnick has observed, law and order may frequently be in tension with each other:

> Law is not merely an instrument of order, but may frequently be its adversary. There are communities that appear disorderly to some (such as Bohemian communities valuing diversity), but which nevertheless maintain a substantial degree of legality. The contrary may also be found: a situation where order is well maintained, but where the policy and practice of legality is not present. The totalitarian social system, whether in a nation or an institution, is a situation of order without the rule of law.[48]

Both views of justice—both law and order—are necessary for the perpetuation of a secure yet free regime. Neither must be allowed simply to predominate. The same is true of the broader issues behind them: majority rule and minority rights. The strength of our nation has always resided in its capacity to superintend judiciously over these conflicting views and tendencies. This has been accomplished, for the most part, through the use of separation of powers and

BERRY'S WORLD

© 1974 by NEA, Inc.

"Don't do anything violent or I'll sue you!"

Reprinted by permission of Newspaper Enterprise Association (or NEA).

checks and balances. Power is so distributed in the government that no one branch or agency is able to tyrannize over the others. The same principles of separation of powers and checks and balances are also present in the criminal justice system. Thus, the courts and corrections have come to emphasize the rights of minorities and individuals to the occasional disadvantage of society—that is, the majority. They have placed a higher priority on rule of law than on order. The police, on the other hand, have come to express the apprehensions and promote the values of the law-abiding majority. They have stressed order to the detriment of the rule of law. Neither, however, has prevailed. Each has been checked by the other, and a balance or accommodation has been reached within the criminal justice system.

As was initially stated in Chapter 1, the tension between law and order, between majority rule and minority rights, has recently taken on a new importance with the introduction of police-community relations programs. For a variety of reasons, the police are by far the most significant element in the criminal justice system. They are found in larger numbers, possess more discretionary authority, are more visible, and affect the lives of more citizens than the courts and corrections, which, in contrast, are racked by a high incidence of plea bargaining, high rates of recidivism, inadequate financial and personnel resources, and archaic administrative practices. As a consequence, the check placed upon the police by the courts and corrections has been insufficient and the balance between majority rule and minority rights has been weighted in favor of majority rule. Thus, police-community relations programs must be understood as an attempt to create within police departments themselves a balance between majority rule and minority rights. This theme will be explored in the chapters that follow. Chapter 3 will explore the attitudes and conditions that influence a policeman's street-level decision making—the exercise of discretionary authority. Furthermore, it will consider the police as representatives of the majority; their identity in attitude and outlook with the middle class and the lower middle class will be discussed. Chapters 4 and 5 will then consider the courts and corrections as protectors of individual and minority rights. Problems in protecting these rights will be explored, thereby underscoring the importance of police-community relations programs for preserving a balance between majority rule and minority rights.

NOTES

1. President's Commission on Law Enforcement and Administration of Justice, *The Challenge of Crime in a Free Society* (Washington, D.C.: U.S. Government Printing Office, 1967), p. 7.

2. National Advisory Commission on Criminal Justice Standards and Goals, *Report on Police* (Washington, D.C.: U.S. Government Printing Office, 1973), p. 10.

3. National Advisory Commission on Criminal Justice Standards and Goals, *Criminal Justice System* (Washington, D.C.: U.S. Government Printing Office, 1973), p. 2.

4. *Challenge of Crime in a Free Society*, p. 10.

5. National Advisory Commission on Criminal Justice Standards and Goals, *Report on Courts* (Washington, D.C.: U.S. Government Printing Office, 1973), p. 12.

6. Ibid., p. 13.

7. In some jurisdictions, however, these formal arguments by the prosecution and defense counsel are made before the judge's instructions to the jury are read.

8. Herbert Jacob, *Justice in America: Courts, Lawyers, and the Judicial Process*, 2nd ed. (Boston: Little, Brown, 1972), p. 126.

9. *Challenge of Crime in a Free Society*, p. 141.

10. American Bar Association Project on Standards for Criminal Justice, *Standards Relating to Probation* (New York: Institute of Judicial Administration, 1970), p. 9.

11. *Challenge of Crime in a Free Society*, p. 130.

12. Robert H. Scott, "Problems in Communication and Cooperation," in *Police and Community Relations: A Soucebook*, ed. A. F. Brandstatter and Louis A. Radelet, (Beverly Hills, Calif.: Glencoe Press, 1968), p. 430.

13. National Advisory Commission on Criminal Justice Standards and Goals, *Report on Corrections* (Washington, D.C.: U.S. Government Printing Office, 1973), p. 5.

14. Ibid., p. 6.

15. Ibid.

16. George L. Kirkham, "A Professor's 'Street Lessons'," *FBI Law Enforcement Bulletin*, March 1974, p. 6.

17. *Report on Corrections*, p. 7.

18. Ibid.

19. *Report on Police*, p. 77.

20. *Challenge of Crime in a Free Society*, p. 262.

21. Francis A. Allen, "The Exclusionary Rule in the American Law of Search and Seizure," in *Police Power and Individual Freedom*, ed. Claude R. Sowle (Chicago: Aldine, 1962), p. 77.

22. 116 U.S. 616 (1886).

23. 232 U.S. 383 (1914).

24. 367 U.S. 643 (1961).

25. Quoted in Jerome H. Skolnick, *Justice Without Trial: Law Enforcement in a Democratic Society* (New York: Wiley, 1966), p. 211.

26. Jerold H. Israel and Wayne R. La Fave, *Criminal Procedure* (St. Paul, Minn.: West, 1971), p. 210.

27. 384 U.S. 436 (1966).

28. Skolnick, *Justice Without Trial*, p. 225.

29. Ibid., p. 197.

30. Ibid., p. 196.

31. *Report on Courts*, p. 7.

32. *Report on Corrections*, p. 18.

33. 143 F. 2nd 443 (6th Circuit 1944).

34. 408 U.S. 471 (1972).

35. 406 U.S. 715 (1972).

36. 15 *Criminal Law Reporter* 3,009 (1974).

37. 309 F. Supp. 362 (E. D. Ark. 1970).

38. 15 *Criminal Law Reporter* 1069 (1974).

39. *Report on Corrections*, p. 145.

40. Ibid., p. 223.

41. The President's Commission on Law Enforcement and Administration of Justice, *Task Force Report: Corrections* (Washington, D.C.: U.S. Government Printing Office, 1967), p. 85.

42. *Report on Police*, p. 74.

43. Albert J. Reiss, Jr., "Professionalization of the Police," in *Police and Community Relations: A Sourcebook*, ed. A. F. Brandstatter and Louis A. Radelet, (Beverly Hills, Calif.: Glencoe Press, 1968), p. 221.

44. Ibid., p. 229.

45. Ibid.

46. *West Virginia State Board of Education* v. *Barnett,* 319 U.S. 624 (1943).

47. *Report on Police*, p. 2.

48. Skolnick, *Justice Without Trial*, p. 8.

BIBLIOGRAPHY

BRANDSTATTER, A. F., and RADELET, LOUIS A. *Police and Community Relations: A Sourcebook.* Beverly Hills, Calif.: Glencoe Press, 1968.

JACOB, HERBERT. *Urban Justice: Law and Order in American Cities.* Englewood Cliffs, N.J.: Prentice-Hall, 1973.

KAPLAN, JOHN. *Criminal Justice: Introductory Cases and Materials.* Mineola, N.Y.: Foundation Press, 1973.

NATIONAL ADVISORY COMMISSION ON CRIMINAL JUSTICE STANDARDS AND GOALS. *Report on Corrections.* Washington, D.C.: U.S. Government Printing Office, 1973.

———. *Report on Courts.* Washington, D.C.: U.S. Government Printing Office, 1973.

———. *Report on Police.* Washington, D.C.: U.S. Government Printing Office, 1973.

PRESIDENT'S COMMISSION ON LAW ENFORCEMENT AND ADMINISTRATION OF JUSTICE. *The Challenge of Crime in a Free Society.* Washington, D.C.: U.S. Government Printing Office, 1967.

————. *Task Force Report: Corrections.* Washington, D.C.: U.S. Government Printing Office, 1967.

————. *Task Force Report: Courts.* Washington, D.C.: U.S. Government Printing Office, 1967.

————. *Task Force Report: Police.* Washington, D.C.: U.S. Government Printing Office, 1967.

RADELET, LOUIS A. *The Police and the Community.* Beverly Hills, Calif.: Glencoe Press, 1973.

SKOLNICK, JEROME. *Justice Without Trial.* New York: Wiley, 1966.

THE POLICE
AND ENFORCEMENT
OF THE LAW

The police are both a reactive and a proactive organization. Police become a reactive force when they respond to calls or complaints from citizens. They are proactive when they initiate a search for criminal violations. Organizationally, the police are designed to be both reactive and proactive in their work. The detective and traffic divisions, the specialized vice and organized crime bureaus, the task force, and even patrol are regarded as proactive units of a police department. However these major divisions of a police department can also be reactive.[1]

When the police act in a reactive role, it is the citizen who initiates the criminal justice system. The citizen makes the vital decision about whether to mobilize the police and to cooperate with them. When proactive, the police make the initial decision about discovering and investigating criminal matters, handling noncriminal matters, obtaining warrants, and booking offenders.[2] However, whether reactive or proactive, the police have the authority for making the most essential decision that sets in motion the criminal process: whether or not to arrest or detain. This is why the patrolman on the beat has considerable discretion; for it is he who must ultimately view a situation, decide whether it is criminal or noncriminal, apply one of 30,000 or so existing laws and statutes, make a decision, and then swiftly act on his decision. Although discretion allowed a police officer in the arrest decision is supposedly circumscribed by common law, statute law, and departmental regulations, the personal characteristics of the police officer have an important bearing on the way the discretion is used.

For better or worse, the police are one of the few organizations where discretion increases as the rank order in the hierarchy decreases. No official in our society, save a police officer or an individual member of a combat team during war, has the discretion and the legal sanction to take the life of another on the spot. No other official may deprive a citizen of his basic freedom by arrest or other form of detainment. In the police, these powers are seldom exercised by higher ranking officers; they are exercised by the lowest members of a police force, the beat patrolman or the detective.

Yet, despite the realities of street-level police decision making, some high police officials subscribe, at least for public consumption, to the idea that police discretion should not exist. A. O. Archuleta, a Utah police chief, argues in a leading American police periodical that "there is never an individual choice to enforce or not to enforce the law." Archuleta goes on to accuse those who support police discretion in whether to arrest an individual or to take him home as "talking about discriminatory law enforcement which is police corruption."[3] More realistically, James Q. Wilson points out that discretion is inevitable

> partly because it is impossible to observe every public infraction, partly because many laws require interpretation before they can be applied at all, partly because the police can sometimes get information about serious crimes by overlooking minor crimes and partly because the police believe that public opinion would not tolerate a policy of full enforcement of all the laws all the time.[4]

Determinants of Police Behavior

The policeman's discretionary authority is the source of much of the police-community relations tension and conflict. For not only is the policeman's role of law enforcement subject to discretionary decision making, but so are the more frequently performed functions of order maintenance and public service. The concept that the police are "the impartial enforcers of all the laws for all persons" is a myth.[5] Although police officers may be admonished by their superiors to "go by the book," experienced patrolmen have learned that you cannot always go by the book because there occur situations about which the book has little or nothing to say.

In their order-maintenance and public service roles, now the predominant tasks of urban police departments, the discretionary authority of beat patrolmen is especially pervasive. This is because a patrolman is occupied most of the time in these, the least controlled, least defined aspects of his job, and the way he performs his work is left almost entirely to his own discretion. His decision-making authority while performing peace-keeping and service tasks suggests that he is a highly trained professional, but in fact he is too often ill prepared for discharging his responsibilities professionally. Thus, some groups in the community have demanded tighter controls over police conduct through a variety of techniques, including civilian review boards and neighborhood control of police.[6]

The nonmechanical nature of police work has made the application of routine bureaucratic standards and norms of conduct unattainable in the course of police-citizen interactions. The basis for police decisions on the street level is essentially linked to the work personality of the individual officer. The work personality is a product of the sum total of the officer's perceptions and attitudes. The occupational behavior of police officers approaches standardization if the perceptions and attitudes of members of the police force are sufficiently alike so as to result in common responses.[7]

Environmental Conditioning

A policeman's work personality, and hence the nature of a community's law enforcement, are environmentally and occupationally conditioned. Community norms and standards often have a bearing on police occupational behavior. For instance, a community may have an ancient statute that forbids kite flying on Sundays. Normally, this law is never enforced. However, if a group of persons who are found to be unacceptable in the eyes of the majority of the community citizens—such as young counterculture youths—decided to fly kites on a Sunday, then the police can respond to the prevailing judgment by arresting this particular group of kite flyers. And they have done so.

Another environmental factor that influences a policeman's work personality has to do with the fact that urban policemen operate in a violent environment, so their job is often a dangerous one. Consequently, the issue of personal safety, or even survival, is a paramount one for a policeman. This means that survival needs invariably play a major part in dictating police behavior.

Because police work is often dangerous, fear is an attitude that accompanies a policeman on his beat. George Kirkham, a college professor who joined the Jacksonville, Florida, police force to learn what it was like to be a police officer at firsthand, learned that fear is intrinsic to police work. He writes:

> Like crime itself, fear quickly ceases to be an impersonal and abstract thing. It became something which I regularly experienced. It was the tightness in my stomach as I approached a warehouse where something had tripped the silent alarm. I could taste it as a dryness in my mouth as we raced with blue lights and siren toward the site of a "Signal Zero" (armed and dangerous) call. For the first time in my life I came to know—as every policeman knows —the true meaning of fear. Through shift after shift it stalked me, making my palms cold and sweaty and pushing the adrenalin through my veins.[8]

Survival for the officer has meant the ability to perceive danger. Skolnick describes this ability as being able to identify "symbolic assailants."[9] The symbolic assailant is a person whose demeanor, actions, and language have become associated by policemen with danger and violence. These identifiable traits are learned by police officers through a history of prior relations with persons fitting these characteristics. From these occupational experiences, a policeman acquires a perceptual shorthand for detecting those persons who are likely to pose a threat to his safety. When dealing with suspects perceived as symbolic assailants, police officers are often influenced in their discretionary behavior by considerations of possible threats to their survival rather than by legal grounds.

Occupational Influences

A policeman's discretionary behavior is also greatly influenced by occupational standards. For example, police departments attempt to provide measurable indices of law-enforcement activities by which to rate their efficiency. Statistics kept by law-enforcement agencies generally deal with the reporting of crime and the "clearance" of these crimes. A crime is cleared when an arrest is made for the crime. The way these statistics are maintained shows a clear bias toward crime fighting as the principal police duty. The emphasis is on dealing with crime productively and efficiently. Thus an officer is expected to conform to the production criteria specified by his department. Production and efficiency are interrelated, and apprehension rates are usually the measure of a police officer's efficiency. Therefore, a police officer's efficiency is judged by his ability to produce apprehensions, and institutional pressure is brought to bear on each policeman to be "productive."

The stress on clearance rates with concomitant productivity pressures have produced some devious working practices. In response to the stress, policemen have either ignored or deviated from formal rules in order to display high productivity. This behavior resembles the condition common in industrial organizations where foremen and production-line workers bypass formal rules in order to meet production quotas.[10]

In the case of the police, deviation from the rule of law in order to maximize their production is facilitated by the low visibility of much of their behavior. Furthermore, laws and measures that impede a policeman's productivity are often viewed as unjustifiable obstacles. Hence due process of law—a set of judicially enforced constitutional guarantees of fair treatment for the suspect—is often not understood in the police culture as protecting civil liberties, but rather as imposing difficult working conditions. Police officials are frustrated by the concept of legal guilt embodied in due process of law and prefer to adhere to their professional judgment about factual guilt, which gives them wide latitude in their discretionary behavior.

The exclusionary rule, a guarantee against unreasonable searches and seizures by prohibiting the introduction at trial of evidence obtained in violation of the Constitution, has been challenged by police officers striving to meet production demands through "creative" apprehension. Caught in a dilemma where their administrative and political superiors insist on production but their judicial superiors restrain their capacity to produce, policemen all too often resolve the problem in favor of productivity, which promises greater organizational rewards.[11]

Police officials in a number of cities admit privately that they either know of, or have themselves been parties to, cases of "creative" apprehension—for example, the planting of evidence on defendants during the course of apprehension. They typically justify this action on the grounds that the defendants are known to be criminals, known to be "guilty" by the policeman on the scene, but have avoided arrest on previous occasions by skillfully "losing" the evidence of their criminality. One policeman has addressed the question of whether this type of police behavior is either morally or legally justified by this response: "I hate to lie to the judge, and I especially hate it because the criminal knows that I'm lying. It hurts the policeman's credibility with the criminal element. But, hell, if I didn't plant evidence sometimes I wouldn't be making very many cases against some bad characters."[12]

Another area in which a policeman's discretionary determinations are applied with scant regard for legalities is where there occurs a perceived attack on a policeman's authority. This type of situation combines both the elements of perceived danger and a challenge to a policeman's manhood and to the authority he represents. When dealing with instances of disrespect for the police, officers have often resorted to physical force as a means of establishing a strong claim of authority and asserting control of the situation.

The intensity of police feelings toward challenges to their authority has led to an increased tendency on their part to join together and to provide a common solidarity against outside influences. In response to what they consider to be an increasing challenge to their authority, policemen have become more self-protectionist as an occupational group. They have not only closed ranks against perceived outside encroachments, but have also entered the political arena, through their unions and guilds, to secure rights and benefits for their membership. Not least among the rights they seek is the freedom from infringement on their group autonomy and especially the preservation of the discretionary authority of the individual policeman. The issue of discretionary authority is defended by policemen as intrinsic to the principles of worker initiative in the police bureaucracy. Significantly, the growth of their political power, through collective action, has enabled the police rank and file to fend off restraints on their individual initiative. The growth of discretionary authority of the individual policeman has now become more than a question of departmental policy or law; it is now a political issue as well.

Decency in Law Enforcement

Police decision making is complex enough in cases where discretion is authorized, let alone in situations where discretion is not authorized. In reacting to perceived dangers and to threats to their authority, policemen often rely on stereotypic symbolic assailants and other perceptual traits of suspiciousness. This leads to judgments that are of questionable validity and provides a controversial basis for subsequent actions. It is the type of police behavior that is most objectionable to citizens.

While it is true that a police officer must establish his authority in most situations that require his intervention, it takes more than the uniform, badge, truncheon, and side arms to command authority. The need to behave as a man in authority is not an excuse for arbitrary police action. To gain control of a situation, the policeman must establish a legitimate right to intervene. There cannot be a substitute for the legitimacy of police actions. In instances where a legal basis is unclear, police discretion should rely on good judgment, prudence, and common sense. It is unfortunate that most police training programs do not inculcate these values. The vast majority of policemen on the streets are products of training techniques that are often culture-bound; once they leave the training environment, their tendency to stereotype symbolic assailants is further reinforced by peer-group socialization in the work environment. So long as the job personality of most police officers continues to reflect survival and authority needs and these needs give rise to perceptual stereotyping and unauthorized discretionary behavior, police-community tensions will continue to be a very serious problem.

Realistically, personal discretion is unavoidable. Because of the wide range of police responsibility there is much that is judgmental in many police-citizen interactions. But despite the ambiguities of police roles, abuses in discretionary authority must be guarded against. A police official must reject the notion that he is endowed with a special authority and that he is above the law when he is acting as the legal guardian of society. Reliance on personal judgments must not allow for personal prejudices to interfere with job-related decisions or else the decisions will inevitably be unjust and discriminatory.

Understandably, there is a fine line between discrimination, or discriminatory decisions, and discretion supported by empirically tested evidence of criminality. While there is real-world evidence that the majority of crimes are committed by blacks, youths, and low-income persons, and while this has justified the need for a larger police presence in areas where these persons predominate, it does not justify a blanket suspicion of all people who fit these categories. To stereotype a certain category of citizens as criminals does violence to the democratic concern for justice and gives credence to those who contend that law enforcement is highly prejudicial.

Suspiciousness is indeed an important quality in police behavior, and when certain groups—such as blacks, young people, and low-income persons—commit a disproportionate share of all reported crimes, this influences the policeman to treat all persons fitting those descriptions with suspicion. This leads to a heightening of police activity of routinely questioning persons in these categories on the street, stopping and frisking them, and detaining them for further interrogation, especially if a crime has been reported in the area where they were stopped. To do otherwise would be considered a dereliction of duty by a policeman. Again, discretionary authority must not be abused and curbstone justice must be avoided in these cases.

The excessive practice of field interrogation will invariably involve a number of law-abiding citizens who fit the category of suspicious persons by virtue of their race or personal appearance. By needlessly antagonizing these citizens, the police deprive themselves of the support of the law-abiding population in the neighborhoods where most of the crime is committed and where most of the peace is breached. It is difficult enough to enforce the law and maintain peace and order in these areas without antagonizing everyone who lives there.[13] There cannot be a substitute for the exercise of good judgment in the determination of truly suspicious persons; and indiscriminate stereotyping of a group of citizens may be expedient law enforcement, but it is detrimental to community relations. Moreover, in a democracy, expediency in law enforcement is intolerable when this does violence to individual freedom and justice.

Whether discretionary behavior is authorized or unauthorized, the application of discretion is nonetheless widely used in police decision making on the street level. Properly understood, police discretion must preserve a delicate balance between community protection and individual rights. Although a great deal of police discretion escapes notice, the person who is the subject of a police decision is well aware of its application. A speeding motorist who has received a courtesy warning instead of a traffic summons has been the beneficiary of police discretion. The addict who is allowed to go free in exchange for providing police with valuable and accurate information about criminals and criminality knows what police discretion is all about. On other other hand, a jaywalker whose action has been unknowingly observed by the police and is not given a summons for his minor transgression is totally unaware that he was momentarily the subject of a police decision.

The latitude allowed a beat patrolman on the street is the inevitable product of the insufficiency, and even the inappropriateness, of many institutional and legal guidelines. Policemen are normally assigned individually or in pairs to patrol a specific territory out of sight of their immediate superiors, let alone command officers at headquarters level. Realities of contemporary policing require these officers to play a variety of roles, and the performance of these roles is made possible by the discretionary behavior of each individual officer. The democratic ideal states that society is governed by laws and not by men. The fact is that in the real world, it is the unavoidable decisions of men that set the legal process in motion. If these decisions have little or nothing to do with the law, then the democratic ideal has nothing to do with reality as it is played out in police-citizen relationships.

Police decision making affects the democratic process in a fundamental way. And these decisions are formed out of a variety of experiential conditions. Ultimately, police-community relations begin with the factors that influence police behavior, and it can be said that these factors predetermine the type of law enforcement that a community obtains.

Police Personality: Attitude Formation

The total range of police occupational experiences shapes the way the law is enforced and the kind of relations that the police will have with the community. A police officer internalizes the effects of these experiences so that they occupy an important part of his value system. Therefore, what a community can expect in the way of police practices and behavior is an attitude shaped by the officer's own occupational experiences.

Much of what has been said and written about the police has presented the view that there is a common attitude among policemen of cynicism, suspiciousness, conservatism, and bigotry.[14] However, the very inconsistency of the evidence supporting these traits as common to the "police personality" makes it difficult to accept these findings uncritically. With approximately 40,000 police agencies in the United States, the occurrence of a single dominant personality type would seem questionable.

The conventional discussions of the police personality normally zero in on the authoritarian aspects of the police character. While there is some consensus that authoritarianism is a dominant police trait, there is division about how this personality trait is developed. Some argue that authoritarian personalities are selected for police work, while others feel that police work itself produces an authoritarian world view. The arguments concerning determinants of the police personality will now be examined.[15]

Selection of Authoritarian Personality Types

One explanation of police authoritarianism is that individuals already possessing authoritarian characteristics are selected for police work in the first place. This kind of selection is done in three ways: (1) self-selection; (2) the screening out of "liberals"; and (3) recruitment from an authoritarian class of people.

The selection process consists of written examinations, physical agility tests, oral interviews, and background investigations. The screening process is probably biased in favor of certain groups despite its purpose as an objective method by which to screen prospective applicants. The bias occurs when, consciously or unconsciously, a police department screens for "compatible" applicants. These are applicants whose mores, attitudes, and opinions coincide with those already existing within the department.

The portion of the screening process that singles out the desired values and norms is in the oral interview and attitudinal questionnaire stage. Unquestionably, the screening process enables the police to identify and therefore to eliminate unstable and undesirable personalities, but it also has the effect of screening out applicants with "incompatible" values according to the value scales of the officials doing the screening. The physical requirements also play a part in excluding still more potential applicants, and these requirements, especially the height requirement, usually cause the exclusion of members of certain ethnic groups such as Chicanos and Oriental-Americans.

It is said that individuals who already possess authoritarian personalities may deliberately select a police career because they feel that police organizations fit their personality needs. These persons may be drawn to police work by the conventional image of a paramilitary organization whose primary concern is to unearth suspicious activities and protect conventional moral standards.

Research supporting the notion that specific personalities are chosen for different occupations is unclear. Although there is evidence that certain personalities will be attracted to certain occupations, this holds true only when the occupations are specifically and narrowly defined. Police work, however, takes in a number of tasks and is not easily defined. The policeman on the street must perform a wide variety of roles and tasks ranging from law enforcer to social worker. However, critics who insist that authoritarian personalities are selected for police work maintain that although the myriad roles of the police defy an easy description for the occupation, the traditional perception of the police role as that of crime fighter is the one that is most associated with police work, and it is this task that authoritarian individuals find appealing.

The absence of police officers with liberal political backgrounds may be attributed to the rigorous character investigations that weed out anyone with any radical political activity in his past. Even if a liberal becomes a policeman, he is not likely to remain in police work. Because police forces are already conservative organizations, the liberal individual will not find much support and reinforcement for his attitudes. The liberal recruit is likely to be ostracized by his peers for his beliefs; moreover, the nature of the organization as a paramilitary bureaucracy that rewards conformity and discourages change may be antithetical to his disposition. Should the liberal choose to remain on the police force, he may try to seek alternative support for his values. For instance, he may seek a place in a department's community relations division. Another alternative for a liberal is to change his belief system. But if the change is too drastic for his self-concept, it may be easier for him to opt out and leave police work altogether.

Some writers feel that police work "naturally" attracts working-class men. This is supported by data showing that most police officers come from working-class or lower middle-class backgrounds. Police work is chosen by persons with these backgrounds because it not only represents an advance in social status, but also provides reasonably good pay, security, and "action" for young men without any special training or education.

It is now becoming common for many police departments to express a preference for applicants who, having successfully passed all formal screening requirements, have had prior law-enforcement experience and some college—either a two-year college certificate or preferably a baccalaureate degree. Preference is also shown for minority recruits, especially blacks. While these departments are not experiencing any difficulty in finding applicants with prior police experience, many of them are having problems attracting large numbers of qualified minority-group applicants and applicants with the desired college education. These recruitment difficulties may be caused by the stereotyping of the police by some segments of society and especially by members of minority groups and college men and women. In some cases, these stereotypes may have been validated by negative interactional experiences with police officials.

Some feel that police bureaucracies, by virtue of their homogeneity, have practically standardized norms and biases. When these attitudes are acted out in the community, they provide the police with an occupational image. This image affects some individuals and groups negatively, and consequently they are not likely to be attracted to an organization that represents attitudes with which they do not wish to be associated. Thus the homogeneity of police forces tends to be self-reinforcing. A police career is appealing to an individual whose norms and biases are consistent with those found in the police. Even without the screening criteria that favor applicants possessing the attitudes and backgrounds that already predominate in police agencies, a law-enforcement career continues to attract a person with class, ethnic, and value ties with incumbent policemen. This fits with the essential human preference for an environment that is comfortable and reinforces one's own perspective.

Police bureaucracies may presently be homogeneous, but this condition is not necessarily a perpetual one. Already the changing ethnic composition of the major cities has prompted police agencies to alter recruitment and selection policies to accommodate members of minority groups. The criteria for "qualified" applicants have become subjected to review. Many young blacks are precluded from police departments because of previous contacts with law enforcement that may have resulted in some form of criminal record, no matter how innocuous. Most present-day department standards would preclude the admission of applicants with prior criminal records. However, because this has tended to exclude a great number of minority applicants, some departments have modified this policy or removed it altogether. If this should become common practice, it may result in fundamental changes not only in the composition of police forces but also in the practices and behavior of policemen. In any event, the injection of a variety of ethnic groups from various social and economic backgrounds will provide police forces with a heterogeneity that has not existed historically.

Another expected change in the composition of police forces concerns the growing number of college men and women who either are seeking or will soon seek admittance into a police career. This is already manifested by the rapidly growing number of law-enforcement courses in junior colleges and four-year colleges around the country. These programs are enjoying large student enrollments, which point to an interest in law-enforcement careers. A factor that has led some college-educated people to seek work in police agencies concerns the supply and demand of college graduates. With the steady growth of the number of college graduates in the nation, the value of a baccalaurate degree has decreased. Consequently, many persons who spend four years in a university in the hope of obtaining junior executive positions are now faced with the prospect of joining the growing numbers of a white-collar proletariat instead. Today's average liberal arts graduate can generally expect no more than a low-paying clerical position, even though the position may carry an impressive title. This situation has directed the attention of many middle-class college graduates to careers in occupations previously disregarded. Law enforcement is one such occupation that is becoming the beneficiary of the devaluation of a college degree.

Arthur Niederhoffer notes that prevailing economic conditions have always had an effect on the makeup of police forces. He states that until the Depression, membership in the police force was a monopoly of the lower class. However, the Depression changed all that; middle-class persons began to choose police careers, where there were numerous openings, rather than seek more prestigious occupations where there were few or no openings, or spend their working day in a bread line. Toward the end of the Depression, police lists

> began to bulge with college graduates—teachers, engineers, lawyers, and even some near-dentists and doctors. Of the 300 recruits appointed to the New York City Police Department in June, 1940, more than half held college degrees. Police rookies of that class still remember the envy that they incurred in apprentice lawyers earning $5 a week and out-of-work teachers afraid to leave the telephone in case the rare call for a day of substitute teaching might come.[16]

With the return of prosperity, there was a sharp decline in the number of college graduates interested in becoming policemen. But now that college graduates are once more experiencing lean times, this trend may again be reversed. In any event, there appears to be a high degree of interest in law-enforcement careers on the part of many students now in college, so that it is reasonable to project a forthcoming growth of college men and women in police ranks.

Occupational Influence on Police Personality

The feeling that police work induces authoritarianism is supported by citing a number of occupationally related factors that form the policeman's personality. The factors used by some critics to describe the police personality are suspicion, cynicism, bigotry, anti-intraception, violence, and conventionalism.

Following the successful completion of the screening process, an applicant is accepted into the police department, where his personality begins to adjust to the occupational environment. The applicant begins his exposure to police values, standards of conduct, and norms in the training phase, the recruit school. If the recruit does not already possess these value attributes, the argument is made that he will now become indoctrinated with them, and the longer the training period, the deeper the imprint they make. Recruit school will provide him "with a set of temporary definitions with which he can function until he becomes more thoroughly oriented."[17]

Formal training devotes a great deal of time to technical subjects such as fingerprinting, traffic accident investigation, narcotics identification, report writing, and defense techniques. A major focus of the early training is on the authority characteristics of a police official, stressing that the police officer must make the public respect him. When attention is given to the human aspects of the police job, the focus is usually on the potential dangers that these human encounters provide. The hazardous nature of police roles is impressed upon the police recruit with lessons devoted to the handling of such volatile encounters as marital disputes, violent individuals, traffic offenders, and drunks. Statistics bear out that most police casualties in the line of duty occur while handling disturbances of this nature.[18]

The assertion is often made that policemen are trained to be suspicious of anything out of the ordinary. The proper attitude of suspicion is to be sensitive to any deviation from the norm, for any such deviation may be indicative of criminal activity. Thus the police recruit is taught a perceptual shorthand that enables him to recognize suspicious traits. The development of this facet of a policeman's working personality enables him not only to identify actual and potential criminal behavior, but also to be on constant guard for signs of danger. Suspiciousness becomes an essential personality trait for police officers, and this attitude is believed to be significant for a policeman's self-preservation as well as for effective law enforcement. To be suspicious of situations or persons that appear out of the ordinary is the first step in a policeman's discretionary behavior. Suspicion keys the decision to investigate, which provides the basis for the arrest decision and the subsequent invocation of the criminal process. Accordingly, a police officer's perceptual shorthand of suspicious behavior is the attitude that triggers the chain of law-enforcement responses.

Deviations from the norm that arouse suspicion are called "attention-getters" by the police. Typical attention-getters that are likely to arouse the suspicion of a policeman would include juveniles loitering, persons running at night, or a person carrying burglar tools. While these activities would be considered suspicious by almost anyone, there are other situations that bring charges of prejudicial law enforcement by some members of the community. Police officers, when looking for things out of the ordinary, are likely to be suspicious of a black person in a white, middle-class neighborhood at night, or of counterculture youths, or youths in general, for that matter. These police attitudes have implications for community relations as they inevitably result in the random stopping and questioning of minority and counterculture persons who may have aroused the interest of a police officer by their behavior or appearance.

There are also charges that police suspicion is often more guided by racial and cultural reasons than by objective factors. If police behavior is motivated by race and class considerations, the argument runs, then these attitudes may have received an early impetus in rookie training.

> Most [training] instructors are police officers, sergeants and above and,
> while versed in day-to-day street tactics and the technical aspects of the job,
> most were trained long ago and may be reluctant to accept newer policies

with regard to police-citizen interaction. While most instructors attempt to be objective, their biases are usually clear, either by virtue of their asides while instructing, their racial jokes, or their obvious contempt toward recent Court rulings.[19]

In defense of suspicion as an occupational personality trait it must be stated that because danger is a recurrent theme of police work, a good police officer, out of necessity, has to develop an intuitive capability to detect the unusual, or what Skolnick calls "perceptual shorthand" to detect "symbolic assailants."[20] This means that the policeman formulates in his mind a set of characteristics or traits that he judges to be criminal, and when he observes them in a person he invariably becomes suspicious. The perceptual shorthand comes out of the police officer's experiences on the street level as well as from values inculcated in him by his peer group. Kirkham, for one, finds suspicion to be a trait essential for a policeman's self-preservation:

> As someone who had always regarded policemen as a "paranoid" lot, I discovered in the daily round of violence which became part of my life that chronic suspiciousness is something that a good cop cultivates in the interest of going home to his family each evening. Like so many other officers, my daily exposure to street crime soon had me carrying an off-duty weapon virtually everywhere I went. I began to become watchful of who and what was around me, as things began to acquire a new meaning: an open door, someone loitering on a dark corner, a rear license plate covered with dirt. My personality began to change slowly according to my family, friends, and colleagues, as my career as a policeman progressed. Once quick to drop critical barbs about policemen to intellectual friends, I now became extremely sensitive about such remarks—and several times became engaged in heated arguments over them.[21]

Since suspicion arises out of the detection of out-of-the-ordinary behavior, groups and individuals who are most likely to behave unconventionally, that is, out of keeping with the dominant standards of behavior, are most likely to invite police suspicion. This inevitably results in negative contacts between police and such groups as minority citizens and the young.

Having successfully completed formal training, a phase that detaches the rookie from his previous life pattern and initiates him into a new one, the recruit enters the world of law enforcement as a commissioned police officer. This is the second phase, which has the rookie interacting with the more experienced men, who provide him, directly and indirectly, with the secrets and customs of the police.[22]

The behavior of the patrolman on the street is influenced far more by his peer group and immediate supervisors than by the upper levels of command. As the recruit begins to be socialized into the occupation, he is often told to discount everything he learned in formal training; it is dismissed as being too idealistic for the real world of police operations. It is at this point that the recruit becomes privy to the tricks of the trade of the veteran officers, and these tricks may even include illegal or unethical practices that are preferred for their expediency in law enforcement. Veteran officers are also likely to teach their personal definition of "criminality" to the younger men. The rookie is taught to identify suspicious behavior according to peer-group perceptions, and if these perceptions are under the influences of prejudices of older officers who feel that certain groups are susceptible to criminality, then these attitudes are probably imparted to the rookie. If the rookie is socialized properly, then he will adopt the attitudes of the veteran officer with whom he is paired. What the veteran officers consider suspicious, the rookie will consider suspicious; the manner in which the older officer reacts to a situation is the way the rookie officer will react.

Police work is generally performed in pairs or in small groups, and because the work is sometimes dangerous there is a dependence of police officers on their partners for their survival. In view of the dependency factor for survival, compatibility in a working team is felt to be essential, and for this reason there is a great deal of pressure for the acceptance and adoption of institutional norms. While there is not a universal harmony in police departments, "there is probably a higher degree of compatibility and agreement on the basic goals and means to those goals, in police work than in any other similar organization, including the armed forces. Those who cannot accept the means and ends of the organization quickly find the job unbearable and either resign or are dismissed."[23] The officers who remain in the occupation will enforce the laws with broad discretion, performing their duties in pairs or small groups and without benefit of much supervision. And the way they operate will be greatly influenced by the values and attitudes derived from their peer group.

One of the first things the recruit learns is that most police organizations can be described as closed systems. Recruitment and selection for entry are conducted only for the lowest level of the organization, and promotions are made from within, with only the members of the organization competing for these positions. A police bureaucracy is an inbred organization, and this lends itself to a commitment to the status quo throughout the hierarchy. The new men learn quickly that reform and new ideas are not encouraged.

The occupational structure that the recruit enters consists of the training division, from where he came as a recruit, the records division, the communications division, and the action branches of each department: patrol, detective, and traffic.

Records, or the bureau of identification, is known as one of the quietest places in a police station. This branch is involved in the application of scientific police work, which in many departments is primarily concerned with fingerprint identification. The communications division is an active branch as it is the center of radio activity and station information. The detective division is a prestige assignment and a highly desired one by most patrolmen. Detectives are not concerned with service activities, and they do not observe an established routine. Each detective works on criminal cases at his own pace, and he is singled out for recognition when he solves an important case—makes a "good pinch." The glamour of the detective division makes an assignment there a highly prized one.

Most officers, however, are assigned as beat patrolmen, generally to a patrol car. A major purpose of police patrol is to provide a visible law-enforcement presence. The visibility is supposed to deter crime and to enable peace keeping. Much police activity takes place through the patrol cars, where the radio is the police officer's link to the police department both in a personal, psychological way and from a physical or action perspective.[24]

While performing their job of preventive patrol, policemen listen to life as depicted over their radio, which is too often cheap and sordid, since the broadcasts primarily concern criminal activity throughout the city. Continued and repetitive cruising through an assigned zone of the city, usually having a minimum number of contacts with citizens on an eight-hour shift, subjects patrolmen to severe boredom and isolates them from the community. The men in the cars eagerly look forward to activity that breaks the monotony of a routine patrol.

Jesse Ruben's study shows that policemen have a variety of ways of coping with occupational boredom. Some policemen "look for action," which is to say they self-initiate citizen contacts and investigations. If the patrol car is not a two-man car with a partner with whom to converse, boredom is combated by stopping to chat with other patrolmen or by backing up other patrol cars sent on a call. Boredom-avoidance practices may even include periodically getting out of an assigned zone and racing along a superhighway for a few moments, sleeping, looking for women, and engaging in sexual intercourse.

Ruben concludes that boredom induced by preventive patrol heightens an officer's tendency to suspicion and cynicism. Furthermore, it produces a psychological attitude that is regressive for good community relations, especially as it concerns minority groups.

> Periods of fantasy engaged in during boring, uneventful patrols sensitize the patrolman to the prejudices preached by some of his peers and supervisors. The negative interchanges between himself and minority-group citizens (and by the nature of his work most of his interchanges are negative) are mulled over again and again while he rides around with nothing else to do. He may begin . . . to fear ghosts, but his ghosts are black. He loses some of his intellectual capacity to discriminate between those black citizens who turn to him for assistance and protection and those who flaunt his authority and break the law. He becomes more susceptible to the view that blacks are "the cause of 99 per cent of crime around here."[25]

It is believed that police work provides a policeman with the roles and experiences that create an attitude of cynicism. The police official faces a world over which he has little control. The city's complexity and congestion, anonymity, affluence and poverty, and abundance of opportunity have all been conducive to the rapid rise of crime and crime rates. Confronting a task that has apparently no solution, the police officer experiences diffuse feelings of hate, envy, and hostility, all of which are exacerbated by a sense of powerlessness against the conditions that have evoked these feelings.

In the police occupation the typical adaptation to these conditions is the attitude of cynicism, a combination of a sour-grapes pattern and diffuse feelings of hate, envy, and impotent hostility. This feeling appears to be historically endemic to policemen. The minister of police under Napoleon regarded the world as composed of scoundrels, hypocrites, and imbeciles, with very few exceptions. A 1939 study of American police found that most policemen subscribe to the belief that the average citizen was always trying "to get away with something," that the common fear of the police was the sole deterrent to a universal lawlessness. Other, later studies confirm this pessimistic view that the police hold of society.[26] Police cynicism, aided by the perception held by officers that their working environment is full of savagery and hypocrisy, is further compounded by a belief among many policemen that the average citizen holds an antipathy toward them.

Supposedly the most contrary expression of police cynicism is their racial prejudice. This is explained by defining prejudice as a form of "directed cynicism." There is some evidence that an antiminority group sentiment among policemen is directly related to the extent of negative interaction that they experience with minority citizens. A study by Algernon Black and Albert Reiss discovered that a greater proportion of policemen made "highly prejudiced" statements in precincts located in minority-group areas than they did in white or racially mixed areas.[27] However, this may be partly attributable to the fact that the crime rate is highest in black neighborhoods, where poverty is also greatest. Additionally, values in minority-group areas are significantly different from those found in majority-population neighborhoods. These factors contribute to a culture shock experienced by policemen patrolling minority-group areas, and this may account for the racial prejudice found among officers.

Critics of police behavior often cite cases of police brutality in minority-group neighborhoods as proof that policemen are bigoted and are acting out authoritarian aggression in these situations. However, there are also other explanations for police violence in the ghetto. Policemen have stated that in order to maintain control of difficult situations in minority-group neighborhoods it is necessary to be tough. James Baldwin, the noted black author, agrees: ". . . the only way to police a ghetto is to be oppressive."[28] Being tough in a ghetto may be a matter of survival. Studies have shown that policemen are more frequently physically or verbally abused in minority-group neighborhoods than in other neighborhoods of the city.[29] Furthermore, policemen are alert to cues indicating criminal activity and trouble. Consequently, policemen often perform their duties in minority-group neighborhoods under great stress and anxiety and are therefore apt to use force not necessarily as an expression of personal prejudice, but as a means of preventing injury to themselves.

Another accusation leveled at policemen is that of anti-intraception. This is to say that they bear an antipathy for idealists, who try to complicate a policeman's "reality" with their "softhearted, visionary" ways. Critics point out that the police have a fondness for violence as the way to deal with problems. Police cynicism provides a ready-made rationale for police brutality: policemen need not have qualms about busting heads of rotten degenerate characters. Additionally, violence becomes the expression of policemen who respond to perceived disrespect. This is pointed out as a manifestation of an unhealthy insecurity about status among police officers.

Policemen, the critics continue, are a conventional lot. One of their primary characteristics is their compulsive adherence to middle-class values. Although policemen are generally recruited from the working class, they try to personify middle-class values as they perceive them. Departmental regulations about haircuts and facial hair are used as examples of this rigid adherence to the most conventional norms.

In their politics the police are supposed to be conservative if not reactionary. While there is some evidence that many police officers are political conservatives, conservatism is not so widespread among police as some would believe. On the basis of evidence gathered on the politics of policemen, it is correct to say that the majority of police officers claim political beliefs that would be considered right of center. However, this is not peculiar to policemen. Studies of political preferences among American citizens reveal that more respondents identify themselves as conservatives than liberals.

Suspicion, cynicism, bigotry, anti-intraception, violence, and conventionalism are aspects of a policeman's personality that are believed to be commonplace in police forces. Arising from the nature of police work, these traits are supposedly transmitted from one generation of policemen to the next. The sum effect of these personality traits is the creation of authoritarianism. Some would go so far as to say that the police system would consider itself a failure if it did not purposely create authoritarian personalities among its men.[30]

Police View of Society

A policeman deals with a number of publics, but his working personality is likely to be largely influenced by the public with whom the greatest part of his occupational energies are spent. His view of society is a sordid one, as provided by the radio in his patrol car and as reinforced by his encounters with felons, drunks, and social outcasts of all types. If the policeman is a hero and a servant of the public, he is also its disciplinarian and avenger, and it is the latter two roles that are emphasized by the occupational norms by which the officer's efficiency is measured.

The negative contacts with the public aided in a large part by the sordid world view that the policeman obtains from his occupational environment have caused the police to draw closer together to form a fraternal bond linked by common experiences that excludes outsiders. "You can't exaggerate the closeness of our dealings with people," says a policeman in Joseph Wambaugh's *New Centurions*.

> We see them when nobody else sees them, when they're being born and dying and fornicating and drunk. We see people when they're taking anything of value from other people and when they're without shame or very

much ashamed and we learn secrets that their husbands and wives don't even know, secrets that they even try to keep from themselves, and what the hell, when you learn these things about people who aren't institutionalized, people who're out here where you can see them function everyday, well then, you really *know*. Of course, you get clannish and associate with others who know. It's only natural.[31]

Solidarity or fraternalism among police officers is furthered by the actual or perceived loss of respect and authority in the community. Police are drawn even closer together because of what they see as a decline in their authority—an essential concern to the self-esteem of many officers—produced by lenient courts, their low status in the community, and the dangers to which they are often exposed.

In reacting to what they feel are challenges and abuses by the outside world, the police close ranks for self-protection. The resultant behavior is an emphasis on the maintenance of respect for the police and the observance of a rule of silence within the organization. The police will seek the attainment of respect and authority in the community even to the extent of doing violence in order to show who is boss. The rule of silence insulates the organization from any disclosure of its practices and allows the police to create an aura of bureaucratic mystique about itself. Rodney Stark writes that police solidarity in our society is obsessive. "Its primary manifestation is a cult of secrecy and loyalty not unlike that attributed to the Mafia. The one overriding rule among the police seems to be: 'Never squeal on a brother officer no matter what he does.' "[32]

Crucially, the code of silence not only is applied against external scrutiny, but also works against internal investigations. A policeman learns very early in his career that there are sanctions applied against those who cooperate with internal control mechanisms. A former patrolman in a large Eastern police department divulged that in his first week in recruit training he was cautioned to watch his tongue: "One of your classmates may be a plant from the internal investigation division." This officer recalled that the group norm he was taught to observe was that the most damaging criticism that one can make of a fellow officer is not that he is brutal or that he is corrupt, but that he is a "fink," willing to break the code of silence.

Another far-reaching consequence for the police personality is that the power granted him to perform his duties, and his constant association with crime and criminals, may tempt policemen to view themselves as "superior to the general race of men."[33] A police official is provided with a unique set of capabilities: he is empowered to regulate the lives of others, a role symbolized by his distinctive uniform and weapons. In view of this power, it would seem to be vital to have safeguards against the potential abuses of police power and to ensure that as instruments of the law policemen act in a way that is closely tied to the law. Niederhoffer claims that this is not necessarily the case. Instead, he states, policemen learn to manipulate the law, which then becomes nothing more than a means to an end.

In performing his special role in the social system, the policeman realizes that for much of his time on duty he is above the law. Paradoxically, society has granted him the license to disregard the law in order to enforce it. He may kill where necessary, he may destroy property and invade privacy; he may make arrests merely on grounds of suspicion; he may disregard traffic regulations. The sense of power often corrupts him into a belief that he is superior to the law.[34]

Trauma of Status Anxiety

Although a great number of policemen are originally from working-class backgrounds, when they become policemen they tend to identify themselves as middle class and typify such middle-class values as getting ahead, looking toward the future, owning a home and a new car, assuming responsibility, and so on. But because so many of them are new to the middle class, they are insecure about their status. Without benefit of such social rewards as prestige and high pay, policemen jealously guard their middle-class standing by clinging to their perceptions of respectability. In effect, their doubts about their social status have made them marginal men.

The insecurity is aggravated by the common belief among police officers that they do not receive the prestige or the recognition to which they are entitled from the general public. There is even a feeling that the prestige of police work has fallen in recent years. Moreover, they believe that they are hampered in their work by the courts, local government, and civil-rights groups and their supporters. These perceptions provide the basis for a policeman's uncertainty about himself and about police work.

Despite the uncertainties that go with police work, status anxiety is not unique to police officers. There is evidence indicating that this attitude may be prevalent among working-class and lower middle-class people in general. The results of a Gallup poll taken in 1969 showed that the "silent majority" displayed feelings of insecurity that paralleled those found among policemen.[35] This study of the attitudes of white working- and middle-class Americans revealed that the sample group was increasingly pessimistic about America's future, with approximately 50 percent of them believing that this country has changed for the worse in the last ten years. Further, the majority of the respondents stated that they believed that things were going to get even worse in the next ten years. They were upset by what they perceived to be a decline in moral and religious standards and in community spirit; they were very much concerned about the increasing crime rate and thought that life was fraught with dangers. The solution to these problems, as recommended by a majority of the sample, was to strengthen police forces around the country.

The possibility of increasing police power did not appear to hold a threat for the sample group; it was felt that the threat was to the wrongdoers and not to the "decent people." This groups of Americans were also despondent over the diminution of their buying power and were jealous of blacks, who they felt were getting more than they deserved from the social and economic system. They indicated that blacks did not work for what they got, but rather obtained advantages on the basis of reverse discrimination.

The study revealed that anger and frustration were greatest in the working class, "families whose breadwinners have at most a high school education, hold blue-collar jobs, and bring home income of $5,000 to $10,000 a year."[36]

All socioeconomic groups sampled expressed a concern about crime, racial violence, deteriorating values, and rising prices. However, the greatest concern and the most extreme opinions were obtained from respondents identified as working class. This suggests that socioeconomic status marginality creates a great deal of frustration and resentment. The attitudes of white middle- and working-class Americans happen to coincide with the personality characteristics attributed to policemen: conventionalism, authoritarian aggression, stereotyping, cynicism, and projectivity. This indicates that policemen should not be singled out as having unique personality traits; in fact, policemen appear to be representative of white working-class and middle-class America. These personality traits are not so much a matter of occupational influences as they are indicative of attitudes of people from a common socioeconomic background. If police are authoritarian, then they are no more so than a great number of American citizens. Authoritarianism, as a personality type, is not unusual in this country. Racial prejudice, conservatism, cynicism, and all the other traits associated with authoritarianism appear to be relatively widespread.

While authoritarianism is not peculiar to policemen, their visibility has apparently singled them out for special attention. Policemen, as individuals, are, in the main, quite ordinary people; their occupation and the authority it wields is what makes them extraordinary. Police behavior is of public concern, not only because police work involves so much interaction with a great number of people or because it takes place in public places, but also because the police are now the focus of attention as never before—in the media, in scholarly journals, in the speeches of politicians, and in the conversation of ordinary citizens.

Interestingly, much of police work is not of interest to the scrutinizers of police behavior. Most of a policeman's time is spent in activities that have little or nothing to do with law enforcement. But because these activities do not conform to the conventional concept of police work, they often go unnoticed. When the policeman is occupied in such duties as breaking up family quarrels, writing reports, assisting motorists, and so on, he is not particularly visible, but it is when he performs tasks that appear to be authoritarian in nature that he becomes visible to police watchers. And when policemen perform job tasks that require a visible display of authority, an outrage against police brutality, harassment, and discrimination often ensues. It is ironic that for a time there was a great deal of attention paid to singling out peculiarities that characterize the criminal mind; now the preoccupation seems to be with finding undesirable personality traits associated with the police mind.

Attitudes Affecting Police Morale

Many, if not all, police departments in this country are experiencing a crisis in police morale. This problem is caused not so much by a lack of money or a lack of personnel, but by a set of conditions that are even more frustrating because they are not susceptible to solution within a police department. The conditions and attitudes that have adversely affected police morale may be summarized as a failure of the system of criminal justice and a failure of public confidence.

The failure of the criminal justice system has had an effect on the behavior of the policeman on the street level. In New York City, for instance, policemen make about a quarter of a million arrests a year. There are fewer than 100 judges in Manhattan Criminal Court, and out of all of the arrests made only 180 felony trials went to verdict in Manhattan in 1970. The average arraignment in New York City takes less than two minutes and most of the persons arrested by the police escape going to trial because of dropped charges, copped pleas, and the failure of witnesses to testify. The conditions caused by a shortage of criminal court judges and overcrowded jails continue to persist because of an apathetic general public.

> [The] whole criminal justice system, with its built-in revolving doors, turns even the best cops somewhat bitter and cynical. Hang around any court room and talk to cops and all have at least one common complaint: they arrest a man, often at great physical risk, they book him, have him arraigned, and go to court with him, and before they can take a sip of coffee from the cardboard container in the hall, the man is on the street again. After awhile the cop wonders why he should bother, why he should take the risks involved—why, in fact, he should try to be a good cop at all.[37]

The failings of the criminal justice system are seen not only in the large number of persons who are arrested and then for one reason or another are not brought to trial, but also in the large number of recidivists that the prisons create. The association of recidivism with criminality has led to the accusation that prisons, their intended purpose notwithstanding, are serving as occasional schools for criminals. The combination of an overburdened court system that often can do no better than to rubber-stamp justice and prisons that develop and expand the force of criminals, leaving them better than ever from their stay behind bars, has done little to gain respect for the criminal justice system and the police officer who is the most visible symbol of that system.

The lack of finanical support for the various yet interdependent components of the criminal justice system has a bearing on the problems that the system is facing. The major portion of the criminal justice dollar is earmarked for police work, and only a scant remainder finds its way to be distributed among courts, jails, and rehabilitation programs. This creates the expectation that the police will perform the major burden of criminal justice, "to do what other components of the system cannot, or will not, do. A cop can arrest. He cannot—must not—convict, and he certainly cannot reform."[38]

Police morale has suffered from the perception among police officers that the other components of the criminal justice system are lenient and permissive to criminals and indifferent, or even punitive, to the victims of crime and to police officers. They believe, too, that these attitudes enjoy the support of some members of the public and the press. George Kirkham, the college professor turned policeman, identifies with these police concerns:

> As someone who had always been gravely concerned about the rights of offenders, I now began to consider for the first time the rights of police officers. As a police officer, I felt that my efforts to protect society and maintain my personal safety were menaced by many of the very court decisions and lenient parole board actions I had always been eager to defend. An educated man, I could not answer the questions of my fellow officers as to why those who kill and maim policemen, men who are involved in no less honorable an activity than holding our society together, should so often be subjected to minor penalties. I grew weary of carefully following difficult legal restrictions while thugs and hoodlums consistently twisted the law to their own advantage. I remember standing in the street one evening and reading a heroin "pusher" his rights, only to have him convulse with laughter half way through and finish reciting them, word for word, from memory. He had been given his "rights," under the law, but what about the rights of those who were the victims of people like himself? For the first time, questions such as these began to bother me.

Kirkham adds:

> The same kinds of daily stresses which affected my fellow officers soon began to take their toll of me. I became sick and tired of being reviled and attacked by criminals who could usually find a most sympathetic audience in judges and jurors eager to understand their side of things and provide them with "another chance." I grew tired of living under the ax of news media and community pressure groups, eager to seize upon the slightest mistake made by myself or a fellow officer. As a criminology professor, I had always enjoyed the luxury of having great amounts of time in which to make difficult decisions. As a police officer, however, I found myself forced to make the most critical choices in a time-frame of seconds, rather than days: to shoot or not to shoot, to arrest or not to arrest, to give chase or let go—always with a nagging certainty that others, those with great amounts of time in which to analyze and think, stood ready to judge and condemn me for whatever action I might take or fail to take. I found myself not only forced to live a life consisting of seconds and adrenalin, but also forced to deal with human problems which were infinitely more difficult than anything I had ever confronted in a correctional or mental health setting. Family fights, mental illness, potentially explosive crowd situations, dangerous individuals—I found myself progressively awed by the complexity of tasks faced by men whose work I once thought was thoroughly simple and straightforward.[39]

Adding to the problems of the system of criminal justice are excessive and often hypocritical laws, many of which are either difficult or impossible to enforce. Crimes involving morals—but not personal injury or theft—force the police into the role of the moral guardians of society. This often means that the police must enforce upon one segment of society the moral beliefs of an-

other. The police are expected to enforce laws against gambling, marijuana, sexual acts between consenting adults, prostitution, and pornography, and yet these activities are often acted out by many of the same citizens who claim to endorse the laws that forbid them. The effect of these morality laws has been the failure of public confidence in law enforcement because the laws are practically unenforceable.

A serious consequence of unenforceable laws has been police corruption. "Immoral" practices such as gambling have been a primary source of police corruption, which has resulted in a great deal of unfavorable publicity for law enforcement. No doubt many of these illegal activities could not go on without police approval. Some police officers are as ambivalent about the morality of these activities as are many other citizens, and with the lure of lucrative payoffs from the operators of illegal enterprises, it is not surprising that police forces have been troubled with corruption in their ranks. Additionally, in their role as crime fighters the police are heavily reliant on informants. This practicality of police work requires that some of the small-fry criminals continue to practice their illegal activities with impunity because they are sources of valuable information that enables the police to apprehend bigger criminals.

Persistent and dedicated efforts directed toward prosecuting violations of moral laws requires an involvement of a large number of police officers and the expenditure of a great deal of public funds. For example, the extent to which police go to control gambling is often disproportionate to the problem. A large number of policemen are utilized for the purpose of obtaining information about the possibility of a neighborhood crap game. Subsequently, after a period of surveillance by a substantial number of officers, the police are able to apprehend a group of men engaged in a game of two-dollar craps in some alley. The irony of this act is that the apprehension may have taken place while some off-duty officers were busily playing poker in their homes.

A zealous enforcement of moral laws often creates enmity toward the police from large segments of the community. Many citizens resent the intrusions of a police agency into their personal lives, and the enforcement of laws involving private morals is highly antagonistic to those who do not culturally subscribe to the legal definition of these activities as crimes. Additionally, the role of guardian of individual morals grants officers a wide discretionary latitude in determining which acts violate the norms of society. The discretion in interpretation may be especially idiosyncratic where the legal definitions are vague, as in the case of pornography, where policemen often act as public censors.

Whitman Knapp, a U.S. district judge who gained a national reputation for heading an investigation that exposed corruption in the New York City Police Department, recently said that the prime cause of police corruption are the laws that society demands be enforced against some of its members but not against others. "We have to stop being lazy and give realistic objectives to our police departments. There is no doubt that those laws (such as gambling and prostitution laws) must be trimmed," Judge Knapp stated.[40]

Moral laws, or "crimes-without-victims laws," have a double-edged effect on police-community relations. These laws are criminogenic in that they create criminality; and they stimulate the corruption process of police forces. Both of these factors serve to alienate the police from the community.

These laws create criminals because they are so numerous and so all-encompassing that if they were to be fully enforced there would be few citizens of this country who could honestly state that they have never violated at least one of these laws during their lifetimes. Furthermore, criminogenic laws are never enforced uniformly or universally. It is extremely rare to hear about police raiding a country club whose members were participating in a high-stakes card game, or to hear about the arrest of citizens in white middle-class neighborhoods who gamble in the privacy of their own homes. Apprehensions for violations of laws against gambling generally occur in the streets and alleys of poor neighborhoods. It happens this way not necessarily because of the individual prejudices of police officers, but because of the differences in social patterns between middle-class neighborhoods and poorer areas. Social activities among the middle classes—including some acts that may be in violation of criminogenic laws—occur within the confines of private residences. On the other hand, lower-class citizens participate in perhaps the very same acts, but they do them publicly. This is because the squalor of slum living conditions—the oppressive heat of un-air-conditioned rooms on hot summer nights, for instance—forces the residents into the streets. Life in the slums—including activities that are judged to be immoral or illegal according to prevailing moral norms—takes place in the streets. Thus criminal activity of all kinds is far more visible in lower-class neighborhoods than it is in other areas, and lower-class citizens are more susceptible to arrest than are other citizens.

The irrationality of many of the criminogenic laws and the inconsistency of their application have created adverse community reaction to their enforcement. The zealous policeman who knows or cares little about the street-life culture of lower-class neighborhoods and rigidly enforces criminogenic laws in these areas not only serves to widen the gulf between the police and the community there, but also makes criminals out of many average citizens. Since all forms of social activities in these neighborhoods take place publicly, some of these activities, while considered innocuous by the norms of the neighborhood, are bound to violate certain laws. Inevitably, a strict interpretation of illegality captures within the net of law enforcement a number of people who would otherwise have escaped this fate if their acts had taken place in private. As a matter of fact, spokesmen of minority-group citizens have attributed the large percentage of arrests among minorities to this kind of selective law enforcement that primarily criminalizes "street people."

The black youth who is suspected by police of being a numbers runner is stopped and frisked by the same officer who is later seen joking with prostitutes and bookies. The black youth is aware that the officer is practicing selective law enforcement and feels victimized by the system of criminal justice. From this interaction with the police he will have a negative feeling for law enforcement and its officials. The black man who is arrested for shooting craps in an alley by the same officer who receives $200 a week from the local bookie or $1000 a week from the local narcotics dealer will unquestionably be hostile to law enforcement. These are serious questions posed by the law and aggravated by officiousness, arbitrariness, or even corruption in police practices; and society has not been able to resolve these problems.

The British police are often cited for having very good relations with the community. Studies have shown that a vast majority of the British public hold their police in high esteem and believe them to be honest, courteous, and doing a good job. William V. Shannon writes in "A New Look at the Police" that the principal reason for this attitude is that British police are not asked to enforce laws that are unenforceable. In Britain gambling is legal, homosexual relations between consenting adults in private is legal, narcotics addicts are treated relatively leniently, prostitutes are not arrested if they stay off the streets, and abortions can be obtained free through the National Health Service. Shannon notes that in this country the vice squad is "a synonym for payoff, and potentially good policemen are demoralized by protection money flowing from illegal but enormously profitable gambling of all kinds." He concludes that "no real improvement in police performance is possible until Americans face up to this corruption and the double standard which produces it."[41]

The conditions that exist in society are beyond the scope of the police. Crime, violence, and disorder have their roots in social and economic conditions that the police did not create. Poverty, racism, and the social and psychological dislocations of urban life are the main contributors to disorder. These are problems with which society as a whole and all levels of government must deal. The police are the agency charged with coping with the symptoms of these conditions. Police are unable to redress the wrongs of society; they can only try to cope with the manifestations of these wrongs. The more difficulties that society creates for the police in the discharging of their duties, by an indifference to the problems that cause disorder, the less likely are the police to perform their duties adequately.

The existence of tensions between the police and segments of society provides a very serious barrier for law enforcement. Some of these tensions are there because of police malpractice, while others occur because the police, as omnipresent symbols of the political system, are singled out as antagonists by groups that oppose the political system and the society associated with it. Individual policemen, no matter what their personal attitudes, are at times confronted by a blanket hatred, especially in areas where "Off the pigs" has been a popular slogan.[42]

The law-abiding citizen is generally unconcerned about the police except when he is victimized by a crime and needs a policeman. Beyond that, the average citizen's most frequent interaction with a police official takes place when he receives a traffic citation. Policemen are placed in a position of being the natural adversaries of many members of minority and counterculture groups and the young because of the high frequency of law violations by these groups. Because of continuing negative contact, little if any support for the police has come from this segment of the population. Rodney Stark states that "the students, protestors, and blacks are filled with hatred of the police. The police are filled with hatred of students, protestors, and blacks. We mix them at our peril."[43] It is the hostility shown the police by some segments of the community and a hostility that is often reciprocated by policemen that lead to the sort of tensions that result in violence.

The conditions and attitudes prevailing in the society at large have had an effect on the work personality of police officials. Faced with active hostility on the part of certain groups on the one hand and with indifference or disrespect by the public whose support they seek on the other, the police perceive themselves as frustrated and embattled by an environment that is not of their making. The feeling of profound isolation from the general public results in police attitudes that are distinctly those of a minority subculture: the magnification of group solidarity. Police solidarity, the camaraderie and fellowship among fellow officers, is what makes wearing the blue uniform worthwhile and gives "the feeling that they are doing a job that is important to society despite working conditions to the contrary."[44] Despite the evidence of low morale among police officers, many of them receive job satisfaction and stimulation through the solidarity of their peer group. Interestingly, this attitude has the earmarks of a classic syndrome of an oppressed minority, in this case, the "blue minority." A police officer recently said: "To a cop, human beings come in six colors: white, black, brown, red, yellow and blue. And we cops are all blue."

Recent actions by organizations of black police officers have shown that there are some cracks in the blue solidarity, with black police officials emphasizing their blackness over their blueness. In several cities black policemen have formed organizations representing them as a racial group rather than joining organizations that represent policemen as an occupational group. Moreover, black officers, through their organizations, have actively opposed some of the policies of police organizations and have allied themselves with black citizens in criticizing police practices in minority neighborhoods.

Although the conditions and attitudes in the community sometimes serve as impediments to a policeman's job, there is a feeling among most policemen that there is no more worthwhile job in urban America. There cannot be any doubt that law enforcement is a challenging and often dangerous occupation for which there is scant reward. Thus the importance of the job and the feeling of self-fulfillment become necessary psychological nutrients that must sustain a policeman in his daily tasks. Kirkham writes that he has often asked himself the questions: "Why does a man become a cop? What makes him stay with it?" He concludes:

> Surely it's not the disrespect, the legal restrictions which make the job increasingly rough, the long hours and the low pay, or the risk of being killed or injured trying to protect people who often don't seem to care.
>
> The only answer to this question I have been able to arrive at is based on my own limited experience as a policeman. Night after night, I came home and took off the badge and blue uniform with a sense of satisfaction and contribution to society that I have never known in any other job. Somehow that feeling seemed to make everything—the disrespect, the danger, the boredom—worthwhile.[45]

NOTES

1. Albert J. Reiss, Jr., *The Police and the Public* (New Haven: Yale University Press, 1972), pp. 88–89.

2. Ibid., p. 115.

3. A. O. Archuleta, "Police Discretion Versus Plea Bargaining," in *Police Chief*, April 1974, p. 78.

4. James Q. Wilson, *Varieties of Police Behavior: The Management of Law and Order in Eight Communities* (New York: Atheneum, 1972), p. 7.

5. Louis A. Radelet, *The Police and the Community* (Beverly Hills, Calif.: Glencoe Press, 1972), p. 82.

6. Ibid., p. 81.

7. Alan Edward Bent, *The Politics of Law Enforcement: Conflict and Power in Urban Communities* (Lexington, Mass.: Heath, 1974), p. 15.

8. George L. Kirkham, "A Professor's 'Street Lessons'," *FBI Law Enforcement Bulletin,* March 1974, p. 6.

9. Jerome H. Skolnick, *Justice Without Trial: Law Enforcement in a Democratic Society* (New York: Wiley, 1966), pp. 45–48.

10. Ibid., p. 180.

11. Bent, *Politics of Law Enforcement.*

12. Ibid., p. 25.

13. Radelet, *Police and the Community,* pp. 83–84.

14. Robert W. Balch, "The Police Personality: Fact or Fiction?" *Journal of Criminology, Criminal Law and Police Science,* March 1972, pp. 106–119.

15. The section dealing with police personality characteristics is derived partially from Balch, "Police Personality," pp. 106–119, and Bent, *Politics of Law Enforcement,* pp. 15–39.

16. Arthur Niederhoffer, *Behind the Shield: The Police in Urban Society* (Garden City, N.Y.: Doubleday, 1969), pp. 16–17.

17. William A. Westley, *Violence and the Police: A Sociological Study of Law, Custom, and Morality* (Cambridge: M.I.T. Press, 1970), p. 189.

18. *The World Almanac* (New York: Doubleday, 1973), p. 967.

19. A. Didrick Castberg, "The Exercise of Discretion in the Administration of Justice" (paper prepared for delivery at the 1972 annual meeting of the American Political Science Association, Washington, D.C., September 5–9, 1972), p. 8.

20. Skolnick, *Justice Without Trial.*

21. Kirkham, "Professor's 'Street Lessons'," p. 8.

22. Westley, *Violence and the Police,* p. 189.

23. Castberg, "Exercise of Discretion," p. 9.

24. Westley, *Violence and the Police,* p. 35.

25. Jesse Ruben, "Police Identity and the Police Role," in *The Police and the Community,* ed. Robert F. Steadman (Baltimore: Johns Hopkins University Press, 1972), pp. 28–31.

26. Niederhoffer, *Behind the Shield,* pp. 98–99.

27. For an account of the Black and Reiss study, "Patterns of Behavior in Police and Citizen Transactions," see Robert W. Balch, "The Police Personality," pp. 106–119.

28. James Baldwin, *Nobody Knows My Name* (New York: Dell, 1962), p. 61.

29. See David H. Bayley and Harold Mendelsohn, *Minorities and the Police: Confrontation in America* (New York: Free Press, 1969).

30. Niederhoffer, *Behind the Shield.*

31. Joseph Wambaugh, *The New Centurions* (New York: Dell, 1972), p. 161.

32. Rodney Stark, *Police Riots: Collective Violence and Law Enforcement* (Belmont, Calif.: Wadsworth, 1972), p. 181.

33. Niederhoffer, *Behind the Shield,* p. 97.

34. Ibid.

35. *Newsweek,* October 6, 1969.

36. Ibid.

37. Pete Hamill, "Patrick V. Murphy: The Future of a Law-and-Order Liberal," *New York,* October 4, 1971, p. 32. Reprinted by permission of Monica McCall, ICM. Copyright © 1971 NYM Corporation.

38. Ibid., p. 34.

39. Kirkham, "Professor's 'Street Lessons'," pp. 7–8.

40. *The Commercial Appeal,* Memphis, April 3, 1973, p. 9.

41. William V. Shannon, "A New Look at the Police," in Radelet, *Police and the Community,* p. 618.

42. Bent, *Politics of Law Enforcement,* p. 31.

43. Stark, *Police Riots,* p. 116.

44. David C. Perry and Paula A. Sornoff, "Politics at the Street-Level: The Select Case of Police Administration and the Community" (paper prepared for delivery at the 1972 annual meeting of the American Political Science Association, Washington, D.C., September 5–9, 1972), p. 36.

45. Kirkham, "Professor's 'Street Lessons'," p. 9.

BIBLIOGRAPHY

AHERN, JAMES E. *Police in Trouble: A Frightening Crisis in Law Enforcement.* New York: Hawthorn, 1972.

BALDWIN, JAMES. *Nobody Knows My Name.* New York: Dell, 1962.

BAYLEY, DAVID H., and MENDELSOHN, HAROLD. *Minorities and the Police: Confrontation in America.* New York: Free Press, 1969.

BENT, ALAN EDWARD. *The Politics of Law Enforcement: Conflict and Power in Urban Communities.* Lexington, Mass.: Heath, 1974.

BORDUA, DAVID J., ed. *The Police: Six Sociological Essays.* New York: Wiley, 1967.

CHEVIGNY, PAUL. *Police Power.* New York: Pantheon Press, 1969.

CROMWELL, PAUL F., JR., and KEEFER, GEORGE, eds. *Police-Community Relations.* St. Paul, Minn.: West, 1973.

CURRY, JESSE E., and KING, GLEN D. *Race Tensions and the Police.* Springfield, Ill.: C. C Thomas, 1962.

NIEDERHOFFER, ARTHUR. *Behind the Shield: The Police in Urban Society.* Garden City, N.Y.: Doubleday, 1969.

RADELET, LOUIS A. *The Police and the Community.* Beverly Hills, Calif.: Glencoe Press, 1972.

REISS, ALBERT J., JR. *The Police and the Public.* New Haven: Yale University Press, 1972.

SKOLNICK, JEROME H. *Justice Without Trial: Law Enforcement in a Democratic Society.* New York: Wiley, 1966.

STARK, RODNEY. *Police Riots: Collective Violence and Law Enforcement.* Belmont, Calif.: Wadsworth, 1972.

STEADMAN, ROBERT F., ed. *The Police and the Community.* Baltimore: Johns Hopkins University Press, 1972.

WESTLEY, WILLIAM. *Violence and the Police: A Sociological Study of Law, Custom, and Morality.* Cambridge: M.I.T. Press, 1970.

WILSON, JAMES Q. *Varieties of Police Behavior.* New York: Atheneum, 1972.

WAMBAUGH, JOSEPH. *The New Centurions.* New York: Dell, 1972.

4

|||||||||||||||||||||||||||||||||||||||||||||||||||||||||||||||||||||||||||||||||||||||||||||||||||||||||||||

THE COURTS
AND THE PROTECTION
OF INDIVIDUAL RIGHTS

Chapter 3 presented the police as both protectors and representatives of the majority. In many instances, however, it appears that the police are prevented from serving the interests of the majority by reducing crime because of the actions of the courts in general and the United States Supreme Court in particular. Thus Quinn Tamm of the International Association of Chiefs of Police has noted:

> The courts in too many cases are ignoring the public's right to protection.
> . . . The fabric of criminal law has become such a patchwork that too
> often the killer-fish escapes through the holes while those responsible for
> netting them become entangled in the ravelings and are rendered impotent.
> . . . Could it be, then, that the deterrent effect of swift, sure and just
> punishment has been lost because the courts have become preoccupied with
> the rights of the individual rather than the rights of society? The scales of
> justice are getting out of balance. Too often the criminal ascends to the role
> of the victim or underdog when he is apprehended and the full force of legal
> machinery directed against him. Too often the original victim of the
> murderer or the rapist or the child molester fades from memory as
> overwhelming public and judicial compassion is lavished on the criminal.[1]

This viewpoint is not limited to those directly involved in law enforcement. Even Senator Sam Ervin, generally known for his defense of civil liberties, has argued that "increasingly in the last decade our law enforcement officers have been limited and often hamstrung in dealing with crimes by high court rulings . . . [which have] stressed individual rights of the accused to the point where public safety has often been relegated to the back row of the courtroom."[2]

It is true that the courts regard their purpose as protecting the individual. As Justice Hugo Black observed in *Chambers* v. *Florida:*

> Under our constitutional system, courts stand against any winds that blow
> as havens of refuge for those who might otherwise suffer because they are

helpless, weak, outnumbered, or because they are nonconforming victims of prejudice and public excitement. Due process of law, preserved for all by our Constitution, commands that no such practice as that disclosed by this record shall send any accused to his death. No higher duty, no more solemn responsibility, rests on this court than that of translating into living law and maintaining this constitutional shield deliberately planned and inscribed for the benefit of every human being subject to our Constitution—, of whatever race, creed, or persuasion.[3]

However, it is an open question how successful the courts have been in protecting these individual rights. This chapter will examine what the Supreme Court has done in the criminal procedural realm to protect the rights of individuals and minorities. It will then consider to what extent the Court has succeeded in this endeavor. Through this analysis, it will become obvious that the Supreme Court, and the lower courts as well, are far less able to protect minority and individual rights—and thereby preserve the balance between majority rule and minority rights—than is generally believed. The need for police-community relations programs to assure that neither the majority nor the minority can come to tyrannize the other will become all the more apparent.

The Constitution and Criminal Procedure

The Supreme Court has played the significant role it has in the development of criminal procedure in large part because of the special emphasis the United States Constitution places upon criminal procedure. Of the twenty-three separate rights spelled out in the first eight amendments, thirteen concern criminal procedure. The Fourth Amendment guarantees the right of the people to be secure against unreasonable searches and seizures and prohibits the issuance of warrants without probable cause. The Fifth Amendment requires prosecution by grand jury indictment for violation of all "infamous crimes" (except certain military prosecutions) and prohibits placing a person "twice in jeopardy" for the same offense or compelling him to be a "witness against himself." The Sixth Amendment lists several rights that apply "in all criminal prosecutions": the right to a speedy and public trial by an impartial jury of the state and district in which the crime was committed, notice of the "nature and cause of the accusation," confrontation of opposing witnesses, compulsory process for obtaining favorable witnesses, and the assistance of counsel. The Eighth Amendment adds prohibitions against the imposition of excessive bails and fines and the infliction of cruel and unusual punishments. Finally, along with these specific guarantees, the Fifth Amendment adds the general prohibition against the deprivation of life, liberty, or property without due process of law. These provisions are not self-defining, however, and a considerable dispute has arisen within the legal community and in the society as a whole over two questions: (1) Do these provisions have equal application in state as well as federal procedures? And (2) what in fact is the substance of some of these constitutional protections? For example, what constitutes an "unreasonable" search and seizure? At what stage does the right to counsel become available? What is a "cruel and unusual" punishment? These questions will be taken up in some detail.

Application of Bill of Rights Guarantees to the States

In the American federal system, both the national and state governments can enact and enforce criminal laws. However, with the exceptions of such federal enclaves as the District of Columbia, over which Congress has plenary legislative authority, the power of the national government to define crimes is strictly limited to its delegated and implied powers. As a consequence, federal criminal statutes are tied to such constitutional grants of legislative power as those relating to taxation, interstate commerce, and the postal system. Although these grants of legislative power have led to the development of a substantial and growing federal code, most of the criminal laws in the United States are state laws. As noted constitutional authority David Fellman points out, "The state is mainly responsible for the maintenance of law and order; most crimes are defined by state legislatures; and enforcement is in the hands of state police and judicial agencies."[4] This is reflected in a comparison of state and federal prison populations. Thus, for example, in 1970 there were 176,384 adult felony offenders in state institutions but only 19,623 such persons in federal penal institutions.

Since the states, and not the national government, are primarily responsible for the enactment and enforcement of criminal law in the United States, a very important question arises: Do the provisions of the Bill of Rights that pertain to criminal procedure in fact apply to the states, where, after all, most criminal proceedings take place? Initially, the answer to this question was an emphatic no. In the famous decision of *Barron* v. *Baltimore* in 1833, Chief Justice John Marshall declared that the first ten amendments of the United States Constitution were enacted as limitations solely upon the national government. Marshall's reasoning was on firm ground. "The opening sentence of the First Amendment begins with the phrase 'Congress shall make no laws . . .' and this would be curious language indeed if it had intended to apply the provisions which followed as limitations upon state action."[5] This understanding was complicated however, with the adoption of the Fourteenth Amendment in 1868. Among that amendment's provisions is the following: No state shall "deprive any person of life, liberty, or property, without due process of law." The bearing of these words on state criminal law is unmistakable: defendants cannot be deprived of life, liberty, or property without due process. However, the words themselves are ambiguous. After all, what constitutes due process? Does it impose on the states the same restrictions the first eight amendments impose on the national government? If so, why? If not, why not? From the outset, the Supreme Court has been troubled by the relationship between the limitations imposed upon state action by the Fourteenth Amendment's due process clause and the limitations imposed upon federal action by the first eight amendments. Three separate views of the appropriate relation between these amendments have been advanced through the years: the fundamental rights interpretation, total incorporation, and selective incorporation. Each will be briefly considered.[6]

The "Fundamental Rights" Interpretation

The fundamental rights interpretation of the Fourteenth Amendment is no longer accepted by a majority of the Supreme Court, but it was for years the prevailing view. It finds no necessary relationship between the Fourteenth Amendment and the guarantees of the Bill of Rights. The Fourteenth Amendment's due process clause is understood as incorporating "traditional notions" of due process, described quite generally by Justice Benjamin Cardozo in *Palko* v. *Connecticut*[7] as those principles "implicit in the concept of ordered liberty." Applied to criminal procedure, this view requires that a state grant the defendant "that fundamental fairness essential to the very concept of justice."[8] While the Bill of Rights is regarded as a likely indicator of "fundamental fairness," it is not necessarily conclusive.

Just as the fundamental rights interpretation of due process does not require incorporation of all the specific guarantees of the Bill of Rights, neither is it limited by the scope of these guarantees. The concern is with fundamental fairness, not mere compliance with the Bill of Rights. Consequently, a state procedure may violate due process even though its operation is not contrary to any specific guarantee in the first eight amendments. For example, Justice John Marshall Harlan, following this interpretation in his concurrence in *Estes* v. *Texas*, was able to declare unconstitutional the use of television in the courtroom even though he believed that practice was not contrary to the defendant's right to an impartial jury or public trial. The crucial question for him was: Did this practice prove to be so potentially prejudicial that it infringed upon the defendant's "fundamental right to a fair trial assured by the due process clause of the Fourteenth Amendment"?[9]

Critics of the fundamental rights interpretation contend that it encourages an ad hoc, personal application of the Fourteenth Amendment. Justice Black was chief among these critics. He argued that "fundamental fairness" is so imprecise a standard that it gives the judiciary "unconfined power" contrary to the basic idea of a written constitution. As he wrote in *Duncan* v. *Louisiana*, "application of the 'vague contours of due process' depends entirely on the particular judge's idea of ethics and morals instead of requiring him to depend on the boundaries fixed by the written words of the Constitution."[10] Supporters of this interpretation reply that its application is not basically subjective, but rests on a consensus of society that can be determined quite independently of the justice's personal views. Various "objective" factors, such as the significance attached to the right by the framers of the Constitution, the subsequent treatment of the right in state courts and legislatures, and the significance attached to the right in other countries with similar jurisprudential traditions, are available to the Court as it determines whether a particular procedural right has been traditionally recognized as an essential ingredient of fairness. "Although these factors do not provide a mathematical calculus for application of the Fourteenth Amendment, proponents of the fundamental rights interpretation argue that they supply as much objectivity as any other standard for interpreting that amendment."[11]

Total Incorporation

The second view of the relationship between the Fourteenth Amendment and the Bill of Rights is the total incorporation interpretation. Although this view has never commanded majority support, it has had considerable influence in shaping the third view, the selective incorporation interpretation, which is currently dominant. Proponents of total incorporation argue that the Fourteenth Amendment was intended simply and exclusively to make the first eight amendments applicable to the states. Not only do they believe that the legislative history and language of the amendment support total incorporation, they also make the pragmatic argument that it avoids much of the subjectivity inherent in a fundamental rights approach by restricting the justices to the specific language of the Bill of Rights.

Critics of total incorporation challenge these contentions. They argue that neither the legislative history nor the language of the amendment supports this view. They point out that the due process clause merely restates a single provision of the Fifth Amendment of the Bill of Rights. They also reject the notion that total incorporation avoids much of the subjectivity inherent in the fundamental rights approach. They criticize Justice Black, this interpretation's leading exponent, for merely shifting the focus of judicial inquiry from the flexible concept of fundamental fairness to equally flexible terms in the specific amendments. They note that such terms as "probable cause," "unreasonable search," and "speedy and public trial" are hardly self-defining and must be interpreted in light of the same contemporary notions of fairness that are considered in applying a fundamental rights standard. Finally, the critics argue that total incorporation imposes an undue burden on the states and deprives them of any opportunity to act as social and legal laboratories—experimenting with reforms designed to enhance the protection and freedoms of the people.

Selective Incorporation

The selective incorporation doctrine represents the third view of the appropriate relationship between the Fourteenth Amendment and the Bill of Rights. It combines aspects of both the fundamental rights and total incorporation interpretations. It accepts the basic premise of the fundamental rights interpretation that the Fourteenth Amendment encompasses all rights, substantive and procedural, that are "of the very essence of a scheme of ordered liberty."[12] It acknowledges that not all rights spelled out in the Bill of Rights are fundamental, and conversely that other rights may in fact be fundamental, even though they are not specifically guaranteed in the Bill of Rights. However, in determining whether an enumerated right is fundamental, this interpretation focuses on the total right guaranteed by the individual amendment, not merely the element of that right before the Court nor the application of that right in a particular case. As constitutional authorities Jerold H. Israel and Wayne R. La Fave observe: "Once it is decided that a particular guarantee within the first eight Amendments is fundamental, that guarantee is incorporated into the Fourteenth Amendment 'whole and intact' and is enforced against the states in every case according to the same standards applied to the federal government."[13]

Proponents of selective incorporation contend that a fundamental right should not be denied merely because the "totality of circumstances" does not disclose "a denial of fundamental fairness" in a particular case. After all, evaluation of the factual circumstances surrounding any particular case is often extremely subjective and discretionary. Moreover, selective incorporation avoids the rigidity and extremism of total incorporation. Critics charge, however, that selective incorporation is nothing more than an artificial and unacceptable compromise between the fundamental rights and total incorporation doctrines that is inconsistent with the logic and historical support of both. Proponents of the total incorporation view charge that it imports the same element of subjectivity as the fundamental rights doctrine. Proponents of fundamental rights, on the other hand, contend that selective incorporation fails to appreciate the special burdens involved in the administration of criminal justice at the state level. They fear that the imposition of a single standard regulating both state and federal administration will result in the placing of an unrealistic constitutional straitjacket on the states or a relaxing of standards as applied to both state and federal officials in order to meet the special problem of the states.[14]

Despite these shortcomings, however, selective incorporation has become the dominant interpretation. Justice William Brennan advanced this view for the first time in 1961 in *Cohen* v. *Hurley,* and by 1963 it had the basic support of at least three justices. In addition, it was accepted by Justices Black and Douglas, who, although they remained supporters of total incorporation, accepted selective incorporation as a lesser evil than the fundamental rights interpretation. With this majority support, it has been instrumental in applying the following Bill of Rights guarantees to the states: protection against unreasonable searches and seizures and the right to have excluded from criminal trial any evidence obtained in violation thereof (*Mapp* v. *Ohio*[15]); the privilege against self-incrimination (*Malloy* v. *Hogan*[16]); the guarantee against double jeopardy (*Benton* v. *Maryland*[17]); the right to assistance of counsel (*Gideon* v. *Wainwright*[18] and *Argersinger* v. *Hamlin*[19]); the right to a speedy trial (*Klopfer* v. *North Caro-*

lina[20]); the right to jury trial (*Duncan* v. *Louisiana*[21]); the right to confront opposing witnesses (*Pointer* v. *Texas*[22]), and the right to compulsory process for obtaining witnesses (*Washington* v. *Texas*[23]). When two earlier cases—*In re Oliver*[24] and *Cole* v. *Arkansas*[25]—incorporating right to a public trial and due notice of the nature and cause of the accusation are added to this list, the only Bill of Rights guarantees directly related to criminal procedure that are presently not incorporated are the Eighth Amendment prohibition against excessive bail and the Fifth Amendment requirement that prosecution of infamous crimes proceed from a grand jury indictment. The occasion has never arisen for the Supreme Court to rule on the prohibition against excessive bail, but most commentators assume that it will be incorporated if the issue is squarely presented.[26] The grand jury requirement, on the other hand, was specifically held not to be guaranteed by the Fourteenth Amendment in the 1884 decision of *Hurtado* v. *California*,[27] and that decision continues to be followed as valid precedent.

Through selective incorporation, the Supreme Court has come to hold that virtually all of the protections enumerated in the Bill of Rights are equally applicable in state as well as federal criminal prosecutions. But what is the substance of some of these protections? What constitutes, for example, an unreasonable search and seizure, a speedy trial, or cruel and unusual punishment? The discussion that follows explores the Supreme Court's understanding of what several of these Bill of Rights guarantees—equally applicable to the federal and state governments—actually require.

Search and Seizure

The Fourth Amendment to the Constitution provides that "the right of people to be secure in their persons, houses, papers, and effects, against unreasonable searches and seizures shall not be violated and no Warrants shall issue but upon probable cause supported by Oath or affirmation, and particularly describing the place to be searched, and the persons or things to be seized." As with many provisions of the Constitution, its language is somewhat ambiguous. It does not prohibit all searches, but only those that are unreasonable. What, however, makes a search unreasonable?

The Court has dealt extensively with this question. The general rule it has developed is that searches are reasonable if they are based on a warrant obtained from a magistrate. Such a warrant may be issued only if the law-enforcement officials can demonstrate through introduction of evidence that probable cause exists that some evidence of criminal activity will be uncovered by the search.[28] In the absence of a search warrant, the Court has held that searches of the person of a defendant are always justified if they are incident to a lawful arrest. The Court has held these searches to be reasonable as they involve the need of an officer to search a defendant to remove weapons (thus protecting the officer's safety) and evidence (thus preventing the defendant from destroying it). This Court ruling does not, however, permit an officer to search just anybody and then use the evidence thereby obtained to justify the original arrest. Generally speaking, the officer cannot use the fruits of a search as justification for the arrest; the grounds for arrest must exist for a search incident to the arrest to be valid.[29]

Recently, in *Terry* v. *Ohio*,[30] the Court has also held that searches of a defendant's person which are not incident to a valid arrest may nevertheless still be reasonable if the officer has good reason to believe that the defendant is armed. These searches, however, are not unlimited in their scope. The recent decision in *Chimel* v. *California*[31] restricts searches of the premises within which the defendant is arrested to those areas "within his immediate control"—that is, within which he might gain possession of a weapon or destructible evidence.[32]

Once the question of what constitutes a reasonable search has been resolved, another question quickly emerges: What remedy should be available to a defendant whose Fourth Amendment rights have been violated—that is, who has been the subject of an unreasonable search and seizure? The Supreme Court has found it necessary, on a number of occasions, to deal with this question. It dealt with it for the first time in 1914 in *Weeks* v. *United States*.[33] In *Weeks,* it declared that the appropriate remedy was exclusion of evidence obtained illegally. The Court did not state that the Fourth Amendment of its own force barred from criminal prosecution the use of items illegally seized. It did not consider the Fourth Amendment to constitute a rule of evidence. However, the Court went on to state that unless such evidence were excluded, the Fourth Amendment would present no effective deterrent to improper searches and seizures. Thus *Weeks* held that as a federal rule of evidence, which in its supervisory function the Supreme Court can lay down for all federal courts, illegally obtained or "tainted" evidence could not be used in a federal prosecution. *Weeks,* however, dealt only with federal prosecutions, and, as the Fourth Amendment was not yet incorporated through the Fourteenth Amendment to apply to the states, most states continued to follow the old common-law rule that relevant evidence was admissible regardless of its source. It was not until *Wolf* v. *Colorado*[34] in 1949 that the Supreme Court had occasion to rule on these state practices. In that decision, Justice Felix Frankfurter, writing for the Court, concluded that freedom from unreasonable searches and seizures was an essential element in the concept of "ordered liberty." The Fourth Amendment was thereby made applicable to the states. However, the Court in *Wolf* refused to apply the exclusionary rule of *Weeks* to state proceedings. It denied that the exclusionary rule had any constitutional status and asserted instead that it was simply a pragmatic remedy developed under the Court's powers to supervise the federal judicial system. It was not until 1961 in *Mapp* v. *Ohio*[35] that the Supreme Court abandoned the *Wolf* doctrine and held the exclusionary rule applicable to state proceedings. The Court had come to conclude that the exclusionary rule, by removing the incentive to disregard the Fourth Amendment, constituted "the only effectively available way . . . to compel respect for the constitutional guarantee." It was no less than "an essential part of both the Fourth and Fourteenth Amendments." The Court discounted Justice Cardozo's argument that the exclusionary rule permitted the "criminal . . . to go free because the constable has blundered," noting that "another consideration, the imperative of judicial integrity," had priority. "Nothing," the Court noted, "can destroy a government more quickly than its failure to observe its own laws."

Self-Incrimination and Coerced Confessions

The Fifth Amendment provides that no person "shall be compelled in any criminal case to be a witness against himself." As with other provisions of the Bill of Rights, this privilege was originally restricted simply to federal prosecutions. In both *Twining* v. *New Jersey*[36] and *Adamson* v. *California*,[37] the Supreme Court rejected the argument that the exception to compulsory self-incrimination was a fundamental right" and hence necessary to a system of "ordered liberty." However, the Court was finally persuaded in 1964 in *Malloy* v. *Hogan*[38] to overrule these long-standing precedents and extend its application through the Fourteenth Amendment to the states as well. Justice Brennan stated for the Court: "The Fourteenth Amendment secures against state invasion the same privilege that the Fifth Amendment guarantees against federal infringement—the right of a person to remain silent unless he chooses to speak in the unfettered exercise of his own will, and to suffer no penalty . . . for such silence." A set of questions now arises: What does the right to remain silent mean? What constitutes being "compelled"? That is, what constitutes coercion in violation of the privilege? What does this privilege mean in relation to police interrogation of suspects?

Although the Court did not rule until *Malloy* that the protection against self-incrimination applied to the states, since 1936 it had placed limitations upon police interrogation techniques and the admissibility of confessions obtained therefrom. In that year, in *Brown* v. *Mississippi*,[39] it overturned the conviction of three defendants whom police had physically tortured in order to extort confessions. The Court made abundantly clear its belief that the use of such confessions violated the due process clause of the Fourteenth Amendment: "The freedom of the state in establishing its policy is the freedom of constitutional government and is limited by the requirement of due process of law. Because a state may dispense with a jury trial, it does not follow that it may substitute a trial by ordeal. The rack and torture chamber may not be substituted for the witness stand."

Brown was reaffirmed in 1940 in *Chambers* v. *Florida*,[40] when the Court again overturned a state conviction because the defendant, although he had not been subjected to blatant physical methods of coercion, had nonetheless been arrested on suspicion without a warrant, denied contact with friends or attorneys, and had been questioned for long period of time by different squads of police officers. *Brown* and *Chambers* were followed by a long line of cases that dealt with the admissibility of confessions on an ad hoc basis. They employed the "totality of circumstances" rule: in the evaluation of the Court, did the circumstances surrounding the obtaining of a particular confession—for example, the age and maturity of the defendant, the nature of the charge, the degree of pressure put upon the defendant, the length of interrogation, etc.—constitute coercion, thereby rendering the trial unfair?[41] As is apparent, the "totality of circumstances" rule did not provide the police or the prosecution with much guidance on what practices did or did not pass constitutional muster. As a result, the Court was continually confronted with a barrage of "coerced confessions" cases dealing with such police practices as attempts to gain the sympathy of the defendant through an old friend on the police force;[42] threats to bring a defendant's wife into custody for questioning;[43] threats to place defendant's children in the custody of welfare officials;[44] and interrogation of a wounded defendant under the influence of a so-called truth serum.[45]

By 1964 the Court sought to establish some general guidelines on the meaning of self-incrimination and coerced confessions, in the hope of thereby freeing itself from this perpetual litigation. *Escobedo* v. *Illinois* provided the Court with the perfect opportunity.[46] In *Escobedo,* the defendant made damaging admissions while being interrogated, after he had asked for and been denied an opportunity to consult with his attorney. In overturning Escobedo's conviction, the Court laid down the following rule:

> We hold, therefore, that where, as here, the investigation is no longer a general inquiry into an unsolved crime but has begun to focus on a particular suspect, the suspect has been taken into police custody, the police carry out a process of interrogation that lends itself to eliciting incriminating statements, the suspect has requested and been denied an opportunity to consult his lawyer, and the police have not effectively warned him of his absolute constitutional right to remain silent, the accused has been denied the "Assistance of Counsel" in violation of the Sixth Amendment to the Constitution as made obligatory upon the states by the Fourteenth Amendment . . . and that no statement elicited by the police during the interrogation may be used against him in a criminal trial.[47]

Escobedo was a big step toward establishment of general guidelines for police interrogation. However, as the passage quoted above indicates, it was still couched somewhat in "the particularized language of the totality-of-circumstances rule."[48] It was not until two years later, in the celebrated case of *Miranda* v. *Arizona,* that the Court finally broke completely with past cases, rejected the ad hoc totality-of-circumstances rule, spelled out specific procedures for the police to follow during interrogation, and declared that any statements elicited in violation of these procedures would be inadmissible.[49] These procedures constituted a "stiff code of conduct for police interrogation."[50] They included the following requirements:

1. A suspect held in custody for interrogation must be informed of his right to remain silent.
2. He must be warned that anything he says may be used against him in court.

3. He must be given the right to consult with an attorney prior to questioning and have his attorney present during questioning if he wishes.
4. He must be told that, if he wants an attorney but cannot afford one, an attorney will be provided for him free.
5. If, after being told this, a suspect says that he does not want an attorney and is willing to be questioned, he may be, provided that he has reached this decision "knowingly and intelligently."
6. If, after being told all of his rights, a suspect agrees to be questioned, he can refrain from answering additional questions any time after they have started, whether or not he has an attorney with him.

Miranda was met with a storm of controversy. It was said to handcuff the police. Even the normally restrained Justice John M. Harlan felt compelled to denounce it orally from the bench when it was handed down. With his face flushed and his voice occasionally faltering with emotion, Harlan branded it a "dangerous experimentation" at a time of a "high crime rate that is a matter of growing concern," a "new doctrine" without substantial precedent, reflecting "a balance in favor of the accused."[51] However, as this consideration of the cases leading to *Miranda* indicates, *Miranda* was not "some quick flash of creative inspiration."[52] It constitutes the formal working out and culmination of the Court's answer to the question "What does compelled testimony mean?" Its attempt to define—and in the defining, to expand—the scope of the protection against self-incrimination represents still another effort by the Court to assure the rights of the individual and minorities.

It must be noted, however, that *Miranda* and its commitment to the rights of individuals and minorities has recently been undermined by two key decisions: *Harris* v. *New York*[53] and *Michigan* v. *Tucker*.[54] *Harris* limited the scope of *Miranda* by holding that statements made to police by a defendant who has not been advised of his *Miranda* rights cannot be introduced in a trial court as evidence of guilt, but can be used to impeach the credibility of the defendant should he testify on his own behalf and, in so doing, contradict his earlier statements. As Chief Justice Burger declared for the majority:

> Every criminal defendant is privileged to testify in his own defense, or to refuse to do so. . . . The shield provided by *Miranda* cannot be perverted into a license to use perjury by way of a defense, free from the risk of confrontation with prior inconsistent utterances. We hold, therefore, that petitioner's credibility was appropriately impeached by use of his earlier conflicting statements.

The 1974 *Tucker* decisions further eroded *Miranda*'s protections. It held that failure to advise the defendant of his right to court-appointed counsel when the other *Miranda* rights were given was not by itself so serious an error as to require suppression of the defendant's statements made during police interrogation. Justice William Rehnquist spoke for an eight-member majority when he observed:

Just as the law does not require that a defendant receive a perfect trial, only a fair one, it cannot realistically require that policemen investigating serious crimes make no error whatsoever. The pressures of law enforcement and the vagaries of human nature would make such an expectation unrealistic. Before we penalize police error, therefore, we must consider whether the sanction serves a valid and useful purpose.

Right to Counsel

The Sixth Amendment declares that "in all criminal prosecutions, the accused shall enjoy the right . . . to have Assistance of Counsel for his defense." As with so many other provisions of the Bill of Rights, the language is in need of interpretation. What, after all, is involved in the right to have assistance of counsel? Does it require, for example, appointment of counsel for indigents—and if so, in what sorts of cases? When that question is resolved, another arises. The Sixth Amendment guarantees the right of counsel "in all criminal prosecutions." It makes no mention of detention, interrogation, preliminary hearings, or other pretrial stages that an accused must face. When does the right to counsel accrue? The Court's answers to these questions will be taken up, as they illustrate again the Court's commitment to the protection of individual and minority rights.

The original meaning of the Sixth Amendment right to counsel was most restrictive. The right extended only to permission for the accused to employ and bring to trial a lawyer of his choosing. It made no provision for the indigent defendant who might want and even badly need assistance of counsel, but who was unable to afford a lawyer. The provision was "permissive only. It imposed no duty on the government to provide free counsel."[55] This interpretation extended well into the twentieth century. As late as 1931, the Wickersham Commission, appointed by President Hoover to investigate law enforcement, stated in its report: "[T]he right guaranteed is one of employing counsel, not one of having counsel provided by the government."[56]

In 1932, however, the Court began to expand this interpretation. In *Powell* v. *Alabama*[57] it held that in capital felony cases, right to counsel was secured by the due process clause of the Fourteenth Amendment. Justice George Sutherland held that in such cases, "the right to have counsel appointed, when necessary, is a logical corollary from the constitutional right to be heard by counsel." Six years later, in *Johnson* v. *Zerbst*,[58] the Court extended this interpretation further and held that right to counsel extends to appointment of counsel for indigent defendants in all federal criminal proceedings, capital or noncapital. "The Sixth Amendment withholds from federal courts, in all criminal proceedings, the power and authority to deprive an accused of his life or liberty unless he has or waives the assistance of counsel." The Court justified this new interpretation by quoting from *Powell*: "The right to be heard would be, in many cases, of little avail if it did not comprehend the right to be heard by counsel." However, this requirement of representation by counsel was not extended to all state criminal proceedings until 1963, in *Gideon* v. *Wainwright*.[59] In that celebrated case, the Court unanimously concluded that right to counsel was fundamental and essential to a fair trial in both. Justice Black declared that precedent, reason, and reflection all "require us to recognize that in our adversary system of criminal justice, any person hailed into court, who is too poor to hire a lawyer, cannot be assured a fair trial unless counsel is provided for him." He noted that since the government hires lawyers to prosecute and defendants with money hire lawyers to defend, it is apparent that "lawyers in criminal courts are necessities, not luxuries."

As a result of *Gideon*, the right to counsel was extended to all indigent defendants in both federal and state felony prosecutions. *Gideon* did not, however, extend this right to "all criminal prosecutions." Petty offenses were still excluded from coverage, and it was not until 1972, in *Argersinger* v. *Hamlin*,[60] that right to counsel was guaranteed in those cases as well. In that decision, the Court noted that the volume of misdemeanor cases was far greater than the number of felony prosecutions. As a result, there was "an obsession for speedy dispositions, regardless of the fairness of the result." Prejudice had crept into this "assembly line justice." The Court cited favorably an American Civil Liberties Union study that concluded that misdemeanants represented by counsel were five times as likely to emerge from police courts with all charges dismissed as were defendants who faced similar charges without counsel. As a consequence, the Court felt compelled to hold that "absent a knowing and intelligent waiver, no person may be imprisoned for any offense, whether classified as petty, misdemeanor, or felony, unless he was represented by counsel at his trial."[61]

For all practical purposes, right to counsel is now assured "in all criminal prosecutions" in the United States, be the defendant affluent or indigent, be the offense serious or petty. However, the question then arises: When in the course of legal proceedings does the right to counsel accrue and how long does it continue? In 1932, in *Powell* v. *Alabama*, Justice Sutherland declared that the defendant "requires the guiding hand of counsel at every step in the proceedings against him." Through the years, the Court has held that that constitutional principle is not limited to the presence of counsel at trial. As it declared in *United States* v. *Wade:* "It is central to that principle that in addition to counsel's presence at trial, the accused is guaranteed that he need not stand alone against the state at any stage of the presecution, formal or informal, in court or out, where counsel's presence might derogate from the accused's right to a fair trial."[62] On the basis of that principle, the Court has ruled that the accused has the right to counsel at such "critical stages" as in-custody police interrogation following arrest;[63] the police lineup held for eyewitness identification;[64] the preliminary hearing;[65] the arraignment;[66] at his appeal;[67] and even at a posttrial proceeding for the revocation of probation or parole.[68] In short, the Court has come to interpret the broad language of the Sixth Amendment provision of right to counsel to mean that in all criminal proceedings, either federal or state, the accused is entitled to representation by counsel at every step where substantial rights may be affected.

Right to a Fair Trial

The Sixth Amendment provides that "in all criminal prosecutions, the accused shall enjoy the right to a speedy and public trial, by an impartial jury of the State or district wherein the crime shall have been committed." Among other provisions, it also grants the accused the right "to be confronted with witnesses against him [and] to have compulsory process for obtaining witnesses in his favor." Once again, the bare language of the amendment leaves many questions unanswered: What is a speedy trial? What constitutes an adequate "criminal prosecution" sufficient to justify trial by jury? What is an impartial jury? And what is the right to confrontation?

The Sixth Amendment assures the accused of the right to a speedy trial. But what is a speedy trial? As the Court has acknowledged, "the right to a speedy trial is a more vague concept than other procedural rights. It is, for example, impossible to determine with precision when the right has been denied. We cannot definitely say how long is too long in a system where justice is supposed to be swift but deliberate."[69] The Court has been reluctant to hold "that the Constitution requires a criminal defendant to be offered a trial within a specified time period." To do so would require the Court "to engage in legislative or rule-making activity." Instead, the Court has identified four factors that have to be balanced against each other on an ad hoc basis: length of delay, the reason for the delay, the defendant's assertion of his right to a speedy trial, and prejudice to the defendant. If in the balance the Court concludes that the defendant was denied a speedy trial, the "only possible remedy" is dismissal of the indictment.[70]

Once the question of a speedy trial has been resolved, others emerge. To begin with, in what type of proceedings is a defendant entitled to a jury trial? The Court has never held that all defendants are entitled to a jury trial. It has reserved that right only for those charged with serious crimes, thereby differentiating between serious and petty crimes. The standard by which the Court determines what constitutes a serious crime is the length of the sentence the law authorizes a judge to impose for a violation. Currently, the standard appears to be six months' imprisonment. If the law authorizes penalties of more than six months, the defendant is entitled to a jury trial; if less, he is not.

If the defendant is entitled to a jury trial, still another question arises: What is an impartial jury? In answering this question, the Court has had to consider three crucial issues: the composition of the jury, prejudicial pretrial and trial publicity, and the question of jury size and the requirement of unanimity. The composition of the jury has been the subject of considerable litigation. For example, the Court employed the equal protection clause of the Fourteenth Amendment to declare formal exclusion of blacks from juries unconstitutional in its 1880 ruling in *Strauder* v. *West Virginia.*[71] In *Eubanks* v. *Louisiana,* it recognized the difficulties involved in proving discrimination and held that a prima facie case of discrimination could be established by showing that only a small percentage of blacks had been called to jury duty despite a large majority of blacks in the total population.[72] In *Swain* v. *Alabama*, although the Court held that a presecutor's use of peremptory challenges to strike all prospective black jurors in a particular case did not constitute denial of due process, it warned that a different result might be reached if it could be shown that the prosecutor regularly followed that practice.[73] The Court has never held, however, that each black defendant is entitled to a jury made up entirely or in part of blacks. "Fairness in selection has never been held to require proportional representation of races upon a jury."[74]

Claims of discrimination in jury selection based on other factors have not fared so well, however. Thus, in *Hoyt* v. *Florida*, the Court held that a state could reasonably exclude all women from jury duty unless they volunteered. The Court accepted as reasonable the state's argument that the woman's role in the home was so significant that the state could reasonably relieve her of jury duty unless she determined herself that such services were consistent with her other responsibilities.[75] Likewise, it upheld New York's use of "blue ribbon juries"—juries used for especially important or complex cases and made up of the more affluent, highly educated members of the community.[76]

Recent Court action affecting the composition of the jury has extended beyond the demographic makeup of the jury and has taken up the question: What of the opinions of the jury? In *Witherspoon* v. *Illinois*, it held that

> in a capital case, a state denies the defendant's right to an impartial jury on the issue of sentence when it automatically excludes all prospective jurors who have "conscientious or religious scruples against capital punishment" without seeking to determine whether their scruples would invariably lead them to vote against imposing capital punishment.[77]

Directly related to the question of the opinions of the jury is the second major issue involved in the right to an impartial jury: protection of the defendant and the jury from prejudicial pretrial and trial publicity. This issue presents the Court with an especially vexing dilemma. What should it do when the constitutionally protected right to a fair trial clashes with the constitutionally protected right of a free press? The British, with whom the Americans share a common criminal law tradition, have been considerably less vexed by this question. They have long since committed themselves to the right of a fair trial over a free press. As a result, any publication of information about a defendant in a criminal case before the trial starts leads to punishment for contempt of court. Upon pain of large fines and lengthy jail sentences, nothing that might conceivably affect the attitude of a potential juror may be reported unless and until it is formally disclosed in court. The Supreme Court has been reluctant to go so far, in large part because of the Bill of Rights' strongly worded First Amendment: "Congress shall make no law . . . abridging the freedom of . . . the press." However, the Court has attempted to provide relief for defendants. Thus, in 1961, in *Irvin* v. *Dowd*, the Court for the first time reversed a conviction on the grounds of prejudicial pretrial publicity.[78] In *Rideau* v. *Louisiana*, the Court went beyond *Irvin* and reversed a conviction without requiring a particularized showing of juror prejudice. It declared that due process had been denied the defendant, who had been refused a request for a change of venue despite the fact that the entire community had been "exposed repeatedly and in depth" to the "spectacle" of the defendant confessing to the crime in a police interview broadcast on local television.[79] Then, in *Sheppard* v. *Maxwell*, the principles of *Irvin* and *Rideau* were extended to publicity during the trial as well.[80] In that decision, the Court declared that the presence of a large, ill-controlled news media contingent can deny a defendant that "judicial serenity and calm" which are essential for a fair trial—even in the absence of proof that the jury was in fact prejudiced by the publicity.

With these decisions both defining and assuring an impartial jury, the Court has felt free to allow the states to depart somewhat from the traditional requirements that juries consist of twelve members and that they render their verdicts unanimously. In *Williams* v. *Florida*, the Court upheld the conviction of a defendant by a jury composed of only six members.[81] In justifying its decision, it noted that

> the essential feature of a jury obviously lies in the interposition between the accused and his accuser of the common-sense judgment of a group of laymen, and in the community participation and shared responsibility that results from that group's determination of guilt or innocence. The performance of this role is not a function of the particular number of the body that makes up the jury. To be sure, the number should probably be large enough to promote group deliberation, free from outside attempts at intimidation, and to provide a fair possibility for obtaining a representative cross-section of the community. But we find little reason to think that these goals are in any meaningful sense less likely to be achieved when the jury numbers six, than when it numbers twelve.

Likewise, in *Johnson* v. *Louisiana*, it departed from the requirement of unanimity.[82] It sustained provisions of both the Louisiana Constitution and the Code of Criminal Procedure, which provide that in criminal cases punishable by hard labor, a vote of nine of the twelve jurors is sufficient to convict or acquit.

The final question raised by the right to a fair trial is the right of confrontation. This right was made applicable to the states via the Fourteenth Amendment in *Pointer* v. *Texas*.[83] The scope of this right is still not fully defined, but *Barber* v. *Page*,[84] *Bruton* v. *United States*,[85] and *Illinois* v. *Allen*[86] are indicative of the Court's thinking on this matter. *Barber* held unconstitutional the admission into evidence of the preliminary hearing testimony of a witness unless the state makes a "good-faith effort to obtain his presence at trial." *Bruton* considered another aspect dealing with the unavailability of witnesses when it took up the admissibility at trial of prior statements of accomplices. It barred admission in a joint trial of a confession of one defendant that implicated both. Although the Court had previously held in *Delli Paoli* v. *United States*[87] that the use of one defendant's confession as evidence against a codefendant violated the codefendant's right to confrontation where the confessor refused to take the stand, it nevertheless held that the confession could be admitted as evidence against the confessor if the jury were specifically warned not to consider it against the codefendant. *Bruton* reversed *Delli Paoli*, and held that the jury instruction did not afford satisfactory protection to the codefendant. *Illinois* v. *Allen,* on the other hand, indicates that the implication of the confrontation guarantee may be limited by the need to consider other values in the administration of justice. It acknowledged that the defendant's presence in the courtroom is an essential element of the right to confront witnesses but that that right may be lost when an obstreperous defendant's conduct is so disruptive as to justify either removing him from the courtroom or binding and gagging him.

Posttrial Procedures

The Supreme Court's efforts to protect the constitutional rights of defendants also extend to such posttrial procedures as sentencing, appeals, and postconviction remedies. Traditionally the Court has not subjected sentencing to the same constitutional limitations applied to the trial process. This was based in part on the historical separation of the trial and sentencing stages. It was also justified on the grounds that fulfillment of the basic objectives of sentencing, especially the emphasis on relating punishment to the individual as well as the crime, requires more flexible procedural standards than those applied in the determination of guilt.[88] However, recently the Court has restricted considerably this flexibility as inconsistent with its reading of the due process and equal protection clauses of the Fourteenth Amendment and the prohibition against cruel and unusual punishments of the Eighth Amendment. Thus, for example, in *Williams* v. *Illinois,* the Court declared that an indigent offender may not be continued in confinement beyond a maximum term specified by law because of his failure to satisfy the monetary provisions of the sentence.[89] Such a practice, the Court held, constituted a denial of equal protection of the laws in that it imposed a far heavier burden on the indigent than on the solvent offender. Likewise, in *Tate* v. *Short,* the Court denied that a state can, consistent with the equal protection clause, limit the punishment to payment of fines if the offender is able to pay, yet convert the fines into a prison term for an indigent offender without means to pay his fine.[90] *Williams* and *Tate* have not gone far enough in restricting the flexibility in sentencing to suit some, however. Federal District Judge Marvin F. Frankel remains extremely critical of "the almost wholly unchecked and sweeping powers we give to judges in the fashioning of sentences," which he finds "terrifying and intolerable for a society that professes devotion to the rule of law."[91] He proposes three alternatives by which this "unbounded discretion" can be checked: sentencing councils, which utilize other judges to advise and assist collectively the sentencing judge on sentencing decisions; mixed sentencing tribunals, which employ panels of three, including a judge, a psychiatrist or psychologist, and a sociologist or educator, to impose sentences; and greater appellate review of sentences.[92]

The impact of the prohibition against cruel and unusual punishments has also been significant. In *Trop* v. *Dulles,* the Court held that denationalization of a native-born citizen convicted by a court-martial of wartime desertion from the military was cruel and unusual punishment. Chief Justice Warren, speaking for the majority, noted that "[t]his court has had little occasion to give precise content to the Eighth Amendment." But, whatever its "precise content," it "is not static. The Amendment must draw its meaning from the evolving standards of decency that mark the progress of a maturing society."[93] In keeping with this commitment to draw the amendment's meaning from "evolving standards," the Court has gone on to brand imprisonment for narcotics addiction[94] and perhaps alcoholism[95] as cruel and unusual punishment. In *Furman* v. *Georgia,* in a five-four decision in which each justice wrote a separate opinion, the Court used this same provision to invalidate the death penalty laws of thirty-nine states and the federal government, although it is possible that new and narrowly drawn death penalty statutes may survive constitutional scrutiny.[96]

Even when the sentencing stage is complete, the constitutionally protected procedural rights of the defendant do not cease. Although the Supreme Court held in *McKane* v. *Durston*[97] that a state is not constitutionally obligated to provide appellate review of criminal convictions, it has also held in *Griffin* v. *Illinois*[98] that if a state does establish appellate review—and all states now have done so—it must be available to all, regardless of financial status. Most constitutional decisions relating to appellate review since *Griffin* have been concerned with the application and extension of the *Griffin* principle, with *Douglas* v. *California,*[99] which held that the state must provide indigent defendants with court-appointed counsel on appeal, being the most significant.

The constitutional limitations on state postconviction remedies are roughly parallel to the limitations applied to appellate review. Several Supreme Court opinions suggest that a state need not provide postconviction remedies; however, once it does, the *Griffin* principle applies here as well. Postconviction relief in federal courts is subject to the limitations of Article 1, Section 9, of the U.S. Constitution, as well as the due process requirements of the Fifth Amendment. Article 1, Section 9, provides that "the Privilege of the Writ of Habeas Corpus shall not be suspended, unless when in Cases of Rebellion or Invasion the public Safety may require it." In *Fay* v. *Noia*[100] the Court interpreted this provision to impose a constitutional duty to maintain the writ unimpaired as well as unsuspended, and it extended significantly the availability of habeas relief for state prisoners "in custody in violation of the Constitution." It held that state prisoners would not automatically be precluded from raising in federal proceedings those constitutional issues that the state courts had refused to consider because of the defendant's failure to comply with state precedural rules.[101]

The Limited Impact of Supreme Court Decisions

From this review of what the Supreme Court has done to guarantee all criminal defendants the provisions of the Bill of Rights, five basic themes emerge. First, its actions have consistently emphasized that criminal procedure involves important aspects of individual liberty of concern not only to the Court but also to society as a whole. As Chief Justice Earl Warren put it,

> no general respect for, nor adherence to, the law as a whole can well be expected without judicial recognition of the paramount need for prompt, eminently fair and sober criminal law procedures. The methods we employ in the enforcement of our criminal law have aptly been called the measures by which the quality of our civilization may be judged.[102]

Second, closely related to this theme is the emphasis on achieving equality in the administration of criminal law. "The Court has recognized the unequal impact of criminal procedure on the poor and racial minorities and has sought to eliminate at least the official aspects of such inequality."[103] This same concern for equality has also been extended to treatment of juveniles. As a result of the 1967 decision of *In re Gault*,[104] juvenile defendants are guaranteed the right to effective and specific notice of charges, to representation by counsel (and appointment of counsel if the defendant is indigent), to confront and cross-examine witnesses, and to exercise the privilege against self-incrimination.

Third, the Court has come to maintain that uniform constitutional standards must be applied in both the state and federal systems. It has repudiated for the most part the notion that the states may properly serve as laboratories, experimenting with novel social and economic schemes.

Fourth, the Court, prompted in part by its elimination of more flexible constitutional standards for the states, has moved toward more broadly stated rulings. Decisions like *Miranda* and *Wade* have gone far beyond the proscription of particular unconstitutional practices and have prescribed affirmative standards of conduct that the Court regards as essential to safeguard against such unconstitutional practices. Thus, for example, *Miranda*, to avoid the potential violation of a defendant's privilege against self-incrimination during pretrial police interrogation, requires that the defendant must be warned of his rights and given the right to consult with counsel before and during any interrogation. *Wade* similarly requires that the state make available to the defendant assistance of counsel in order to protect him against the unconstitutional manipulation of a lineup identification procedure.

Fifth, the impetus for the development of these criminal procedural rights has come from the Court itself. Many of the lawyers who brought these cases to the Supreme Court were far less interested in developing general legal doctrines protective of the rights of defendants than they were in winning the cases for their particular clients. Yet the Court took these rather run-of-the-mill cases and used them as vehicles for the enunciation of broad legal policy, protective of the rights of individuals and minorities generally.[105] Nonetheless, despite these efforts by the Court to provide for both liberty and equality through broadly stated rulings to the federal and state criminal justice systems alike, there is still a "rather wide gap between what the court says ought to be done and what in fact is actually done."[106] The lessons gained from the experiences of the exclusionary rule provide a good example.

To repeat, the exclusionary rule provides for exclusion from a criminal prosecution of any evidence obtained in violation of the Constitution. The primary justification in favor of the exclusionary rule is that exclusion of evidence obtained by illegal means will deter law-enforcement officials from illegal behavior. Yet as Professor Dallin H. Oaks has noted, there is no convincing evidence in support of this justification.[107] Chief Justice Warren Burger, while sitting on the United States Court of Appeals for the District of Columbia, went even further:

> Some of the most recent cases in the Supreme Court reveal, almost plaintively, an unspoken hope that if judges say often and firmly that deterrence is the purpose, police will finally take notice and be deterred. As I see it, a fair conclusion is that the record does not support a claim that police conduct has been substantially affected by the suppression of the prosecution's evidence. . . . I suggest that the notion that suppression of evidence in a given case effectively deters the future action of the particular policeman or of policemen generally was never more than wishful thinking on the part of the courts.[108]

There are a number of limitations on the deterrent effectiveness of the exclusionary rule. To begin with, in terms of direct corrective effect, the exclusionary rule benefits only the defendant incriminated by illegally obtained evidence. It provides no compensation, however, for the injury suffered by the victim of an illegal search that turns up nothing incriminating. In short, it provides nothing for the innocent but freedom for the guilty. This irony has helped to generate disrespect for the law. As Chief Justice Burger has observed:

> The operation of the Suppression Doctrine [Exclusionary Rule] unhappily brings to the public gaze a spectacle repugnant to all decent people—the frustration of justice. . . . If a majority—even a substantial minority—of the people in a given community . . . come to believe that law enforcement is being frustrated by what laymen call "technicalities," there develops a sour and bitter feeling that is psychologically and sociologically unhappy. . . . I do not challenge these rules of law [which apply the Suppression Doctrine]. But I do suggest that we may have come the full circle from the place where [Justice Louis] Brandeis stood, and that a vast number of people are losing respect for law and the administration of justice because they think that the Suppression Doctrine is defeating justice.[109]

A second reason for the limited deterrent effect of the exclusionary rule is that it is a sanction limited to evidence offered at trial. As Jerome Skolnick has suggested, a variety of goals or motivations other than obtaining convictions may prompt arrest and search and seizure. The police may be interested in developing informants and information upon other offenders.[110] They may also wish to impose punitive sanctions, as is common in gambling and liquor law violations. The upper echelons of police departments are often as concerned with keeping the lid on in high-crime areas as with convictions; consequently, an officer who searches a suspect without probable cause on the basis of a furtive movement may gain the approval of his superiors, even though the evidence obtained is inadmissible. A large proportion of police behavior is traceable to these motivations for arrest and search and seizure, and is not likely, therefore, to be responsive to any deterrent effect of the exclusionary rule.

A third limitation on the deterrent effectiveness of the exclusionary rule is that it fosters "police perjury." "Creative arrest ticket writing," as it is referred to in the vernacular, may be employed to mask the use of proscribed techniques of investigation, interrogation, arrest, search, and handling of prisoners. Jerome Skolnick has observed that the police officer may often feel compelled to "reconstruct a set of complex happenings in such a way that, subsequent to the arrest, probable cause may be found according to appellate court standards. In this way, as one District Attorney expressed it, 'the policeman fabricates probable cause.' "[111] This fabrication of probable cause is perhaps best demonstrated through an examination of the "plain view doctrine."

The plain view doctrine is a fundamental part of search and arrest procedure.[112] Specifically, it allows officers who have a right to be where they are—for example, in a public place, in a home by consent or by warrant, stopping a traffic violator—to seize any contraband or other evidence of a crime they can observe, even when the original approach may have been for other reasons. Furthermore, such legally seized evidence may be used for criminal prosecution in court. Therefore, when it is crucial that the seized evidence must be constitutionally supported on the basis of the plain view doctrine, the facts of the case must clearly represent the search on those grounds. Examples of such cases might include the following:

a. An officer stops a driver on the highway for speeding; as the patrolman approaches the vehicle, he observes several gallons of untaxed liquor in the back seat. The officer has an obligation to ticket the violator, which gives him the right to scan visually the back seat to check for hidden assailants for his own protection. Seeing the untaxed whiskey, a violation of both state and federal statutes, the officer is entitled to make an immediate arrest, seizing the evidence in his view. Exclusion of "real evidence," such as the liquor in this arrest, would virtually eliminate related charges.[113]

b. An officer, checking buildings late at night, drives behind a department store, where he observes a man leaning over into the trunk of an automobile. The officer parks his patrol car and walks over to the other vehicle on the parking lot. Using his flashlight, the officer illuminates first the man and then the contents of the open trunk, discovering that the vehicle is loaded with new merchandise in boxes from the nearby department store. Placing the man under arrest and seizing the boxes as evidence, the officer verifies that a burglary had in fact occurred by having a second police unit he summoned check the store.

c. Any number of cases where an officer describes the defendant as a "known" burglar, drug pusher, robber, etc. This is an extension of the old

English system of branding persons with hot irons as "known" social undesirables, criminals, and the like. This label, applied to any suspect, may explain high levels of observation and even provide the key element in the decision to make an arrest based on certain actions.

An examination of these three cases indicates that they all involve direct evidence as well as so-called real evidence. The officer discovers direct evidence when he uses his five senses—sight, hearing, smell, taste, touch. The central issue is that direct evidence gives rise to real evidence; that is, what an officer finds (sees, hears, etc.) is what he later presents as courtroom exhibits (guns, drugs, goods, etc). Through the use of "police perjury," it is possible to present real evidence in a criminal prosecution, in spite of an illegal search, if the circumstances of its discovery such as "plain view" are altered to meet legal standards for reasonable search and seizure.

Each of the three "plain view doctrine" seizures that made arrests and successful prosecutions possible in the sample cases could have been examples of police perjury in reaction to the exclusionary rule. For example:

a. The officer seizing the untaxed liquor might have made a search by lifting up a blanket covering the whiskey jugs in the rear seat floor; he could simply have failed to mention the blanket, forgetting it was there.

b. The officer in the darkened parking lot might have seen a suspicious male shutting his car trunk. He might have forced the suspect to reopen the trunk so that he could have a better look inside. This, however, would be an illegal search under the circumstances stated; the evidence would have been useless in court.

c. The officer might not have been aware of the past nature or even the existence of any criminal record on the part of the defendant. However, if he discovered this later, it would be easy enough to include it in official records when in fact it formed no part of the basis for the original action.

The sample cases presented here suggest how and when "police perjury" might occur. However, as a number of empirical studies have established, the occurrence of police perjury is more than merely conjectural. Law students at the Columbia Law School analyzed the evidentiary grounds for arrest and subsequent disposition of misdemeanor narcotics cases in New York City for six-month periods before and after the *Mapp* decision. Table 4.1 summarizes their findings. The sharp reduction in the number of arrests, especially by the Narcotics Bureau, gives some evidence of illegal searches and seizures, but this evidence is inconclusive. Of much greater interest, however, are the summaries in Table 4.2 of the officers' accounts of how the evidence for the arrest was discovered. It is curious that suspects possessed of narcotics drugs should suddenly

TABLE 4.1 Misdemeanor narcotics arrests by New York City Police, 1960–1962

| | Six-Month Period | | |
Job assignment	Before Mapp	After Mapp	Difference
Narcotics Bureau	1,468	726	−51%
Uniform Division	316	330	+ 4%
Plain-clothes Detail	507	625	+23%
TOTAL	2,291	1,681	−27%

Source: Dallin H. Oaks, "Studying the Exclusionary Rule in Search and Seizure," *University of Chicago Law Review,* vol. 37 (1970), p. 697.

TABLE 4.2 New York City Police officers' allegations regarding discovery of evidence in misdemeanor narcotics offenses, 1960–1962

| | Percent of Arrests | | |
| | Six-Month Period | | |
How evidence found	Before Mapp	After Mapp	Difference
I. Narcotics Bureau:			
(a) Hidden on person	35	3	−32
(b) Dropped or thrown to ground	17	43	+26
II. Uniform:			
(a) Hidden on person	31	9	−22
(b) Dropped or thrown to ground	14	21	+ 7
III. Plain-clothes:			
(a) Hidden on person	24	4	−20
(b) Dropped or thrown to ground	11	17	+ 6

Source: Dallin H. Oaks, "Studying the Exclusionary Rule in Search and Seizure," *University of Chicago Law Review,* vol. 37 (1970), p. 698.

become so much more inclined to dispose of this evidence by dropping or throwing it to the ground at the very time the Court extended to them the protection against unreasonable searches and seizures. As the law students were forced to conclude from all of this, the police were induced to commit police perjury in an attempt to legalize their arrests and thereby avoid the effect of the exclusionary rule.[114] To the extent that the exclusionary rule encourages police officers to give such deliberately false testimony about the circumstances of arrests or searches and seizures, it not only fails to achieve its own objectives, but it also corrupts law-enforcement personnel and degrades the entire criminal justice system.

Still a fourth reason for the limited deterrent effect of the exclusionary rule is that it encourages police imposition of extrajudicial punishments. Dallin Oaks reports that police are on occasion forced to control gambling through the use of harassment. Suspects are searched without probable cause. If gambling paraphernalia is found, they are arrested, and the police confiscate the contraband and money (and the defendant's car, if it was involved) without any intention of applying the criminal law. The suspects are promptly freed, and no prosecution ensues since the search was illegal. The confiscated property is, however, retained. The police are forced to these means of punishing, harassing, and generally making life difficult for the gamblers because of the strict requirements of the laws of search and seizure and the light penalties imposed on gambling offenses.

Finally, a fifth limitation on the deterrent effectiveness of the exclusionary rule is that it permits police to immunize criminals to prosecution by deliberately overstepping legal bounds in obtaining vital evidence. Samuel Dash, now prominent for his service as general counsel to the Senate Select Committee on Presidential Campaign Activities (the Watergate Committee), studied the high proportion of defendants released after they were granted motions to suppress in gambling cases in Chicago in 1950. He credited this to "corruption." He witnessed the same police and the same defense involved day after day in the same routine of motion to suppress, testimony, and release, and concluded that "the raids are made to immunize the gamblers while at the same time satisfying the public that gamblers are being harassed by the police."[115]

The Supreme Court itself has recently become increasingly aware of these limitations. Thus Chief Justice Burger, in *Bivens* v. *Six Unknown Named Agents,* proposed an elimination of the exclusionary rule and the development of a "meaningful and effective remedy against unlawful conduct by government officials."[116] He conceded that private damage actions against individual police officers are inadequate in this respect. Consequently he urged Congress to develop an administrative or quasi-judicial remedy against the government itself to afford compensation and restitution for persons whose Fourth Amendment rights have been violated. Burger saw two advantages in such a statutory scheme: it would eliminate the "universal capital punishment we inflict on all evidence when police error is shown in its acquisition"; and it would provide some remedy for completely innocent persons who are sometimes the victims of illegal police conduct. Burger proposed that Congress enact a statute along the following lines:

1. It should waive sovereign immunity as to the illegal acts of law-enforcement officials committed in the performance of assigned tasks.
2. It should create a cause of action for damages sustained by any persons aggrieved by conduct of governmental agents in violation of the Fourth Amendment or statutes regulating official conduct.
3. It should create a quasi-judicial tribunal, perhaps patterned after the United States Court of Claims, to adjudicate all claims under the statute.
4. It should substitute this remedy for the exclusion of evidence secured for use in criminal cases in violation of the Fourth Amendment.

5. It should direct that no evidence, otherwise admissible, shall be excluded from any criminal proceeding because of violation of the Fourth Amendment.

Other members of the court are increasingly coming to share Chief Justice Burger's disenchantment with the exclusionary rule. Thus, in *United States* v. *Robinson*,[117] Chief Justice Burger and Justices Blackmun, Powell, Stewart, and White joined Justice William Rehnquist in refusing to limit the search of those arrested for traffic violations to a frisk for weapons and ruled that a full search of anyone in custodial arrest is not only an exception to the warrant requirement but is also "reasonable" under the Fourth Amendment. They thereby sustained the conviction of the defendants for possession of narcotic drugs found during these searches. This same six-member majority formed again in *United States* v. *Calandra*[118] in refusing to apply the exclusionary rule to grand jury proceedings. Justice Powell contended for the majority that the historic and integral role of the grand jury in ensuring effective law enforcement would be compromised by its introduction.

Studies on the deterrent effectiveness of *Miranda* suggest the same limitations on the Court's power to influence police behavior and thereby protect individual and minority rights. Research conducted in Washington, D.C., and New Haven, Connecticut, indicates that police fail to observe the spirit and often the letter of *Miranda*. Both studies suggest that when officers do give the warnings, they do so in a ritualistic fashion not designed to encourage the suspect to exercise his rights.[119] The work of Neil Milner supports their findings. He concludes that the "effectiveness of Supreme Court-imposed restraints on police behavior . . . is mitigated by the milieu in which the police officer operates, by the characteristics of the police decision-making process, and by the relationship police have with their reference groups."[120] Jonathan Casper has summarized the principal findings of these studies:

> The court spoke in its *Miranda* opinion of redressing the balance between law enforcement officials and the suspect, of permitting him to make intelligent choices about how to proceed without coercion and with the advice of competent counsel should he so desire it. The studies on the impact of *Miranda* suggest that this goal has not been reached. The decision was no doubt a movement towards this goal, but the dynamics of the legal system—the gap between the "ought" of doctrine and the "is" of behavior— again demonstrate that the protection of civil liberties depends upon much more than the words of the court.[121]

Two Models of the Criminal Process

What accounts for this discrepancy between Supreme Court rulings and police behavior? What explains the Court's inability to play a vital and effective role in the balancing of majority rule versus minority rights? Herbert L. Packer, in one of the most influential contributions to the understanding of the administration of criminal justice, has suggested that the answer to these questions is to be found in the fact that there are, in the United States, two distinct views, two alternative ways of looking at the goals and procedures of the criminal process: the crime control and the due process models.[122] Each model will be briefly discussed.

"The value system that underlies the crime control model is based on the proposition that the repression of criminal conduct is by far the most important function to be performed by the criminal process."[123] This model regards the criminal process to be the positive guarantor of social freedom. In order to achieve this high purpose, it focuses primary attention on the efficiency with which the criminal justice system operates to screen suspects, determine guilt, and secure appropriate dispositions of persons convicted of crime. This emphasis on efficiency encourages informality, uniformity, and, above all, a presumption of guilt. The importance of informality to achieve efficiency is obvious. "The process must not be cluttered up with ceremonious rituals that do not advance the progress of the case."[124] Since the facts can be more quickly established through informal interrogation at the police station than through the formal process of examination and cross-examination in a court, the crime control model prefers extrajudicial processes to judicial processes, informal operations to formal ones. Uniformity is also stressed; routine, stereotyped procedures are imperative if large numbers are to be handled. Thus the crime control model is an administrative, almost a bureaucratic model.

> The image that come to mind is an assembly-line conveyor belt down which moves an endless stream of cases, never stopping, carrying the cases to workers who stand at fixed stations and who perform on each case as it comes by the same small but essential operation that brings it one step closer to being a finished product, or, to exchange the metaphor for the reality, a closed file.[125]

However, this assembly-line justice of the crime control model can operate efficiently only if an early determination is made of probable innocence or guilt. It is necessary that the probably innocent be screened out, thereby allowing the probably guilty to be passed quickly through the remaining stages of the process. "The key to the operation of the model regarding those who are not screened out" is what Packer calls "a presumption of guilt."[126] It is this presumption of guilt that makes it possible for the crime control model to deal effectively with a large volume of crime. It supposes that the screening processes of police and prosecutors are reliable indicators of probable guilt.

> Once a man has been arrested without being found to be probably innocent or, to put it differently, once a determination has been made that there is enough evidence of guilt to permit holding him for further action, then all subsequent activity directed toward him is based on the view that he is probably guilty.[127]

If Packer likens the crime control model to an assembly line, he likens the due process model to "an obstacle course. Each of its successive stages is designed to present formidable impediments to carrying the accused any further along in the process."[128] The due process model places a much higher priority on reliability than on efficiency. It "resembles a factory that has to devote a substantial part of its input to quality control. This necessarily cuts down on quantitative output."[129]

Reliability becomes all the more important when the due process model's doctrine of legal guilt is understood. According to this doctrine, an accused is not guilty of a crime merely because he, in fact, did what he is said to have done. The doctrine of legal guilt requires more than mere factual guilt. Rather, an accused is guilty if and only if the state can prove—under various procedural restraints dealing, for example, with the admissibility of evidence, the burden of proof, and the requirement that guilt be proved beyond a reasonable doubt— that he did in fact commit the crime. "None of these requirements has anything to do with the factual question of whether the person did or did not engage in the conduct that is charged as the offense against him; yet favorable answers to any of them will mean that he is legally innocent."[130]

In this concern for reliability and legal guilt lies the explanation for the presumption of innocence basic to the due process model. Thus, even if a murderer were to kill his victim in plain view of a large number of people and were to declare to the police when they arrive, "I did it and I'm glad," the due process model would presume the subject to be innocent, for the presumption of innocence is not a "prediction of outcome" but "a direction to officials about how they are to proceed."[131] It directs them to ignore the presumption of guilt in their treatment of the suspect and to close their eyes to what will frequently seem to be factual probabilities. It encourages them to prefer reliability as measured through the determination of legal guilt in an adversary proceeding to efficiency.

These two models are, as Packer describes them, polarities; they represent competing schemes of values. They do not constitute "a program for action," but rather are "an aid to analysis," useful in providing an answer to the question of why "the courts' prescriptions about how the process ought to operate does not automatically become part of the pattern of official behavior in the criminal process."[132] With them, the answer to this question is quite simple: Although the due process model is preached—by the Court, by high school civics texts, and by politicians on Law Day—the crime control model is actually practiced. It is practiced because it is of value and utility for each element in the criminal justice system to do so.

Plea Bargaining

The extent to which the crime control model is practiced is evident by the fact that plea bargaining takes place in over 90 percent of all criminal prosecutions in the United States. In plea bargaining—or "copping a plea," as it is called in the vernacular—the defendant agrees to plead guilty in exchange for a lesser sentence. It is efficient in that it spares the criminal justice system of the need for a trial. Yet it is clearly in conflict with the due process model, for the defendant who enters such a plea not only admits guilt but also surrenders his "entire array of constitutional rights designed to protect a criminal defendant against unjustified conviction, including the right to remain silent, the right to confront witnesses against him, the right to trial by jury, and the right to be proven guilty by proof beyond a reasonable doubt."[133] There are a variety of reasons that have led defendants, as well as other participants in the criminal justice system—the police, the prosecutor, the judge, and the defense attorney—to prefer plea bargaining according to the crime control model to an adversary proceeding according to the due process model. The reasons of each of these participants will be explored.

The reasons that induce a defendant to waive his procedural rights assured by the Court interpretations of the Bill of Rights and plead guilty are numerous. To begin with, he may simply wish to acknowledge his guilt and willingness to take his medicine. Alternatively, he may prefer the relative anonymity of the copout ceremony to the potential publicity of a trial. More likely than not, however, he will plead guilty because he has negotiated his right to require the prosecution to prove guilt at trial for a lesser charge or sentence. There are five ways by which this plea negotiation can take place. First, the defendant can agree to plead guilty in return for a lesser or a different charge. The motivation for doing so is that it may affect the trial judge's sentencing discretion. For example, the offense to which the defendant pleads guilty may have a lower maximum penalty, thereby assuring the defendant that his sentence cannot be longer than a given period of time. Or the offense may have a lower minimum sentence thereby enabling the defendant to be eligible for parole earlier. This motivation is especially apparent in California, where there is considerable incentive for a defendant to plead guilty to lesser charges for which punishment will be confinement for a particular period of time in a county jail rather than to go to trial, where conviction will in all probability subject him to the indeterminate sentences of the state prison system. Reduction or change in charge may also have advantages for the defendant independent of sentencing. Thus, to avoid being labeled a child molester or a homosexual, the defendant may be willing to plead guilty to a charge such as disorderly conduct or assault.

A second way by which the plea negotiation can take place is for the defendant to plead guilty to a single charge in a multiple-charge indictment in return for the dropping of all other charges. The recent Watergate-related convictions are illustrative of this. So is the plea bargaining involving former Vice-President Spiro T. Agnew. Agnew agreed to resign as vice-president and plead no contest (nolo contendere) to a single count of income tax evasion in return for a government agreement to quash all other indictments that may have been pending.

A third way for plea negotiations to occur is for the prosecutor to agree to recommend a sentence to the judge for the original charge in return for the plea. Although this recommendation is generally not binding on the judge, he may routinely follow it. In these cases, the defendant trades his trial rights for the prosecution's promise to attempt to influence the sentence by means of a recommendation.

A fourth way by which plea negotiation can take place is for the defendant simply to throw himself on the mercy of the sentencing court. Actually, it involves no real bargaining at all between the prosecution and the defendant, and is typically practiced either by those who are unaware of the advantages that may be gained by bargaining with the prosecution or by those who are aware that under existing practice, their sentences will be shorter if they plead guilty and who do so with that expectation.

Finally, a fifth form of plea negotiation involves judge shopping. In many jurisdictions, there are wide sentencing disparities among judges. A defendant may agree to plead guilty in exchange for assurances from the prosecution that he will be brought before a particular judge for sentencing.

These incentives for the defendant to engage in plea bargaining have, to a certain extent, been neutralized by the tendency of prosecutors to "overcharge." Overcharging takes place when the prosecutor charges a defendant with a variety of counts, not with the intention of obtaining a conviction for each count, but in an effort to induce the defendant to plead guilty to a few of the charges in exchange for dismissal of the rest. Overcharging can be either horizontal or vertical. Horizontal overcharging may include charging the defendant with a separate offense for every criminal transaction in which he is alleged to have participated. For example, an embezzler who has falsified evidence in his employer's books over a long period of time may face an indictment with hundreds of counts. It may also include several offenses arising out of a single act. Thus, the defendant who commits an armed robbery may be charged with six different counts:

1. robbery first degree
2. assault second degree
3. assault third degree
4. grand larceny
5. carrying a dangerous weapon
6. petit larceny

Similarly, one accused of burglary may be charged with three separate counts:

1. burglary third degree
2. possession of burglar's tools
3. unlawful entry of a building

Vertical overcharging, on the other hand, follows a fairly uniform pattern. It typically occurs when a prosecutor charges robbery when he should charge larceny of the person, or auto theft when he should charge joy riding—a less serious offense that does not involve an intention to deprive the owner permanently of his property.

This tendency of the prosecutor to overcharge has reduced somewhat the benefits a defendant can derive form the plea bargain. Yet, despite this, plea bargaining is still preferred to an actual trial, where, if the defendant is convicted, a far harsher sentence is likely. Consider the answer of one serious offender to the question "You think you did about as good as you could [through plea bargaining]?"

> I think I made out like a bandit. I mean I had forty years hanging, the maximum. They could have gave me a ten-to-twenty on just one of them, because twenty years is the maximum on burglary. They could have gave me ten-to-twenty; they could have gave me anything. They gave me twenty, nineteen, on the way down. Or they could have gave me a one-to-two or two-to-five, but whatever he offers you, you better take it, because if you don't, you're going to get more than he offered; so take what you get . . . yeah, I mean from forty years down to one year you know—good.[134]

The sentence of the defendant who pleads guilty is likely to be less severe than the sentence of the defendant who is convicted after trial. There are a number of reasons for this. Perhaps the chief among these is that the sentencing judge considers the plea of guilty as evidence of repentance. The defendant pleading guilty is less culpable than the one denying guilt in that his very confession demonstrates a readiness to accept responsibility for his criminal acts. Judges commonly feel that such a confession of wrongdoing is indicative of a repentant attitude and thus constitutes an important first step toward rehabilitation of the accused. A second reason that a judge may award a defendant convicted at trial a more severe sentence than one pleading guilty is the notion that the former has very likely committed perjury in his defense. This inference can be drawn, of course, only when the defendant has taken the stand. It presumes the occurrence of perjury from the fact of conviction. Since the defendant is also a perjuror, additional punishment is deserved. The perjury rationale for increased sentences can be viewed from two perspectives. It may be viewed as an additional sentence imposed by the judge because the defendant has committed the second crime of perjury, or it can be viewed as an appropriate sentence for the defendant because his perjurous conduct increases the difficulty of reformation. After all, perjury is a culpable act that bears upon the character of the accused. A third reason for entitling a defendant pleading guilty to some discount in punishment is the aid his plea provides to the efficient administration of justice. Finally, a fourth reason that may contribute to shorter sentences for

By permission of John Hart and Field Enterprises, Inc.

those who plead guilty is that the brutal circumstances that frequently accompany criminal activity are not emphasized by the prosecution or vividly recounted at trial. In a copout ceremony, the defendant is more antiseptic; he appears less a threat to society. For all these reasons, a defendant is often well advised to enter into a plea bargain. The following conversation between a public defender and his client in New York City's former Manhattan House of Detention (the Tombs) captures this well:

> "Well, it's very simple. Either you're guilty or you're not. If you're guilty of anything, you can take the plea and they'll give you a year and under the circumstances that's a very good plea and you ought to take it. If you're not guilty, you have to go to trial."
> "I'm not guilty. . . ."
> "Then you should go to trial. But the jury is going to hear that the cop followed you into the building, the super sent him to apartment 3-A, he arrested you there, and the man identified you in the hospital. If they find you guilty, you might get fifteen years."[135]

The prospect of the harsher sentence the defendant might face if he is unable to prove his innocence at trial is quite an incentive to engage in plea bargaining, especially if the defendant has been unable to post bail bond. Bail is a procedure for releasing arrested persons on financial or other condition to ensure their return for trial. It typically operates as follows: An arrested person is brought by the police before a committing magistrate or judge, who fixes an amount of money as security for his appearance at trial. In some courts, bail schedules set an amount for each offense, and if the defendant can post that amount, the judge seldom considers the case individually. In either case, if the defendant can post the required amount or can pay a bondsman to post it for him, he is released until trial. If he cannot, he remains in jail

Under normal bail procedures, where a bail bond is obtained from a private bail bondsman, the accused pays 10 percent to the bondsman, who then becomes financially responsible to the state for the defendant's appearance at trial. If the defendant fails to appear, the bail bondsman forfeits the entire amount of the bond. If, on the other hand, the defendant appears, he does not recoup the 10 percent he has paid to the bondsman. It is in this way that the bondsman makes his living. Because of the loss of the 10 percent premium, when bail is set at more than $500 it often becomes more than most defendants can afford. For example, in New York City, 25 percent of all defendants fail to make bail at $500, 45 percent fail at $1500, and 63 percent at $2500.[136] Although the proportion of defendants who fail to make bail varies widely from place to place, the President's Commission on Law Enforcement and Administration of Justice reports that it is often substantial. Table 4.3 summarizes their findings for both representative large and small counties.

The results of these bail procedures, which leave a substantial proportion of defendants in jail because they cannot post bond, has been the promotion of plea bargaining, the crime control model, and the presumption of guilt. These procedures may induce a defendant who has already spent a number of months

TABLE 4.3 Felony defendants unable to make bail in representative large and small counties

Large Counties	Percent
Large counties:	
Cook (Chicago)	75
Hennepin (Minneapolis)	71
Jefferson (Louisville)	30
Philadelphia (Philadelphia)	14
Small counties:	
Brown, Kans.	93
Rutland, Vt.	83
Putnam, Mo.	36
Anchorage, Alaska	28
Catoosa, Ga.	6

Source: President's Commission on Law Enforcement and Administration of Justice, *Task Force Report: The Courts* (Washington, D.C.: U.S. Government Printing Office, 1967), p. 37.

in jail because he is unable to post bond to plead guilty even though the defendant knows himself to be innocent. If the sentence is short and if he is given credit for the time he has already served awaiting trial, he may be subject to immediate or imminent release. However, if he protests his innocence, he may have to spend an additional two to three months in jail awaiting a formal trial, at which, if he is convicted, he may receive a far more severe sentence in prison —where pretrial jail does not count. The pressures to plead guilty are great: plead guilty and you are free; plead not guilty and you remain in jail.

Present bail arrangements not only encourage plea bargaining, they also promote the crime control model and its presumption of guilt. Professor Caleb Foote and his associates conducted pioneer studies on the varying dispositions between bailed and nonbailed defendants in Philadelphia and New York. Their findings support this contention. In Philadelphia, for instance, they traced the disposition of 529 serious criminal cases where the defendants were free on bail. Of that number, 275 were convicted. Of these, only 61, or 22 percent, were sentenced to prison. In contrast, of 417 similar cases where the defendants were held in jail before trial, 340 were convicted and 200, or 59 percent of them were sentenced to prison.[137] In New York, the same pattern was present. Of a sample of 2,000 defendants, the grand jury dismissed about 24 percent of those defendants free on bail but 10 percent of those in jail. Jailed defendants pleaded guilty about 90 percent of the time while those awaiting trial on bail did so only about 70 percent of the time. At trial, jailed defendants were acquitted about 20 percent of the time, in contrast to those free on bail, who were acquitted 31 percent of the time. Finally, suspended sentences were received by only 13 percent of jailed defendants who were tried and convicted but by 54 percent of bailed defendants who were tried and convicted.[138] These figures are explained in large part by the fact that the period before trial is a crucial stage in the administration of criminal justice. A jailed defendant is limited in what he can do to assist in the preparation of his defense. He may be confined at an inconvenient location or have insufficient time available to work with his attorney, with investigators, or with witnesses. He has no opportunity to make amends with complaining witnesses in an effort to have the charges dropped. He cannot help locate witnesses or evidence. He earns no money that can be used to help in his case. More recent figures gathered in conjunction with the Manhattan Bail Project stress just how crucial this stage is. Table 4.4 compares disposition by charge for defendants who were free pending trial and those who were in jail at the time of adjudication.

The effect of detention is clear. Table 4.5 compares the sentences received—

TABLE 4.4   Case dispositions, by jail status and charge

	At liberty before trial			Detained before trial		
Charge	Percent convicted	Percent not convicted	Total cases	Percent convicted	Percent not convicted	Total cases
Assault	23	77	126	59	41	128
Grand larceny	43	57	96	72	28	156
Robbery	51	49	35	58	42	100
Dangerous weapons	43	57	23	57	43	21
Narcotics	52	48	33	38	62	42
Sex crimes	10	90	49	14	86	28
Others	30	70	47	78	22	23

Source: National Advisory Commission on Criminal Justice Standards and Goals, *Report on Corrections* (Washington, D.C.: U.S. Government Printing Office, 1973), p. 100.

TABLE 4.5   Sentence, by jail status and charge

Charge on which guilt determined	At liberty before trial			Detained before trial		
	Suspended sentence (percent)	Prison (percent)	Total cases	Suspended sentence (percent)	Prison (percent)	Total cases
			FELONIES			
Assault	42	58	26	6	94	73
Dangerous weapons	30	70	10	9	91	11
Larceny	42	48	40	7	93	107
Narcotics	41	59	17	—	100	16
Robbery	22	78	18	3	97	59
Others	43	56	14	12	88	17
			MISDEMEANORS[a]			
Assault	68	32	134	13	87	159
Dangerous weapons	49	51	65	25	75	43
Larceny	72	28	195	14	86	357

Source: *Report on Corrections*, p. 99.

[a] Although all charges enter the court as felonies, the charges are often reduced and defendants plead guilty to misdemeanors.

suspended sentences with or without probation versus prison sentences—between those in detention and those at liberty. This discrepancy in disposition and sentencing is made all the more serious since pretrial detainees are often indiscriminately mixed with persons convicted of crime. The result of this, as Justice Douglas has observed, is "equivalent to giving a young man an M.A. in crime."[139]

These discriminatory aspects of pretrial confinement have made the need for reform imperative. So too have the huge economic costs imposed on units of government that must clothe and feed those detained for want of bail. New York City is a good example. Each year an estimated 60,000 persons spend an average of thirty days each in pretrial detention. Since the cost per day per inmate may be cautiously estimated at $6.25, this means that New York City annually spends over $10 million on pretrial confinement. This money could well be used elsewhere in the criminal justice system—providing, for example, additional courtrooms, judges, prosecutors, and court staff sufficient to reduce the heavy volume of cases that has made plea bargaining necessary in the first place. Programs of reform have been initiated to eliminate these human and economic costs. In general, they are of three basic types. In a few jurisdictions, Oakland, California, for example, police are encouraged to issue citations in lieu of making arrests, thereby diminishing the amount of detention from the moment the defendant comes into contact with the criminal justice system. In many more cities and counties, programs that allow selected defendants to be released simply on their own promise to appear for trial—release on own recognizance (ROR) programs —have proved successful. Finally, in a few locations, Illinois being an example, bail bondsmen have been replaced and defendants are allowed to deposit 10 percent of their bond with the court, most of which is returned when they appear for trial. These reform programs, however, are rare exceptions. And, as a result, bail, along with all the other above-mentioned reasons, has encouraged defendants to participate in plea bargaining and to act consistent with the crime control model. The limited ability of the Supreme Court to protect individual and minority rights becomes all the more apparent.

Plea bargaining would not be as widely practiced as it is if it received only the support of defendants. However, it has found favor with virtually all the participants of the criminal justice system, including the police, the prosecution, the judge, and even the defense attorney.

The police, although they often complain about plea bargaining, have many reasons for supporting it. To begin with, they save time spent waiting around and testifying in trials. More importantly, plea bargaining is useful in clearing cases—that is, "solving" crimes—and thereby improves the department's clearance rate, one of the most commonly used indicators in evaluating police performance by superiors, political figures, and the public at large. On many occasions, a defendant charged with a particular offense will admit to a number of other crimes with an agreement that he will be charged with, plead guilty to, and probably be punished for his most recent arrest. In this way the police are able to clear several other cases on the basis of admissions by the defendant. Another important reason police have for supporting plea bargaining is that it suppresses legal issues. A plea of guilty deprives the defendant of the opportunity to raise questions about the character of the evidence against him or the activities of the police in their treatment of him. Since 90 percent of all cases end in plea bargaining, the police know that following procedural rules about searches and seizures and interrogations is not as overwhelming a concern as it would be if every defendant were likely to use every procedural imperfection as a weapon in his defense. Thus the plea bargain buries much police conduct not conforming to legal doctrine.

The prosecutors also gain from plea bargaining. As with the police, guilty pleas avoid time-consuming trials and suppress legal issues in potentially damaging challenges to the state's case. Moreover, the use of guilty pleas, even at the cost of conviction on lesser charges, takes all the risk out of the prosecution and assures the prosecutor a high batting average, so useful at election time.

Some of the same reasons that prompt prosecutors to support the plea bargain apply to the judges as well. They share the prosecutor's desire to avoid "the time consuming, expensive, unpredictable snares and pitfalls of an adversary trial."[140] They see the plea bargain as essential if any progress is to be made in overcoming the huge backlog of cases, with their mounting delays. Moreover, as Abraham Blumberg has pointed out, the defendant's plea of guilty enables the judge to engage in a social-psychological fantasy, "the accused becomes an already repentant individual who has 'learned his lesson' and deserves lenient treatment."[141]

Even the defense attorney, whether a public defender or privately retained, is likely to favor plea bargaining. The defense attorney who bargains for his client is often pursuing more than the best possible deal for his client. He may also be pursuing personal goals and acting as a representative of the organizational matrix that the criminal court comprises. Many attorneys who specialize in criminal work in trial courts depend for their income upon turning over a relatively large number of cases representing clients paying small fees. Since plea bargaining is an efficient and quick method of turning over a large number of cases, it has considerable appeal. Moreover, no one else in the court structure is more strategically located or ideally suited to promote plea bargaining than the defense attorney. In recognition of this, both prosecutors and judges—who also gain from plea bargaining—frequently cooperate with the defense attorney in ways designed to assist his efforts to persuade the defendant to plead guilty. For example, prosecutors may engage in overcharging as a part of an elaborate sham staged for the benefit of the defense attorney. These additional charges are easily and routinely eliminated in plea negotiations. Yet they help the defense attorney to justify his fee. He can tell the defendant, "Look, there were five felony charges against you, but I went to bat for you and got the prosecutor to go all the way down to one. I've gotten you quite a deal, please don't blow it." Judges can also provide similar assistance. Thus they will typically recess the case of a defendant who is in jail awaiting plea or sentence if his attorney requests such action. Ostensibly, this may be done for some seemingly valid reason, but the real purpose may be to permit the attorney to press for collection of his fee, which is likely to go uncollected if it is not obtained prior to the conclusion of the case.

Other factors also bind the defense attorney to the court and encourage him to induce his client to plead guilty. If he is a court regular, he is likely to develop interpersonal relationships and dependencies in his dealings with the prosecutors and judges. Thus he may not push the prosecutor too hard on one case in order to gain a favor that can be collected in another case. Moreover, since the defense attorney's contact with his client is typically brief, while his contact with the prosecutors and judges is continuous, the pressures to become a "double agent" are all the more intense.[142] The operation of the crime control model, with its presumption that someone brought this far into the criminal process is guilty, spares the defense attorney much anxiety. Since his client is probably guilty, he is acting in his client's interest by encouraging him to plead guilty in return for some consideration.

Thus the use of plea bargaining tends to serve the best interests of all participants of the criminal process. The police, prosecutors, judges, and defense attorneys benefit by it; so, it appears, does the guilty defendant, who obtains in return for his acquiescence and participation a more favorable disposition. There are only two losers: the innocent defender and society as a whole. The clearly innocent defendant finds himself enmeshed in the operation of the crime control model with its presumption of guilt and its emphasis on efficiency over reliability. Once enmeshed in this process, there is little opportunity to escape unscathed. As Abraham Blumberg has pointed out: "It would appear at least tentatively that once one is caught up in the system as an accused (indicted) individual, there is little chance of escaping conviction."[143]

The loss to society as a whole is less visible but no less serious. The frequent result of plea bargaining is that defendants are not dealt with as severely as might otherwise be the case. This leniency reduces the deterrent impact of the law. Likewise, plea bargaining endangers society's interest in protection by making the correctional task of rehabilitation more difficult. To the extent that plea bargaining limits the sentencing alternatives of the court, it may encourage sentences inconsistent with correctional goals, thereby generating further conflict in the interrelationships among the components of the criminal justice system. Plea bargaining may also have another effect on correctional efforts: it may reinforce the defendant's belief that he can manipulate the criminal justice system and, as a result, minimize his motivation to participate in correctional programs. Jonathan D. Casper provides a most perceptive insight into this problem:

> The situation the defendant faces in the period preceding his eventual plea is, in many respects, an extension of his life in the streets. You scuffle around, trying to accumulate a little wealth or power; you con others and are conned by them; you exploit those you can and are exploited by those

who are more powerful; you use people for your own ends and are, in turn, used by others. You lie, you cheat, you care little about abstract moral principles. How you make out on the street depends upon what you've got and how you use it. In addition, luck and fate are crucial elements of life in the streets. Often the events that occur are accidental: You come into some money easily; you get burned and lose it. You are to a large extent at the mercy of others and of fate. You try to get what you want; but whether you get it or not often has little to do with your efforts.

These same characteristics seem to the defendants to characterize their experience within the legal system. Their initial arrest is often simply the product of bad luck: They are arrested for an activity that they have been engaging in frequently. Something goes wrong, and they get caught. They then must attempt to make the best of their situation and use the techniques that they already know well in order to attempt to ameliorate their plight. The other participants in the system seem to be doing the same things. They are going about their jobs in fashions that seem to the defendants quite similar to the hypocritical and manipulative ways in which they themselves treat people. And they are probably correct.[144]

Society suffers from the plea bargain in still another respect. Reliance on the crime control model and its presumption of guilt transfers considerable sanctioning authority from the courts to the police, who "make the major decisions about sanctions by deciding whether to pull someone into the machinery of justice."[145] It critically affects that separation of powers which must exist within the criminal justice system if a balance between majority rule and minority rights is to be preserved.

An End to the Plea Bargain?

These costs to innocent defendants and to society as a whole prompted the National Advisory Commission on Criminal Justice Standards and Goals to propose the abolition of plea bargaining altogether.

> As soon as possible, but in no event later than 1978, negotiations between prosecutors and defendants—either personally or through their attorneys—concerning concessions to be made in return for guilty pleas should be prohibited. In the event that the prosecution makes a recommendation as to sentence, it should not be affected by the willingness of the defendant to plead guilty to some or all of the offenses with which he is charged. A plea of guilty should not be considered by the court in determining the sentence to be imposed.[146]

To accomplish this, the commission recommended reducing the huge backlog of cases that has made plea bargaining necessary through decriminalization of "victimless crimes," increased use of screening and pretrial diversion, and expanded funding for the criminal justice system sufficient to provide the manpower and facilities necessary to handle this volume. Each of these recommendations is, however, open to criticism. Removal of criminal sanctions from

TABLE 4.6 Number and percent of arrests for victimless crimes in 1972

Crime	Number	Percent
Drunkenness	1,676,800	19.2
Disorderly conduct	696,800	8.0
Narcotic drug laws	527,400	6.0
Liquor laws	279,300	3.2
Runaways	266,800	3.1
Curfew and loitering	141,400	1.6
Gambling	78,600	0.9
Vagrancy	66,000	0.8
Suspicion	56,000	0.6
Prostitution	51,600	0.6
Total known victimless crimes	3,840,700	44.1

Source: *Crime in the United States: Uniform Crime Reports, 1972* (Washington, D.C.: U.S. Government Printing Office, 1973), p. 119.

such victimless crimes as marijuana use, prostitution, pornography, drunkenness, and gambling would certainly help to reduce the heavy volume of cases the criminal justice system is required to process. Statistics of the FBI reveal that the total number of arrests in the United States in 1972 was 8,712,400, of which 1,724,400 (20 percent) were for the seven "index crimes": murder, rape, robbery, assault, burglary, larceny, and auto theft. The total number of arrests for victimless crimes was 3,840,700 (44 percent of the total). Table 4.6 itemizes the number and percentage of arrests by particular victimless crimes. Despite this advantage, however, decriminalization of victimless crimes is an extremely controversial proposal and is unlikely to gain the support of the majority. Screening and diversion of cases, although they have allowed Philadelphia to reduce the incidence of guilty pleas in its criminal courts from 90 percent to 32 percent, share the same defect as plea bargaining: they are departures from the due process model and deprive the defendant of many of the rights courts can protect. Expanded funding is surely desirable but not likely. The commission's optimism in this respect deserves mention: "Basic to the Commission's position on plea negotiations is its conclusion that lack of resources should not affect the outcome of the processing of a criminal defendant and that it is not unrealistic to expect that the criminal justice system can and will be provided with adequate resources."[147] This comment contrasts strikingly with the realism of Chief Justice Burger's comments to the American Bar Association:

> There is another factor. It is elementary, historically and statistically, that systems of courts—the number of judges, prosecutors, and of courtrooms— has been based on the premise that approximately 90 per cent of all defendants will plead guilty leaving only 10 per cent, more or less, to be tried. . . . The consequence of what might seem on its face a small percentage change in the rate of guilty pleas can be tremendous. A reduction from 90 per cent to 80 per cent in guilty pleas requires the assignment of twice the judicial manpower and facilities—judges, court reporters, bailiffs,

clerks, jurors, and courtrooms. A reduction to 70 per cent trebles this demand.[148]

The Supreme Court's response to the plea bargain has been in keeping with Chief Justice Burger's statement. In *Boykin* v. *Alabama*[149] and *McCarthy* v. *United States*[150] the Court held that as a matter of constitutional law, a plea of guilty is valid so long as the trial court record affirmatively showed that the plea was intelligent and voluntary. Then, in *Brady* v. *United States* in 1970, despite plea bargaining's tie to the crime control model, the Court's held that a plea was not involuntary when made in response to an assurance of a more lenient disposition.[151] For all practical purposes, it thereby validated plea bargaining. Since then, the Court has been content to try to improve the system of plea bargaining rather than to eliminate it. Thus, in *Santo Bello* v. *New York*, it held that if a guilty plea is entered in reliance upon a prosecutor's promise, due process of law requires that that promise be kept or that the defendant be given some relief— for example, an opportunity to withdraw the guilty plea.[152]

The Court's most comprehensive effort to restore the protections of the Bill of Rights to plea bargaining came in April 1974, in a set of amendments the Court proposed to the Federal Rules of Criminal Procedure. Although these amendments apply only to the federal courts, it is likely that as litigation continues, these same procedures will be required in state judicial systems as well. These amendments set forth the following requirements: They forbid the trial court to participate in the plea negotiations between the attorney for the government and the attorney for the defendant. Once, however, a plea agreement has been reached which contemplates entry of a plea of guilty in the expectation that a specific sentence will be imposed or that other charges before the court will be dismissed, the trial court shall require the disclosure of the agreement in open court at time the plea is offered. At that juncture, the trial court may accept or reject the agreement, or defer its decision as to acceptance or rejection until it has had an opportunity to consider the presentence report. If the trial court accepts the plea agreement, it shall inform the defendant of this fact and dispose of the case as provided for in the plea agreement. If, however, the trial court rejects the plea agreement, it shall inform the parties of that fact, advise the defendant personally in open court that the court is not bound by the plea agreement, afford the defendant the opportunity to withdraw his plea, and advise the defendant that if he persists in his plea of guilty, the disposition of the case may be less favorable to the defendant than that contemplated by the plea agreement. Except for good cause, notification of the trial court of the existence of a plea agreement should be at the arraignment. Notwithstanding the acceptance of the guilty plea, the trial court still shall satisfy itself that there is a factual basis for the plea. And finally, throughout the proceedings at which the defendant enters his plea, a verbatim record shall be made which shall include the court's advice to the defendant, the inquiry into the voluntariness of the defendant's plea, and the inquiry into the accuracy of the guilty plea.

Along with these efforts to make the plea bargain more visible and to extend greater protection to the defendant in this process, the Supreme Court and especially its chief justice have been striving to promote better and more efficient judicial administration capable of confronting the enormous volume of cases without succumbing to the plea bargain and other behavior consistent with the crime control model. Progress in this respect, however, has been limited. Chief Justice Burger bemoaned this fact before the American Bar Association.

> [I]n the final third of this century, we are still trying to operate the courts with fundamentally the same basic methods, the same procedures and and the same machinery . . . [that] were not good enough . . . [at the turn of the century]. In the supermarket age we are trying to operate the courts with cracker-barrel corner grocer methods and equipment—vintage 1900.[153]

Examples of these "cracker-barrel corner grocer methods" are numerous, but the court's reluctance to adopt modern management and record-keeping systems is especially obvious. At a time when computerized data processing could print out a daily calendar for the judges in each division of court; could provide additional information on case loads so that the judges' time could be properly scheduled; could determine how many cases each attorney has and when each case is scheduled for its next court hearing; could be used for legal research, yielding data, for example, on how many defendants were arrested for carrying guns during a certain period and what happened to them in court; and could be of benefit to court administrators, enabling them to determine accurately how well each division is coping with its business, whether methods need to be changed, or whether more judges or support personnel are needed, most courts continue to waste considerable time and effort keeping most records and preparing most dockets in longhand.[154]

There are a number of problems that have mitigated against better and more orderly judicial administration. Three are of particular importance. First, the courts are almost totally dependant on political processes for their resources. Responsibility for complex social problems is often placed on the courts without giving them the requisite resources necessary for their effective resolution. Second, the traditional adversary theory requires the judges to play passive roles and thereby makes the courts almost wholly dependent for the administration of justice upon the performance, quality, and availability of the American lawyer. And third, the statutory division between courts of limited jurisdiction and courts of general jurisdiction prohibits flexible administration. This division results in a most inefficient utilization of manpower and facilities by prohibiting an equitable distribution of cases among the various courts. As long as these problems continue, judicial administration will remain inefficient. Plea bargaining, although improved and made more visible by the Supreme Court as it has been, will continue to be practiced; so will the crime control model, both at the expense of the due process model. The protection to individual and minority rights afforded by the Bill of Rights and superintended over by the Supreme Court will, for the most part, remain unexercised, as they are presently unexercised in 90 percent of all cases. The balance between majority rule and minority rights will remain tilted in favor of the majority.

NOTES

1. Quinn Tamm, "Police Must Be More Free," in *Violence in the Streets,* ed. Shalom Endleman (Chicago: Quadrangle, 1968), pp. 398–399.

2. Sam Ervin, "*Miranda* v. *Arizona:* A Decision Based on Excessive and Visionary Solicitude for the Accused," *American Criminal Law Quarterly,* 5 (1967):125.

3. 309 U.S. 227 (1940).

4. David Fellman, "The Supreme Court's Changing View of Criminal Defendants' Rights," in *Crime in Urban Society,* ed. Barbara N. McLennan (New York: Dunellen, 1970), pp. 96–97.

5. 7 Pet. (U.S.) 243 (1833).

6. Jerold H. Israel and Wayne R. LaFave, *Criminal Procedure* (St. Paul, Minn.: West, 1971), p. 5.

7. 302 U.S. 319 (1937).

8. *Lisenba* v. *California,* 314 U.S. 219, 236 (1941).

9. *Estes* v. *Texas,* 381 U.S. 532 (1965).

10. *Duncan* v. *Louisiana,* 391 U.S. 145 (1968).

11. Israel and La Fave, *Criminal Procedure,* p. 9.

12. *Cohen* v. *Hurley,* 366 U.S. 117 (1961); Justice Brennan dissenting.

13. Israel and La Fave, *Criminal Procedure,* p. 15.

14. *Baldwin* v. *New York,* 399 U.S. 66 (1970); Justice Harlan dissenting.

15. 367 U.S. 643 (1961).

16. 378 U.S. 1 (1964).

17. 395 U.S. 784 (1969).

18. 372 U.S. 335 (1963).

19. 407 U.S. 25 (1972).

20. 386 U.S. 213 (1967).

21. 391 U.S. 145 (1968).

22. 380 U.S. 400 (1965).

23. 388 U.S. 14 (1967).

24. 333 U.S. 257 (1948).

25. 333 U.S. 196 (1948).

26. Israel and La Fave, *Criminal Procedure*, p. 24.

27. 110 U.S. 516 (1884).

28. Jonathan D. Casper, *The Politics of Civil Liberties* (New York: Harper & Row, 1972), p. 230.

29. Although, in light of *United States* v. *Robinson*, 94 S. Ct. 467 (1973), and *Gustafson* v. *Florida*, 94 S. Ct. 488 (1973), once a defendant is in custody, he may be subjected to a full search; any evidence obtained thereby can be used to bring new charges against him.

30. 392 U.S. 1 (1968).

31. 395 U.S. 752 (1969).

32. On the basis of *Katz* v. *United States*, 389 U.S. 347 (1967), it appears that for electronic surveillance to be regarded as reasonable, warrants are also required, at least in the absence of considerations of national security.

33. 232 U.S. 383 (1914).

34. 338 U.S. 25 (1949).

35. 367 U.S. 643 (1961).

36. 211 U.S. 78 (1908).

37. 331 U.S. 46 (1947).

38. 378 U.S. 1 (1964).

39. 297 U.S. 278 (1936).

40. 309 U.S. 227 (1940).

41. Casper, *Politics of Civil Liberties*, p. 259.

42. *Spano* v. *New York*, 360 U.S. 315 (1959).

43. *Rogers* v. *Richmond*, 365 U.S. 534 (1961).

44. *Lynumn* v. *Illinois*, 372 U.S. 528 (1963).

45. *Townsend* v. *Sain*, 372 U.S. 293 (1963).

46. 378 U.S. 478 (1964).

47. 378 U.S. 490–491.

48. Casper, *Politics of Civil Liberties*, p. 261.

49. 384 U.S. 436 (1966).

50. C. Herman Pritchett, *The American Constitution*, 2nd ed. (New York: McGraw-Hill, 1968), p. 631.

51. Henry J. Abraham, *Freedom and the Court: Civil Rights and Liberties in the United States*, 2nd ed. (New York: Oxford University Press, 1972), p. 125.

52. Fellman, "Supreme Court's Changing View," p. 111.

53. 401 U.S. 222 (1971).

54. 94 S. Ct. 2357 (1974).

55. M. Glenn Abernathy, *Civil Liberties Under the Constitution*, 2nd ed. (New York: Dodd, Mead, 1972), p. 181.

56. U.S. National Commission on Law Observance and Enforcement, *Report on Prosecution* (Washington, D.C.: U.S. Government Printing Office, 1931), p. 30.

57. 287 U.S. 45 (1932).

58. 304 U.S. 458 (1938).

59. 372 U.S. 335 (1963).

60. 407 U.S. 25 (1972).

61. Since Argersinger had been convicted of carrying a concealed weapon and sentenced to ninety days in jail, the Court left unconsidered the question of whether counsel is also required even in situations where there is no prospect of imprisonment. However, Justice Louis F. Powell in his concurrence did take up this question and concluded that the requirements of the Sixth Amendment apply whether the loss of liberty is involved or not.

62. 388 U.S. 218, 226 (1967).

63. *Escobedo* v. *Illinois*, 378 U.S. 478 (1964); *Miranda* v. *Arizona*, 384 U.S. 436 (1966).

64. *United States* v. *Wade*, 388 U.S. 218 (1967); *Gilbert* v. *California*, 388 U.S. 263 (1967).

65. *Coleman* v. *Alabama*, 399 U.S. 1 (1970).

66. *Hamilton* v. *Alabama*, 368 U.S. 52 (1961).

67. *Douglas* v. *California*, 372 U.S. 353 (1963).

68. *Mempa* v. *Rhay*, 389 U.S. 128 (1967).

69. *Barker* v. *Wingo*, 407 U.S. 514 (1972).

70. This severe remedy was reaffirmed by the Court in *Strunk* v. *United States*, 412 U.S. 434 (1973).

71. 100 U.S. 313 (1880).

72. 356 U.S. 584 (1958).

73. 380 U.S. 202 (1965).

74. *Akins* v. *Texas*, 325 U.S. 398 (1945).

75. 368 U.S. 57 (1961).

76. *Fay* v. *New York*, 332 U.S. 261 (1947).

77. 391 U.S. 510 (1968).

78. 366 U.S. 717 (1961).

79. 373 U.S. 723 (1963).

80. 384 U.S. 333 (1966).

81. 399 U.S. 78 (1970).

82. 406 U.S. 356 (1972).

83. 380 U.S. 400 (1965).

84. 390 U.S. 719 (1968).

85. 391 U.S. 123 (1968).

86. 397 U.S. 337 (1970).

87. 352 U.S. 232 (1957).

88. Israel and La Fave, *Criminal Procedure,* p. 70.

89. 399 U.S. 235 (1970).

90. 401 U.S. 395 (1971).

91. Marvin E. Frankel, *Criminal Sentences: Law Without Order* (New York: Hill & Wang, 1973), p. 5.

92. Ibid., pp. 69–85.

93. 356 U.S. 86 (1958).

94. *Robinson* v. *California,* 370 U.S. 660 (1962).

95. *Powell* v. *Texas,* 392 U.S. 514 (1968).

96. 408 U.S. 232 (1972).

97. 153 U.S. 684 (1894).

98. 351 U.S. 12 (1956).

99. 372 U.S. 352 (1963).

100. 372 U.S. 391 (1963).

101. Israel and La Fave, *Criminal Procedure,* p. 75.

102. *Coppedge* v. *United States,* 369 U.S. 438 (1962).

103. Israel and La Fave, *Criminal Procedure,* p. 80.

104. 387 U.S. 1 (1967).

105. Casper, *Politics of Civil Liberties,* p. 279.

106. Theodore L. Becker and Malcolm M. Feeley, *The Impact of Supreme Court Decisions,* 2nd ed. (New York: Oxford University Press, 1973), p. 3.

107. Dallin H. Oaks, "Studying the Exclusionary Rule in Search and Seizure," *University of Chicago Law Review,* 37 (1970):665–753.

108. Warren Burger, "Who Will Watch the Watchmen?" *American University Law Review,* 14 (1964):11–12.

109. Ibid., p. 22.

110. Jerome Skolnick, *Justice Without Trial: Law Enforcement in a Democratic Society* (New York: Wiley, 1966), p. 224.

111. Ibid., p. 215.

112. U.S. Department of Justice, *Handbook on the Law of Search and Seizure* (Washington, D.C.: U.S. Government Printing Office, 1971), p. 21.

113. Fred E. Inbau, *Evidence Law for the Police* (Philadelphia: Chilton, 1972), pp. 1–5.

114. Comment, "Effect of *Mapp* v. *Ohio* on Police Search-and-Seizure Practices in Narcotics Cases," *Columbia Journal of Law and Social Problems,* 4 (1968):87.

115. Samuel Dash, "Cracks in the Foundation of Criminal Justice," *Illinois Law Review,* 46 (1951):391–392.

116. 403 U.S. 388 (1971).

117. 414 U.S. 218 (1973).

118. 414 U.S. 338 (1974).

119. Richard J. Medalie, Leonard Zeitz, and Paul Alexander, "Custodial Police Interrogation in Our Nation's Capital: The Attempt to Implement *Miranda*," *Michigan Law Review* 66 (May 1968):1347–1422; and Michael Wald et al., "Interrogations in New Haven: The Impact of *Miranda*," *Yale Law Journal*, 76 (July 1967):1519–1648.

120. Neil Milner, "Supreme Court Effectiveness and the Police Organization," *Law and Contemporary Problems*, 36, no. 4 (Autumn 1971):467.

121. Casper, *Politics of Civil Liberties*, pp. 265–266.

122. Herbert L. Packer, *The Limits of the Criminal Sanction* (Stanford: Stanford University Press, 1968), pp. 149–173.

123. Packer, *Limits of the Criminal Sanction*, p. 158.

124. Ibid., p. 159.

125. Ibid.

126. Ibid., p. 160.

127. Ibid.

128. Ibid., p. 163.

129. Ibid., p. 165.

130. Ibid., p. 166.

131. Ibid., p. 161.

132. Ibid., p. 150.

133. National Advisory Commission on Criminal Justice Standards and Goals, *Report on Courts* (Washington, D.C.: U.S. Government Printing Office, 1973), p. 42.

134. Jonathan D. Casper, *American Criminal Justice: The Defendant's Perspective* (Englewood Cliffs, N.J.: Prentice-Hall, 1972), p. 65.

135. James Mills, "I Have Nothing to Do with Justice," *Life Magazine*, March 21, 1971, p. 62.

136. President's Commission on Law Enforcement and Administration of Justice, *Task Force Report: The Courts* (Washington, D.C.: U.S. Government Printing Office, 1967), p. 37.

137. Caleb Foote et al., "Compelling Appearance in Court: Administration of Bail in Philadelphia," 102 *University of Pennsylvania Law Review* 1031 (1954).

138. Caleb Foote et. al., "A Study of the Administration of Bail in New York City," 106 *University of Pennsylvania Law Review* 693 (1958).

139. *New York Times*, April 4, 1963, p. 37, col. 5.

140. Abraham S. Blumberg, *Criminal Justice* (Chicago: Quadrangle, 1970), p. 65.

141. Ibid.

142. Ibid., p. 113.

143. Ibid., p. 31.

144. Jonathan D. Casper, *American Criminal Justice*, p. 81.

145. Herbert Jacob, *Urban Justice: Law and Order in American Cities* (Englewood Cliffs, N.J.: Prentice-Hall, 1973), p. 117.

146. National Advisory Commission on Criminal Justice Standards and Goals, *Report on Courts* (Washington, D.C.: U.S. Government Printing Office, 1973), p. 46.

147. Ibid.

148. Chief Justice Warren Burger, "The State of the Judiciary, 1970," *American Bar Association Journal* 56 (October 1970):931.

149. 395 U.S. 238 (1969).

150. 394 U.S. 459 (1969).

151. 397 U.S. 742 (1970).

152. 404 U.S. 257 (1971).

153. Burger, "State of the Judiciary," p. 929.

154. See Ralph A. Rossum, "Problems of Municipal Court Administration and the Stress of Supreme Court Decisions: A Memphis Case Study," *American Journal of Criminal Law*, 3, no. 1 (Spring 1974).

BIBLIOGRAPHY

ABERNATHY, M. GLENN. *Civil Liberties Under the Constitution*, 2nd ed. New York: Dodd, Mead, 1972.

BECKER, THEODORE L., and FEELEY, MALCOLM M. *The Impact of Supreme Court Decisions*, 2nd ed. New York: Oxford University Press, 1973.

BLUMBERG, ABRAHAM S. *Criminal Justice.* Chicago: Quadrangle, 1970.

CASPER, JONATHAN D. *American Criminal Justice: The Defendant's Perspective.* Englewood Cliffs, N.J.: Prentice-Hall, 1972.

———. *The Politics of Civil Liberties.* New York: Harper & Row, 1972.

Criminal Law Reporter.

DOWNIE, LEONARD. *Justice Denied: The Case for Reform of the Courts.* Baltimore: Penguin, 1971.

FRANKEL, MARVIN E. *Criminal Sentences: Law Without Order.* New York: Hill & Wang, 1973.

ISRAEL, JEROLD H., and LA FAVE, WAYNE R. *Criminal Procedure.* St. Paul, Minn.: West, 1971.

JACOB, HERBERT. *Urban Justice: Law and Order in American Cities.* Englewood Cliffs, N.J.: Prentice-Hall, 1973.

KAPLAN, JOHN. *Criminal Justice: Introductory Cases and Materials.* Mineola, N.Y.: Foundation Press, 1973.

MCLENNAN, BARBARA L., ed. *Crime in Urban Society.* New York: Dunellen, 1970.

NATIONAL ADVISORY COMMISSION OF CRIMINAL JUSTICE STANDARDS AND GOALS. *Report on Courts.* Washington, D.C.: U.S. Government Printing Office, 1973.

PACKER, HERBERT L. *The Limits of the Criminal Sanction.* Stanford: Stanford University Press, 1968.

PRESIDENT'S COMMISSION ON LAW ENFORCEMENT AND ADMINISTRATION OF JUSTICE. *Task Force Report: Courts.* Washington, D.C.: U.S. Government Printing Office, 1967.

PRITCHETT, C. HERMAN. *The American Constitution,* 2nd ed. New York: McGraw-Hill, 1968.

RADZINOWICZ, LEON, and WOLFGANG, MARVIN E., eds. *Criminal and Justice,* vol. 2: *The Criminal in the Arms of the Law.* New York: Basic Books, 1971.

SKOLNICK, JEROME. *Justice Without Trial: Law Enforcement in a Democratic Society.* New York: Wiley, 1966.

United States Reports.

CORRECTIONS: SUCCESS THROUGH FAILURE

David Rothenberg has described prisons as the "only business that can succeed by its own failures. It needs men returning to its fold so it can perpetuate itself."[1] The same can be said of the correctional system generally. The President's Commission on Law Enforcement and Administration of Justice considers that the "ultimate goal of corrections under any theory is to make the community safer by reducing the incidence of crime. Rehabilitation of offenders to prevent their return to crime is in general the most promising way to achieve this end."[2] By this measure, the correctional system is an abysmal failure. According to the most recent statistics of the FBI's Uniform Crime Reports, 65 percent of those arrested from 1970 to 1972 had been arrested before. Of the 228,032 offenders brought to the attention of the computerized criminal history file of the National Crime Information Center,

> 184,809 had been arrested two or more times. These individuals had an average criminal career of four years and 11 months (number of years between first and last arrest) during which time they were arrested an average of four times each. The 228,032 offenders had a total of 867,000 documented charges during their criminal careers, with 244,329 reported convictions and 87,358 imprisonments of six months or more.[3]

Corrections is a failure. This has profound consequences not only for the criminal justice system generally but for police–community relations programs especially. Alexander Hamilton's words bear repeating: "Give all the power to the many they will oppress the few. Give all the power to the few they will oppress the many. Both therefore ought to have power that each may defend itself against the other."[4] Within the criminal justice system, the police have come to represent the many, attempting to provide security and order for the

law-abiding majority. The courts and corrections, on the other hand, have together come to represent the few. The courts, through their emphasis on due
process, seek to protect the accused individual from the caprice, excitement, and
prejudice that occasionally afflict the majority, whose laws he is alleged to have
violated. Correctional agencies, through programs of treatment and custody,
seek to reintegrate the accused individual into society so that he may live a
peaceful life, productive and satisfying to himself and others. (The correctional
system's emphasis on the few and disregard for the many is particularly apparent in its preoccupation with the offender and its general disregard for the
victims of his crimes through programs of compensation or restitution.) With
the failure of the courts (as described in Chapter 4) to provide adequate protection for the individual and minorities, the failure of corrections to reintegrate
the offender into society becomes all the more serious. Courts and corrections
have been unable to insure a proper balancing of the tension between the many
and the few, between majority rule and minority rights. The need for police–
community relations programs that can infuse this tension within the police
themselves becomes, as a result, all the more imperative. The factors that account for the failures of the correctional system and that add to the responsibility of the police will be explored at some length in this chapter.

The Purpose of Criminal Sanctions

One of the major problems faced by the correctional system arises from the fact
that there is no agreement in answer to the question "Why punish crimes?"
Three very different justifications for criminal punishment are possible: retribution, deterrence, and rehabilitation. Each of these justifications is in conflict with
the others; yet the correctional system in the United States has attempted to
promote all of them, and, as a result, has failed to achieve any of them.

Retribution rests fundamentally on the idea that it is right for a wicked
man to be punished. It contends that a man should be responsible for his actions
and ought to receive his just deserts.[5] Deterrence, in contrast, is based on the
view that punishment, either actual or threatened, will inhibit those who are
otherwise disposed to commit crimes. It operates on a utilitarian premise: punishment is justified insofar as it can be shown that more good is likely to result
from inflicting than from withholding it. The good that is sought from such
punishment is the prevention or the reduction of a greater evil, crime. An important distinction must be drawn between special deterrence—after-the-fact
inhibition of the person being punished—and general deterrence—inhibition in
advance through threat and example.[6] Finally, rehabilitation justifies punishment as necessary for the reformation of the offender, that is, as necessary to
change his personality so that he will conform to the dictates of the law. As such
it is offender-oriented rather than offense-oriented. It denies that there is a

generally postulated equivalent between the offense and the punishment, as is the case in either the retributive or deterrent thories of punishment. Rather, it seeks to punish—perhaps a better word would be treat—each offender as an individual whose special needs and problems must be fully known and attended to if he is to be dealt with effectively.

All three of these justifications for criminal punishment are in conflict with each other. Thus, too much emphasis on rehabilitation undercuts deterrence; too much concern for retribution interferes with rehabilitation; and too much stress upon deterrence, especially general deterrence and its inhibition in advance by example, obscures retribution's concept of desert. Each justification tends to neutralize the effect of the others. The presence of each of these contradictory justifications deprives correctional personnel of any standard or goal against which they can measure the success of their correctional endeavors. These problems, summed up in the question "Why punish?" confront every aspect of the correctional system, but perhaps nowhere are they felt more acutely than in the prisons.

Prisons

Perhaps the most immediately obvious method of punishment today is institutionalization. However, institutionalization is a relatively modern practice. "Before the 18th century, prisons were not used to punish but detain the accused until the debtor paid his debt, the rapist was castrated, the thieves' hands were cut off, or the perjuror's tongue was torn out."[7] It was in Pennsylvania, founded by the Quaker William Penn, that initial attempts to substitute institutionalization for such mutilations and barbarism were begun. Institutionalization, however, has never really succeeded. As high recidivism rates make abundantly clear, prisons have for the most part atrophied the offenders' capacity to live successfully in the free world. Nonetheless, prisons have persisted to the present and have in fact increased tremendously in number. The reasons for this are all too obvious: despite their many dreadful shortcomings, a civilized country like the United States can neither turn back to the barbarism of an earlier time nor find a satisfactory alternative. As the National Advisory Commission on Criminal Justice Standards and Goals points out, "For nearly two centuries, American penologists have been seeking a way out of this dilemma."[8] While penologists have sought a way out of the dilemma posed by the failure of prisons on the one hand and the want of a satisfactory alternative on the other, prisons in the United States have increased in size and number. There are presently in the United States some 196,000 prisoners in 358 major state adult correctional institutions or prisons. Both the characteristics of these inmates and the types and practices of these correctional institutions in which they are imprisoned must be explored more fully in order to appreciate the magnitude of the failure of prisons.

GENERAL CHARACTERISTICS OF INMATES

It is difficult to present a profile of the typical offender, as individual offenders differ strikingly. Some seem irrevocably committed to careers of crime; others hold quite conventional values or are aimless or uncommitted to any goals. Many are disturbed or frustrated; others are alcoholics, addicts, sex deviants, or senile. Despite this diversity, however, several broad characterizations are possible. To begin with, most offenders are male. In 1972, 5,955,783 males were arrested as compared with 1,057,411 females, a ratio of approximately 6 to 1.[9] Men are not only arrested far more often, but they are sentenced to prison in far greater numbers. On December 31, 1970, there were 190,794 males in state and federal prisons and correctional institutions as compared with 5,635 females, a ratio of approximately 34 to 1.[10] This fact is explained in part by the different kinds of crimes females are more likely to commit. Table 5.1 records the distribution of total arrests by sex in 1972. However, the amount of female crime is increasing more rapidly than male crime; it increased by 1.9 percent from 1971 to 1972, a time during which male crime rose only 0.5 percent. This increase is even more dramatic among those under eighteen years of age. There, female crime increased by 2.3 percent and male crime by only 0.4 percent.[11] This may be due in large part to the fact that feminists are assuming in increasing numbers traditional male roles and behavior patterns, including the life of crime. Yet, despite this increase, it is likely that most crime will continue to be committed by and most prisons will remain filled with males.

Most offenders are also young, between the ages of fifteen and thirty. Juveniles alone comprise nearly one-third of all offenders under correctional treatment, with approximately 63,000 in institutions and 285,000 in community-based correctional schemes on an average day. Table 5.2 presents the total arrests by age group in 1972. Although more sixteen-year-olds were arrested in 1972 than any other age group, the average offender sentenced to prison for one year or more is 26.1 years of age.[12]

Many come from urban slums. Members of racial and other minority groups that have suffered economic and social discrimination are likely to end in prison in disproportionate numbers. In 1972 blacks were arrested for 53.7 percent of all serious crime so categorized by the FBI's Uniform Crime Reports and 31.5 percent of all property crimes.[13] Perhaps because of this economic and social discrimination, most offenders are also educationally deprived. Although recent studies indicate that intelligence does not differ significantly between offenders and the general population from which they are drawn, the average institutionalized offender is estimated to be about three grades retarded in school.[14] Table 5.3 shows that over 80 percent of adult felony inmates have less than a high school education. Along with the educational deficiencies, offenders also

TABLE 5.1 Total arrests, distribution by sex, 1972

Offense charged	Number of persons arrested			Percent male	Percent female
	Total	Male	Female		
TOTAL	7,013,194	5,955,783	1,057,411	84.9	15.9
Criminal homicide:					
(a) Murder and nonnegligent manslaughter	15,049	12,727	2,322	84.6	15.4
(b) Manslaughter by negligence	2,986	2,635	351	88.2	11.8
Forcible rape	19,374	19,374	—	100.0	—
Robbery	109,217	102,117	7,100	93.5	6.5
Aggravated assault	155,581	135,050	20,531	86.8	13.2
Burglary—breaking or entering	314,393	298,156	16,237	94.8	5.2
Larceny—theft	678,673	476,974	201,699	70.3	29.7
Auto theft	121,842	114,974	6,965	94.3	5.7
Violent crime[a]	299,221	269,268	29,953	90.0	10.0
Property crime[b]	1,114,908	890,007	224,901	79.8	20.2
Subtotal for above offenses	1,417,115	1,161,910	225,205	82.0	18.0
Other assaults	307,638	265,588	42,050	86.3	13.7
Arson	10,645	9,635	1,010	90.5	9.5
Forgery and counterfeiting	44,313	33,322	10,991	75.2	24.8
Fraud	96,713	68,100	28,613	70.4	29.6
Embezzlement	6,744	4,972	1,772	73.7	26.3
Stolen property; buying, receiving, possessing	71,754	64,807	6,947	90.3	9.7
Vandalism	129,724	119,353	10,371	92.0	8.0
Weapons; carrying, possessing, etc.	119,671	110,910	8,761	92.7	7.3
Prostitution and commercialized vice	44,744	11,591	33,153	25.9	74.1
Sex offenses (except forcible rape and prostitution)	51,124	46,536	4,588	91.0	9.0
Narcotic drug laws	431,608	364,938	66,670	84.6	15.4
Gambling	70,064	63,937	6,127	91.3	8.7
Offenses against family and children	52,935	48,006	4,929	90.7	9.3
Driving under the influence	604,291	562,859	41,432	93.1	6.9
Liquor laws	207,675	178,169	29,515	85.8	14.2
Drunkenness	1,384,735	1,284,677	100,058	92.8	7.2
Disorderly conduct	582,513	498,110	84,403	85.5	14.5
Vagrancy	55,680	36,384	19,296	65.3	34.7
All other offenses (except traffic)	966,722	811,177	155,545	83.9	16.1
Suspicion	41,475	31,566	9,909	76.1	23.9
Curfew and loitering law violations	116,126	92,389	23,737	79.6	20.4
Runaways	199,185	86,856	112,329	43.6	56.4

Source: *Crime in the United States: Uniform Crime Reports, 1972,* p. 129.

[a] Violent crime is offenses of murder, forcible rape, robbery, and aggravated assault.
[b] Property crime is offenses of burglary, larceny, and auto theft.

TABLE 5.2   Total arrests by age, 1972

Age group	Number	Percent	Age group	Number	Percent
All ages	7,013,194	100.0	22	262,982	3.7
Under 15	665,887	9.5	23	232,559	3.3
Under 18	1,793,984	25.6	24	216,690	3.1
Ages 18 and over	5,219,210	74.4	25–29	736,398	10.5
10 and under	80,551	1.1	30–34	583,558	7.6
11–12	149,785	2.1	35–39	450,929	6.4
13–14	435,551	6.2	40–44	433,116	6.2
15	359,504	5.1	45–49	381,191	5.4
16	403,311	5.8	50–54	299,747	4.3
17	365,282	5.2	55–59	192,199	2.7
18	352,707	5.0	60–64	119,412	1.7
19	318,227	4.5	65 and over	101,775	1.5
20	288,896	4.1	Not known	12,991	.02
21	285,833	4.1			

Source: *Crime in the United States: Uniform Crime Reports, 1972*, p. 126–127.

TABLE 5.3   Comparison of educational levels, general population, and institutionalized inmates

Years of school completed[a]	Percent of general population	Percent of inmate population
Completed college	8.4	1.1
Some college	9.4	4.2
Completed high school	27.5	12.4
Some high school	20.7	27.6
5–8 years of elementary school	28.0	40.3
0–4 years of elementary school	6.0	14.4

Source: President's Commission on Law Enforcement and Administration of Justice, *Task Force Report: Corrections*, p. 2.

[a] By persons aged 25–64.

tend to lack vocational skills. Table 5.4 indicates a higher proportion of unskilled laborers among prisoners than in the labor force as a whole.

Although offenders may be identified by these characterizations, they tend to be institutionalized for a variety of offenses. Table 5.5 presents a percentage breakdown of a typical prison population on the basis of the crimes for which each offender has been sentenced.

CLASSIFICATION OF PRISONS

Prisons vary as much as prisoners. Basically, there are three types of prisons: maximum security, medium security, and minimum security. Each will be briefly assessed. Throughout the nineteenth century, most prisons built in the United States were maximum security prisons. Their aim was simple: to keep the prisoners in and the public out. They featured high walls, cagelike cells,

TABLE 5.4 Comparison of occupational experience, general labor force and institutionalized inmates

Occupation	Percent of general labor force	Percent of institution-alized inmates[a]
Professional and technical workers	10.4	2.2
Managers and owners, including farmers	16.3	4.3
Clerical and sales	14.2	7.1
Craftsmen, foremen	20.6	17.6
Operatives	21.2	25.2
Service workers, including household	6.4	11.5
Laborers (except miners)	10.8	31.9

Source: President's Commission on Law Enforcement and Administration of Justice, *Task Force Report: Corrections,* p. 3.

[a] All data are for males only.

TABLE 5.5 Crimes for which the typical prison population is sentenced

Crimes	Percent of total prison population
Burglary	24.1
Larceny	16.1
Robbery	9.9
Auto theft	9.8
Rape	7.1
Other sex offenses	6.2
Forgery	4.6
Weapons offenses	4.2
Offenses against family	2.9
Homicides	2.6
Embezzlement	2.3
Escape from prison	2.2
Aggravated assault	2.1
Other	5.9

Source: Vernon Fox, *Introduction to Corrections* (Englewood Cliffs, N.J.: Prentice-Hall, 1972), p. 130.

factory-like shops, a minimum of recreational opportunity, and practically nothing else.

Many of these fortresses were constructed well, have lasted long, and today comprise the backbone of America's correctional system. Although remodeled and expanded, fifty-six of these nineteenth-century institutions are still in use. They constitute virtually half of the maximum security prisons existing in the United States and house approximately 75,000 of the 110,000 felons in maximum security institutions.[15] The significance of these institutions is underscored by the fact that 56 percent of all state prisoners in America today are in structures built to serve maximum security functions. (See Table 5.6.)

TABLE 5.6 Prison population by security classification

Classification	Number of inmates	Percent of total prison population
Maximum	109,920	56
Medium	57,505	30
Minimum	28,484	15
TOTAL	195,910	100

Source: National Advisory Commission on Criminal Justice Standards and Goals, *Report on Corrections* (Washington, D.C.: U.S. Government Printing Office, 1973), p. 344.

Maximum security prisons are geared to the fullest possible supervision, control, and surveillance of inmates. Prisoners in such institutions are invariably surrounded by a masonry wall or double cyclone fence with armed guard towers. This concern with security and control exists within the walls as well, where doors, which afford privacy, are replaced by steel grilles, where toilet stalls are unscreened, and where showers are taken under supervision.

A maximum security prison consists of more than mere structural considerations, however. It is also characterized by a preoccupation with custody. This even extends to dining, where prisoners often must sit on fixed backless stools and eat without knives or forks at tables lacking in condiments. Since custody and control may be jeopardized by contact with the outside world, precautions are taken to prevent actual physical contact with visitors. Relatives must communicate with inmates by telephone and see them through double layers of glass. When actual physical contact is allowed, it is under the watchful eyes of guards, and body searches precede and follow such visits. The National Advisory Commission on Criminal Justice Standards and Goals has captured perfectly the dominant philosophy underlying maximum security prisons: "Trustworthiness on the inmate's part is not anticipated; the opposite is assumed."[16]

Since the early twentieth century, the thought has gained currency that perhaps not every prisoner constitutes the same risk to society or needs to be subjected to the supervision, control, and surveillance of a maximum security prison. This thought, together with the emergence of the rehabilitative justification for criminal punishment and the increased use of probation and parole, has stimulated a general commitment to and widespread construction of medium security prisons, especially in the past quarter century. Thus, 51 of the existing 110 medium security correctional institutions in the United States have been built since 1950. Today more than 57,500 offenders, or 30 percent of the entire American prison population, are housed in such facilities. (See Table 5.6.)

It is in these medium security prisons that most rehabilitative efforts are conducted. To a greater extent than either maximum security or minimum security institutions, they expose inmates to a variety of programs designed to help them become useful members of society. Yet security is not overlooked. All have strong parameters, either in the form of masonry walls or double cyclone fences, and guard towers. All feature locks, bars, concrete, schedules, head counts, and electronic devices to maintain internal security.

Recently, campus-type plants have been designed in an attempt to eliminate much of the cramped oppressiveness of most security-conscious confinement. These new medium security institutions are typically marked by widely separated buildings connected by meandering pathways, terraced landscapes, and small attractive residences that house inmates in single rooms. They are likely to have schools, vocational educational buildings, gymnasiums, and athletic fields that compare favorably with those of the best community colleges.[17] However, these new institutions have generated considerable controversy. No one seriously argues that prisons should be degrading; that would be counterproductive. Yet no one seriously wants them to be resorts, either. For good political as well as moral and criminological reasons, prisons cannot be permitted to become so attractive that they act as inverse deterrents, encouraging people to engage in criminal conduct in order to be confined in them. At what point prisons become that attractive is difficult to determine, and the controversy that swirls around these new medium security prisons is centered precisely on this difficulty.

Minimum security institutions are generally identified by one common feature: they are relatively open, with custody ensured more by classification than prison hardware. There are 103 such institutions in the United States which range from large drug rehabilitation centers to small farm, conservation, and forestry camps located throughout rural America. Altogether, they house approximately 28,500 offenders, or 15 percent of all prison inmates (see Table 5.6). It was to prisons such as these that the former members of President Nixon's White House staff, convicted for their involvement in the Watergate affair and related crimes, were sent.

While concern with security is often all but lacking at minimum security prisons, so is most attention to the correctional needs of the offenders. A number of these institutions have been established to serve the economic needs of society. There prisoners are kept busy picking cotton, cutting lumber, raising livestock, building roads, and maintaining parks and state buildings. They seldom provide educational or service opportunities other than work—and even the work, predominantly rural in character, bears no relationship to the work skills required for urban life. Whatever therapy they do provide primarily results from the fact that they are open facilities that spare men the corrosive experiences of a stifling prison environment, separate the young and unsophisticated from the predators, and substitute control based on trust for control based on steel and concrete.

Characteristics of Prison Life

Although prisons vary widely in security, facilities, and correctional philosophy, life within them for the typical inmate is often much the same. To begin with, it is marked by a complete lack of privacy. Typically a prisoner spends his entire day with other prisoners, with no opportunity to get away from them or the guards. Second, life in prison tends to be very boring. Many prisoners spend sixteen hours a day or more in their cells. For those who enjoy reading, this does not constitute the problem it does for others. But many prisoners lack the educational background and perhaps even the native resources that are required to enjoy a great deal of reading. (See Table 5.3.) Third, life also tends to be extremely regimented. Prisoners march from place to place; they eat when they are told, whether they are hungry or not; they are provided periods of recreation whether they want them then or not. Regimentation serves an important custodial function, but it also discourages thinking and thereby inhibits that adaptability and independence so essential for a successful return to society. Fourth, and more disturbing than these other aspects, life in prison is very dangerous. Many inmates' predatory instincts are not neutralized merely by incarceration. Their aggression is simply transferred from civil society to prison society. Although prisons have always been dangerous, they are becoming increasingly so, as judges continue to send to prison a lower and lower percentage of first offenders and nonviolent criminals.

Prisons are becoming burdened with the least stable elements of the criminal population. This concentration of unstable and violent prisoners, combined with the unavailability in prison of sexual outlets (at least heterosexual outlets), has led to a fifth and perhaps the most disturbing characteristic of prison life: it is marked by a very high rate not only of homosexuality but also of homosexual rape and assault. As Allen J. Davis notes:

> Sexual assaults are epidemic in some prison systems.
> Virtually every slightly built young man committed by the court is sexually approached within a day or two after his admission to prison. Many of these young men are overwhelmed and repeatedly "raped" by gangs of inmate aggressors. Others are compelled by the terrible threat of gang rape to seek protection by entering into a "housekeeping" relationship with an individual tormenter. Only the toughest and more hardened young men —and those few so obviously frail that they are immediately locked up for their own protection—escape penetration of their bodies.[18]

A few typical examples of these sexual assaults in the raw, ugly, and chilling language of witnesses and victims themselves may help to convey the seriousness of this problem. One victim described his attack as follows:

> I was lying in my bed when seven or eight inmates came to my bed, pulled the blanket off me, put it on the floor and told me to pull my pants down and lay face down on the blanket. I said, "No" and was punched in the face by one of the inmates. The inmate that punched me stated if I did not get on the floor the other inmates would gang up on me.
> I got on the floor and my pants and shorts were pulled off. Two inmates spread and held my legs apart while two more inmates held my hands in front of me. While I was being buggered from behind another inmate would make me suck his penis. This continued until all the inmates had attacked me and I heard one of them say it was 1:30 A.M. so let's go to bed. They put

me on the bed, covered me with the blanket, and one of them patted me on the behind saying, "Good boy. We will see you again tomorrow night." ·

While I was being molested I was held by the neck and head and threatened with bodily harm if I yelled or screamed. They stated that they would beat my head on the floor if I made any outcry.[19]

Allen Davis estimated that during the twenty-six-month period under investigation, there were approximately 2,000 sexual assaults, involving some 1,500 individual victims and 3,500 individual aggressors in Philadelphia's prisons.[20] These assaults are, of course, not unique to Philadelphia. Interviews with thirty-six former inmates of Chicago's Cook County Jail reveal the following vicious and brutal degradation:

Eight of the thirty-six ex-inmates had been victims of beatings, some so serious they caused concussions and fractures.

They witnessed about seventy-five beatings.

They said there was about one beating each day.

Four of the thirty-six ex-inmates admitted that they had been victims of sexual attacks.

They had witnessed about seventy-five sexual attacks.

They said it was reported that about a dozen guards were involved in trafficking in drugs.

They generally reported that "you can get all the marijuana you want if you have the money."

Eight of them had witnessed or were involved in incidents of burning, during which four inmates were set on fire.[21]

Such barbarity is not confined simply to state and local facilities. *The National Catholic Reporter,* in an article entitled "Discipline by 'Rape' at U.S. Prisons," charged that authorities at Lewisburg Federal Penitentiary used the threat of homosexual rape to intimidate young Selective Service violators who were protesting prison regulations and conditions. The draft resisters were threatened with assignment to "the jungle," prison dormitories where known homosexual attackers were quartered.[22]

Guards, for the most part, are unable and unwilling to stop these assaults. The reason is quite clear: guards have much more to fear from prisoners than prisoners do from guards. This requires some explanation. Contrary to popular belief, prison guards are not armed, at least not those who walk among the prisoners. The reason is obvious: they are so close to the prisoners that they can be jumped at any time and have their weapons used against them. Thus the only armed guards in prisons tend to be those in the guard towers or at other crucial places away from the prisoners.

Unarmed and among unstable and violent prisoners, every guard is fully aware that his life can be snuffed out at any moment. After all, an inmate does not have a great deal to fear from killing a guard. Since *Furman* v. *Georgia,* capital punishment cannot be used as a threat. Moreover, even if capital punishment is restored, convicting a prisoner for killing or assaulting a guard is extremely difficult. After all, the only witnesses are likely to be other prisoners.

Although a very few would be willing to testify for the prosecution, they are subject to impeachment on the grounds that they are convicted felons. Most, however, can be expected to testify for the defense, often with perjured testimony. A prisoner has very little to fear from a perjury prosecution if he is already doing time for a major crime like armed robbery. Moreover, perjury prosecutions of prisoners are extremely rare. Prosecutors regard it as a waste of taxpayers' money to go through the process of convicting one who is already in prison and can be kept there for a good long time by the parole authorities. This reluctance is reinforced by the knowledge that juries typically take the view that no harm will really be done by an acquittal, since the man is going to stay in prison anyway.

For all these reasons, it is hard to convict a prisoner for assaulting a guard. Every guard knows this, and so does every prisoner. This knowledge is sufficient to discourage most guards from engaging in acts of brutality. Every guard who circulates among the prisoners knows that if too many prisoners come to dislike him, and if any one of them has both a short fuse and access to knives (and virtually all prisoners do), his life is in constant jeopardy. This knowledge is also sufficient to dissuade guards from exercising real control over homosexual aggressors and other perpetrators of violence behind bars. As a consequence the horrors and degradation go on, with the most unfortunate of consequences: "[T]he degradation of prisoners prevents the possibility of their rehabilitation, even in the rare situations where the necessary rehabilitative resources are available . . . [I]n situations where rehabilitative resources are unavailable, degradation tends only to further dehabilitate."[23] All of these characteristics of prison life—its boredom, its dangers, its regimentation, and its brutality—make corrective efforts very difficult. But so do a number of other factors as well, including problems of classification, allocation of manpower, the plight of prison industries, shortcomings in vocational training, the size and location of prisons, and their isolation from the community.

OTHER OBSTACLES TO SUCCESSFUL CORRECTIONS

For as long as prisoners have been separated on the basis of sex, age, and type of offense, classification may be said to have existed. "Classification, in the prison world, is an organized and coordinated way of continuously evaluating the inmate and assigning him to appropriate placement and activity within the institutional system."[24] A properly operating classification procedure can provide the inmate with more significant safeguards than those offered by concrete, steel, and raw custodial power. Thus, for example, through work options and diversification in housing, classification can keep neophytes from hardened criminals. It can surround the aggressive homosexual and the predatory mugger with extensive security features while at the same time allowing cooperative and stable offenders the opportunity to engage in productive labor and to live in secure low-cost barracks. Classification realizes that not every prisoner needs to be confined in a prison secure enough to hold the most violent and antisocial offender. Thus it provides for a system that has as much or as little control as is required. It "substitutes intelligent discrimination for unmodulated regimentation."[25] In so doing, it serves the interests of both the inmate and the correctional system.

Much of the good that classification can accomplish is left undone, however, in large part because of the way manpower is allocated in American prisons. Classification is an effort to subject inmates to as little custody as necessary, so that the rest of their prison experience may be directed to treatment designed to restore them to civilian life. However, only 20 percent of correctional personnel are engaged in treatment or rehabilitative activities; the remaining 80 percent are preoccupied with custody.[26] Table 5.7 presents the ratio of the 20 percent charged with treatment and rehabilitation to the number of offenders they are supposed to be treating. It highlights more dramatically than words this particular correctional problem. The overwhelming case loads this 20 percent is required to bear are more than enough to render any serious treatment efforts impossible and to defeat the best of classification schemes.

The rehabilitative problems of prisons go beyond classification and manpower and extend to prison industries and vocational training programs as well. Prison industries have as their goals the development in each inmate employed in these industries of (1) a set of attitudes favorable toward work and the work situation; (2) minimal qualifications necessary to hold a job (i.e., general job skills, the ability to follow instructions and safety rules); and (3) attitudes favorable to living a law-abiding life.[27] Yet despite these laudable goals, prison industries have, for the most part, been failures.

Part of the reason for the failure of prison industries has been political. They have been consistently fought by organized labor, out of an undisguised fear that prison-made goods will compete with union-made products on the free market. With the assistance of the Depression of the 1930s, the unions scored a number of decisive victories. Pointing to high rates of unemployment and the instability of the market, they were able to mount considerable political pressure

TABLE 5.7 Ratio of rehabilitative personnel to inmates

Position	Number of inmates per staff member
Classification worker	365
Counselor	758
Psychiatrist	1,140
Psychologist	803
Physician, surgeon	986
Social worker	295
Teacher: academic	104
Teacher: vocational	181
Vocational rehabilitation counselor	2,172

Source: Joseph S. Campbell et al., *Law and Order Reconsidered* (Washington, D.C.: U.S. Government Printing Office, 1973), p. 573.

on both the Congress and state legislatures to pass legislation designed to restrict prison labor. Most of these laws remain in effect today.

As a result of these laws, prison industries are restricted to the maintenance of the facilities of the prisons themselves; the manufacture of goods for use by the institution or by other governmental agencies within the state, as for example the making of license plates; the production of farm equipment or agricultural commodities for sale where state law permits; and the care of state public works. However, even these markets have been for the most part untapped. For example, few public school systems or state colleges and universities make an appreciable proportion of their purchases from state prisons. Again there are reasons for this. As the President's Commission on Law Enforcement and the Administration of Justice observes:

> Political pressure brought to bear by private industry and by labor
> organizations still remains one of the basic impediments to the development
> of prison industries. These pressures are effective despite a model law
> enacted in many states which makes it an offense punishable by fine or
> incarceration for a state purchasing official to procure goods from the
> private market without first assuring that it cannot be provided by prison
> industries.[28]

But political pressure has not been the only reason for the failure of prison industries in this or other respects. In many cases, prison industries have failed because their goods are inferior in design and workmanship to those available on the open market. This is not particularly surprising. When labor is forced and unrewarded either in terms of money or pride of accomplishment, there is little reason to strive for diligence or skill. On top of this, prison industries are often unreliable in delivery and, despite access to cheap labor, they are often required to charge more than the price of products from private industry. This is the consequence of a limited market, which is insufficient to support the size of a plant needed to achieve quality control and economy of scale, and an unskilled labor force. (See Table 5.4.) In brief, they are for the most part small, inefficient industrial operations.

Vocational training programs have much the same goals as prison industries: to repair the inmate's educational and vocational deficiencies so that he may be successfully reintegrated into the community after his release. Like prison industries, however, vocational training programs have also met with considerable failure. Although many in fact learn marketable skills while in prison, they find they must face a sizable number of legal discriminations against them when they get out. Many prisons train men to be barbers; yet, in most jurisdictions, a man cannot be a barber if he is a felon. Likewise, a number of prisons train men for jobs for which bonding by an insurance company is required, despite the fact that insurance companies typically will not bond someone who has a felony conviction on his record. When an ex-inmate finds that his training and diligence have not provided him with more promising occupational opportunities, the result of such well-intentioned but unsuccessful vocational rehabilitation programs is likely to be frustration and contempt for society.

The size and location of prisons also contribute to their inability to correct or rehabilitate offenders. Traditionally, prisons have been very large, often accommodating 2000 to 4000 inmates. This is in keeping with America's belief that bigness somehow means quality. The inevitable consequence of this bigness, however, has been regimentation, uniformity, and depersonalization. Such practices are clearly counterproductive to any successful reintegration of the offender into society.

Prison location as well as size is also a factor affecting rehabilitative success. Most prisons are located in sparsely populated areas. This is a throwback to the nineteenth century, when rural settings were usually chosen for correctional institutions. At that time, there were good reasons for this remoteness. America, after all, was predominantly a farm country, and there was little contrast between urban and rural life styles. Moreover, since prisons were viewed as places of quarantine, the farther from population centers they were, the better. However, what was once thought to be an advantage is now clearly a liability. America has become increasingly urban, so that today over 139 million people or 68 percent of its total population live in its 243 standard metropolitan statistical areas (SMSAS).[29] Accompanying this urbanization has been the emergence of unique life styles and values, the products of ethnic and cultural diversity, which interfere with understanding and communication between urban and rural dwellers.

Furthermore, the justification for criminal punishment has fundamentally changed. The concern is no longer with quarantining the offender, but with rehabilitating and reintegrating him into society. This urbanization and this new correctional philosophy have exposed prisons located in sparsely populated areas to a number of rather severe criticisms. First, they are unable to take advantage of urban academic and social services or medical and psychiatric resources. Second, they have difficulty in recruiting professional staff members—teachers, psychologists, sociologists, social workers, researchers, nurses, dentists, and physicians—to work in rural areas. Third, they interrupt the offenders' contacts with friends and relatives, which are important to the reintegration process. Fourth, they are unable to provide meaningful work-release and study-release programs. Fifth and most importantly, they are likely to be dominated by rural white guards and administrators unable to understand or communicate with black, Chicano, Puerto Rican, and other urban minority inmates.[30]

What is needed if correctional institutions are to become more effective is the development of regional prisons. These small-unit community-oriented institutions would be located in the cities from which the bulk of their inmates would come and would be able to employ available subprofessionals and volunteers to help overcome the isolation of correctional staff. Their small size and relative informality would facilitate the use of work- and study-release programs, furloughs, and field trips. But the likelihood that these institutions will be established on a large scale is slim indeed. As the National Advisory Commission on Criminal Justice Standards and Goals has noted: "Urbanites resist the location of prisons in the cities. They may agree on the need for 'reintegration' of the ex-offender, but this objective is forgotten when city dwellers see a prison in their midst as increasing street crime and diminishing property values."[31]

In short, regional or community prisons are a fine idea as long as they are found in someone else's community. This raises one of the most difficult problems that confront corrections today: community ambivalence toward the entire correctional enterprise. The community, or at least the responsible portion of it, is acutely aware that if offenders are to be successfully reintegrated into the community, they must be exposed to what is good, decent, and just in the community, so that they may become animated by these same values. But at the same time the community is reluctant to open itself too much to these offenders, who, after all, are convicted felons. Correctional officers must deal with this community ambivalence, much as police must deal with considerable community ambivalence, as well. The task is not easy, however, and successes have been few.

With most prisons still located in rural settings and with community ambivalence toward corrections generally unabated, prisons continue to be isolated from the community, and rehabilitation remains problematic. But, although less can be done in this context than in one in which the concept of regional prisons is both widely accepted and practiced, a number of programs designed to break down this isolation from the community is available and, where instituted, has met with some success.

Most of these programs involve some method or measure of temporary release. Furloughs from the institution for a few days are one example. Although they have been used most extensively in juvenile institutions in order to permit the young to attend such family occasions as Christmas, Thanksgiving, weddings, and funerals, their use among adults is increasing, if for a different reason. They can facilitate release arrangements, allowing the inmate to contact potential employers. Mississippi and Michigan have both made extensive and successful use of furloughs; they report that less than 1 percent fail to return.

Other programs involving temporary release include work-release and study-release. Work-release programs allow inmates to go from the institution into the community and work at civilian jobs, returning to the institution at night. Work-release has a number of advantages. It permits the inmate to work for pay in the free community but spend his nonworking hours in the correctional institution. It is an alternative to total confinement and reshapes the conceptions of the prisoner while reducing the financial burden on the taxpayer and maintaining the labor force in the free community. It helps to maintain family ties and generates constructive attitudes and behavior on the part of inmates. The program is popular and successful; cancellation of work-release for serious misbehavior —which generally involves absconding—occurs in only 15 percent of the cases. Perhaps the major limitation to current work-release programs is that since so few prisons are located near the home communities of most inmates, most work-release jobs are temporary, and inmates must leave them when they are paroled or discharged.[32]

Study-release programs operate in a manner similar to that of work-release programs. The only difference is that inmates attend high schools, vocational and technical schools, junior colleges, or universities. They, too, have proven to be popular and successful. Their reception at the federal prison at Danbury, Connecticut, is a good example; approximately 10 percent of its entire population is attending school at night to complete high school or take vocational courses.

The relative success of furloughs and work- and study-release programs, however, should not be allowed to obscure the colossal failure of America's prisons. The magnitude of this failure is told in the statistics of repeat offenders in the FBI's Uniform Crime Reports. During the period 1970–1972, 228,032 offenders were arrested in the United States. Of that number, 148,809 or 65 percent had been arrested before. Table 5.8 presents the number of persons arrested for each type of crime and the percentage of that number who were repeat offenders. It should be kept in mind that these figures are conservative and underestimate the amount of crime committed by these offenders. They are based on arrest figures, and during 1972 only 20 percent of serious crimes committed that year were cleared by arrest. Nevertheless, certain generalizations concerning recidivism or criminal repeating are possible. Repeaters range from 77 percent for the robber to 34 percent for the embezzler. The predatory criminal offenders have the highest recidivism rates, with 77 percent of the robbers, 73 percent of the murderers and auto thieves, 71 percent of the burglars, and 68 percent of those charged with assault being repeat offenders. On the basis of sex and race, males and blacks have the highest incidence of criminal repeating,

TABLE 5.8 Percent repeaters by type of crime, persons arrested, 1970–1972

Crime	Number arrested	Percent arrested before
Robbery	12,892	77
Forgery	7,568	74
Murder	2,994	73
Auto theft	10,378	73
Burglary	12,619	71
Fraud	9,348	69
Assault	12,936	68
Stolen property	9,111	65
Gambling	5,688	65
Rape	1,888	63
Weapons	12,403	62
Larceny	23,250	61
Narcotics	44,833	60
Embezzlement	3,330	34
All other offenses	58,844	66
TOTAL	228,032	65

Source: U.S. Department of Justice, *Crime in the United States: Uniform Crime Reports, 1972* (Washington, D.C.: U.S. Government Printing Office, 1973), p. 38.

TABLE 5.9 Percent repeaters by sex and race, persons arrested, 1970–1972

Sex	Total	Race White	Race Black	Race Other
Total:				
Number of persons arrested	228,032	137,554	86,837	3,641
Percent repeaters	65	62	70	58
Male				
Number of persons arrested	197,990	121,592	73,210	3,188
Percent repeaters	68	65	73	60
Female				
Number of persons arrested	30,042	15,962	13,627	453
Percent repeaters	50	46	54	44

Source: U.S. Department of Justice, *Crime in the United States: Uniform Crime Reports, 1972* (Washington, D.C.: U.S. Government Printing Office, 1973), p. 39.

with 68 percent of those males arrested and 70 percent of those blacks arrested being recidivists. (See Table 5.9.)

ALTERNATIVE TO INCARCERATION

If prisons were successfully fulfilling the purpose of corrections—that is, if they were making the community safer by reducing the incidence of crime—perhaps the degradation and horror they spawn could be tolerated. But as these high rates of recidivism make abundantly manifest, prisons have not been successful; quite to the contrary, they have failed miserably. Through their failure, they have forfeited their claim to centrality in the correctional system. Alternatives to incarceration are now vying for prominence. These alternatives will be examined with care, for they hold in store the future prospects and problems of corrections.

Shorter Sentences

No one seriously argues that prisons should be abolished altogether. Their ability simply to confine especially violent and antisocial offenders and their deterrent effect make it imperative that they be preserved. However, for all the reasons explored above, the following principle has evolved: "Incarcerate only when nothing less will do, and then incarcerate as briefly as possible."[33] This principle does not represent a radical departure from current correctional practices. It fully accepts the propriety and necessity of prisons and makes full use of existing facilities and personnel. Nevertheless, imposition of shorter sentences does constitute an alternative to the present degradation and alienation caused by long-term imprisonment.

Incremental though this alternative is, the experiences of a number of states suggest that shorter sentences in fact allow for the more successful reintegration of offenders into society and, as a consequence, lead to lower rates of recidivism. When the 1963 Supreme Court decision of *Gideon* v. *Wainwright,* which guaranteed the right to counsel to all indigent defendants in felony cases, required the state of Florida to discharge 1,252 prisoners long before their normal release dates, the Florida Department of Corrections selected for study 110 of these early releases and 110 full-term releases matched in detail for equally serious criminal histories and other significant factors. Twenty-eight months after discharge, 13.6 percent of the *Gideon* early-release group had been rearrested, while for the full-term release group, the figure was 25.4 percent. The California Women's Board of Terms and Paroles provides another example. In 1959 it changed its parole policies, reducing the median time served from twenty-four months in the mid-1950s to twelve months by 1965. The prison return rate in 1959 for those parolled two to three years earlier and who had served an average of twenty-four months was 35.3 percent. The prison return rate in 1964 for those parolled two to three years earlier and who had served only seventeen to twenty months was 28.8 percent.[34]

Thus, the alternative of shorter sentences tends to lead to lower rates of recidivism. The National Advisory Commission on Criminal Justice Standards and Goals has recently offered a proposal to reduce these rates even further. It

Reproduced by special permission of PLAYBOY Magazine; copyright © 1971 by Playboy.

TABLE 5.10 Sentence and actual time served by first releases[a] from state correctional institutions in 1970

Column:	1	2	3	4	5	6
	1–5 Years (Percent)		5–10 Years (Percent)		10+ Years (Percent)	
State	Sentenced	Served	Sentenced	Served	Sentenced	Served
Arizona	34.56	88.54	42.44	9.22	23.00	2.44
California	15.21	81.32	66.51	16.13	9.49	2.55
Colorado	21.30	95.70	32.45	3.42	46.25	.88
Connecticut	51.59	97.86	42.39	1.58	6.02	.56
Delaware	87.00	98.65	10.31	.90	2.24	.45
Georgia	56.68	88.80	27.84	9.48	15.47	1.72
Hawaii	4.26	80.85	17.02	13.83	78.72	5.32
Idaho	47.26	94.56	32.88	3.40	19.86	2.04
Illinois	48.47	89.00	30.16	8.00	21.37	3.00
Kansas	8.50	91.51	39.44	6.73	52.05	1.76
Kentucky	72.55	94.14	12.20	5.28	15.25	.58
Louisiana	56.98	88.84	26.97	9.84	16.04	1.32
Maine	76.95	95.20	13.26	3.00	9.80	1.80
Maryland	78.97	97.17	15.12	2.14	5.91	.69
Massachusetts	14.66	92.30	65.43	6.47	19.91	1.23
Minnesota	21.94	5.81	39.35	31.61	38.71	62.58
Mississippi	63.38	87.36	19.89	6.69	16.73	5.95
Missouri	74.81	96.05	19.39	2.74	5.80	1.21
Montana	54.70	95.30	25.17	4.03	20.13	.67
Nevada	38.53	93.51	29.87	6.49	31.60	0.00
New Hampshire	54.44	97.78	34.44	2.22	11.11	0.00
New Mexico	8.54	86.65	47.49	10.83	43.97	2.52
New York	57.40	89.79	28.26	7.61	15.86	2.59
North Dakota	68.47	96.40	19.82	2.70	11.71	.90
Ohio	5.43	84.77	19.95	10.74	74.62	4.49
Oklahoma	73.80	95.57	17.82	3.61	8.37	.82
Oregon	65.90	95.62	25.09	4.26	9.01	.12
South Carolina	64.41	92.62	20.46	5.16	15.12	2.22
South Dakota	86.19	95.24	38.10	4.29	4.29	.48
Tennessee	61.69	90.20	19.46	8.33	18.84	1.47
Utah	10.55	90.45	21.11	9.55	63.84	0.00
Vermont	70.37	100.00	25.93	0.00	3.70	0.00
Washington	3.06	95.78	2.75	3.06	94.19	1.16
West Virginia	0.00	87.15	10.10	10.76	89.90	2.08
Wyoming	73.72	94.89	16.06	3.65	10.22	1.46

Explanation of table:
Column 1: Percent of first releases sentenced to 1 to 5 years.
Column 2: Percent of first releases who actually served less than 6 months to 5 years.
Column 3: Percent of first releases sentenced to 5 to 10 years.
Column 4: Percent of first releases who actually served 5 to 10 years.
Column 5: Percent of first releases sentenced to 10 or more years.
Column 6: Percent of first releases who actually served 10 or more years.

Source: National Advisory Commission on Criminal Justice Standards and Goals, *Report on Corrections* (Washington, D.C.: U.S. Government Printing Office, 1973), p. 144.

[a] A first release is a prisoner released for the first time on his current sentence.

proposed that state legislatures authorize a maximum sentence of five years for felonies other than murder unless the courts find that a particular offender is in a special category, for which a longer period of incarceration is allowed. Initially, this proposal is likely to generate considerable controversy. After all, many states authorize extended periods of confinement for many offenses. Individual sentences can range to fifty years or more. Yet, even though long sentences are authorized, few offenders actually serve extended periods of time.

Table 5.10 shows the gap between sentences imposed and sentences served. It shows that although a substantial proportion of offenders released in 1970 had been sentenced to five years or more, only a relatively small percentage had actually served more than five years. It indicates that the National Advisory Commission's proposals would not substantially alter the pattern of present sentencing practices. Table 5.10 also points out the merits of this proposal. It reflects the broad disparity in sentences that currently exists. And it highlights the considerable discretion that parole boards exercise. While some discretion is essential if parole boards are to be able to individualize sentences and release individuals when they are ready, the longer an offender is subjected to this discretion, the more frustrated and dependent he becomes and the less likely he is to be successfully reintegrated into society. The commission's proposal seeks to allow this discretion to operate where it is related to legitimate correctional goals, but to limit it and check it where it is likely to be arbitrary and counterproductive.

There is much to be said in favor of the commission's call for shorter sentences. Serious consideration by state legislatures of this alternative to present correctional practices would result in a number of advantages. It would call attention to one of the basic causes of sentence disparities: the present condition of criminal codes themselves. Most states pass criminal statutes without reviewing other provisions of their criminal code. The result is discrepancies of almost comic proportion. Thus,

> in Colorado, for example, a recent legislatively sponsored inquiry revealed the following rather shocking provisions: one convicted of first degree murder must serve ten years before he first becomes eligible for parole; one convicted of a lesser degree of murder may be forced to serve fifteen or more years. Destruction of a house by fire is punishable by a maximum of twenty years; destruction of the same house with explosives carries a ten year maximum. Stealing a dog is punishable by a maximum of ten years; killing the dog, by six months and a $500.00 fine. . . .
>
> A recent study in Iowa revealed that no complete revision of the criminal code had occurred since 1860, and that as a result of piecemeal enactment of specific provisions without adequate comparison to others already on the books, the following provisions could be found: "larceny of domestic animals and kidnapping a person carry the same maximum sentence. Maiming a domestic beast and maiming or disfiguring a human may result in a similar five-year maximum. The burning of an empty isolated dwelling may lead to a twenty-year sentence while the burning of a

church or a school carries only a 10-year maximum." . . . The model Penal Code Inquiry into burglary statutes reveals that in California a boy who broke into a passenger car to steal the contents of the glove compartment subjected himself to a maximum of 15 years: if he stole the entire car, he could be only sentenced to ten. . . .[35]

Thus, the mere consideration by state legislatures of the commission's proposal of a maximum prison sentence of five years would be beneficial; it would bring these disparities to their attention. Moreover, if this consideration were to lead to legislative enactment, still additional advantages would accrue. The damage that long-term imprisonment works on the inmate would be reduced, and with it the likelihood that he would return to a life of crime. The sentence served by an offender would no longer depart appreciably from the sentence initially imposed, and the offender would come to know that in this as well as other respects, the law says what it means and means what it says. And finally, the amount of discretion over the fate of an offender that a parole board exercises, and the length of time that it exercises it, would be restricted, thereby freeing the offender somewhat from his dependence on the board, alleviating his frustrations, and enhancing his opportunity for successful reintegration into society.

There is only one serious question that can be raised with respect to this proposal for shorter sentences: Will this milder punishment sufficiently deter either the actual or the potential offender? The same question can be raised with respect to all alternatives to long-term imprisonment, including probation and parole. The following response is typically given to this question: Deterrence of actual offenders has not been accomplished, even with today's longer sentences. Statistics on criminal repeating from the FBI's Uniform Crime Reports are testimony to that. (See Table 5.8.) Deterrence of potential offenders likewise is not supported by evidence. Deterrence appears to vary with the nature of the offense and the offender. Thus, while punishment may deter white-collar crime, it seems to have little effect on crimes of passion. Indeed, there is evidence to suggest that the swiftness and certainty of punishment have much greater deterrent effect than the severity of punishment. Thus, the response to this question continues, the deterrent effect of long prison sentences is merely speculative. And, as the National Advisory Commission insists, "in a free society, long prison sentences can not be justified on the basis of speculation concerning deterrence, particularly where the detrimental effects of imprisonment for the individual offender are known and demonstrable."[36]

Society must bear the burden of proof that these increased restrictions on liberty deter crime. This sentiment of the commission is most interesting. It reflects the thinking of most correctional personnel who seek alternatives to lengthy incarceration. The society, because of its commitment to liberty, in its response to crime and the criminal must err on the side of individual liberty and against the security of society. This sentiment fully acknowledges both the fundamental tension between majority rule and minority rights that pervades the entire criminal justice system and corrections' identity with individual and minority rights. It clearly presents corrections as the protector of these rights, protecting them against the hostile interest of the majority of the society.

Community-Based Corrections

While the alternative of shorter sentences has some merit, many correctional officials are of the opinion that it does not go far enough. They seek community-based corrections, which includes all correctional activities that take place in the community, as the only viable alternative to the present policy of confinement. They provide the following rationale: A man who has committed a crime and has been caught and convicted suffers a considerable blow to his self-esteem, which he may mask with bravado or indifference. He is likely to believe, and with good reason, that conventional persons will reject him, and as a result he may seek out the unconventional. If he is confined to prison, he has no choice; he must associate with the unconventional. However, if he is kept in the community, probation and parole resources will be there to assist him in maintaining and strengthening his contact with the conventional, law-abiding public. His full reintegration into the community will thereby be enhanced.

The National Advisory Commission on Criminal Justice Standards and Goals considers community-based corrections to be "the most promising means of accomplishing the changes in offender behavior that the public expects—and in fact demands of corrections."[37] In fact, it regards this "alternative to incarceration" as so fundamental and basic to the future of corrections that it has joined with the National Council on Crime and Delinquency (NCCD) in suggesting that imprisonment and not community-based corrections should be regarded as the exceptional: "Imprisonment must be viewed as an alternative to community treatment."[38]

They offer three principal justifications for their confidence in and commitment to community-based corrections. First of all, community-based corrections is humanitarian. Custodial confinement in prison places the offender in physical jeopardy, narrows his access to personal satisfaction, and destroys his self-confidence. Although these unfortunate consequences are brought on by the offender's own criminal actions, that in no way alters their reality. To the extent that these unfortunate consequences can be abetted by the use of community treatment, humanitarian objectives are realized. Second, community-based corrections is justified in terms of its restorative capacity. Those who have been the subjects of community corrections are far less likely to become recidivists. The President's Commission on Law Enforcement and the Administration of Justice in its general report noted that various studies have established the success of community treatment.

> One summary analysis of 15 different studies of probation outcomes indicates that from 60–90 percent of the probationers studied completed terms without revocation. In another study, undertaken in California,

11,638 adult probationers who were granted probation during 1956 and 1958 were followed up after seven years. Of this group, almost 72 percent completed their probation terms without revocation.[39]

Third, community-based corrections can be justified in economic terms. It costs from ten to thirteen times more to maintain an offender in a prison than it does to supervise him in custody.[40] This saving in and of itself should not be decisive. After all, the objective of correctional programs is to protect the public, not simply to save money. But since community treatment also appears to ensure and even increase present levels of public protection, this fiscal consideration lends additional justification for community-based alternatives to incarceration.

For community-based corrections to work properly, for its justification to grow in stature, active and full community cooperation and involvement are simply imperative. This is not easy to achieve, as it requires the reversal of a pattern of the recent past. In an earlier era, citizens directly exercised law enforcement and correctional responsibilities. New England had its banishments and public pillories, and the frontier West had its citizen posses. However, as the United States grew in size and complexity, these functions were delegated to public servants; the police force and sheriff's staff replaced the posse, the court system replaced church tribunals, and jails and prisons replaced pillories and summary executions. The delegation of these functions to a professional criminal justice system has become so complete that the public now has little sense of responsibility for them. In fact, the criminal justice system has come to be viewed as an adversary, a set of institutions to be opposed and outwitted rather than a service controlled by and organized to serve the interests of individual citizens and the general public. All one has to do is consider what the youth have to say about police and what the adult public does to circumvent everything from tax laws to traffic regulations to appreciate to what extent the American public regards the criminal justice system in terms of "them" and "us."[41]

This attitude must be reversed if community-based corrections is fully to succeed. Until citizen responsibility and participation are again generated, this flickering candle will remain the brightest light on the correctional horizon. Community involvement is needed both in policy-making and direct service roles. Citizen involvement in policy making often takes the form of service on task forces or study groups that serve a general advisory role to the government. Direct services often involve the utilization of volunteers. Use of citizen volunteers in correction is massive, with citizen volunteers outnumbering professionals five to one. More, however, are needed to fill the ever greater demand for big brothers, pen pals, group programs of many kinds, basic and continuing education offerings, and legal services. These two roles complement each other. The citizen who works as a volunteer will gain increased understanding, which will make him a more effective voice in policy making; at the same time, the informed citizen will be more likely to serve as a volunteer, for he understands the need for contact and communication between the community and the offender. This citizen involvement in policy making and direct services is essential for all three community-based correctional alternatives to confinement: probation, parole, and diversion.

Probation

Probation may be defined as a sentence that does not involve confinement but which instead places the offender under supervision in the community subject to the authority of the sentencing court. The beginnings of probation in the United States are usually traced to Boston, where in 1841 a shoemaker by the name of John Augustus volunteered to offer employment to certain persons convicted of misdemeanors if the judge would suspend their sentences. By 1858 he had bailed out 1152 men and 794 women and girls.[42] Augustus and several other volunteers whom he recruited introduced such innovative practices as investigation and screening, interviewing, supervision of those released, and services such as employment, relief, and education. Their efforts proved to be successful, so much so that in 1878 Massachusetts enacted legislation that formally established probation and enabled Boston to appoint its first paid probation officers. By 1900, six states had legislation that provided for probation; four dealt with adult probation and two were limited to children.

Probation came into its own, however, in the twentieth century. In 1907 there were approximately 795 probation officers in the United States. By 1970 there were nearly 25,000. This development was aided considerably by the juvenile court movement. As early as 1919, thirty-seven states and the District of Columbia had children's court acts, and forty states had probation for juveniles. By 1925, probation for children was available in every state, something that did not occur in the case of adult probation until 1956. Today more than half the adult offenders sentenced to correctional treatments are placed on probation. The President's Commission on Law Enforcement and Administration of Justice reported that in 1965, of the 1,282,386 offenders under correctional control that year, 53 percent, or 684,088, were on probation, with the remaining 47 percent, or 598,298, in institutions or on parole.[43] In fact, about 75 percent of all convictions result in probation. However, since probation is typically a one-time disposition while institutional confinements are often cumulative, with the 65 percent repeaters in prison, the actual count of those on probation at any given time drops to about 53 percent.[44]

Probation consists of two basic operations: the presentence investigation, conducted to determine which offenders will receive the sentence of probation, and supervision of probationers. The presentence investigation is performed by the probation officer to ascertain the family and social background of the offender and to uncover his strengths and his weaknesses with a view toward working out a treatment program. It typically includes evaluations of the offender's background, social relationships, occupational strengths and weaknesses, school background, criminal background, and all other factors pertinent to the sentencing decision. The presentence investigation report is then submitted to the judge after the offender has been convicted but before he is sentenced in order to assist the judge in his sentencing decision. Specifically, the presentence investigation report can serve five functions: First, it can aid the court in determining the appropriate sentence. Second, if the court sentences the offender to probation, it can aid the probation officer in rehabilitative efforts during probation supervision. Third, if the court sentences the offender to confinement, it can assist the correctional institution in designing a classification and treatment program for him. Fourth, it can furnish the parole board with information pertinent to the offender's release on parole. And fifth, the presentence investigation report can serve as a source of information for systematic research.[45]

Presentence investigation reports have proved to be of great value to the sentencing judges, so much so that they follow the probation officer's recommendation for disposition about 95 percent of the time. When the judge and probation officer differ, it is often the result of differences in perspective. The probation officer may place greater emphasis on the rehabilitation of the offender than on such community attitudes as the Gallup Poll uncovered in 1971, when it found that three-fourths of the population sampled regarded present sentences as too lenient.[46] The judge, on the other hand, is typically an elected official and is likely to be much more aware of these sentiments.

Once the presentence investigation is complete and the offender has been sentenced to probation, the second basic operation of probation begins: supervision. Supervision involves a combination of both treatment and enforcement functions. It employs such community resources as family agencies, child care or welfare agencies, child guidance clinics, mental hygiene clinics, vocational guidance agencies, and social group work agencies in an attempt to rehabilitate the probationer for a full, productive, and law-abiding life. At the same time, it engages in surveillance and information-gathering in efforts to control the activities and behavior of the probationer. Both are necessary. Thus, for example, if a probationer is beginning to break contact with employment and family, this may be the beginning of a deteriorating social relationship that the probation officer may wish to deal with through intensive counseling and treatment, through placement of the probationer in jail for a short time, or, in extreme cases, through revocation of probation. Yet a balance between treatment and control must be maintained. The American Correction Association has concluded that such a balance is fundamentally dependent upon the following four principles:

1. Reform comes from within the person; the probationer must, therefore, participate in any treatment program designed to assist him.
2. This program must be individualized to meet his particular needs, problems, capacities, and limitations.
3. To be of greatest benefit both to the probationer and to the community, this program should become part of the legally binding condition of probation.
4. Helping the probationer to understand his own problems and enabling him to deal adequately with them is the goal of supervision.[47]

Unfortunately, a balance between treatment and control presently does not exist for most probationers. In fact, most receive both inadequate treatment and inadequate control. The reason is simple: probation officers have traditionally labored under unmanageable case loads. The average size of case loads in probation is around a hundred. According to the President's Commission on Law Enforcement and the Administration of Justice, probation officers with over a hundred cases are responsible for approximately 76 percent of all misdemeanor cases and 67 percent of all felonies.[48] The consequences of such heavy case loads have been unfortunate. For example:

> A probation officers meets with an eighteen-year-old probationer who has stolen a car. The boy begins to talk, explaining that he began to "slip into the wrong crowd" a year or so after his stepfather died. He says it would help him to talk about it. But the probation officer has no time. The waiting room is filled, and the boy is not scheduled for another fifteen-minute conference until next month.

> A probation officer feels that a thirty-year-old man on probation for burglary is heading for trouble. He frequently misses work and is reported to hang around a bar with a bad reputation. The officer believes that things must be straightened out now, before it is too late, so he tries unsuccessfully two or three times to reach the probationer by phone. He considers going out to look for him but decides against it, as he is already overwhelmed preparing presentence investigation reports and revocation of probation papers on other probationers whom he has not had the time to reach.

> A young probation officer presents to his supervisor a plan for "something different," a group counseling session to operate three evenings a week for juvenile probationers and their parents. He is told to forget it, as he has more work than he can presently handle preparing presentence investigation reports for the judge.

Because the probation officer is too overworked to provide either treatment or control services, the offender is left on his own. If he does not succeed, both he and the community lose. To minimize these losses, the President's Commission recommended that the average ratio of offenders to probation officers be reduced to 35.[49] This recommendation was in keeping with the findings of the Saginaw Project, conducted in Michigan from 1957 to 1962, where probation officers assigned relatively low case loads achieved excellent results, even though only 20 percent of those convicted were sentenced to prison.[50]

Even lower case loads will not alleviate altogether the imbalances between treatment and control; a few offenders will continue to violate the conditions of their probation. On these occasions, probation may be revoked. The revocation process, however, must adhere to certain minimal standards. In *Mempa* v. *Rhay*, the Supreme Court held that right to counsel must extend to probation revocation.[51] In a more recent case, *Morrissey* v. *Brewer,* the Court spelled out in detail the procedural aspects constitutionally required for parole revocation. For a revocation hearing to meet the minimum requirements of due process, it must include written notice of the claimed violations of parole, disclosure to the parolee of evidence against him, opportunity to be heard in person and to present witnesses and documentary evidence, right to confront and to cross-examine adverse witnesses, a neutral and detached hearing body, and a written statement by the fact finders as to the evidence relied on and the reasons for revoking parole.[52] These same protections were subsequently extended to revocation of probation hearings in *Gagnon* v. *Scarpelli*.[53] "We hold that a probationer, like a parolee, is entitled to a preliminary and a final revocation hearing, under the conditions specified in *Morrissey* v. *Brewer*."

For the most part, however, probation does not end in failure or revocation. The President's Commission reports that in California, of 11,638 adult probationers on probation during 1956 to 1958, 72 percent completed their period of probation without revocation.[54] In fact, probation constitutes perhaps "the most successful phase of the correctional process."[55] Its success extends beyond low revocation rates to low recidivist rates as well. For example, Professor Ralph W. England did a follow-up study on a sample of 500 federal offenders placed on probation by federal district court judges in the Eastern District of Pennsylvania. The sample was drawn from a universe consisting of all offenders whose probation was successfully terminated between January 1, 1939, and December 31, 1944. England found that only 87 or 17.7 percent of the 490 remaining ex-probationers (10 had died before they had been off probation for a minimum of six years) had been reconvicted for either a felony or a misdemeanor or both from the end of their probationary term to December 31, 1950. Seventy-three percent of the reconvictions were for misdemeanors, such as gambling, theft, and disorderly conduct.[56] These figures are consistent with other studies of postrelease recidivism among both adult and juvenile offenders, which show success or nonrecidivism rates of 72, 79, 88, and 83 percent.[57]

These studies typically have not been obtained under controlled conditions. Neither have they distinguished among the types of offenders who succeeded or the types of services that were rendered. Nevertheless, all of these success rates are high, especially when compared with the colossal failure of the prisons. Probation continues to have many problems. What constitutes essential and pertinent information for a presentence investigation report? How can the tension caused by the presentence investigation between the due process model and the crime control model be relaxed? How can more realistic case loads be achieved for probation officers? It nevertheless remains, as the National Advisory Commission realistically assessed, the "brightest hope for corrections."[58]

Parole

The success of probation has had its effect on parole. The classic definition of parole was given in the Attorney General's *Survey of Release Procedures*: it is the "release of an offender from a penal or correctional institution, after he has served a portion of his sentence, under the continued custody of the state and under conditions that permit his reincarceration in the event of misbehavior."[59] Parole resembles probation in a number of respects. Both represent a break with the classical theory of criminal law and attempt to adjust the correctional response to the circumstances of the offense and the characteristics of the offender. Both respond to crime and criminology by the employment of treatment in the form of guidance and assistance to the offenders. Both involve gathering and presenting of information about the offender to a decision-making authority with power to release him to community supervision under specific conditions. Finally, both probation and parole provide that if the offender violates these conditions, he may be placed in, or returned to, a correctional institution.

Parole, however, also differs from probation in a number of significant respects. To begin with, parole is granted to the offender who has been incarcerated in a correctional institution before his release; probation, on the other hand, is usually granted by a judge in lieu of any kind of confinement. Perhaps because of this, parole is less "purely" treatment-oriented and more punitive than probation. As Edwin Sutherland and Donald Cressey point out:

> Probationers are considered as undergoing treatment while under the threat of punishment, should they violate the conditions of their probation. But probation is granted by the courts as a substitute for punishment as well as for mere suspension of sentence. Parolees are considered as "in custody" and undergoing both punishment and treatment while under the threat of more severe punishment—return to the institutions from which they have been released. Without the threat of return to prison, release from prison before the maximum term was served would merely represent the workings of the indeterminate sentence, not parole. Since parole is expected to punish and to treat, the conflicts between punishment and treatment which are found in prisons are also found in parole.[60]

Probation and parole also differ in the matter of who makes the decision. Parole is an administrative decision, while the granting of probation is a judicial determination. This fact is often obscured by the occasional use of shock probation. On these occasions, a sentencing judge may require as a condition of probation that an offender spend some time in an institution before he is released under community supervision. The argument usually advanced to justify this practice is that it gives the offender a taste of incarceration that tends to deter him from further criminal activity. However, since it subjects the offender to the destructive effects of institutionalization, disrupts his life in the community, and stigmatizes him with the onus of having been in prison, this practice has come under increasingly severe criticism, and the National Advisory Commission recommended that it be discontinued. With the exception of this practice of shock probation, however, the power to determine when an offender is to be released from prison, to determine the conditions of his supervision, and to decide if parole revocation hearings should be ordered typically passes from the sentencing judge to an agency within the executive branch. In the case of adults, this agency is usually the parole board.

The system of parole originated in the nineteenth century, when penal philosophy shifted in emphasis from punishment to reformation. In the United States the first formally recognized parole system was set in motion in July of 1876 with the opening of Elmira Reformatory in New York State.[61] The Elmira system quickly spread to other states. It extended to Ohio in 1884, and to twenty-four other states by 1898. By 1922, parole laws had been passed by forty-five states, and when Mississippi enacted parole legislation in 1944, it finally extended throughout the entire country. Not every state has identical parole laws or practices, and states vary widely in the proportion of prison inmates released under parole supervision. Thus, Washington, California, Kansas, and New Hampshire release 100 percent of their prison inmates under parole supervision, while Oklahoma and Nebraska release less than 20 percent under parole supervision. Despite these wide variations, however, parole is the predominant mode of release for prison inmates today. In 1970 almost 83,000 felons left prison, and of that number, 72 percent were released on parole.[62]

The fundamental objective of parole, as well as the measure of its success, is reduction of recidivism. After all, almost every offender who is sentenced to a correctional institution is eventually released. National Prisoner Statistics from the Federal Bureau of Prisons show that very few inmates die in prison. The figures for 1970 are typical; in that year, when the total U.S. prison population averaged about 196,000 inmates, there were only 663 deaths in prison.[63]

Since virtually every offender is eventually released, parole can prove to be extremely valuable in reducing recidivism. It can provide supervision and control in order to reduce the incidence of criminal activity while the offender is completing his sentence in the community, and it can provide assistance and services to the parolee so that noncriminal behavior continues once that sentence is complete. The success with which parole can provide this supervision and assistance and promote lower recidivism rates is wholly dependent upon (1) how well it selects inmates for parole, (2) the sort of preparole preparation it provides, and (3) the adequacy of the supervision it gives to the parolees once they are released into the community. Enormous problems in each of these three functional areas have to date greatly limited the success of parole.

The duty of determining which prisoners shall be released on parole, and when, typically falls on the parole board. Parole boards, like parole systems generally, can vary greatly from state to state. Basically, however, there are three principal types of boards: first, a special parole board limited to one institution and usually composed of institutional staff members or at least the warden of the institution, who serves as a member of the board; second, a general state parole board, located in the state Department of Correction, with authority to release from any state institution; and third, a general state parole board, located outside the Department of Correction, with authority to release from any state institution. Recently the trend has been toward centralization of parole authority in one general board and removal of it from the state Department of Correction. This development has received a mixed response. Although it has generally been supported by the prison staff on the grounds that it relieves them of a troublesome responsibility that interferes with their efficiency in institutional work, it has been condemned by others on the grounds that no other agency knows better than the prison staff when a prisoner should be released. This controversy aside, in forty-one states today the parole board is an independent agency; in seven states it is a unit within a larger department of the state; and in two states it is the same body that regulates correctional institutions. In no jurisdiction is the final power to grant or deny parole to adults given to the staff directly involved in the operation of the correctional institution. The same cannot be said for juveniles, however; in thirty-four states the great majority of releasing decisions directly involve the staffs of training schools.[64]

The elimination, at least in the adult field, of parole boards restricted to considering release of only inmates confined to a single institution is perhaps a good thing. After all, those boards are usually dominated by the institutional staff. Such domination may lead a board to grant parole as a reward for good conduct in the prison rather than as a correctional device. It may also lead the board to seek to maintain discipline by means of threats with respect to chances for parole or to grant parole indiscriminately when the institution is over-crowded. Any of these eventualities represents a complete frustration of the primary purpose of parole—the reduction of recidivism. However, parole boards that are entirely independent not only from particular institutions but also from state Departments of Correction are equally capable of overlooking this primary purpose. These boards often appear less concerned with the progress of the inmate than with the possible reactions of the public toward parole. A recent study conducted by the National Council on Crime and Delinquency of nearly half the parole board members in the United States indicates that along with reduction of recidivism, three other concerns enter into board members' decisions on parole: equitable punishment, impact on the system, and reactions of persons outside the correctional organization. Moreover, these factors "assume such importance in certain cases that risk becomes secondary."[65] Thus a well-known inmate may be denied parole repeatedly because of strong public feelings, even though he might be an excellent risk. Alternatively, an offender convicted of a relatively minor crime may be paroled even though a poor risk, because in the opinion of the board he has already been punished enough to pay for his crime. Such considerations can only minimize the effectiveness of parole and limit the correctional impact it could have on offenders. Table 5.11 shows those items considered by at least 20 percent of the parole board members surveyed as being among the five most important in parole decisions.[66]

Once an offender has been selected for parole, by whatever criterion and by a board however organized, a new set of problems affecting prerelease programs arises. The longer an inmate has been incarcerated, the more dependent he becomes. Prison provides an externally imposed discipline; it feeds and clothes the inmate and provides an order or routine to his life. It provides a certain security and assurance that may have never before been experienced. All of these factors, however, make it increasingly more difficult for the inmate upon his re-

TABLE 5.11 Items considered by parole board members to be most important in parole decisions

Item	Percent including item as one of five most important
1. My estimate of the chances that the prisoner would or would not commit a *serious crime* if paroled.	92.8
2. My judgment that the prisoner would *benefit* from further *experience* in the institution program or, at any rate, would become a better risk if confined longer.	87.1
3. My judgment that the prisoner would *become a worse risk if confined longer.*	71.9
4. My judgment that the prisoner had already been *punished enough to "pay"* for his crime.	43.2
5. The probability that the prisoner would be a *misdemeanant* and a burden to his *parole supervisors,* even if he did *not commit any serious offenses on parole.*	35.3
6. My feelings about how my decision in this case would affect the *feelings or welfare of the prisoner's relatives or dependents.*	33.8
7. What I *thought the reaction of the judge might be if the prisoner were granted parole.*	20.9

Source: National Advisory Commission on Criminal Justice Standards and Goals, *Report on Corrections* (Washington, D.C.: U.S. Government Printing Office, 1973), p. 394.

lease to function normally and productively in society. Consequently, a variety of parole preparation programs have been established which attempt to prepare the inmate for reentry into society. These programs are extremely important, for most parole violations occur shortly after release from prison, with approximately 68 percent of them occurring within six months and approximately 90 percent during the first year.[67]

The potential of prerelease guidance has not been realized in most instances, however, and the reason for this also accounts for most of the other failures in community-based corrections: lack of manpower. In the United States, there are approximately 1.3 million people under correctional authority. Of these, one-third are in institutions and the remaining two-thirds are supervised in the community on probation or parole. However, the ratios of staff and costs are inverse to the proportions: only one-seventh of the staff and one-fifth of the money are available to deal with the two-thirds of the offenders who are in the community.[68] As a result, most prospective parolees do not get the sort of guidance and counsel they may need and want. They leave prison and face the initial critical period of reentry into society with more apprehensions than necessary concerning community acceptance, employment, family relationships, and relationships with police and parole officers. It is not strange that most parole violations and revocations occur during the first six months after release from prison.

Whether or not preparole counseling has adequately prepared the prospective parolee for reintegration into the community, once he is released he is placed under the supervision of a parole officer. However, parole supervision, like probation supervision and the correctional system generally, is plagued with a variety of problems that limit its effectiveness. To begin with, there is no general consensus concerning what the purpose of parole supervision actually is. As we noted earlier, parole has always been more punitive than probation. Parole is expected both to punish and to treat. Different understandings of supervision have arisen which place varying degrees of emphasis on punishment or treatment. One understanding, although rapidly disappearing, is that parole is a system of leniency that grants early release to many dangerous criminals who should continue to suffer punishment. It considers most parolees unrehabilitated and likely to commit new crimes if given the opportunity. Thus, supervision requires more surveillance than assistance. Parole work becomes police work. It requires that the parole officer coerce the parolee into conformity by means of punishment or the threat of punishment.

A second understanding of parole supervision is based on the assumption that reformation is practically complete when the offender leaves the prison and that the function of the parole officer is to watch the parolee to ascertain whether he is maintaining the conditions of his parole. As Sutherland and Cressey have characterized it, this understanding of supervision amounts to "watchful waiting."[69] Although parole officers possessed of this understanding will give direct help and assistance to the parolee in locating jobs and solving other problems, will occasionally feel compelled to lecture him, and when doing so will employ both praise and blame, they are reluctant to do so too often. They fear too frequent contact will destroy the parolee's initiative and confidence in himself. Finally, a third understanding of supervision is based on the notion that the essential work of promoting the parolee's adjustment has to be done after his release from prison. This requires the active assistance of the parole officer, not so much to prevent the parolee from exercising his own initiative as to assist and direct him in exercising it so that it will not result in further criminal activity. Unlike the second understanding, this view contends that reformation in the form of self-resolution to "make good" is not always sufficient to prevent recidivism. Parole supervision in the form of assistance is needed to improve the welfare of the parolee by helping him in his individual adjustment, within the limits of his capacity. Parole work in this view becomes social work.

In practice, all three understandings of supervision tend to be present to some degree in every parole system. The presence of these widely divergent understandings within the same parole system is the source of many of parole's difficulties. After all, these different understandings of supervision impose on the parolee very different kinds of degrees of control and elicit in return very different kinds of responses. The first understanding of supervision is primarily punitive and coercive and generates intense negative feelings of alienation. On the other hand, the third understanding tends to be more humanitarian and normative; it appeals to the parolee's better nature. In turn, it tends to generate a much more positive response. If a parolee accustomed to either the first or the third understanding of supervision were suddenly to be subjected to the other, his response would likely reflect frustration, anxiety, and suspicion. The parolee accustomed to surveillance and punishment would not be able to understand his parole officer's new-found interest in assistance and treatment and would be likely to view this change in supervision with mistrust and apprehension. Likewise, the parolee accustomed to assistance and treatment would probably respond to punitive measures with feelings of betrayal, frustration, and confusion. Yet shifts in supervision of the kind described here occur daily in parole systems everywhere. There is no consensus on how parole supervision should be conducted, and the result is confusion, mistrust, and apprehension among parolees and, not surprisingly, a high rate of failure for parole.[70]

As with so many other problems in community-based corrections, the difficulties attending parole supervision are intensified by manpower shortages. Parole supervision is often little more than nominal, for very few states have a sufficient number of officers to make adequate supervision possible. A recent study found that there are only about 2100 parole officers and administrative staff responsible for adult parole services in the United States and another 1400 assigned to parole for juveniles.[71] This study further indicated that adults released on parole are supervised in case loads averaging sixty-eight. Table 5.12 shows the estimated size of case loads in which parolees are presently being supervised.

Since in at least thirty states where probation and parole services are combined, parole officers must also conduct presentence investigations in probation cases, the amount of individual supervision that can be given to each parolee is even further restricted. With supervision, of either the surveillance or assistance variety, so restricted, the parolee, unrehabilitated by prison, unprepared by prerelease programs, and unsupervised once in the community, is likely to adopt

TABLE 5.12 Percentage distribution of parolees, by size of case load in which supervised

Case-Load size	Juvenile parole (percent)	Adult parole (percent)
Under 50	28.2	7.9
51–60	4.7	25.4
61–70	48.8	20.7
71–80	5.7	23.2
Over 80	12.6	22.8

Source: President's Commission on Law Enforcement and Administration of Justice, *Task Force Report: Corrections* (Washington, D.C.: U.S. Government Printing Office, 1967), p. 70.

again the only way of life he knows—the way of life that got him into trouble with the criminal justice system in the first place. This regrettable consequence is all too well documented by a whole range of empirical studies. Thus, Sheldon and Eleanor T. Glueck analyzed the careers of 500 young male offenders paroled from the Massachusetts reformatory and found a parole violation rate of 60.6 percent.[72] Other studies of parole violations indicate somewhat lower rates than those found by the Gluecks. For example, 47 percent of the 7582 male offenders paroled in California in 1965 had been declared violators by 1966.[73] Of those men paroled from the Illinois State Penitentiary between 1926 and 1943, 44 percent were violators. And of 1015 inmates released from federal prisons in 1956, only 35 percent were classed as failures by 1960.[74]

These parole violation rates refer only to the period of parole and do not include criminal activity after the offender is released from parole. However, studies of the subsequent careers of ex-inmates beyond the period of parole are no more encouraging. Sheldon and Eleanor Glueck continued to follow the careers of their sample of 500 young adult male offenders for a period of fifteen years. They found that 79 percent committed new crimes during the first five-year period after parole, 68 percent during the second five-year period, and 68 percent during the third five-year period. Other studies have found a lower but still distressingly high incidence of crime, and the President's Commission on Law Enforcement and Administration of Justice was led to conclude that "the best current estimates indicate that, among adult offenders, 35–40 percent of those released on parole are subsequently returned to prison."[75]

Pretrial Diversion

Because of the high failure rates of parole and the even higher failure rates of prisons, correctional measures that seek to minimize penetration into the criminal justice system are becoming increasingly prominent. Thus, probation in lieu of institutionalization is now imposed in approximately 75 percent of all criminal cases. Another correctional measure that minimizes penetration even further, pretrial diversion, is also gaining increased attention. Pretrial diversion refers to "halting or suspending before conviction formal criminal proceedings against a person on the condition or assumption that he will do something in return."[76]

While formal pretrial diversion is relatively new, informal diversion by citizens and police has always existed. For a variety of reasons, many illegal acts that come to the attention of citizens are never reported to the police. The extent to which this informal diversion takes place is made apparent by a 1974 Law Enforcement Assistance Administration study, which reveals that the actual crime rate in America's major cities is actually three to five times greater than the Federal Bureau of Investigation's Uniform Crime Reports would indicate.[77] Police also employ informal diversion. In many situations, arrest is clearly inappropriate. This is especially true when the police are trying to resolve conflicts between husbands and wives, landlords and tenants, businessmen and customers, or management and labor. They are likely to employ instead such alternatives to arrest as reprimanding the suspected offenders or referring them to their families or other agencies. Pretrial diversion is merely an attempt to formalize these previously discretionary actions. It is an attempt to minimize penetration into the criminal justice system at the earliest possible stages. It has much to recommend it.

To begin with, it possesses a number of distinct advantages when compared to probation, prison, or parole. First, unlike these other correctional alternatives, pretrial diversion can help to reduce the heavy volume of cases that the courts must process. In so doing, it can ease the pressure on the criminal justice system to resort to the crime control model and the plea bargain to handle this volume, and thereby can help bulwark the efforts of the United States Supreme Court to protect the criminal procedural rights of the defendant. Second, by taking the offender out of the criminal process before conviction, diversion imposes no stigma of conviction, which makes rehabilitation and reform all the more difficult. This desire to avoid the stigma of a criminal conviction often provides the offender with all the incentive he needs to fulfill all the conditions of his diversion program. Third, and perhaps most importantly, pretrial diversion can avoid subjecting the offender to the depravity of either prison or jail. Probation, of course, can save the offender from prison, but not necessarily from jail.

Many probationers have been unable to post bond, and as a result have spent their time awaiting trial in jail. Pretrial diversion, by minimizing the offender's penetration into the criminal justice system, can spare the offender this possibility. A national jail census conducted in 1970 by the U.S. Bureau of the Census under an agreement with the Law Enforcement Assistance Administration found that there were 4,037 locally administered jails in the United States with authority to retain adult persons for forty-eight hours or longer. As of March 15, 1970, these local jails held a total of 160,863 persons, including 153,063 adults and 7,800 juveniles. Of that number, 83,079 (52 percent) were pretrial detainees or otherwise not convicted; 8,688 (5 percent) had been convicted but were awaiting further legal action such as sentencing or appeal; and the remaining 69,096 (43 percent) were serving sentences of varying lengths.[78]

For those persons held in these jails, the conditions are generally abominable. There is no distinction made in most jails between the accused, who, as the National Jail Census found, comprise 50 percent of the jail population, and the convicted. Those charged with minor offenses are frequently permitted to associate with those accused or convicted of serious crimes. Often the youthful offender is thrown in with older, more experienced criminals. Consequently, even if he is acquitted, he is more capable of committing antisocial acts upon his release because of what he has learned during his confinement. As Daniel Glaser has observed: "While reformatories and prisons are often called 'schools for crime,' it is a far more fitting label for the typical urban jail."[79]

Quite apart from the lack of segregation between the accused and the convicted, other jail inadequacies are strikingly apparent. The National Jail Census found many of them to be old, lacking in facilities, overcrowded, and understaffed. There are 3,319 jails in the United States at either the county level or in municipalities of 25,000 or larger population. Of the 97,891 cells these jails contain, nearly 25,000 were constructed more than fifty years ago. Of that number, nearly 12,000 are over seventy-five years old, and 5,416 have been in use longer than a century.[80] Most jails are not only old, they are also lacking in facilities. Eighty-six percent of the county and large urban jails in the United States provide no facilities for exercise or other recreation for their inmates. Nearly 90 percent have no educational facilities. Only 50 percent provide medical facilities; 25 percent have no visiting facilities; and there are 47 institutions (about 1.4 percent) that are without an operating flush toilet.[81]

Within these antiquated and ill-equipped institutions, there are frequently overcrowding problems. Ten percent of all jails designed to hold between 100 and 299 inmates typically exceed capacity. In fact, thirty-one jails that by design can accommodate 100 or more persons were overcrowded in excess of 100 persons on the survey date. This includes fourteen jails that were built for 300 or more inmates and which also exceed their capacity by a like amount. These dismal physical facilities have been accompanied by a lack of adequate staff. Jail employees are almost invariably undertrained, too few in number, and underpaid. The National Jail Census found that the nation's jails employed 28,911 full-time equivalent persons on March 15, 1970, for an average of about 5.6 inmates per jail employee. The March 1970 payroll was $18 million for an average of $617 per full-time employee.[82] Jail employees typically emphasize custody over treatment. After all, most are sheriff's deputies or police personnel imbued with the law-enforcement psychology of a policeman who seeks to arrest offenders and get them into jail rather than the rehabilitative psychology of a correctional worker who seeks to prepare the inmate to get out of jail and take his place in a free community of law-abiding citizens.

The lack of segregation between the accused and the convicted, the outmoded facilities, the overcrowding, and the inadequate staff all combine to produce the same horrors, the same degradation, and the same homosexual abuse so prevalent in prison. And the victims of such barbarity are often those only accused, and not convicted, of crime. Of all the correctional alternatives, only pretrial diversion, by minimizing penetration into the criminal justice system in such a way that jail becomes unnecessary, can eliminate these destructive excesses.

Pretrial diversion is thus free from many of the disadvantages of probation, parole, and imprisonment. It also has much to commend it quite apart from the relative merits or demerits of these other correctional measures, however. It presents opportunities for treatment and supervision not otherwise available. These opportunities are perhaps best introduced by considering a hypothetical case in which first informal prosecutorial diversion and then formal pretrial diversion are employed. Consider the case of Frank Smith, a twenty-year-old black male who is married and has two children. He has satisfactory employment but has recently become addicted to the use of heroin and finds himself in desperate need of money to support both his family and his drug habit. Frank has never before been in trouble with the law but is unable to find an adequate solution to this problem. He goes to a local department store and cashes a check for $200, knowing full well that he does not have adequate funds to cover it. The department store discovers that the check is not good and notifies the police, who arrest Frank. He is later charged with passing bad checks.

Immediately following his arrest, the wheels of justice begin to turn, but it will take one year for formal prosecution to be completed. Frank is allowed to make bond and is released from jail. He is advised that if he will pay off the check, the prosecutor will consider suspending prosecution, but since this is informal prosecutorial diversion, no supervision is provided.

Awaiting trial on bond, Frank decides to straighten out his life and make restitution so that he will not be prosecuted to completion. However, after six months Frank has not saved enough money to pay his attorney, make the required restitution, provide for his family, and support his drug addiction. Afraid that if he does not make restitution immediately, he will be faced with additional problems, he decides to commit another offense in order to secure the money. This decision is not a rational one, but Frank is still addicted to heroin, and this addiction has almost totally debilitated Frank to the point where rational thought is practically an impossibility.

Following the perpetration of the second offense, Frank is rearrested and subsequently charged. The formal prosecution for the first offense is resumed as well as prosecution for the second offense. Frank is unable to make bond on the second offense and awaits trial in the county jail. When his case finally comes to trial, Frank is convicted and sentenced to the state prison. Since he has not been able to work, his family has been dependent upon welfare support throughout his incarceration.

Had a formal pretrial diversion program been available. Frank's fate might have turned out quite differently. In fact, it might have turned out like this: Following Frank's arrest, he is interviewed by a representative of the local diversion program and his problem of drug addiction is discovered. A program of drug treatment, supervision, employment and restitution is proposed, and Frank agrees to participate in this program. Formal prosecution is suspended until completion of the proposed program, at which time consideration will be given to complete dismissal of the charges.

Frank is initially referred to a community drug treatment center, where he receives medical attention during detoxification and begins to participate in a drug treatment program including regular counseling, supervision, and support. When his drug problem is under control, Frank returns to his employment with the assistance of his counselor from the diversion program and begins again to earn money. With his employment, Frank is able to support himself and his family as well as to make restitution for the bad check. All the while he is receiving treatment for his problem of drug addiction.

At the end of one year, Frank is well on the road to rehabilitation from his drug addiction. He has made complete restitution, is employed, and has earned the support of his counselors and employer. The case is reviewed by the formal justice system and, on the basis of Frank's accomplishments, the charges are dropped.

Obviously this is a hypothetical case, but it does point out some of the promise of pretrial diversion. Unlike other correctional alternatives, it does not have to wait until the slow and time-consuming judicial process is finally completed before it can begin its assistance to and supervision of the offender. As a result, at least in this hypothetical case, the victim of the first offense is appeased, there are no new victims, and the best interests of society are served. Pretrial diversion provides the opportunity for immediate counseling and treatment. It permits little problems to be uncovered and resolved before they become big problems. Pretrial diversion can also provide the opportunity for another correctional measure—it can allow the offender to make restitution to the victim of his criminal activity.

As in the hypothetical case, one of the conditions of a diversion program can be restitution or compensation to the victim. For the most part, the fate of the victim has generally been ignored by corrections. This is in keeping with the idea that the focus of corrections is the accused individual and its purpose is his rehabilitation. After all, in the balancing of majority rule and minority rights—in the tension between the many and the few—corrections has typically been more concerned with the protection of individual and minority rights than with the protection and compensation of the occasionally aggrieved majority. However, the needs of the victim and any concern for restitution have also been overlooked by the majority of society as well. As the oft-quoted adage notes: "The victim is the Cinderella of the criminal law." He has been largely without redress for the harm that he suffers. Supposedly the punishment of the offender assuages the victim's wounded feelings and dampens his desire for revenge. However, modern corrections' emphasis on rehabilitation rather than punishment has weakened even these dubious grounds for what might formerly have

By permission of John Hart and Field Enterprises, Inc.

been considered satisfaction to the injured. Of course, even this is denied the victim of the offender who goes unapprehended.

Recently, however, a new sensitivity for the fate of the victim and a new concern for restitution has emerged. In large part, this is the result of rapidly escalating crime rates and the increasing anxiety that accompanies the growing recognition that anyone may be a victim—any time and anywhere, regardless of the precautions taken. This is also the consequence of a growing awareness on the part of correctional officers that restitution has considerable value from a penological point of view. Restitution focuses the offender's attention on the harm he has caused. It forces him to come to grips with the consequences of his antisocial behavior. A variety of restitution schemes have recently been proposed. However, with the exception of restitution as a condition of a pretrial diversion program, all of these schemes have serious defects.

One scheme would call for restitution as a condition for probation: only when the convicted offender has provided compensation to the victim is he eligible for probation. The problem with this scheme, as with so many other restitution schemes, is that it is dependent to a great extent upon the offender's ability to give redress; as a consequence, it clearly favors the rich and willing over the poor and willing.[83]

Another scheme would be to give a portion of the fines collected to the victim. After all, there is no logical or penological justification for the retention by the state of the entire sum levied upon the offender. The use of this economic sanction as a rehabilitative measure would bring home to the offender the price charged for his transgression and give him an increased awareness of his responsibility to the individual he has harmed. However, as with restitution for probation, the obvious drawback of this proposal is that it again favors those with the ability to pay over those without this economic advantage. To minimize the economic advantage more affluent offenders enjoy under these schemes, other proposals advance day fine systems or attachment of prison earnings. But day fine systems are dependent upon the availability of suitable and remunerative work, often lacking in those rural areas where prisons are typically situated. Likewise, attachment of prison earnings can function effectively only when the offender is adequately remunerated for his labor while incarcerated, something the present state of prison industries is unable to do.

Still other schemes are proposed, including both private and public insurance plans. These plans have a number of advantages. First, they can satisfy immediately the victim's claim to compensation without reference to the means or desires of the offender. Second, they provide a comparatively uncomplicated claims procedure. And third, they can provide relief to many victims of unknown, unapprehended offenders. Such insurance programs, however, allow the offender to ignore the consequences of his harmful acts and are therefore less penologically valuable. Likewise, they are vulnerable to fraud when supposed "victims" blame unknown "offenders" for their own acts of carelessness or malfeasance.

Restitution through pretrial diversion programs can avoid almost all of these problems. It forces the offender to come to terms with the harm his criminal act has caused. By minimizing the offender's penetration into the criminal justice system, it spares him a conviction that makes employment—so necessary to provide restitution—more difficult. If he is unemployed or possessed of an addiction problem, pretrial diversion's guidance and assistance services can help him overcome these problems and become positively directed and productive.

The advantages of pretrial diversion should not be allowed to obscure its shortcomings, however. Although it is proposed as a method by which to reduce the heavy volume of cases that the criminal justice system must process and which leads it to embrace the crime control model and the plea bargain, diversion is itself based on crime control model principles. Thus, pretrial diversion involves the disposition of criminal charges without a conviction. The disposition does not imply a finding of not guilty; rather, it often assumes guilt. This, of course, runs contrary to the tenets of the due process model, but this is only the beginning. Program restrictions regarding which offenders are eligible for diversion may violate the equal protection clause of the Fourteenth Amendment of the United States Constitution. The defendant's right to a speedy trial must be waived in order to have sentence withheld. As with presentence investigations, the issue of self-incrimination emerges when the defendant, still presumed to be innocent, may be required to discuss the details of his alleged offense with his diversion counselor. Pretrial diversion may also dilute the deterrent effect of punishment.

Studies of existing diversion programs generally show that pretrial diversion does not adversely affect specific deterrence; that is, it does not lead to higher recidivism rates among participating offenders. In fact, quite the opposite is the case. The results of the Vera Institute's Manhattan Court Employment Project show that the rearrest rate over a twelve-month period for offenders successfully completing diversion programs was 15.8 percent, as compared to 46.1 percent for a comparison control group taken from the general court population.[84] However, as we noted earlier in this chapter, deterrence can be specific or general, and the effect of pretrial diversion programs on general deterrence is much more problematic. The same question of the effect on general deterrence is, of course, raised by probation. However, with pretrial diversion, it becomes much more acute. After all, with probation, the offender is at least convicted, and as Herbert Packer points out, "The very fact of criminal conviction is itself a form of punishment, particularly to the relatively law-abiding citizen."[85] Pretrial diversion removes even the punishment of conviction, and the effect this will have on general deterrence remains to be determined.

Courts and corrections in the American criminal justice system have a primary responsibility to represent the interests and rights of individuals and minorities who for whatever reason find themselves accused or convicted by the majority of society for violating its laws. As both Chapter 4 and this chapter should by now have made abundantly clear, courts and corrections have not been particularly successful in preserving this balance between majority rule and minority rights. Corrections especially has failed. Unclear concerning what the proper purpose of penal sanctions is, corrections has engaged concurrently in retribution, deterrence, and rehabilitation. In doing so it has merely neutralized the benefits that each of these justifications may provide. It has produced in those under its control feelings of frustration, demoralization, cynicism, and illegitimacy, which are all too frequently reflected in high rates of recidivism. Rather than protecting and promoting the interests and rights of those under its control, corrections has far too often added to their burden, and thereby ultimately to society's.

Community-based correctional alternatives have both problems and promise. However, until such time as the community is willing fully to accept the offender into its midst for rehabilitation and support these efforts with adequate manpower and revenues, the problems are likely to outweigh the promise. Even pretrial diversion, with its presumption of guilt and its clear identification with the crime control model, is not altogether protective of the individual. As a consequence, the need for police departments through police-community relations programs to develop a sensitivity for the rights and interests of individuals and minorities adequate to offset the failure of courts and corrections becomes increasingly more apparent. Only in this way will the American commitment to a balance between the few and the many, the rights of the minority and the power of the majority, be preserved in the criminal justice system.

NOTES

1. David Rothberg, "Prison Is a Real Education," *New York Times*, December 3, 1971.

2. President's Commission on Law Enforcement and Administration of Justice, *Task Force Report: Corrections* (Washington, D.C.: U.S. Government Printing Office, 1967), p. 16.

3. U.S. Department of Justice, *Crime in the United States: Uniform Crime Reports, 1972* (Washington, D.C.: U.S. Government Printing Office, 1973), p. 36.

4. Max Farrand, ed., *The Records of the Federal Convention of 1787*, (New Haven: Yale University Press, 1937), vol. 1, p. 288.

5. Herbert Packer, *The Limits of the Criminal Sanction* (Stanford: Stanford University Press, 1968), p. 39.

6. Ibid.

7. James S. Campbell, Joseph R. Sahid, and David P. Stang, *Law and Order Reconsidered*, A Staff Report to the National Commission on the Causes and Prevention of Violence (Washington, D.C.: U.S. Government Printing Office, 1973), pp. 341–342.

8. National Advisory Commission on Criminal Justice Standards and Goals, *Report on Corrections* (Washington, D.C.: U.S. Government Printing Office, 1973), p. 343.

9. *Uniform Crime Reports, 1972*, p. 129.

10. "National Prisoner Statistics," *National Prisoner Statistics Bulletin,* 49 (April 1972):6.

11. *Uniform Crime Reports, 1972,* p. 130.

12. Vernon Fox, *Introduction to Corrections* (Englewood Cliffs, N.J.: Prentice-Hall, 1972), p. 59.

13. *Uniform Crime Reports, 1972,* p. 131.

14. Fox, *Introduction to Corrections,* pp. 64, 66.

15. *Report on Corrections,* p. 343.

16. Ibid.

17. Ibid., p. 345.

18. Allen J. Davis, "Report on Sexual Assaults in the Philadelphia Prison System and Sheriff's Vans," in *Crime and Justice,* eds. Leon Radzinowicz and Marvin E. Wolfgang, vol. 3: *The Criminal in Confinement* (New York: Basic Books, 1971), p. 141.

19. Davis, quoted in Campbell et al., *Law and Order Reconsidered,* p. 577.

20. Davis, "Report on Sexual Assaults," p. 142.

21. Campbell et al., *Law and Order Reconsidered,* p. 578.

22. "Discipline by 'Rape' at U.S. Prisons," *National Catholic Reporter,* April 23, 1969, p. 6.

23. Campbell et al., *Law and Order Reconsidered,* p. 576.

24. *Task Force Report: Corrections,* p. 182.

25. Ibid.

26. Campbell et al., *Law and Order Reconsidered,* p. 573.

27. John R. Stratton and Jude P. West, *The Role of Correctional Industries: A Summary Report,* Law Enforcement Assistance Administration, U.S. Department of Justice (Washington, D.C.: U.S. Government Printing Office, 1972), p. 4.

28. *Task Force Report: Corrections,* p. 55.

29. With the exception of New England, a standard metropolitan statistical area (SMSA) is a county or a group of contiguous counties that contain at least one city of 50,000 inhabitants or more, or "twin cities" with a combined population of at least 50,000. In New England, SMSAs consist of towns or cities, rather than counties.

30. *Report on Corrections,* p. 354.

31. Ibid.

32. *Task Force Report: Corrections,* pp. 56–57.

33. *Report on Corrections,* p. 223.

34. John Kaplan, *Criminal Justice: Introductory Cases and Materials* (Mineola, N.Y.: Foundation Press, 1973), p. 564.

35. *American Bar Association Standards for the Administration of Criminal Justice, Sentencing Alternatives, and Procedures* (Chicago: American Bar Center, 1967), pp. 49–50.

36. *Report on Corrections,* p. 145.

37. Ibid., p. 221.

38. Ibid., p. 231–232.

39. President's Commission on Law Enforcement and Administration of Justice, *The Challenge of Crime in a Free Society* (Washington, D.C.: U.S. Government Printing Office, 1967), p. 166.

40. Fox, *Introduction to Corrections*, p. 104.

41. *Report on Correction*, p. 226.

42. Fox, *Introduction to Corrections*, p. 13.

43. *Task Force Report: Corrections*, p. 27.

44. Fox, *Introduction to Corrections*, p. 104.

45. Ibid., p. 106.

46. "The Public: A Hard Line," in *Newsweek*, March 8, 1971, p. 39.

47. American Correction Association, *Manual of Correctional Standards* (Washington, D.C., 1966), p. 107.

48. *Challenge of Crime in a Free Society*, p. 169.

49. Ibid., p. 167.

50. Fox, *Introduction to Corrections*, p. 113.

51. 389 U.S. 128 (1967).

52. 408 U.S. 471 (1972).

53. 411 U.S. 778 (1973).

54. *Challenge of Crime in a Free Society*, p. 166.

55. Fox, *Introduction to Corrections*, p. 120.

56. Ralph W. England, "A Study of Postprobation Recidivism Among 500 Federal Offenders," *Federal Probation*, 19, no. 3 (1955):10–16.

57. Frank R. Scarpitti and Richard M. Stephenson, "A Study of Probation Effectiveness," *Journal of Criminal Law, Criminology, and Police Science*, 59, no. 3 (1968):361–362.

58. *Report on Corrections*, p. 311.

59. *Attorney General's Survey of Release Procedures* (Washington: U.S. Government Printing Office, 1939), vol. 4, p. 4.

60. Edwin H. Sutherland and Donald R. Cressey, *Criminology*, 8th ed. (Philadelphia: Lippincott, 1970), pp. 584–585.

61. Charles L. Newman, *Sourcebook on Probation, Parole, and Pardons*, 3rd ed. (Springfield, Ill.: C. C Thomas, 1968), pp. 33–35.

62. *Report on Corrections*, p. 389.

63. *National Prisoner Statistics: Prisoners in State and Federal Institutions for Adult Felons, 1968–1970* (Washington, D.C.: Federal Bureau of Prisons, April 1972), p. 6.

64. Sutherland and Cressey, *Criminology*, pp. 586–87.

65. *Report on Corrections*, p. 394.

66. These figures are most interesting, and lend support for the need for police–community-relations programs. Even those phases of corrections such as probation and parole which are more offender-oriented and which seek to correct as opposed to punish the offender so that he may be reintegrated into society still take account of public expectations and

feelings. Just as corrections is primarily concerned with the individual but still seeks to accommodate majority sentiment, so too police can represent the majority and carry out its legislative enactments and yet at the same time promote harmonious relationships with individuals and members of minority groups through police–community-relations programs. A balance or accommodation between majority rule and minority rights is thereby preserved in both of these elements of the criminal justice system.

67. Fox, *Introduction to Corrections,* p. 265.

68. Campbell et al., *Law and Order Reconsidered,* p. 573.

69. Sutherland and Cressey, *Criminology,* p. 593.

70. See Amitai Etzioni, *A Comparative Analysis of Complex Organizations* (New York: Free Press, 1961), for a broad-based theoretical discussion of the need for consistency and congruence in compliance mechanisms.

71. *Task Force Report: Corrections,* p. 70.

72. Sheldon Glueck and Eleanor T. Glueck, *500 Criminal Careers* (Cambridge: Harvard University Press, 1930), p. 169.

73. Sutherland and Cressey, *Criminology,* p. 598.

74. Daniel Glaser, *The Effectiveness of a Prison and Parole System* (Indianapolis: Bobbs-Merrill, 1964), pp. 19–20.

75. *Task Force Report: Corrections,* p. 62.

76. National Advisory Commission on Criminal Justice Standards and Goals, *Report on Courts* (Washington, D.C.: U.S. Government Printing Office, 1973), p. 27.

77. Law Enforcement Assistance Administration, U.S. Department of Justice, *Crime in the Nation's Five Largest Cities* (Washington, D.C.: U.S. Government Printing Office, 1974), pp. 28–29.

78. U.S. Department of Justice, Law Enforcement Assistance Administration, *National Jail Census, 1970* (Washington, D.C.: U.S. Government Printing Office, 1971), p. 1.

79. Daniel Glaser, "Some Notes on Urban Jails," in *Crime in the City,* ed. D. Glaser (New York: Harper & Row, 1971), p. 241.

80. *National Jail Census,* p. 4.

81. Ibid., p. 3.

82. Ibid., p. 1.

83. Gerhard O. W. Mueller and H. H. A. Cooper, *The Criminal, Society, and the Victim,* Law Enforcement Assistance Administration, U.S. Department of Justice, Selected Topic Digest no. 2 (Washington, D.C.: U.S. Government Printing Office, 1973), p. 7.

84. *Report on Courts,* p. 29.

85. Packer, *Limits of the Criminal Sanction,* p. 46.

BIBLIOGRAPHY

CAMPBELL, JAMES S.; SAHID, JOSEPH R.; and STANG, DAVID P. *Law and Order Reconsidered.* A Staff Report to the National Commission on the Causes and Prevention of Violence. Washington, D.C.: U.S. Government Printing Office, 1969.

FOX, VERNON. *Introduction to Corrections.* Englewood Cliffs, N.J.: Prentice-Hall, 1972.

FRANKEL, MARVIN E. *Criminal Sentences: Law Without Order.* New York: Hill & Wang, 1973.

HART, H. L. A. *Punishment and Responsibility.* New York: Oxford University Press, 1968.

KAPLAN, JOHN. *Criminal Justice: Introductory Cases and Materials.* Mineola, N.Y.: Foundation Press, 1973.

LAW ENFORCEMENT ASSISTANCE ADMINISTRATION. *National Jail Census. 1970.* Washington, D.C.: U.S. Government Printing Office, 1971.

LEINWALD, GERALD., ed. *Prisons.* New York: Pocket Books, 1972.

LEWIS, ORLANDO F. *The Development of American Prisons and Prison Customs, 1776–1845.* Montclair, N.J.: Patterson Smith, 1967.

MUELLER, GERHARD O. W., and COOPER, H. H. A. *The Criminal, Society, and the Victim.* Selected Topic Digest, no. 2. Law Enforcement Assistance Administration, U.S. Department of Justice. Washington, D.C.: U.S. Government Printing Office, 1973.

NATIONAL ADVISORY COMMISSION ON CRIMINAL JUSTICE STANDARDS AND GOALS. *Report on Corrections.* Washington, D.C.: U.S. Government Printing Office, 1973.

————. *Report on Courts.* Washington, D.C.: U.S. Government Printing Office, 1973.

NEWMAN, CHARLES C. *Sourcebook on Probation, Parole, and Pardons,* 3rd ed. Springfield, Ill.: C. C. Thomas, 1968.

PACKER, HERBERT L. *The Limits of the Criminal Sanction.* Stanford: Stanford University Press, 1968.

PRESIDENT'S COMMISSION ON LAW ENFORCEMENT AND ADMINISTRATION OF JUSTICE. *The Challenge of Crime in a Free Society.* Washington, D.C.: U.S. Government Printing Office, 1967.

————. *Task Force Report: Corrections.* Washington, D.C.: U.S. Government Printing Office, 1967.

RADELET, LOUIS A. *The Police and the Community.* Beverly Hills, Calif.: Glencoe Press, 1973.

RADZINOWICZ, LEON, and WOLFGANG, MARVIN E., eds. *Crime and Justice,* vol. 2: *The Criminal in the Arms of the Law.* New York: Basic Books, 1971.

————. *Crime and Justice,* vol. 3: *The Criminal in Confinement.* New York: Basic Books, 1971.

ROTTENBERG, SIMON, ed. *The Economics of Crime and Punishment.* Washington, D.C.: American Enterprise Institute for Public Police Research, 1973.

STRATTON, JOHN R., and WEST, JUDE P. *The Role of Correctional Industries—A Summary Report.* Law Enforcement Assistance Administration, U. S. Department of Justice. Washington, D.C.: U.S. Government Printing Office. 1972.

SUTHERLAND, EDWIN H., and CRESSEY, DONALD R. *Criminology,* 8th ed. Philadelphia: Lippincott, 1970.

UNITED STATES BUREAU OF PRISONS. *The Jail: Its Operation and Management.* Washington, D.C.: U.S. Government Printing Office, 1973.

————. *National Prisoner Bulletin: National Prisoner Statistics.* Washington, D.C.: U.S. Government Printing Office, 1972.

EXPLORING
COMMUNITY TENSIONS

6

|||||||||||||||||||||||||||||||||||||||||||||||||||||||||||||||||||||||||||||||||||||||||||||||||||||||||

THE POLICE
AND THE COMMUNITY

Police functions serve as extensions of political authority. The formal rules governing public behavior in society originate as political decisions by governmental bodies that subsequently filter down to the public. The rules formalized by duly constituted public officials are ultimately implemented at the grass-roots level by the police, the legitimized agents of public authority at this level. This makes law-enforcement officials the extended arm of the political system and the link between the rules devised by the system and social conduct in the community. Fundamentally, the police are duly designated agents of social control in society.

Police forces are also empowered by the state to uphold the state's sovereignty. They are employed by political agencies that seek protection from the acts of private citizens that are threatening to governmental authority. For instance, during the social unrest of the 1960s, many self-styled revolutionaries, such as the Weatherman, committed themselves to the overthrow of the state. In more recent times the Symbionese Liberation Army held similar aims. Thus policemen serve to guard the standards of legality adopted by the state from members of the general public who would seek to substitute their own criteria of legality for those of the state.

Crucially, the ability of police to exercise their authority is directly related to the public acceptance of the legitimacy of the political system. The way members of the public perceive their political institutions has a great deal to do with the capacity of police officers, as agents of the government, to enforce the laws. The erosion of support for a political system's legitimacy undoubtedly has a greater immediate effect upon policemen than on any other group of public officials. It is the police who are the first to contend with restive groups that have rejected the legitimacy of political institutions and the decisions that emanate from them. Policemen, as front-line representatives of governmental power, are the first ones to face negative sentiments from some segments of the public from which political officeholders are relatively insulated. Harlan Hahn writes that "if private citizens lack a sense of allegiance to the political institutions that comprise the polity, they are unlikely to respect the position of policemen who personify those institutions."[1]

Classical theory of sovereignty in a democratic polity holds that although political authority is exercised by elected public officials, actual rule is retained by the people. Moreover, the way the citizens perceive the state affects its political legitimacy and obligations. Thus the viability of the police mission is closely linked to essential questions of political authority and legitimacy. Police officials, like all other government officials, must rely on widespread citizen support in order to receive compliance with their directives. Policemen and other government officials must be able to obtain extensive approval of their activities in order to retain legitimacy. It would become extremely difficult for the police to function if there were a widespread challenge to the political legitimacy of governmental institutions or a popular belief that these institutions were undeserving of loyalty.

Public Attitudes

A great deal of concern about the police is expressed in much that is being said and written today. There are individuals and groups in society who expect police to handle simultaneously race relations and civil rights, the youth revolution, and a rising crime rate, among other problems. In effect, the police are blamed for many of society's ills, either for their inability to cope with them or for overreacting or underreacting to them. These negative impressions of the police have caused serious morale problems among active duty policemen, and thereby have made it difficult for police departments to recruit new officers.[2]

James Q. Wilson states that the problem of police morale stems from two characteristics of the policeman's role. First, most of his interaction with citizens is in an adversary relationship. Second, the police official is expected to perform roles that are often incompatible. Although the public has high expectations, they are uncertain about what they really want from him. Moreover, some communities want only certain laws enforced symbolically: for example, the laws applying to gambling, prostitution, homosexuality, and so on. Or the dominant culture group may want some of these laws enforced only in areas populated by members of minority groups or minority cultures. Police morale is also adversely affected when police officers feel that they are ill prepared in education or training to perform the roles and duties that are expected of them.[3]

The common belief among many policemen that they operate in an unsympathetic, critical, and uncomprehending community leads them to isolate themselves from the community and to seek peer-group alliances with fellow officers. The need for emotional and ideological sustenance against what is perceived as a hostile environment imbues the policeman with elements of secrecy and sometimes of ritual and other manifestations of subgroup traits. Louis Radelet supports psychologist Hans Toch's contention that police suffer from a minority group syndrome: ". . . police officers sense . . . [hostile] attitudes by civilians and their defensive reaction is typical of minority groups: they become self-righteous. They seek the exclusive company of one another, and 'regale one another with their own virtues, sometimes enhancing these to superman proportions. Self-regard and pride slide into chauvinism, especially . . . built on a foundation of persistent self-doubt.' "[4]

Public opinion has a bearing on the ability of police departments to attract new recruits. As public officials, policemen often suffer from the stereotyping of public servants as less curious, competent, intelligent, and industrious than others.[5] Moreover, contemporary police officers hold a lowly position on the status scale. Two surveys, one taken in 1947 and the second in 1963, placed police in relatively low status positions on a list of ninety occupations. The first study had the police in position fifty-five. Sixteen years later their position had come up only eight places, to forty-seven. However, Arthur Niederhoffer suggests that one of the reasons for the low placement of police officers in these surveys may be due to the fact that respondents identify the police occupation with the beat patrolman, who is the most visible representative of the police agencies. Niederhoffer concludes that the police occupation, "symbolized by the proletarian cop at the base of the occupational pyramid, is accorded the low prestige that is the lot of the working class in America."[6] To test this hypothesis he administered a survey to sixty-five Queens College students (sophomores and juniors) who were asked to rank occupations according to the prestige they attached to each. What was significant about this questionnaire was that he separated the various police ranks among eighteen other occupations. The results of Niederhoffer's survey differed greatly from those that appeared in the earlier studies. Although the police patrolman was ranked seventeenth out of twenty-three occupations, police captain and lieutenant ended up in the top half of the occupations, not very far behind the level of the professions. As the results of the survey in Table 6.1 show, when an opportunity is provided to make distinctions between subordinates and superiors, respondents are not apt to lump all policemen together in the usual low rank.

However, there is other evidence to show that the police are not regarded very high on prestige ranking of occupations.[7] One of the reasons for the low status of police officers is what Richard N. Harris calls the "moral division of labor." "Respectable" persons in the community fully recognize the need for certain jobs. Disposal of garbage, processing rejected or dead persons, and enforcing the law are all jobs that are distasteful to some members of society. These functions, they believe, are better left to those who are not so offended by doing "dirty work."[8] As a result, police agencies have had trouble attracting re-

TABLE 6.1 How Queens College students ranked selected occupations

(N = 65; 1 equals highest rank; 23 equals lowest rank)

1. Doctor	13. Government worker
2. Lawyer	14. Private detective
3. Psychologist	15. Salesman
4. Sociologist	16. Carpenter
5. Teacher	17. Police patrolman
6. Accountant	18. Farmer
7. FBI agent	19. Plumber
8. Police Department captain	20. Auto repairman
9. Police Department lieutenant	21. Clerk in a store
10. Lieutenant, U.S. Army	22. Taxi driver
11. Police Department detective	23. Private, U.S. Army
12. Police Department sergeant	

Source: Arthur Niederhoffer, *Behind the Shield: Police in Urban Society* (Garden City, N.Y.: Doubleday, 1969), p. 24.

cruits from socioeconomic classes other than the working and lower-middle classes.

Negative perceptions of policemen and police work are nothing new. The following sample of newspaper accounts shows that there has been a historic dissatisfaction with law-enforcement officials:

> [Boston, 1733] At town meeting, an application was made to have Matthew Young appointed watchman, that he and his children do not become a town charge.[9]

> [Boston, 1821] Several burglaries having been committed, some persons were very severe on the Watch, and said "They care for nothing but their pay, and are sure to get that; give us a private Watch." Others said, "A private Watch like the one in 1816, as soon as the stores are closed, would be found at the Exchange, sipping coffee. The only safe way is for merchants to watch themselves." Others said, "Who will work faithfully all night for the bare stipend of fifty cents?"[10]

> [Concord, New Hampshire, 1892, report of the chief] A few years ago there existed in this city a strong prejudice against the police department, which at this time has not entirely disappeared. People who are constantly finding fault with the police are standing in their own light, for they are their servants and they would be supported.
>
> No police department that does its work fearlessly can hope for general favor. Every year hundreds of individuals are arrested and punished for violation of known laws, and it is not expected that they or their friends will call a mass meeting and pass resolutions commendatory to the department or any of its members.[11]

> [San Francisco, 1892, report of the chief] For a long time we were troubled with complaints from prisoners of losing property that was taken from them in the search when they were booked at the stations. After a good deal of trial I hit upon an expedient that prevented all such leakage.

Whenever anything is taken from a prisoner now it is carefully described on the register sheet opposite his name by the officer in charge of the book.[12]

Public attitudes can either help or hinder law enforcement. Law-enforcement effectiveness is dependent upon the citizens' willingness to cooperate with the police and other agents of the criminal justice system. Recent data show that there is a large degree of public apathy with respect to law enforcement. This attitude was revealed in a survey in April 1974, which indicated the actual crime rates in five cities—Chicago, Detroit, Los Angeles, New York, and Philadelphia—to be several times higher than the police statistics reports, because many of the crimes are never reported by the public. The Justice Department's Law Enforcement Assistance Administration (LEAA) completed a study based on interviews with 22,000 residents and 2,000 business firms in each of the five cities. In Philadelphia the crime rate (now including estimated *unreported* crime) was found to be five times as high as originally believed. In the other cities there were two to three times as many crimes as were reported to police. The reasons given by the respondents for not reporting criminal acts to police were as follows:[13]

Victim felt nothing could be done about it	34%
Not important enough	28%
Police would not want to be bothered	8%
Too inconvenient	5%
Private personal matter	4%
Afraid of reprisal	2%
Reported to someone else	7%
Other reasons	12%

Donald Santarelli, LEAA administrator, reported that "the crime survey results demonstrate in an astounding number of instances Americans simply do not think it is worthwhile to report to public authorities that they have been victims of criminal acts." He concluded: "In my judgment the data transmits a strong message of public apathy toward its criminal justice institutions bordering on contempt."[14] That such an attitude prevails among broad segments of society indicates a failing in police-community relations. If the residents of large American cities are so apathetic that they are reluctant even to report instances of their own victimization, it is difficult to expect extensive community assistance in fighting crime or preserving the peace. It must be recalled that thirty-eight persons looked on while Kitty Genovese's killer stalked her and slowly murdered her in New York City several years ago. The gut reaction to such an occurrence is that while it happened in New York, it certainly "can't happen here." The LEAA data show that not only can it indeed happen here, but it has and it will again.

The concern about public apathy is not limited to the police departments of large cities. Chief J. R. Kimble of San Carlos, California, reports that the biggest problem his department faces is public indifference. "We [the San Carlos depart-

ment] are trying to stimulate community interest through contacts with the service clubs, social organizations, private groups, and individuals on the street. We are hoping to reestablish the principle that it is an honorable thing for a community to police itself."[15] Albert J. Reiss, Jr., in his book *Police and the Public,* states that much depends upon the citizen's willingness to cooperate with the police and other agencies of criminal justice. "Citizens exercise considerable control over the policing of every-day life through their discretionary decision to call or not to call the police."[16]

The citizens' attitude about the police is of grave importance to a society confronted with growing crime rates and urban violence. The President's Commission on Law Enforcement[17] warns that lack of confidence among a significant portion of the public has serious consequences for the police. These attitudes affect police recruiting and morale, discourage a policeman's enthusiasm about doing his job well, and may even cause some officers to leave police work. Poor police-community relations, the commission notes, impedes the police in the law-enforcement process. Citizens hostile to the police are not likely to provide information, to report law violations and suspicious persons, or to testify against lawbreakers.

The commission also reported that public hostility has an effect on police behavior. "For example, it may make officers reluctant to act; it may also induce the use of unnecessary force, verbal abuse, or other improper practices."[18] Working in an unfriendly environment may cause a policeman to abuse his authority. The injudicious use of police authority because of poor police-com-

195

munity relations reinforces the hostility of the citizens who are subjected to this authority and in turn instigates further abuses of police authority. Consequently, police-community hostility may not only be self-perpetuating, but escalating as well.

Adverse police-community relations also have implications for a policeman's personal safety. A large number of assaults on policemen have come about as a result of community hostility toward the police. Police work, already a dangerous endeavor, is made even more so by poor community relations.

> Though the number of incidents which result in police injury is a small proportion of total police contacts with the public, the prospect of facing danger in hostile neighborhoods is constantly present. Like any other person, the officer resents having to work day in and day out, frequently for low pay and in danger, for people who often verbally abuse him or silently dislike him.[19]

The commission report concluded that, most significantly, when the police and the public are at odds, policemen tend to choose to join with other policemen for social support, isolating themselves from the public and its changing needs.

The concern about public evaluations of police has made police departments sensitive about developing methods that would improve police practices and thereby gain favor with the public. One of the strategies frequently employed is that of police "professionalism." A "professional" police department, according to James Q. Wilson, is one that is governed by values that call for impersonal rules in the application of law enforcement.[20] It is a managerial view calling for rationality, efficiency, and impersonality. Jerome Skolnick describes it as a view that "envisages the professional as a bureaucrat, almost as a machine calculating alternative courses of action by a stated program of rules, and possessing the technical ability to carry out decisions irrespective of personal feelings."[21] Richard Chackerian notes that the managerial view of police professionalism

> has come to mean an emphasis on standardized testing in recruitment and promotion, lateral entry to allow selection of 'the best man' regardless of tenure in the organization, and an emphasis on college and in-service training. Each of these emphases is designed to maximize technical competence as well as to enforce commitment to the ideal of maintaining public order within the constraints imposed by due process of law.[22]

Chackerian's recent study of public attitudes toward the police in five Florida cities cautions against relying on the managerial view of police professionalism as necessarily leading to improved community attitudes toward law enforcement. The study discovered that, according to the sample used, most of the citizens did not hold unfavorable opinions about law enforcement in the first place. However, highly significant was the finding that where there was citizen dissatisfaction, it generally correlated with a feeling that government was remote and that a professionalized police department seemed incapable of coping with the high incidence of crime. Additionally, instead of showing an interest in law-enforcement questions that are likely to center around fairness, due process, and equity, a large number of the respondents indicated a preoccupation with high arrest rates as measures of police effectiveness.[23]

The preoccupation with crime fighting and evaluating police departments on the basis of their arrest productivity has influenced the police to emphasize this one role and to neglect their many others. When the pressure for arrest productivity in a police department is coupled with public apathy about reporting criminal activity, a curious situation about crime reporting may occur in a community. For example, in an effort to reduce local crime, the city of Orange, California, decided to award its police officers with a 1 percent salary increase if the crime rate for rape, robbery, burglary, and auto theft was reduced by 3 percent from the same period in the preceding year. The plan went on to provide for a 2 percent increase in salary if crime was reduced by 6 percent. Additional salary adjustments were to be made if reduced crime rates were sustained for a period of twenty consecutive months. Interestingly, if the citizens of Orange, California, are as reluctant to report crimes as are citizens of other American cities, then police salaries in this community are likely to increase not so much from their efforts to reduce crime as from an apathetic citizenry who will not be reporting the real extent of crime. The practicalities of this experiment of relating police salaries to prevailing crime rates appears to be dubious in light of available evidence about the lack of citizen cooperation with law-enforcement agencies in urban America.

Police graft and corruption contribute to the poor attitude that the general public holds about the police. There have been a substantial number of exposés of police corruption in American cities. A recent exposé concerned the Chicago police. Following a rather lengthy investigation, sixty Chicago police officers were indicted for bribery and extortion. As of April 1974, forty of them have been convicted while eight others have been acquitted. The Chicago scandal resulted in the removal of that city's superintendent of police. In reporting the affair, *Newsweek* observed that while morale in the Chicago Police Department had nearly collapsed, the police seemed to be less distressed by the revelation of corruption in their ranks than they were by the investigation of the corruption. *Newsweek* went on to chastise the policemen by stating: "They're going to have to realize that integrity must come before their mistaken loyalty toward each other."[24]

The attitude of excessive loyalty to their peers is not peculiar to Chicago policemen. A special crime commission report released in April 1974, dealing with corruption in the Philadelphia Police Department, indicated that the commission was "plagued by roadblocks at every turn," placed there by officers either interfering or not cooperating with the investigation. The report identified 127 officers who received illegal cash payments. Out of a total of 8,226 men in the Philadelphia police force, the report listed at least 400 of them who should have been indicted, fired, or disciplined for illegal practices.

Despite studies revealing that some segments of the population are dissatisfied with the police, there are also other polls and public opinion surveys that show that an overwhelming majority of the public has a high regard for the work of the police. The President's Commission on Law Enforcement published a number of surveys that consistently demonstrated that a large portion of the public rated law-enforcement officials as either "good" or "excellent."[25] However, from the standpoint of evaluating police-community relations, the validity of these data is questionable. In a heterogeneous society such as ours, it does not matter that a majority may hold the police in high regard. So long as there are segments of the public that hold a negative view of the police, then this should have consequences for police relations with the community in a real sense. Majority rule, in the case of the police image in the community, does not provide a true picture of policing in democratic society. The existence of hostile minorities has serious repercussions for police work. Law-enforcement effectiveness can occur only to the extent that all members of the public respect the law and to the extent that law-enforcement officials discharge their duties honestly and fairly. Police work is appreciated most where these conditions exist and least where they do not. Undoubtedly, crime rates diminish or rise to the degree that law enforcement is both respected and respectable.

Values of a Democratic Society

A key to police-community relations may have to do with what the community expects from the police and what the police expect from the community. One divergence in perception and attitude that causes problems in police-community relations is the matter of conflict about police role expectations and police role perceptions. When this conflict takes place between the police and the community, it can be said that there is "dissonance" between the community and the police. But in a heterogeneous society there are divergences in perception and attitude among members and groups within a community, and these differences may occur over law enforcement. When divergences concerning law-enforcement practices are pronounced, there occurs dissonance within the community itself. As a result, law enforcement is often caught in the middle of community dissonance; if police officials perform their roles according to the expectations and desires of one group, they are bound to alienate another. This is an essential problem facing law enforcement in democratic society.

Sharp division among members of the general public about the roles policemen are expected to perform is now common in urban America. A majority of the citizens believe that real police work consists of "crime fighting"; all other police tasks are treated as superfluous. James Q. Wilson lends support to this perception in *Varieties of Police Behavior*, in which he lists order maintenance and law enforcement as essential police roles and dismisses social services from consideration. He states that such services "are intended to please the client

JULES FEIFFER

and no one else." Wilson feels that the only police activities that are worthy of concern are those "which the client cannot be allowed to judge for himself: in short, with police efforts to enforce laws and maintain order."[26]

In "Dilemmas of Police Administration," Wilson describes order mainte-nance duties as likely to include quelling domestic disturbances, handling noisy drunks, stopping barroom brawls, and dealing with street disturbances. Often in order-maintenance functions there may not be a clear violation of the law. In situations where the law is ambiguous, a policeman may choose to intervene on the basis that a form of conduct violates community norms or standards.[27]

Police discretion in the order-maintenance role occurs because of varying community definitions of "peace" and "order." For instance, in counterculture or minority neighborhoods, street-level activities may appear "disorderly" to members of the dominant group, even though these activities may not be in clear violation of the law. Consequently, if an officer applies majoritarian standards of good behavior and conduct in these areas, he is likely to antagonize the people in the community where his intervention takes place for enforcing cultural standards other than their own. The resulting hostility of the residents of the community toward the police inevitably impairs the role of law enforcement. The police are not likely to receive support from these citizens in uncovering activities that are in clear violation of the law. Thus, while the police are busily suppressing street-corner activity that offends middle-class norms—activity that may be perfectly harmless and in keeping with the neighborhood's cultural pat-tern—the less visible criminal activity may be flourishing in the streets and alleys and on rooftops of the community. In one of these neighborhoods where "order" is being maintained, prostitutes may be strolling on "peaceful" streets; bookies may be taking bets in alleys; and junkies may be scoring with dope pushers on rooftops.

Sometimes a trade-off has to be made between the order-maintenance and law-enforcement roles for the most effective policing, and police discretion must be exercised wisely and judiciously. If not, the short-run gain of order main-tenance could be made at the expense of the police's law-enforcement capabili-ties within a community.

In the law-enforcement role the condition of legality is generally clear-cut. When he is performing this role the police officer applies legal sanctions, usually by arresting persons who injure or deprive innocent victims. Examples of un-lawful activities that lead to the application of legal sanctions include robbery, rape, burglary, purse snatching, mugging, and auto theft. In these cases the task of the police officer is appropriately established: he is to make an arrest after an act has been committed, or he is to prevent the act from occurring in the first place. His task is to fight or deter crime and criminals. However, the police are handicapped in the performance of this fundamental role. To begin with, because of the apathy of the general public, a large number of crimes go unre-ported. Second, police resources are limited. And third, the police and citizens are adversaries in some communities. In these communities, citizens do not just withhold information about criminal activities; they sometime provide aid and comfort to criminals.

Social services by the police may be slighted in some quarters as superfluous, but nevertheless these services have become necessary in order to gain public confidence in neighborhoods where compliance with the law is minimal. Compliance with the law rests upon the consent of the governed, and those who must administer or enforce the law depend upon public trust and approval in the execution of their responsibilities. It follows that police officers have the obligation not only to serve, but also to gain the respect of all segments of the community. Hahn argues that with the existence of two distinct subgroups in society it may be more crucial for police officers to gain the confidence and cooperation of habitual offenders or persons who are frequently in conflict with the law than to secure the approval of high-status and so-called law-abiding groups. This view is based on the belief that without a minimal amount of cooperation and respect from the principal "clients" of police officials, the performance of police work can be made extremely hazardous and difficult. Recognizing that the alienation of high-status segments of the population might be at the cost of losing a valuable source of political influence, Hahn nonetheless emphasizes that policemen must strive to obtain the compliance of persons toward whom police practices are directed, even if this causes conflict with the dominant, "law-abiding" subgroup.[28]

The method by which the police can gain the approval of their principal clients, according to Hahn, involves providing this group with community services. This entails performing functions "analogous to the services provided by other government bureaus" for purposes of gaining the confidence and political support from segments of the community to whom these functions are directed. Hahn believes that an engagement in these activities by law-enforcement personnel is likely to gain tangible benefits for law enforcement as well as to provide needed social benefits for some groups.

> [Calls] for such services are most likely to originate in segments of the community—such as low-income families, minority groups, and young people—that tend to be most critical of police behavior. Unlike relatively affluent residents, those groups may lack the necessary means of obtaining private professional help from clergymen, physicians, lawyers, and psychiatrists to meet personal needs and emergencies.[29]

However, Hahn concludes that police authorities have failed to take advantage of opportunities for improving community relations through the performance of community service activities. Instead, policemen have joined in the prevailing attitude that their primary task is that of controlling crime, and regard service functions as either demeaning or inappropriate. Thus, by emphasizing the punitive aspects of their responsibilities, police forces have further alienated themselves from subgroups with histories of negative contacts with law enforcement.

It should be noted that the social service role is not a new one for the police. Police departments began providing various services to citizens who were thought to be likely instigators of public disorder in the 1800s. Police in New York, Philadelphia, and Boston in the mid-nineteenth century "were heavily engaged in over-night lodging services, in addition to supplying coal for poor families, soup kitchens for the hungry, and jobs as domestics for girls they thought might be lured away from prostitution."[30] Subsequently, however, police involvement in these services came under attack by organized charities either because they felt that it was inappropriate for the police to render such services or, more likely, because they wanted to have a monopoly over social services.

The conflict over police role expectations is complicated by another variance in community expectations: the means that the police should employ either in law enforcement or in order maintenance. Some people believe that the police should stamp out crime even at some cost in civil liberties; others feel that civil liberties must be maintained even at some cost in crime. This is the fundamental conflict between law and order. In homogeneous communities where there is common agreement on the norms of behavior for both citizen and policeman, there exists no such conflict. But in the heterogeneous society that makes up urban America there is no general agreement on the meaning of law and order.[31]

Law and order are found to be in opposition because the ideal of law implies a set of procedural guarantees that restrain the methods and procedures that may be employed for maintaining public order. The procedures of criminal law stress the protection of individual liberties by regulating the conduct of law-enforcement officials. These procedures include such issues as the law of arrest, the law of search and seizure, the elements and degree of proof, the nature of a lawful accusation of crime, the right to counsel, and the fairness of trial. Public order, on the other hand, is not so much an ideal of legality as it is an ideal of conformity. "Order" is a vague term, but it generally means the elimination of threats to personal security by controlling criminal behavior. Thus, Hahn states: "the individual freedoms afforded all citizens by the law may be depicted as antithetical to the interests of the broader community in preserving public order."[32]

An example of the conflicting community demands for "law" and "order" occurred in San Francisco in connection with police methods used for the apprehension of the "Zebra" murderers. Zebra was the police code name for the special radio frequency used to coordinate police operations directed at solving a series of racially motivated homicides. Between December 1973 and April 1974 white citizens were being randomly attacked on the streets of San Francisco. Twelve whites were killed and eight wounded during this period. In each instance the assassin was reported to be black.

In response to a terrified and outraged white community, San Francisco's Mayor Joseph Alioto ordered the city's police to stop and search all black citizens who fitted a general description of the killer or killers. More than six hundred black men were questioned during the intensive police search, which lasted one week. The operation aroused resentment from the black community and liberal groups, who were able to obtain a court injunction against it. Shortly after the searches were stopped, four black men were arrested and charged in the case, and the Zebra murders ceased. One of the American Civil Liberties Union (ACLU) attorneys who was involved in the legal efforts to stop the field interrogation practice stated that the incident demonstrated "that in time of stress, a black man has no rights that a white man need respect."[33]

Because public order is an amorphous goal, it is subject to a great deal of discretionary interpretation, leaving the decision as to what behavior violates order pretty much up to the individual policeman on the street level. With public order as a guide to police behavior, the priority for police forces has been the achievement of managerial efficiency in the task of maintaining order. Managerial efficiency is obtained with an efficient, technically sophisticated police organization. Skolnick writes that if the police are to adhere to a devotion to a legal as opposed to a managerial professionalism, two concepts must be observed:

> First, the police must accustom themselves to the seemingly paradoxical but fundamental idea of the rule of law, namely, that the observance of legal restraints may indeed make their task more difficult. That's how it is in a free society.
>   Second, the civic community must support compliance with the rule of law by rewarding police for observing constitutional guarantees, instead of looking to the police merely as an institution responsible for controlling criminality. In practice, regrettably, the reverse has been true.[34]

Skolnick maintains that a police observance of legality would reduce unreasonable police interrogations, friskings, detentions, and other invasions of privacy to which members of minority and counterculture groups are often subjected. Coupled with this change in the orientation of many police departments is the need for the development of new conceptions of the police role, writes Skolnick. He suggests that it is imperative for police to learn why certain groups commit most crimes. With their authorized capacity for considerable discretion, Skolnick is hopeful that the discretion is used constructively rather than destructively. One of the most constructive innovations in police roles, he writes, was the creation of police-community relations programs within police departments.[35] The public stand on law and order varies with attitudes related to antisocial behavior and the way the police should deal with it. Those who hold individuals morally and legally responsible for their acts take a punishment approach to the treatment of antisocial behavior. Those who blame environmental factors for antisocial behavior tend to prefer a rehabilitative approach. The punitive attitude toward antisocial behavior is generally associated with a preference for law-enforcement practices that may be contrary to existing law. The police tend to identify with the majoritarian ideal of order. This is because police officers enjoy support and cooperation in sections of the community where the standards they enforce are shared by the members of the community. This affinity between law-enforcement officials and citizens most often occurs in white middle-class neighborhoods that are representative of the dominant mores and norms that are integrated into the society's legal system.

With police values strongly reinforced by the values of the larger society, police behavior seeks to coincide with dominant-group attitudes and expectations. This is not hard to do, since, in the main, policemen and dominant-group citizens have shared values.[36] Radelet states:

> many policemen as well as many others who hold strongly to established
> values are inclined to react strongly against those who wish to change
> these values. Student rebels and black or white extremists are regarded
> as threats to stability. The larger society actually encourages the police
> to exercise their discretion in handling such threats in ways that would
> probably not be tolerated by more "respectable" adversaries.[37]

Policing in the urban community is a vexing occupation because, in essence, there does not exist such a thing as an urban "community," but rather a number of communities each with its own set of values and expectations about police practices and behavior. Fundamentally there are at least two communities: a majority and a minority one. The majority community is preoccupied with its safety and protection from criminal elements. This community provides the political system with its major source of legitimacy by supporting the system and its rules. The police, as agents of the political system, also have the support of the majority community, especially because the police and this community have the same conceptions of norms, standards, and values and an affinity for public order.

The minority community, made up of racial minorities and counterculture and dissident groups, does not feel that the political system represents them and therefore tends to withhold its support of the system. Moreover, there are times when segments of this community do more than just withhold support; they perform acts that are designed to bring down the system and the community that supports it. Police, identified as agents of the dominant system and the society that nurtures it, are the front-line targets of groups that believe themselves to be maligned by the majoritarian culture and the laws that spring from it. The police, in this scenario, are agents of the majority community and are authorized by that community to apply their standards and mores in a minority community that does not wholly subscribe to these rules of social conduct. Consequently, police officers play a crucial role in the relationship between the majority and minority communities.

Thus, police-community relations is not simply a question of gaining cooperation and support among minority groups that are alienated from government and its laws and those who must administer and enforce those laws. It is also crucially an attempt to resolve the tensions between the majority and the minority in American society. The police happen to be the intervening bridge between communities that do not interface directly with each other. In effect, the police are caught in the middle of conflicting communities with conflicting values and standards of conduct.

The view that law-enforcement officials are agents of the majority or dominant group in society is argued on the basis that interaction between police and the public is not evenly distributed throughout society. This is because the types of offenses that normally invite police intervention are the ones that are most commonly committed by lower-class citizens. Supporting this contention, Hahn argues that law, for the most part, reflects the distribution of political influence within society. This pattern often represents the ability of high-status groups to protect themselves from the stringent restrictions of the criminal code and from demeaning encounters with the police. Thus, Hahn continues, many violations of the law by middle-class people, such as fraud in either commercial transactions or the completion of income tax returns, typically do not entail police intervention or enforcement. And the provisions of the criminal law seem generally to be structured so that law-enforcement procedures, traffic regulations excepted, are directed at relatively low-status segments of the society.[38] Hahn concludes that majority-group citizens see the police as primarily imposing social controls on persons of lower social status than themselves. The problem of crime is essentially viewed by the dominant group as a conflict between "law-abiding" and "criminal" segments of the population. Within this perceptual framework it follows that the majority group may be prepared to do away with established civil liberties of the so-called criminal element for the sake of their own safety. Hahn cautions that "[police] involvement in any popular movement that fails to respect the traditional guarantees of individual rights might compel police officers to become violators rather than enforcers of the law."[39]

Police and the Forces of Change

One of the fundamental issues in the relations of the police with the public in a democratic society is that the police are "caught between those who desire a change and those who resist change."[40] The policeman as a street-level bureaucrat is at the "cutting edge of social change" as expressed by restless human action.[41] Provided with a vague mandate to "maintain order," the policeman finds that the definitions of "order" fluctuate over time. In the course of a career in a police department, a police official is continually provided with a new set of ground rules for dealing with the community. Social change, especially as it concerns people-to-people relations, has complicated social control in our society. The counterculture conflict in large cities has added a new role for the police officer: conflict management. The problems and demands of minority groups in recent history provide an unparalleled challenge to the American devotion to the ideal of cultural pluralism. How the majority reconciles the minorities is a question that not only confounds students of this kind of tension, but also serves as a vivid and real concern to the street-level policeman who must serve as an umpire in the management of social conflict.[42]

Forces of social control operating in pluralist societies have always had the problem of how to deal with the various subcultures. In societies where there is a dominant set of norms and values and groups within the community whose customs or behavior are different, there is the potential for conflict. The question becomes whether social control will rely upon dominant culture norms or upon more flexible definitions. In either case the decision is unlikely to please everyone. The police official is the one who must confront this dilemma in his daily task of effecting social control on the street level.

The policeman must work in all neighborhoods—in areas where conventional norms prevail and in others where values and behavior are inimical to those who subscribe to conventional standards of conduct. If the police closely identify with the dominant culture pattern and enforce the laws accordingly—and there is evidence that they often do—then their contact with unconventional subcultures will likely result in conflict. In a very real sense, policemen feel that their role as agents of social control is undermined not only by the dynamic shifts in social values and direction but also by the conflicting demands on their roles by the differing subcultures. Police, more than any other governmental agents, are at the point of contact for both social change and social difference.[43]

Police and the Lower Classes

In view of the difficulties facing law-enforcement officials in the contemporary urban environment it is not surprising that the greatest tension between police and the community occurs with the lower classes, among whom social change and social difference are most strikingly manifest. Because of the presence of these tensions, policemen are often accused of being prejudiced in their dealing with residents of lower-class neighborhoods. However, this may not be an altogether fair evaluation of police behavior in these areas. Lower-class people may have traits that induce "justifiable antipathy" from persons who do not share their characteristics or their behavior patterns.

Edward Banfield posits the novel theory of the inevitability of a lower class characterized by "present-orientedness." He writes that the "culture of poverty" is produced by "extreme present-orientedness, not lack of income or wealth." Banfield defines lower-class present-orientedness as improvidence, irresponsibility, "without strong attachments to family, friends, or community," and an inability or unwillingness "either to control impulses or to put forth any effort of self-improvement."[44]

Realistically, it would be difficult to determine whether a policeman's negative attitude toward a lower-class person is influenced by racial prejudice—since a large number of lower-class persons are nonwhite—or by class prejudice. Banfield states that although, in principle, "it is easy to distinguish racial prejudice from class prejudice as well as prejudice from justifiable antipathy, doing so in practice would usually require a wisdom greater than Solomon's. Concretely, racial and class prejudice are usually inextricably mixed, and so are prejudice and justifiable antipathy."[45]

Both racial prejudice and class prejudice have important implications for police behavior. Prejudice—an irrational attitude of hostility on the basis of supposed characteristics—forms an uncontrollable hostility on the part of a prejudiced person toward the subject of his feelings. This attitude is especially dangerous when held by a policeman, who possesses so much authority. Unquestionably, a police official who is racially prejudiced should not, at the very least, be allowed to patrol in a neighborhood whose residents are subjects of his hostility. Of course, the problem is that it has been difficult to discover these attitudes of hostility in police officers or to be certain that any aspects of hostility are based on irrational prejudice instead of a rationally derived attitude of antipathy.

Class prejudice—a rational attitude of hostility on the basis of objective characteristics—is referred to by Banfield as justifiable antipathy. If a police official possesses this kind of attitude, it seems possible to rationalize the antipathy so that it is directed toward persons who are deserving of it. Nothing could be more damaging to police-community relations in lower-class neighborhoods than for a police officer to hold a blanket class prejudice against all of the residents.

Racial prejudice, of course, is not only damaging to community relations, but is dangerous as well, for the racially prejudiced officer is not so much enforcing the law or dominant-group standards as he is likely to express his personal hostility toward a group and have his action legitimized by his association with governmental authority. Every effort should be made by law-enforcement agencies to see that their officials do not demean governmental authority by words or acts that are motivated by race prejudice.

Rationally, not all lower-class persons have characteristics that are offensive to middle-class values. Banfield defines lower-class types as cognitive, situational, and volitional.[46] The cognitive lower-class person is one who is psychologically incapable of taking account of the future or of controlling his impulses. He or she is culturally disturbed and is incorrigibly present-oriented. It is this kind of lower-class person who, according to Banfield, is beyond redemption.

Next, the situational lower-class person can be future-oriented, but finds it either extremely difficult or unprofitable. Those who find it difficult to be future-oriented are persons whose lack of education or training causes them to be poor. However, these are honest, responsible, and provident people who work hard and try to plan for the future. Many of America's immigrant groups started out in the situational lower class when they first came to this country. Eventually, most of the immigrants were able to escape poverty by hard work, persistence, and assimilation into the dominant culture. It has been the historic pattern for the second-generation immigrants to rise above the socioeconomic level of their parents. Many successful men and women in America today are the direct descendants of immigrants; other successful persons were themselves immigrants. For example, Henry Kissinger was a refugee from Nazi Germany and came to this country with his family as a young boy.

An example of the person who may find it unprofitable to leave the lower class would be a pimp or a dope peddler. Although these persons may have the ability to hold respectable jobs that would enable them to escape their lower-class environment, their chosen occupation is so profitable that they prefer to stay in the neighborhood where they practice their occupation.

Finally, a volitional lower-class person is one who prefers the lower-class life style. An example of this type of person would be a middle-class youth who chooses to live in a tenement and opts for the street-life culture of a lower-class neighborhood. He acquires a wardrobe usually purchased from an army surplus store, rejects the values and norms of his family, and tries to integrate into the lower-class life style. As a convert to the lower class, this person is sometimes the most dedicated adherent of present-orientedness.

It is essential for police officers to be able to distinguish among lower-class persons. If a patrolman is assigned to a lower-class neighborhood he must remember that he is a servant of the people in that area as well as a peace keeper and an enforcer of the law. He is bound to fail in all roles if by an attitude of hostility toward all residents he ends up alienating the law-abiding citizens as well as the violators of the peace and of the law. Since a great deal of the reported crime takes place in lower-class neighborhoods, the task for law enforcement is sufficiently difficult without having to operate in an environment that is totally hostile as well as somewhat lawless.

The greatest victims of lower-class neighborhood crime are lower-class citizens themselves. They are in great need of police protection; a need that is no less than that of citizens in middle- and upper-class neighborhoods. Without their cooperation and respect, a police officer cannot perform his duties effectively. To gain support for law enforcement from citizens in lower-class neighborhoods necessitates a police-community relations effort that, at the very least, recognizes that there are decent people in every socioeconomic group, including the lower classes.

The conditions of poverty are beyond the scope of the police. This would necessitate means that would increase the productivity and the earning power of those who are poor, and these means require policies and attitudes on the part of the entire political system that may not be practicably attainable. However, police can treat decent people with respect and dignity no matter what their economic condition. It would be helpful if some police officials would recall that they themselves may have come from families that were situationally poor. Reflections and remembrances of this kind may prevent the further isolation of police officers, trying to live up to the middle class, from the community they are assigned to protect.

Police Field Practices

The action of individual officers on the street level have an important bearing on attitudes that the community holds about the police. This relationship is especially relevant in lower-class or minority-group neighborhoods, whose residents are the most sensitive about police practices because they are the ones who are most likely to have contact with the police.

There has been a great deal written and said about alleged police misconduct or discrimination. Although many of the allegations are unfounded, there is enough evidence to support the existence of police practices that do damage to police-community relations. Many of the practices that alienate the community are established police policies, such as the use of arrests for investigative purposes. The use of dogs in police work is especially useful for controlling crowds, but this practice is known to be harmful to community relations. Many of these practices take place in minority-group and poor neighborhoods because the crime rates are highest in these areas. Consequently, minority groups and the poor claim that they are singled out for abusive treatment by the police. They use this to justify their hostility to law-enforcement officials.

Negative contacts between the police and the minority and poor communities provide potentially explosive social and criminal problems. Realistically, it is impossible for the police to discharge their duties of enforcing the law and preserving the peace without incurring some resentment and hostility. The very nature of police work places them in an adversary position with persons who must come in contact with policemen. However, while some police practices are intrinsic to police work and are justifiable despite the antagonisms they produce in the community, other methods used in accomplishing police functions may be of dubious propriety and needlessly antagonistic. Moreover, it may be useful for police departments to evaluate their policies governing police practices to analyze better the competing considerations of police efficiency versus community relations. Some policies may be appropriate as well as essential police techniques and yet be extremely harmful to community relations. The tension that sometimes exists between police efficiency and police-community relations is a factor that should be weighed before establishing policies governing police practices.[47]

The many pressures of the crowded urban environment make it difficult for the policeman to perform calmly and with restraint in all street situations. The composure of a police officer is especially tested in a high-crime-rate or slum neighborhood. In these neighborhoods particularly, a policeman's authority is continuously being challenged by persons anxious to perceive any weakness or fear. In dangerous neighborhoods, an officer may be taunted, threatened, or even physically injured.

> Even if an officer is of the highest quality, his work and the people with whom he must deal may cause him to become disillusioned or angry. If he

is not of the highest quality or if he has not been properly trained, if he is prejudiced or hot headed, he may succumb to his anger or resentment and physically or verbally abuse someone who offends him.[48]

The police official is often the subject of disrespect and abuse because of hostility toward the political system he represents. As the symbol of the system's authority, he becomes the front-line target of the hostility, and his authority is constantly tested. Interestingly, police authority is not only challenged by minority groups and lower-class persons, but is a subject of some controversy in liberal circles. George Kirkham, the university professor who joined a Florida police department to learn what it was like to be a police officer, changed from one who questioned police authority to one who realized that it was indispensable:

> As a university professor I had always sought to convey to students the idea that it is a mistake to exercise authority, to make decisions for other people, or rely upon orders and commands to accomplish something. As a police officer myself, I was forced time and again to do just that. For the first time in my life, I encountered individuals who interpreted kindness as weakness, as an invitation to disrespect or violence. I encountered men, women, and children, who, in fear, desperation, or excitement, looked to the person behind my blue uniform and shield for guidance, control, and direction. As someone who had always condemned the exercise of authority, the acceptance of myself as an unavoidable symbol of authority came as a bitter lesson.[49]

Generally, the most hostile police-citizen contact involves youths. Youths commit a large proportion of crimes. They spend a great deal of their time on the streets, making themselves noticeable to patrolling officers. They congregate in groups, inviting the suspicion of policemen and posing the threat that they are difficult to control. Youths have a lot of leisure time that they often spend in such local gathering places as recreation centers, discotheques, pool halls, and street corners. However, they are a potential source of aid to law-enforcement officers because they often acquire information that is useful to the police.

Their antipathy toward the police may stem from racial, class, or experiential animosity, as well as from youth's natural dislike for authority. A fundamental reason for the hostility between the police and youths lies in the need for the police to receive respectful behavior and the youths' need to assert their autonomy. To a policeman respect symbolizes the acceptance of his authority. Youths, however, have an equal need to establish and maintain their autonomy, which for lower-class gang boys means a claim to a "turf"—a street corner, a city block, or other geographical area—as the inviolable site of their activities.

The struggle for control over turf provides the backdrop for hostile encounters between police and juveniles. The turf claimed by a gang is not only an area for their private hangout, but also the policeman's beat. Police suspicion of youths gathering together in groups, or because of their furtive actions, is supported by common sense and experience, as well as an occupationally oriented need to preserve public order and to solve crimes. But when youths are approached by police authority they feel themselves both challenged and demeaned, and may react with hostility and defiance. This uncooperativeness and insulting demeanor is a challenge to the policeman. Sometimes officers react in ways that may not have legal basis but which nonetheless protect their authority. Police actions motivated by the need to assert authority result in the creation of resentment and disrespect. An interview with a San Francisco juvenile gang is illustrative of this kind of relationship:

> One day we were standing on the corner about two blocks from school and this juvenile officer comes up. He say, "Hey, you boys! Come here!" So everybody else walked over there. But this one stud made like he didn't hear him. So the cop say, "Hey, punk! Come here!" So the stud sorta look up like he hear him and start walking over. But he walking over real slow. So the cop walk over there and grab 'im by the collar and throw him down and put the handcuffs on him, saying, "When I call you next time, come see what I want!" So everybody was standing by the car and he say, "All right, you black . . . ! Get your . . . home!" Just like that. And he handcuffed the stud and took him to juvenile hall for nothing. Just for standing there looking at him.[50]

This incident suggests that the demeanor of a suspect may have an important effect on police decisions in cases of arrest. A study of juvenile offenders claims that police officials are in agreement that "defiance on the part of a boy will lead to juvenile court quicker than anything else."[51] Demeanor is not only a factor in juvenile dispositions but has also been found to be related to charges against prostitutes, speeders, and other offenders.[52]

The President's Commission on Law Enforcement advised that improved relations with juveniles would occur if policemen avoided ethnic slurs and recognized and made allowances for the "exuberance and the naturally combative and non-conforming attitudes of adolescents."[53] This does not mean that policemen should be necessarily softer or more lenient, but rather that they should "allow adolescents to escape the uncomfortable spotlight of constant suspicion."

Other forms of reported police abuses range from simple discourtesy to the unwarranted use of excessive force against persons of all ages. Surveys have confirmed that some officers treat citizens in an insulting manner. The use of racial pejoratives, such as "nigger," "coon," "boy," and "Pancho," angers members of minority groups and develops counterprejudice against law-enforcement agencies and officers. Although discriminatory statements are condemned by responsible police administrators, the use of such language is reported to be widespread among police forces. The President's Commission on Crime in the District of Columbia revealed that "offensive terms such as 'boy,' or 'nigger' are too often used by officers of the department" and that "in most cases the language is chosen deliberately to demean the citizen and demonstrate the superiority of the officer."[54] Nonracial slurs also produce a negative response from citizens. Police use of such terms as "punk," "jerk," "loudmouth," "freak," "wino," or "stupid" to whites and nonwhites alike does little to improve relations with the general public.

Unjustified use of force by police officials—or police brutality—has been a significant problem for a number of years. Evidence of police brutality was reported as early as 1931 by the Wickersham Commission (National Commission on Law Observance and Enforcement), and these findings have been reiterated in a number of commission reports published since then.

The President's Commission on Law Enforcement and Administration of Justice, in its 1967 report on the police, stated that physical abuse is not as serious a problem as it was in the past. However, it did provide data suggesting that there still exist a number of cases involving excessive use of force. For their study, commission observers accompanied police officers on regular patrol in a number of major cities, principally in high-crime and slum precincts, for periods ranging from five to eight weeks. Commission observers witnessed 5,339 police-citizen encounters, which included police contacts with suspects, witnesses, victims, and bystanders. From observing these encounters the commission reported that

> there were 20 instances where officers used force where none was clearly required or where its use was plainly excessive. Of the incidents observed, most did not appear to be based upon racial prejudice. More than half of those subjected to excessive force were white. Almost all of the victims appeared to be poor. They included drunks, sexual deviates, or juveniles who were regarded by the police as hoodlums, and most appeared to contest verbally the police officer's authority.[55]

Minority-group members have indicated in a number of surveys that they believe that discrimination is practiced against both middle-class and poor persons from minority groups. It is extremely difficult to substantiate these allegations, since an officer's decision in any particular situation may be based on a variety of factors. Since a large number of the poor and members of minority groups live in high-crime areas, it is normal that police officers would routinely arrest or stop large numbers of persons in these groups. The high crime rate among the poor and minority groups makes it consistent for them to have a high arrest rate. However, police administrators must ensure that all decisions to stop or arrest persons must be based on objective evidence of suspiciousness, proof of guilt, or threat of danger to the officer or public, and that the decisions must adhere to legal requirements.

A major source of friction between the police and minority groups is the use of field interrogations. Field interrogation is believed by the police to be a necessary method for investigating and preventing crime, especially since crimes in progress are rarely encountered in police work. Police officials believe that by stopping and questioning suspicious persons they can forestall much crime. Minority-group leaders, on the other hand, claim that field interrogations are mainly conducted in slum communities. Moreover, they feel that these interrogations are used indiscriminately and are conducted in an abusive and demeaning manner.

The controversy surrounding the use of field interrogations as a routine police practice is aided by the lack of statutory clarity about the extent of police authority used to stop persons for purposes of criminal investigation. In many states there is no specific statute that defines this practice. However, some states have specific statutory provisions granting policemen authority to stop suspicious persons. Some departments have adopted the policy of "aggressive patrol," which encourages officers routinely to stop and question persons who appear suspicious. Minority-group leaders and their sympathizers throughout the country contend that field interrogations are principally motivated by racial and cultural factors. There is almost unanimous agreement among these groups that field interrogation is a major source of police-community tension. The controversy surrounding the widespread use of field interrogations of black men during San Francisco's Zebra murders is illustrative of this attitude.

The President's Commission on Law Enforcement found that field interrogation, often used in conjunction with aggressive preventive patrol, is a prevalent tactic used by many police departments. The commission also found that field interrogations are occasionally used in a way that discriminates against minority groups, the poor, and the young. Finally, field interrogations were observed to be frequently conducted in a discourteous or otherwise offensive manner.[56]

Carl Werthman and Irving Piliavin found that youths of all races were singled out for field interrogations. Their study revealed that field interrogations by the police are often motivated by suspicion based mainly on a person's clothing, hair length, and walking mannerisms. White youths, for instance, were subjected to the interrogations not necessarily because of manifest evidence of criminality, but because of their personal appearance. The study concluded that the juveniles did not object to being stopped and interrogated for illegal activity: "If you done some thing and you be lying and yelling when the boys from juvy come around and they catch you lying, well, what you gonna do? You gonna complain 'cause you was caught? Hell, man, you can't do that. You did something and you was caught and that's the way it goes." However, they resented field interrogation in the absence of criminality—when "we were just minding our own business when the cops came along." They were especially angry for being stopped because of their hair or clothes: "Hell, man, them cops is supposed to be out catching criminals! They ain't paid to be lookin' after my hair!"[57]

An indiscriminate or discriminatory use of the arrest power by police officials is also a source of police-community tension. Some departments commonly employ the practice of arresting persons as a means of detaining them while an investigation of their possible involvement in criminal activity is being conducted. This practice occasionally takes on wholesale proportions when dragnet arrests are made on suspicion after the commission of a serious crime or crimes in a community. Because cases of wholesale arrests have occurred primarily in minority neighborhoods, this has led to charges of discriminatory law enforcement.

In some cities police employ the practice of harassment arrest when they have insufficient evidence to obtain a conviction or when they believe that the courts will end up giving the arrested persons a light sentence. This technique is employed primarily to annoy persons who are involved in vice practices such as gambling, prostitution, and illegal liquor sales. The use of the arrest power to harass persons also takes place in cases of racially mixed couples. To foreclose this practice, police departments must establish policies specifically forbidding harassment arrests and directing officers to make arrests only if probable cause exists that a crime has been committed.

The President's Commission on Law Enforcement stated that almost one-half of all arrests made each year in the United States were for minor crimes such as vagrancy, disorderly conduct, use of obscene language, loitering, failure to move on, blocking the street or sidewalk, drunkenness, drinking in public, and curfew violations.[58] This practice is more injurious to an individual than an unwarranted field interrogation, since it goes beyond merely stopping a suspect and leads to his arrest and confinement, at least until he makes bail.

The application of minor crimes statutes is often demanded by the community rather than instigated by the police. These statutes are employed as a means of ridding a community of undesirable or unsightly persons, or to harass persons engaged in vice activities. The police, on their own initiative, like to use these statutes in order to detain a suspect during an investigation of a more serious crime and as a way to regulate street activity in lower-class neighborhoods.

Slum neighborhoods experience the largest number of arrests for failure to move on, loitering, blocking the sidewalk, and public drinking. The large number of officers assigned to these neighborhoods, because they are high-crime areas, accounts for the spillover of law enforcement into apprehensions for minor crimes in these areas. Residents of these neighborhoods sometimes complain that there is overpolicing of minor transgressions while major crimes such as robbery, rape, and burglary go unpoliced. Police departments justify a strict enforcement of minor crime statutes in poor areas as a means of keeping order in areas where it is difficult to keep order. In any case, the practice of such arrests exacerbates tensions between police officers and the residents of lower-class neighborhoods.

Police use of firearms in the course of apprehension strains community relations and on several occasions has been the spark that set off serious urban disturbances. Alarmingly, few police departments have clear guidelines on when officers may apply deadly force in the discharge of their duties. The President's Commission on Law Enforcement reported that a study in a medium-sized city found that "officers fired guns more than 300 times in a two-year period and over one-third were during automobile chases involving juveniles."[59] The commission also revealed that police use of firearms in unwarranted numbers of cases occurs in other cities as well.

Police Tactical Procedures

The behavior or conduct of individual policemen is not the sole determining factor in police-community relations. Departmental procedures employing techniques directed at promoting efficiency, reducing crime, or putting down riots have a bearing on police-community relations. For instance, in order to fight crime in high-crime areas, a department may employ a large number of officers in saturation patrols or use trained dogs and handlers in these neighborhoods. To maximize an efficient utilization of its manpower, a department will employ motorized instead of foot patrols or one-man patrol cars rather than two-man cars. These practices, while efficient and economical, have sometimes antagonized segments of the community, or at least have minimized opportunities for friendly contacts with the public, and these are the contacts that form the crux of good community relations.

Police forces are increasingly patrolling in cars rather than on foot. Foot patrols, a service that personalized contacts between a patrolman and the citizens on his beat, are being eliminated by police administrators because they are considered to be far less efficient than radio police cars, which can cover larger areas and respond more quickly. Philadelphia's Mayor Frank Rizzo, formerly the city's police commissioner, expressed his criticism of foot patrols on the basis of efficiency measures:

> The day of preventing crime is over. We have to have the ability to apprehend and this is what we do in Philadelphia. Foot patrols are expensive and limited to a relatively small area even with communications . . .
> We've got more foot beat men than we had before now. Let's be practical. You put a policeman in a residential area and he walks around and says "hello" and shakes hands—and what good does he do? This is not policing.[60]

The change-over to motorized patrol, while demonstrably more efficient for law-enforcement purposes, has at the same time affected police-community relations. Motor patrol has cut down the opportunities for policemen to maintain a relationship with citizens in nonenforcement situations. A study of a police department that relied almost exclusively on motorized patrol found that the officers "had little opportunity to build up an intimate familiarity, much less an identification, within a neighborhood."[61] The passing of the foot patrol has not only denied positive community contacts through informal and friendly exchanges with citizens, but has also impeded police officers in developing a greater understanding of the culture and opinions of the people in the areas they patrol. The loss has deprived the police of an opportunity to present a positive image to the community; it has also impaired an appreciation by policemen of individuals in a patrol area as human beings and "not as a nameless part of a racial, religious, or ethnic group."[62]

In order to reconcile the needs for greater efficiency and greater informal contact with the public, police departments could provide alternative patrol techniques. The use of motor scooters for patrol purposes would facilitate contact with residents. Foot patrolmen could be employed in high-crime, high-density areas. Finally, a two-man patrol car can have one partner walking a beat with a portable radio used for communication with the man in the car. Or a patrolman on a scooter or in a one-man car could park his vehicle occasionally and with a portable police radio walk around a neighborhood for a while. In this manner, a department could have the flexibility of having foot patrolmen using cars to increase their mobility.[63]

Another efficiency consideration has been the increasing shift from two-man to one-man patrol cars. The rationale for this practice is that a department could employ its scarce personnel to cover more area at less cost. The one-man car in itself poses no problem for police-community relations unless it has an effect on police behavior. From a positive standpoint, it has been suggested that an officer patrolling alone cannot be influenced by a partner to display his *machismo* (manliness) in street-level encounters. Consequently, he is more likely to use persuasion rather than force in law-enforcement or peace-keeping situations.

On the other hand, when an officer patrols alone in areas where there is great hostility to the police, his nervousness or fear may lead him to use a night stick or even a gun unnecessarily. Moreover, in these hostile neighborhoods a one-man car may be placing an officer in deadly danger. It has been suggested that when an officer patrolling alone is faced with a difficult arrest or a confrontation, then additional cars can be dispatched to the scene. However, there are times when dangerous situations occur spontaneously and there is no time to call for help. In any event, the use of one-man patrol should be evaluated carefully by departments to ensure that this does not place officers in positions of extreme danger or lead to behavior that is harmful to relations with the community.

In recent years, large police departments have employed special units in an effort to control crime. These units are called tactical forces, tactical patrol forces, task forces, tactical mobile units, or tac squads, but they essentially perform the same tasks. Tactical units are responsible for such special functions as patrolling in high-crime areas, controlling disturbances and riots, and handling demonstrations and other large crowds. In most of these units, the men are carefully selected for their physical ability and intelligence, and are specially trained.

These units create community-relations problems when they are encouraged by departments to be exceedingly aggressive. For example, a tactical unit in a large southern city is encouraged to compete for the number of arrests among its platoons. Accordingly, the men in the unit are expected to beat the bushes for crime. This has resulted in a large number of arrests that were thrown out of court for violations of due process and for other suspect practices.[64]

Since the 1960s dogs have been increasingly used by law-enforcement agencies for deterring crime, for protecting the officer, and for accompanying a police handler on patrol in high-crime areas. A number of police forces have reported that their dog-handler teams have been very successful in performing their designated missions. However, the use of dogs to control crowds, for civil-rights demonstrations, and on routine patrol in minority areas has aroused considerable hostility. In cities where the police make frequent use of their canine corps, such as Washington, D.C., minority-group citizens have made the use of dogs one of their principal complaints against the police. On the other hand, surveys indicate that there are also large numbers of minority citizens who favor the use of police dogs for their deterrent effect on crime.

Because a canine corps can provide the police with some protection in high-crime areas, it would be imprudent to reject out of hand this method of crime control and peace keeping. However, it is questionable whether dogs should ever be used to control crowds, and where dogs are deployed in populated areas, great caution should be exercised in their handling. Finally, it has been shown in several cities that when the use of dogs for routine patrol is carefully explained to the citizens, a large number of residents have accepted their use as beneficial to public safety.[65] Fundamentally, the modern police dog is not mean, and reacts fiercely only upon command. Off duty, the dogs double as family pets.

The method that a police force uses to handle a crowd has been a subject of considerable public contention. The assembling of a large number of police personnel in keeping with good law-enforcement practice for preventing a riot has on several occasions been regarded by minority and perhaps other groups as a provocation. To rectify this source of tension with the community, the police can eliminate the possibility of provocation by holding some units out of sight of the crowd at some distance from the scene. These units can then be released for duty in other areas when tensions are abated.

It is important that the police hold crowds in as unprovocative a manner as they can possibly muster. Many riots have been triggered by unseemly police action. Some riots could have been prevented if police-community relations had been genuinely good. Unquestionably, the police are not the sole source of discontent among some communities. There are socioeconomic and other factors that may lead to a riot, and the police have little to do with these causes of public violence. However, police action should never be the provocation of a disturbance. In the case of peaceful demonstrations, one of the major responsibilities of the police is to ensure that the constitutional rights of the demonstrators are respected. This responsibility includes cooperating with all legal demonstrations even though the participants or their cause may be personally repugnant to police officers. Police actions at a demonstration should be fair and impartial. Legal demonstrators must be protected against the illegal action of bystanders, but if laws are violated by the demonstrators, then official action must be taken against them.

When a riot or a disturbance is in progress, then the primary consideration must be to end it. The police are faced with two alternatives for action. The first, a common police technique with considerations of efficiency and expediency in controlling riots, involves the use of massive amounts of force and the dispersal of the rioters into small groups as quickly as possible. The use of batons, dogs, tear gas, and even firearms, if needed, are part of the riot-control tactics of this option. The other alternative is one that regards police-community relations with as much importance as the need to end the riot. The example of the way the New York City police handled a riot during the summer of 1966 is illustrative of this alternative:

> When a mob formed, the police did not try to break it up directly. They blocked off the streets but left open an avenue of "escape" for the mob. The mob then generally dissipated. No shots were fired by the police in answer to sporadic sniping and the emphasis was on restraint. Despite a week of disturbances, no major riot resulted, police casualities were light, and the department earned considerable praise from the community.[66]

Police Accountability

Chackerian noted that one of the ways that citizens evaluate police service is by their sense of access to government. The feeling among citizens that "one can make claims directly to government officials and that they will be considered on their merits rather than in terms of personal benefits or harm to the official"[67] is related to a high evaluation of law enforcement. The police have the same obligation as any other governmental agency in a democracy to be accessible to the public. The accessibility of police forces is not only a means of satisfying the citizenry, but also an important means of making the police accountable to the community for their actions.

Emmette Redford states that in a democratic society the general public must have elements of protection from the arbitrary practices of public administrators. These elements consist of: (1) notice—the right to know; (2) the opportunity to be heard—the right to access; (3) the rule against bias—the right to a fair forum; and (4) independent review—the right to appeal.[68] In the case of the police, a governmental agency with legal and symbolic authority, a sure way to ensure that their policies and practices comply with the law is to have sufficient controls that allow for Redford's elements of protection. Police malpractice can be minimized by careful personnel screening, effective training, continuous retraining, and competent supervision. The department that clearly enunciates its community-relations policies and has mechanisms to ensure that its members adhere to them should hold down the number of complaints it receives from citizens. Yet despite these measures, there will always be some citizen complaints about police treatment, both warranted and unwarranted. And, in all probability, there will always be some misconduct by individual policemen, whether this misconduct is reported or not. The way police departments and the community should handle complaints—the way police forces should be made accountable for their actions—is one of the most controversial issues of urban politics.

In the American political system, founded on principles of separation of power and checks and balances, the operations of administrative agencies that exercise governmental authority must be held to effective legislative, executive, and judicial review and control. The operations of the police, as an agency of government, must be subject to these accountability measures not only because they are charged with carrying out legislative, executive, or judicial mandates, but also because there are important areas where the police are left with discretion to develop their own policy within broad legislative or judicial guidelines. Furthermore, the discretionary authority of the individual police officer is generally exercised autonomously, and these personalized decisions may affect the lives and the freedom of a number of citizens. Should these street-level decision be made capriciously or prejudicially and the citizen have no recourse against them, then the democratic process becomes more rhetoric than substance. In their responsibility to uphold the law, the police must be held accountable to ensure that they discharge their official responsibility within the limits of the law.

The extent of control over the police by political authority varies with the level of government at which police operations take place. In the United States, although cities and counties are legally creatures of the states under state constitutions, states have, for all practical purposes, allowed these jurisdictions to run themselves without interference or oversight. This underscores a strong cultural commitment to local autonomy in this country, and this commitment has been extended to local control of law enforcement. Thus, other than the ultimate sanction found in state law, authority over urban police departments in both administrative direction and policy formation is in the hands of city councils and city executives. Local political authorities have become responsible for police administration in this country despite the fact that police are primarily involved in the enforcement of state laws rather than of city ordinances.[69] With the exception of the rare instances when states run the local police, the administrative leadership of local police agencies is appointed by the city executive and city council.[70]

Normally, the organizational chain of command in a police department starts out with the patrolman on the beat at the base of the hierarchical pyramid, moves up through the command channels to the administrative leadership—a single executive or a board or commission—and finally ends with the mayor or city manager at the apex of the pyramid. The city council's role in police administration usually pertains to the appointment or confirmation of the appointment of the department head of the police force, performing legislative investigation of police malpractices, and perhaps participating in the disciplining and removal of the administrative head of the police.

This close relationship of police forces to partisan political influence has historically had a negative effect on police service. The exercise of direct control over police agencies by political authorities has provided instances of incompetence, lax enforcement, and the improper use of police authority. Elected officeholders with the prerogative of assignment and promotion of police personnel have exchanged immunity to enforcement for political favors, and, in some cities, utilized the police to assist them in winning elections.[71]

Owing to the predominance of political interest in the mayor-council form of government and the history of graft and incompetence in local government, reform movements have played a major role in providing alternatives to existing governmental forms and practices. One of the most successful reforms was the creation of the city manager form of city government. This form of local government has been put forth as the most suited to offer competent public service. The manager, a professional public administrator, has the authority to choose the most capable person available to be the executive head of a police department; he then turns over to that person the responsibilities and authority required for the effective running of a police organization. "With the complete separation of the legislative and administrative functions of government provided by this pattern of municipal organization, political interference with police administration is reduced to a minimum."[72]

But the city manager form of government is not prevalent in the large cities where urban problems are most critical and where law-enforcement needs are most urgent. These cities traditionally maintain the highly politicized mayor-council form of government, where political interests and interference with administrative agencies are most active.

In recent years, efforts to divest from police agencies the undesirable practices that have been associated with direct political control have sought to provide the police with some degree of operational independence. In order to reconcile the need for popular control over police forces while at the same time enabling them to function independently of undue interference, cities have turned to the establishment of variously constituted administrative boards. However, these organizational patterns have tended to obscure the responsibilities of control over the police, and consequently there has been a countervailing movement for more direct controls by elected officials or by a city manager who is in turn responsible to a city council. The vacillations and uncertainties concerning the most appropriate arrangements for control over the police have occurred in many urban communities.

In cities where changes in organization patterns of control have been developed with the intent of isolating the police from political interference, the changes have had, in some instance, the effect of making the police impervious to the legitimate demands of citizens. On the other hand, where the police are still directly responsible to elected officials, there is a growing sensitivity about accusations of political interference in police operations, so that city mayors have sought to provide their police forces with complete autonomy.

Indeed, the mayors of several of the largest cities, considering police department autonomy to be a virtue, have campaigned for re-election on a platform stressing the independence which they have granted to their police agencies. A mayor's apprehensions are created by his knowledge that any action on his part affecting the police, no matter how legitimate, may be characterized as political or partisan interference. The consequence is that we are now in a period of uncertainty as to the best relationship between police and the city government, the issue aggravated by the situation of unrest in large urban areas.[73]

Neither the courts nor public prosecutors play an active part in the development of administrative policies to effect control over police practices. Although trial judges have acted as something resembling chief administrative officers of the criminal justice system by controlling the use of the criminal process through their power to dismiss cases, this role has not been expanded to include responsibility over police policies. Even if trial judges, in excluding evidence determined to have been obtained illegally, are placed in the role of controlling police practices, the process of judicial review is more a matter concerning the propriety of the actions of an individual policeman than a review of the departmental administrative policy.

The public prosecutor, state's attorney, or district attorney is considered to be the chief law-enforcement officer under the statutes of some states. But despite this official designation he is not generally held responsible for the overall supervision of the police. In effect, the public prosecutor's sole interest in police operations is generally confined to those cases likely to end up in a criminal prosecution. This excludes the non-prosecution–oriented activities of the police that provide a large amount of the total police effort.

Internal Controls

Without the benefit of adequate external controls over police operations, the attention must focus on the availability of internal procedures that deal with police misconduct. Effective internal police procedure is surely the best way to ensure that police personnel are living up to general concepts of fairness and departmental policies concerning proper police conduct. Internal discipline is the swiftest and most effective means of control because it is imposed within the hierarchy and by the officer's own superiors. If properly carried out, internal disciplinary procedures can demonstrate to the public that a department's policies regarding community relations are taken seriously and enforced.

Unfortunately, in many departments disciplinary action against violations of departmental rules occur more frequently and with greater severity than are actions against police officers charged with misconduct toward citizens. For example, a police department issued reprimands to two officers for firing their weapons at a suspect in violation of departmental policy; for a similar offense a civilian would at least have been charged with assault with a deadly weapon. Meanwhile, a policeman who "during a five-month period cohabited with a divorced woman" was suspended from the department for twenty-two days.[74]

Most large police departments have formal machinery for investigation of policemen and police activity. The development of specialized investigative machinery within departments arose out of the historic problem of fighting corruption in American police forces. If internal investigation units were as diligent in ferreting out misconduct against citizens as in ferreting out corruption, they would provide a great service to community relations.

However, these units are handicapped in their investigations of both corruption and misconduct by the cult of secrecy that prevails in police departments. While there is evidence that police are wary of "outsiders," they are even more so toward police officers whose job it is to investigate other police officers. No one is more despised by police in any department than a "snitch," "shoo-fly," or "fink" —euphemisms used for personnel assigned to internal investigative units.[75] The President's Commission on Law Enforcement made note of this attitude and stated: "Policemen all too often, because of misplaced loyalty, overlook serious misconduct by other officers. This has relevance to community relations as well as corruption."[76]

To circumvent the prevailing ethos of secrecy in police departments, an ethos that tries to hide irregularities not only from the public but also from internal control mechanisms, the Boise, Idaho force issued an order that serves to encourage the reporting of misconduct among officers by other officers. The order provides a model for other departments to follow.

> REPORTING VIOLATIONS OF LAWS, ORDINANCES, RULES, OR ORDERS
> If you know of other members or employees violating laws, ordinances, or rules of the department, or disobeying orders, you shall report same in writing to the chief of police via official channels. If you believe that the information is of such sensitivity or such gravity that it must be brought to the immediate personal attention of the chief of police you may bypass official channels.[77]

It is speculative as to whether administrative policy, by itself, can alter a deeply entrenched socialization process that rejects procedures that call for the breaking up of peer-group solidarity. So long as police officers stubbornly cling to the inviolability of their code of secrecy, little can be done, in truth, to correct actual or possible misconduct by police personnel. However, policemen should know that by allowing police misconduct to exist with impunity, a negative image, affecting all law-enforcement officers, will persist.

Realistically, no department will be immune to some misconduct at times by some of its personnel. However, every department is expected to discover the misconduct, take corrective action, and learn from the experience. Law-enforcement agencies are primarily in the business of dealing with the public, and if their efforts are to be effective they must have the public's trust. Complaints by citizens offer the department a unique opportunity to develop a channel of communication that will make possible the discovery of problem areas within the department. The way a department deals with such complaints provides a pretty good measure of its regard or lack of regard for community relations.

Because of the importance of having meaningful channels of communication with the public, citizen complaints should be encouraged. Although this source of information is important to police departments, the President's Commission on Law Enforcement found that many departments have procedures that tend to discourage rather than to encourage the filing of complaints.

> Unfortunately, police officers and departments often regard a citizen complaint as an attack on the police as a whole rather than a complaint against an individual officer, and therefore, attempt to discourage citizens from filing them. Discouraging citizen complaints not only deprives a department of valuable information but also convinces the public that the kinds of practices complained about are condoned or even expected.[78]

Many police departments do not have a designated special unit for dealing with complaints. As a rule, citizen complaints are referred to a department's internal investigating unit where there is one. The lack of means available in some departments for processing citizen complaints is a tacit way of discouraging complaints against police officers.

Citizens who file complaints about police malpractice often do it at their own risk. In the nation's capital, statistics show that a large number of those who reported police misconduct were themselves charged with the misdemeanor of filing a false report.[79] Similar procedures were used to discourage complainants in other cities as well. Another device used to discourage complaints against the police is to charge a person with resisting arrest or disorderly conduct whenever the person brings a charge of brutality against an officer. Evidence of a variety of techniques used to either harass or intimidate a complainant against police practices indicates a tendency to discourage complaints against police.[80] This has led to a widespread distrust of internal police control procedures, particularly by minority groups around the country.

Control by Civilian Procedures

The dissatisfaction with police internal review procedures, as voiced by minority groups, has led to the urging of the creation of civilian review boards to investigate civilian complaints and to determine their validity. Control over police operations as provided by civilian review boards concerns having complaints about police malpractice channeled through a publicly constituted committee of citizens. The boards are advisory only, without the power to decide cases. They serve as reviewing agencies of actions taken by police departments in response to citizen complaints. The right to review includes a right to recommend remedial action. However, civilian review is not a substitute for investigation and disciplining by the department. It is designed to aid a department in these matters by having civilian members of a community reviewing in a nonpolice environment cases of alleged police misconduct and the police department's handling of these cases.

The kinds of services performed by civilian review boards can be illustrated by the history of Philadelphia's Police Advisory Board, which lasted eight years and three months. During its life span the board heard 207 cases out of 1004 complaints filed. Thus, only 20.6 percent of the complaints against police malpractice came before a hearing, the rest being either informally settled or dismissed. Out of the 207 cases that reached the board, punishment was recommended in 24.1 percent of the cases, with 30 instances of an oral or written reprimand advised and 20 recommendations of temporary suspension. On a yearly average, recommendations of punishment occurred in about 6 cases that reached the hearing stage. The board never advised dismissal.[81]

Civilian review boards have had a troubled history. Many of these agencies have been handicapped by insufficient staff and delays in receiving reports from police departments. Moreover, a number of the boards have had successful campaigns waged against them by police associations and their political allies. For example, the Philadelphia Police Advisory Board underwent a series of court suits instigated by the Philadelphia Lodge of the Fraternal Order of Police. Finally, in 1969, Mayor Tate of Philadelphia issued an executive order formally disbanding the board as a Christmas gift to the men of the police department.[82] In New York City a civilian review board lasted just four months. It was dissolved after the Patrolmen's Benevolent Association, representing the largest police force in the nation, was able to persuade the electorate to vote out the board.[83] Civilian review boards have also suffered by becoming major issues in political campaigns in a number of cities, with "law and order" candidates manifestly opposing them.

In several cities around the country there are human relations commissions and other similar local agencies that assist the community with problems in racial or religious discrimination. Some of these agencies serve as conduits for citizen complaints about treatment by the police. Other human relations agencies, while they do not regularly process citizen complaints, are requested by the mayor or city council or even the police department itself to investigate especially serious incidents involving police malpractice. Cities that do not have formal channels for the processing of citizen complaints against the police have, from time to time, employed the offices of human relations commissions. This is a useful practice in view of the unavailability or incapacity of most formal agencies to control the police and serves at least to demonstrate a willingness on the part of the elements of the political system to improve relations with the public.

Without effective means for "someone to watch the watcher," there has arisen an interest in the use of an ombudsman, a person or office, originally created in Scandinavian countries, empowered to gain redress against administrative abuse. Sweden's ombudsman is often held up as a paradigm. He is chosen by Parliament and is usually a jurist. He has eight lawyer assistants. Although he does not possess the power to order administrative officials to take action, he can order prosecutions. In practical terms, his power is mainly derived through public reprimand or criticism, which is enough to prompt administrative action. He also aids complainants in obtaining compensation for damages either from the government or from an official of government. The ombudsman has jurisdiction over all national officials, including judges, and over municipal officials. The only officials excluded from his jurisdiction are ministers of the government.

Complaints against public agencies or officials are made in writing to the ombudsman, without having to have first been directed to the administrative agency. The ombudsman then asks for all relevant documents and for an explanation from the appropriate agency. He can supplement the documents received by holding a hearing or asking the police to investigate further. Crucially, the ombudsman can initiate an investigation without a complaint having been filed.[84]

The Swedish ombudsman's role is not limited to the protection of the public. He serves to help protect administrative officials as well:

> One important aspect of the Ombudsman's activity that is frequently overlooked is the rejection of unwarranted complaints. Obviously it is of great interest to the official attacked that accusations of abuse are not left open, and that it is made evident by an impartial agency that the complaints were not justified. Also, it is of great importance that accusations made in the press, or otherwise, regarding abuse by the authorities are taken up for investigation by an agency free of bureaucratic influence, and that these investigations are available and the true facts made known to the general public. Since the Ombudsman gives the grounds for decisions rejecting complaints, the petitioner will receive an explanation of what to him appeared to be wrong. By the rejection of unwarranted complaints after proper investigation and on grounds clearly stated, the Ombudsman contributes to strengthening public confidence in the authorities and thus to the feeling of well-being in the society.[85]

The urgency with which political control is perceived by some citizens has led to demands for "neighborhood governments" from some quarters. Most of the calls for neighborhood government are founded on the question of neighborhood and community control of the police. Those who advocate decentralizing the police and placing them under neighborhood authorities, elected by the residents of the neighborhood, see this as a way of making the police more responsive to specific communities and to eliminate the middle-class bias that dictates law-enforcement practices. In effect, neighborhood-controlled police forces are held up as agencies that would be more sensitive to the idiosyncratic cultural patterns of communities that deviate from the majoritarian cultural standards and norms.

Arguments against the neighborhood police force concept point out that so long as there is a standard definition of lawful and unlawful behavior as supported by the laws of a society, it is impractical to urge an idiosyncratic law enforcement. Furthermore, there is the question of how a neighborhood police force would evaluate conduct uniformly when various socioeconomic groups live within a community. For example, how would a policeman in a neighborhood department distinguish between the acceptable behavior of a middle-class black as opposed to the behavior of a lower-class black who may be living on the same block? And how is a community to be defined? Is it to be defined on racial grounds or on class grounds?

Finally, what would happen if a citizen in a community with a neighborhood police department that is sympathetic to minority life styles ventured into a different community with a police force upholding a different set of values? What would happen if this person acted in a way that was deemed unacceptable in the new community, although it was acceptable in the neighborhood in which he resides? How would the courts react to his arrest in a neighborhood outside his residence? There is also the possibility that each community will use its own police force to exclude ciitzens of other communities. The questions concerning a multiplicity of police forces upholding a multiplicity of standards boggles the mind. At any rate, these kinds of concerns about police accountability underscore a citizen dissatisfaction with existing controls over police operations and practices and emphasize the importance of police-community relations programs. As Joseph F. Zimmerman points out, police-community relations programs are designed to improve communications between the neighborhoods and the police and to provide for the more sensitive delivery of police services without the need for administrative decentralization or neighborhood or community control and the problems they raise.[86]

Police in Politics

The obscure nature of control mechanisms over police operations has yet another element with which to contend: the affiliation of police and politics. If the function of government can be accurately described as the exercise of power, then the police department, an agency of government, is one of the instruments of this power. Major friction in police-community relations result when some citizens view with dissatisfaction the way police forces use power. The need for police accountability is a means to provide a countervailing mechanism to police power. Simply stated, one aspect of good community relations is to have effective means, both internal and external, to impose a restraining force on police actions. The critical issue in the relations between police and community in a democratic society is fundamentally a political one: the achievement of balance between police power and restraint. From the available evidence of a paucity of restraining mechanisms on the police, the balance seems to be heavily tipped in favor of police power.

The police are aided in their power relationship with the community by actively participating in the political process. This is hardly surprising owing to a historic association of police forces with local government politics. In the days when political machines and bosses ran the cities, the police were known to cooperate with the politicians in power in permitting election irregularities, graft, and corruption because of city hall's power of appointment and promotion in police departments. Furthermore, the police have a reputation as upholders of the political and social status quo. A number of examples of their antilabor, antiminorities, and antidissent activities on behalf of the prevailing policies of the time are cited in support of this contention. These illustrations of political policing by no means exhaust the full range of police involvement in politics. Radelet distinguishes between several styles of political policing: administrative, partisan, cultural, and fraternalistic.[87] Most of these political roles played by the police have served to increase their power at the expense of the forces providing for their restraint.

In *administrative* politics, a police administrator maintains relationships with political decision makers in government—mayors, city managers, city councils, and so on—for the realization of departmental needs and goals. Radelet sees this function as not only perfectly legitimate but also as integral to effective public administration. This political role is directed toward influencing public opinion for the sake of improving the quality of police work and police service. Police executives must become active participants in the political process because police departments cannot depend on political support from an identifiable constituency. For a constituency to be partisan in promoting the value of police work, there must be a politically active group that enjoys the advantages of police service. Hahn states, "[In] fact, the only distinct clientele that occupies a special relationship to police forces are violators of the law, who are essentially hostile to law enforcement officers and who may possess the least political influence of any group in the society."[88]

Police involvement in politics in the narrow, *partisan* sense has police forces playing a part in the spoils and patronage of a political regime. Police departments, in this role, may serve as an extension of a political machine by having officers act as precinct captains and perform a number of services that ensure the perpetuation of the political regime in power. Police involvement in *cultural* politics takes place when they enforce local standards and values rather than having their actions directed by law. This is tied closely to a policeman's discretionary authority, which, in this sense, is more often influenced by dominant-group mores than by other judgmental factors.

Last, and the most pervasive power relationship, is what Radelet calls *fraternalistic* politics. This political role is expressed through police unions, guilds, and social organizations that have provided the police with a great deal of political power in local politics. These fraternal organizations have given police departments, as institutions, the power to contend with existing control mechanisms over police operations, such as they are, as well as providing policemen, as workers in police institutions, with the political power that has been protective of their autonomy and freedom.

The phenomenon of police unionization has served to crystallize the self-perception of policemen as craftsmen demanding freedom from infringement on their autonomy in the discharge of their occupational responsibility. Police fraternal organizations, through strength of numbers and demonstrated solidarity, have been able to neutralize controls over police officials by both internal and external means. These organizations have advanced the principle of worker initiative on the part of the police rank and file. In order for the police to preserve their worker initiative, they have had to fend off restraints imposed by institutional controls as well as the rule of law. Police organizations, through collective action, have been successful in many cases in challenging all actors, either within the police bureaucracy or in the political system, who are sympathetic to the needs for constraint and review of individual police practices.

Police organizations possessing a great deal of political power have the capability to negotiate autonomy with civil authorities in the political system and with the administrators of police departments.

> Police organizations wield power on several different levels. As labor organizations they employ standard weapons of economic warfare such as strikes, threat of strikes, and slow-downs, or rather, modified and imaginative versions of these practices. The police version of economic pressure consists of "job actions": the "blue flu" or threat of the "blue flu," slow down in ticket writing, over-enforcement of the laws, or varying enforcement of the law. At another level, still as labor organizations, they act as vehicles for negotiating and presenting employee viewpoints to management. Finally, they operate as political organizations employing traditional political techniques for gaining their objectives. On this level they have been extremely active in lobbying, supporting political organizations friendly to their aims, overtly working for pro-police candidates, as well as working against those whose policies and ideologies are rejected by the police rank and file.[89]

In line with their activities to preserve the autonomy and authority of police officials, police organizations have devoted their efforts to combating external control over police operations. Their most notable victories came in the fight against the Philadelphia and New York civilian review boards. In Philadelphia their efforts were mainly confined to obtaining court injunctions against the operation of the board, and after eight years of litigation the Philadelphia chapter of the Fraternal Order of Police was rewarded by Mayor Tate, who disbanded the board by an executive order.

In New York City, the Patrolmen's Benevolent Association was the driving force behind the collection of signatures on a petition calling for a referendum on a civilian-controlled complaint review board. The PBA was supported in its opposition against the review board by the Conservative party, American Legion posts, parents' and taxpayers' groups, and the Brooklyn Bar Association. In support of the board were such groups as the New York City Civil Liberties Union and a number of civil-rights, civic, religious, and labor organizations. The surface argument against the board was that it threatened police efficiency and morale, and would contribute to a breakdown in public order and safety by handcuffing the police in their dealings with criminal elements. The pro-board coalition justified the civilian review agency for the sake of restoring public confidence in the police.

> But underneath the surface of official statements was one issue that dominated all others—race. Because it was generally regarded by the public and the press as a means to satisfy Black and Puerto Rican demands, a civilian review board became identified as a civil rights issue. The result of this identification was to make the referendum a measure of the degree of "white backlash," that is, resentment by white voters against Blacks and rights for Blacks.[90]

The vote in the referendum was 1,313,161 against civilian review and 765,468 for the board, with whites voting against the board and blacks overwhelmingly favoring civilian review.

In a number of other cities police organizations have been instrumental in mobilizing a bias against civilian review. In their struggle to preserve police autonomy, these organizations have employed the tactic of suggesting that police accountability measures such as civilian review are primarily beneficial to minority groups and lawless elements. The argument has often been posed in terms of a dichotomy between public order and public disorder. The successes experienced by police organizations indicate that the politics of race has an important relationship to attitudes regarding law enforcement in urban areas. The exploitation of the white-black racial dichotomy has been useful to police organizations and their allies in their efforts to preserve police autonomy.

Ironically, although the police represent the majority culture on the street level, the majority or dominant group in society also does not have any effective means to make the police accountable. By playing the majority off against minorities on behalf of their autonomy, the police have become impervious to controls from practically any source. This poses an awesome threat to the principles of democratic society: the achievement of a balance of power and restraint on all agencies of government and especially in the case of an agency with the extraordinary capabilities and authority that the police possess.

In view of this dilemma, how can society expect fairness and decency from its law-enforcement agents? This problem could be treated from within police departments by providing policies and mechanisms directed toward police practices that stress the need for good community relations. Most important, these institutional procedures must be supported by investigative processes and an open line of communication with the public to ensure compliance. Fundamentally, police forces and especially police administrators should consider community relations as the key index by which to measure the effectiveness of their departments. To do less is to allow some individual officers to behave antisocially and illegally with relative impunity. A firm commitment to practices that will serve to provide good police-community relations is one way to ensure that the police operate within the law and in the best interest of society as a whole.

NOTES

1. Harlan Hahn, ed., *Police in Urban Society* (Beverly Hills, Calif.: Sage, 1971), pp. 24–25.

2. Louis A. Radelet, *The Police and the Community* (Beverly Hills, Calif.: Glencoe Press, 1973), p. 103.

3. Ibid., pp. 115–117.

4. Ibid., p. 122.

5. Vern L. Folley, *American Law Enforcement* (Boston: Holbrook, 1973), pp. 194–195.

6. Arthur Niederhoffer, *Behind the Shield: The Police in Urban Society* (Garden City, N.Y.: Doubleday, 1969), p. 22.

7. Alan Edward Bent, *The Politics of Law Enforcement: Conflict and Power in Urban Communities* (Lexington, Mass.: Heath, 1974).

8. Richard N. Harris, *The Police Academy: An Inside View* (New York: Wiley, 1973), p. 3.

9. Edward H. Savage, *Police Records and Recollections, or Boston by Daylight and Gaslight for 240 Years* (Boston: John P. Dalen, 1973), p. 26.

10. Ibid., p. 60.

11. George W. Hale, *Police and Prison Cyclopaedia* (Boston: Richardson, 1893), pp. 250–251.

12. Ibid., p. 420.

13. *The Commercial Appeal*, Memphis, April 15, 1974.

14. Ibid.

15. "Police Chiefs Speak Out," *Public Management*, December 1968, p. 290.

16. Albert J. Reiss, Jr., *The Police and the Public* (New Haven: Yale University Press, 1972), pp. 69–70.

17. President's Commission on Law Enforcement and the Administration of Justice, *Task Force Report: The Police* (Washington, D.C.: U.S. Government Printing Office, 1967), pp. 144–145.

18. Ibid.

19. Ibid., p. 145.

20. James Q. Wilson, "The Police and the Delinquent in Two Cities," in *City Politics and Public Policy*, ed. J. Q. Wilson (New York: Wiley, 1968), p. 174.

21. Jerome H. Skolnick, *Justice Without Trial: Law Enforcement in a Democratic Society* (New York: Wiley, 1966), p. 236.

22. Richard Chackerian, "Police Professionalism and Citizen Evaluations: A Preliminary Look," *Public Administration Review*, March/April 1974, pp. 141–142.

23. Ibid., pp. 141–148.

24. "Chicago's Rogue Cops," *Newsweek*, December 3, 1973, p. 85; and *The Commercial Appeal*, Memphis, April 16, 1974.

25. *Task Force Report: The Police*, pp. 145–149.

26. James Q. Wilson, *Varieties of Police Behavior: The Management of Law and Order in Eight Communities* (New York: Atheneum, 1972), pp. 4–6.

27. James Q. Wilson, "Dilemmas of Police Administration," *Public Administration Review,* September–October, 1968, p. 407.

28. Hahn, ed., *Police in Urban Society,* p. 27.

29. Ibid., p. 28.

30. Radelet, *Police and the Community,* p. 36.

31. Ibid., pp. 40–41.

32. Hahn, ed., *Police in Urban Society,* p. 19.

33. *The Commercial Appeal,* Memphis, July 5, 1974, p. 14.

34. Jerome H. Skolnick, "The Police and the Urban Ghetto," in *Police-Community Relations,* eds. Paul F. Cromwell, Jr., and George Keefer (St. Paul, Minn.: West, 1973), p. 191.

35. Ibid.

36. Alan Edward Bent, *The Politics of Law Enforcement: Conflict and Power in Urban Communities* (Lexington, Mass.: Heath, 1974), pp. 89–108; also see Robert W. Balch, "The Police Personality: Fact or Fiction?" in *Police-Community Relations,* eds. Cromwell and Keefer, pp. 127–158.

37. Radelet, *Police and the Community,* p. 124.

38. Hahn, ed., *Police in Urban Society,* p. 16.

39. Ibid.

40. Radelet, *Police and the Community,* p. 495.

41. Victor G. Strecher, *The Environment of Law Enforcement: A Community Relations Guide* (Englewood Cliffs, N.J.: Prentice-Hall, 1971), p. 53.

42. Radelet, *Police and the Community,* p. 213.

43. Strecher, *Environment of Law Enforcement,* p. 68.

44. Edward C. Banfield, *The Unheavenly City: The Nature and Future of Our Urban Crisis* (Boston: Little, Brown, 1970), pp. 125, 217.

45. Ibid., p. 78.

46. Ibid.

47. This section relies heavily on the President's Commission on Law Enforcement and Administration of Justice, *Task Force Report: The Police* (Washington, D.C.: U.S. Government Printing Office, 1967), pp. 178–193.

48. Ibid., p. 179.

49. George L. Kirkham, "A Professor's 'Street Lesson,'" *FBI Law Enforcement Bulletin,* March 1974, pp. 4, 6.

50. *Task Force Report: The Police,* p. 180.

51. Ibid.

52. Ibid.

53. Ibid., p. 180.

54. Ibid.

55. Ibid., p. 182.

56. Ibid., pp. 184–185.

57. Carl Werthman and Irving Piliavin, "Gang Members and the Police," in *The Police*, ed. David Bordua (New York: Wiley, 1967), pp. 56–98.

58. *Task Force Report: The Police*, p. 187.

59. Ibid., p. 189.

60. Sally Grimes, "Foot Patrolmen Losing Out to Red Cars," *Philadelphia Bulletin*, February 4, 1971, p. 3.

61. *Task Force Report: The Police*, p. 190.

62. Oscar Handlin, "Community Organization as a Solution to Police-Community Problems," *Police Chief*, March 1965, p. 22.

63. *Task Force Report: The Police*, p. 190.

64. Bent, *Politics of Law Enforcement*, p. 26.

65. *Task Force Report: The Police*, pp. 191–192.

66. Ibid., p. 193.

67. Chackerian, "Police Professionalism," p. 147.

68. Emmette S. Redford, *Democracy in the Administrative State* (New York: Oxford University Press, 1969).

69. See chap. 4, "Police Accountability: Dilemmas of Democratic Control," and especially pp. 63–76, in Bent, *Politics of Law Enforcement*.

70. Ibid., p. 67. In earlier times state legislatures took over the control of police departments because of alleged failures of city authorities to maintain proper standards of order. Consequently, the police departments of New York, Chicago, Boston, Cleveland, Detroit, Baltimore, Cincinnati, St. Louis, New Orleans, and Kansas City, among others, were at one time or another administered by state legislatures.

71. *Task Force Report: The Police*, p. 30.

72. V. A. Leonard and Harry W. More, *Police Organization and Management*, 3rd ed., Police Science Series (Mineola, N.Y.: Foundation Press, 1971), p. 21.

73. *Task Force Report: The Police*, p. 30.

74. Ed Cray, *The Enemy in the Streets* (Garden City, N.Y.: Doubleday, 1972), p. 302.

75. William A. Westley, *Violence and the Police* (Cambridge: M.I.T. Press, 1970), pp. 109–191.

76. *Task Force Report: The Police*, p. 194.

77. Ibid.

78. Ibid., p. 195.

79. Cray, *Enemy in the Streets*, p. 263.

80. *Task Force Report: The Police*, pp. 194–195.

81. Stephen C. Halpern, "The Role of Police Employee Organizations in the Determination of Police Accountability Precedures in Baltimore, Philadelphia, and Buffalo" (a paper pre-

pared for delivery at the 1972 annual meeting of the American Political Science Association, Washington, D.C., September 5–9, 1972), pp. 3–7.

82. Bent, *Politics of Law Enforcement*, pp. 82–84.

83. Ibid., p. 73.

84. *Task Force Report: The Police*, p. 202.

85. Alfred Bexelius, "The Ombudsman for Civil Affairs," in *The Ombudsman, Citizen's Defender*, ed. Donald C. Rowat (London: Allen & Unwin, 1965), p. 24.

86. Joseph F. Zimmerman, *The Federated City: Community Control in Large Cities* (New York: St. Martin, 1972), pp. 43–49.

8.7. Radelet, *Police in the Community*, p. 492.

88. Hahn, *Police in Urban Society*, p. 26.

89. Bent, *Politics of Law Enforcement*, p. 77.

90. Murray S. Stedman, Jr., *Urban Politics* (Cambridge, Mass.: Winthrop, 1972), p. 276.

BIBLIOGRAPHY

BANFIELD, EDWARD C. *The Unheavenly City: The Nature and Future of Our Urban Crisis.* Boston: Little, Brown, 1970.
————. *The Unheavenly City Revisited.* Boston: Little, Brown, 1974.
BENT, ALAN EDWARD. *The Politics of Law Enforcement: Conflict and Power in Urban Communities.* Lexington, Mass.: Heath, 1974.
BORDUA, DAVID, ed. *The Police.* New York: Wiley, 1967.
CRAY, ED. *The Enemy in the Streets.* Garden City, N.Y.: Doubleday, 1972.
CROMWELL, PAUL F., JR., and KEEFER, GEORGE, eds. *Police-Community Relations.* St. Paul, Minn.: West, 1973.
FOLLEY, VERN L. *American Law Enforcement.* Boston: Holbrook, 1973.
HAHN, HARLAN, ed. *Police in Urban Society.* Beverly Hills, Calif.: Sage, 1971.
HALE, GEORGE W. *Police and Prison Cyclopedia.* Boston: W. L. Richardson, 1893.
HARRIS, RICHARD N. *The Police Academy: An Inside View.* New York: Wiley, 1973.
JURIS, HARVEY A., and FEUILLE, PETER. *Police Unionism: Power and Impact in Public-Sector Bargaining.* Lexington, Mass.: Heath, 1973.
LEONARD, V. A., and MORE, HARRY W. *Police Organization and Management,* 3rd ed. Police Science Series. Mineola, N.Y.: Foundation Press, 1971.
NIEDERHOFFER, ARTHUR. *Behind the Shield: The Police in Urban Society.* Garden City, N.Y.: Doubleday, 1969.
RADELET, LOUIS A. *The Police and the Community.* Beverly Hills, Calif.: Glencoe Press, 1973.
REDFORD, EMMETTE S. *Democracy in the Administrative State.* New York: Oxford University Press, 1969.
REISS, ALBERT J., JR. *The Police and the Public.* New Haven: Yale University Press, 1972.
ROWAT, DONALD C., ed. *The Ombudsman, Citizen's Defender.* London: Allen & Unwin, 1965.

SAVAGE, EDWARD H. *Police Records and Recollections, or Boston by Daylight and Gaslight for 240 Years.* Boston: John P. Dalen, 1973.

SKOLNICK, JEROME H. *Justice Without Trial: Law Enforcement in a Democratic Society.* New York: Wiley, 1966.

STEDMAN, MURRAY S., JR. *Urban Politics.* Cambridge, Mass.: Winthrop, 1972.

STRECHER, VICTOR G. *The Environment of Law Enforcement: A Community Relations Guide.* Englewood Cliffs, N.J.: Prentice-Hall, 1971.

WESTLEY, WILLIAM A. *Violence and the Police.* Cambridge: M.I.T. Press, 1970.

WILSON, JAMES Q., ed. *City Politics and Public Policy.* New York: Wiley, 1968.

————. *Varieties of Police Behavior: The Management of Law and Order in Eight Communities.* New York: Atheneum, 1972.

ZIMMERMAN, JOSEPH F. *The Federated City: Community Control in Large Cities.* New York: St. Martin, 1972.

7

POLICE AND MINORITY GROUPS

The concept of police-community relations is generally associated with the relationships that police have with minority groups, and especially with blacks. This is understandable because relations between the police and minorities in the larger cities of this country have been noticeably discordant for a number of years. Complaints about police practices and behavior are most frequent and strident among members of minority groups. Ironically, this comes at a time when police forces are becoming most sensitive to community relations and in a period when law enforcement is enjoying its greatest technical competence and efficiency.

A number of factors have, singly or together, served to complicate the relationships between the police and minority citizens. They include the urban demographic pattern in the United States, which has seen an increase in lower-class and minority residents in the central cities; the historical relationship between the majority whites and the minority nonwhites, with the tensions produced by having two separate sets of values and patterns of behavior in the larger American culture; and the tensions between the minority subcultures and the police occupational subculture.[1] The encounters between police and minority-group citizens are often dictated by cultural forces that dominate these situations and which are beyond the control of either the police or the minority group. These differing cultural perspectives predetermine the roles of each side and lead to mutually antagonistic personal contacts. The police are compelled to enforce the standards and mores of the dominant group in society, while minority groups display cultural patterns that are antithetical to conventional norms. Within this context, they are made to be natural adversaries.

In a more personal, practical way, the police also have more contact with blacks and members of minority groups than with other persons in urban areas.

It is in the minority-group neighborhoods that the crime rate is highest, the peace is broken more frequently, and the residents require the most assistance from governmental agencies. The high occurrence of law violations in minority-group areas has made necessary the presence of a larger number of police officers than are required in white neighborhoods. The large numbers of policemen and their frequent contact with minority citizens have made the police a highly visible institution in minority-group neighborhoods.

The daily face-to-face encounters with minority citizens take place in a number of contexts other than law enforcement. In minority neighborhoods, policemen perform such duties as personal counseling, breaking up family disputes, and acquainting the citizens with the ground rules and codes of personal behavior of the majoritarian culture. For many nonwhites this provides the only contact with the majority culture. Louis Radelet states:

> for most blacks, the white world remains rather remote and inaccessible. The white policeman has made his presence felt in the neighborhoods where all or most of the residents are black. He is visible and he is *there,* and he is perceived as the custodian of "Whitey's law" and "Uncle Charley's system," indeed as the *personification* of that system. Therefore, the police officer—even if he is black (in which case he may be perceived as a "fink" or an "Uncle Tom")—takes the brunt of the frustrations, the anger, the hostility, and the bitterness vented by blacks over their lot. He is seen as a symbolic agent of patent injustice, a "kept man" of the system—clearly "the enemy"—never to be trusted under any circumstances.[2]

Fundamentally, the police often serve as the guardians of the dominant value system and its laws. The police and minority groups are placed in an adversary position because minorities create a strain on society as they press for equity in the allocation of social, economic, and political rewards. By challenging the system, and by the methods used to realize change, some minority groups have come in frequent conflict with the police. The confrontations that arise out of the challenges to "old" value systems have had elements of hostility and danger in them, and this has caused police-minority relationships to be governed by distrust, anxiety, and hatred. "The police and some minority groups often view each other as enemies—each group representing an obstacle to what the other is trying to achieve."[3]

Police contact with black citizens has probably been the most negative of all police-minority group interaction. Jack Kuykendall believes that this is caused by the intense visibility and concentration of blacks and the fact that they are the principal power-challenge group in society. He writes:

> Their use of pressure tactics has resulted in rewards being administered by the dominant group. Blacks have institutionalized militancy through white recognition, and other minorities are emulating black successes. However, the blacks' adaptive capacity is limited and has not correspondingly increased with the success of pressure tactics. Therefore blacks become even a greater threat because power is redistributed only on the basis of institutionalized aggression.[4]

The theory that explains police-minority group conflict in terms of the broader conflict between dominant-group power and those who seek a reallocation of power focuses on the law—what it stands for and how it is applied—as the source of the conflict. It is held that the law is an instrument of dominant-group interests, which includes the regulation of individual behavior and the allocation of power in society. In effect, the law serves the dominant group in two ways: first, "power laws" ensure the ascendancy of the dominant group; second, laws that regulate individual behavior punish individual deviancy—behavior found reprehensible by the dominant group. Consequently, minority groups are handicapped when they compete for power, and their behavior in seeking power is often found to be in violation of laws governing personal conduct. These frustrations have resulted in a great deal of personal and social disorganization in minority cultures. In compensation for the scarcity of legitimate structures for their members, minorities have developed illegitimate opportunity structures. Thus, the theory maintains, with laws often set against minority groups, they are inevitably broken, causing perceptions in the majority-group culture of inherent minority-group deviancy. The negative stereotyping provides the dominant group with a rationale for keeping its laws as they are.

The police play a crucial role in the relationship between the majority, or dominant group, and minority groups. When they are involved in enforcing dominant-group–influenced laws they are acting as a power-maintenance agency.

> Cast in this role they have an institutionalized self-conception as a moral and just power group. The police and some minority groups are traditionally in conflict by virtue of extensive and visible minority deviancy and perceptions of minorities as distorted by on-going experiences, and when trying to maintain the power distribution desired by the dominant group they are, in effect, fighting a "holy war."[5]

On an abstract level the police come in conflict with some minority groups when they act as the enforcers of dominant-group laws and standards; on a more personal level, policemen perceive the minorities as threats both to themselves as individuals and to the police as an institution. Thus, in their contact with minorities, police actions may not even coincide with the law, but rather with their personal values. The minority citizen also has a negative perception of the police. To many minority-group members, policemen represent a system that controls their lives; one that discriminates against them and denies them equity in life's opportunities and power.

> The police-minority contact situation often becomes a vicious circle perpetuating negative reinforcement of each group by the other. The police by their power position *are* oppressive, and when minorities begin to exert pressure for redistribution of power, conflict results. This conflict becomes personalized in the interaction of the minority-group member and police officers. When either can be "read" as manifesting what the other already believes, the situation becomes negative and enhances the possibility of

negativism in future contact. Repeated situations may preclude positive contacts of any nature between police and minorities.[6]

Police Perceptions of Minority Groups

One of the things about minority groups that affronts a police officer is the extent of perceived personal and social disorganization within their culture. Unfortunately, the police often fail to understand that this is primarily a phenomenon among lower-class persons rather than characteristic of minority groups as a whole. However, the association of these undesirable characteristics with minority groups is facilitated by the high percentage of minority citizens, especially blacks, in the lower class.

Edward Banfield, as noted in an earlier chapter, defines the lower-class subculture as "extreme present-orientedness." He describes the lower class as "improvident, irresponsible, without strong attachments to family, friends, or community, and unable or unwilling either to control impulses or to put forth any effort of self-improvement."[7] Boone Hammond gives an example of black lower-class values: "The ideal male type in this culture is the pimp or procurer who lives off the proceeds of seven or eight women, and never has to engage in . . . manual labor."[8] Hammond lends support to Banfield's thesis of lower-class present-orientedness by finding that in the black lower-class subculture "deferred gratifications are not seen to be of any utility . . . In a culture where dreams never come true and middle-class oriented goals are seldom achieved, a man's thoughts do not go too far into the future."[9]

The police officer who is assigned to a lower-class, minority neighborhood is often unprepared for the environment he encounters. Recruited primarily from the working or middle class, he is a stranger to the subculture of poverty and especially black poverty. The policeman in this environment comes equipped with his own set of subculture perspectives produced by his personal background and occupational socialization, and he tends to reject cultural patterns dissonant with his own.

> What comes across clearly to the black resident in this policeman's territory is a harsh, moralistic indictment of the Negro way of life, seen in the words, expressions, and gestures of the officer. Remember this Negro man has not been insulated from American aspirations for success; he has come to this big city which seemed to promise so much, and has found no way to even begin to climb upward from his low point in the social system. He knows how he lives and he needs nobody to tell him that his standards fall below conventional levels; he settles for less in every way, including what he demands of himself; but he feels deep dissatisfaction, frustration, and a certain self-condemnation when he thinks about it for too long . . . For the moment the policeman's reaction becomes an embodiment of the hostile, superior stare of middle-class society—of those who have made it, and have it made.[10]

Some policemen are racially prejudiced. But, according to James Q. Wilson, even if there were no prejudiced policemen, blacks and other minority groups would still regard their treatment by police as unfair. A high proportion of violent crimes are committed by blacks. Arrest figures show that blacks are ten times more likely to commit murder and eight times more likely to commit assault than are whites. Because of the high crime rate among blacks, blackness itself is likely to arouse the suspicion of policemen. Although this is a stereotype reaction, it is a standard police job-related reaction. With the association made between skin color and crime, and the high density of residents in minority neighborhoods, nonwhites are more likely to experience an adversary contact with the police than are whites.[11]

According to Jerome Skolnick, the stereotyping of ethnic groups, like the *modus operandi* of criminals, has become a conventional technique of investigation.[12] With a dark skin providing the police with a statistically significant cue to potential criminality, contacts with minority citizens are increased. This kind of police behavior is believed to be unjust by minorities, and they have responded with hostility toward and hatred of the police. The reaction of minority citizens to police practices in their neighborhoods triggers a vicious circle of mutual antagonism. Hostility by the citizens reinforces a policeman's stereotype of nonwhite criminality as well as fueling a reciprocating hatred, fear, and social isolation of the police from the minority community. In the ghetto, the police are viewed as an army of occupation; for the policeman in the ghetto, his job is one of unending combat. From the vantage point of both the minority-group citizen and the police officer, their relationship is warfare—enemy to enemy.[13]

The hostility the police encounter in minority neighborhoods, expressed by verbal as well as physical abuse, has made fear an important element in police work in these areas. Fear for their personal safety has given rise to two types of police behavioral patterns. One has been an avoidance of as much contact as possible with minority-group residents, to the extent of overlooking certain crimes and proceeding with extreme caution in answering calls for assistance.[14] The second type of fear-induced behavior is overly aggressive action. An extreme example of overaggressive action is provided by Algernon Black when he relates an incident that occurred when two officers responded to a call from a woman who said that three black men were burglarizing an apartment in her building. The officers knocked on the door of the apartment and shouted, "Open up, police!" Receiving no answer, one of the officers shot the lock out of the door and then kicked it open. The second policeman charged into the apartment firing his revolver in all directions. When the shooting had stopped, the officers found two black men lying flat on the floor and one black man hiding in a closet. The men had avoided the police bullets, which were fired at chest height, by falling to the floor and hiding in the closet. A search of the apartment revealed no evidence of illegal behavior. Further investigation revealed that the three men were simply renting the apartment.[15]

Although police overreaction has been a main contributor to police-minority community tensions, policemen defend this kind of behavior, claiming that it is both vital and proper and denying that it is reflective of racial prejudice.[16] They cite cases of ambushes of policemen by minority persons and minority over-reaction to routine police practices as reasons for police fear and hostility. The personal danger to police officers, black and white alike, has in large measure caused some policemen to overreact in minority neighborhoods. A young officer in a California department, who is also a graduate student at a local academic institution, described how the hostility of minority citizens changed his own attitude toward them:

> I was a college graduate before I joined the department. . . . All through the Academy I couldn't wait to get out on the street to make certain that all of the people got even-handed treatment. I was really eager to right all the wrongs in society. But, being on the streets changed all that. . . . The hatred, the unreasoning hostility that blacks hold for police changed that. . . . They have a wall between themselves and us. There's just no getting through. . . . They would just as soon see you dead than doing your job. You should see the hatred. . . . They insult you and taunt you and threaten you. You take your life in your hands to be out there. And it doesn't make any difference if you're a white or a black cop. The attitude of the people toward all cops is the same. If anything, they give black cops a harder time. . . .

The policeman's job personality is strongly influenced by both the middle-class values he holds and the occupational norms and expectations he acquires. Police organizations are social-control agencies responsible for combating criminal activity and maintaining order. They perform their functions through the enforcement of laws; but criminal law is both substantive and procedural. Substantive laws define criminal acts while procedural laws, to some extent, determine guidelines for police behavior. In maintaining order, a sense of social appropriateness is as much a part of a policeman's frame of reference as is the criminal law. Consequently, police responses are not just circumscribed by the law, but are often a function of police perceptions of what constitutes public order as well as an organizational responsiveness to a cultural criteria of un-acceptable levels of order.

In many ways it is the police organization that provides its members with the basic values that influence occupational behavior. The police organization, like other formal organizations, has its own normative standards, customs, socialization process, and goals. Police organizations provide their personnel with the definition of standards of acceptable performance, socialize them with the traits of curiosity and suspiciousness as essential skill requisites, and sensi-tize the members of the organization to stereotype characteristics as cues to potential criminality. Thus, when the policeman goes out into the streets to perform his job, he is imbued with occupational pressures that define his effi-ciency on the basis of apprehensions, and in order to meet the productivity ex-pectation of the organization he relies heavily on such occupationally socialized attributes as suspicion and stereotyping.

Working alone or in pairs on the streets, policemen are continuously aware of the dangerous nature of their job as well as conscious of their authority position. The aspects of danger and the need to maintain authority force police officers to seek to gain and maintain control in every street-level encounter. To this end an officer is willing and able to use force. Furthermore, a policeman has to perform a variety of roles in a wide range of situations. As a result, he exercises a great deal of personal discretion.

> This provides a latitude in responding to calls, but can also result in insufficient control over the response employed by the officer. In many situations the role gives the officer the opportunity to do exactly what his personal values dictate: He becomes the sole arbitor of guilt or innocence —he becomes the "law."[17]

In addition to the police occupational subculture that shapes the policeman's job personality, the characteristics of his personal background and the attitudes of the dominant culture play a determining role in an officer's street behavior. The attitudes of large segments of the dominant white society toward minority-group gains in political power in recent years have had an effect on the way the police treat minority citizens in their daily encounters. This is because many policemen hold the same views toward minority citizens as do other members of the white middle- and working-class society. And if the prevailing dominant-group attitude toward minorities is negative, it is likely to have an effect on the style and practice of law enforcement.

Recent political and social gains achieved by black citizens have met with hostility from some segments of white society. A number of working-class whites believe that the quasi-revolutionary tactics used by black groups to gain political power have succeeded at their expense. They feel that blacks are now receiving more attention from all levels of government than are working- and middle-class whites. Additionally, there is the sentiment among a number of whites that blacks are advantaged by practices of reverse discrimination. Some whites feel that blacks are being hired for jobs that formerly would have gone to middle- and working-class whites. For these reasons, many white people believe that they are now the "forgotten Americans" and have come to resent blacks for what they perceive as gains achieved at their expense. The support shown by a large number of white working-class persons for George Wallace in the 1968 presidential election and in the 1972 Democratic primaries provides an indication of the frustration of this group of citizens at what they see as a "benign neglect" of their needs and demands by the American political system. White backlash is of particular significance because a large number of police officers come from middle- and working-class backgrounds and undoubtedly bring their class values and perceptions to their jobs.[18]

A fundamental reason for police-minority tensions is that there is a high degree of separation between the dominant conventional culture, which produces most policemen, and minority culture—especially the lower-class or poverty-level black subculture. Victor Strecher states that policemen working in a black ghetto are subjected to a culture shock. He describes culture shock as a "personal disorientation through the loss of familiar cues [which] is due to unprecedented working problems as well as to the cultural strangeness and resulting communications problems."[19] He adds that "[whenever] a policeman works in a social setting greatly different from the one in which he was born and reared, he faces many of the same tensions and complexities as those encountered by foreign service personnel working for the first time in a strange country."[20]

Strecher believes that the culture shock syndrome goes through five discernible stages and the policeman operating in an urban ghetto undergoes each of the stages. The first stage, called the honeymoon period, is when the officer is fascinated with the novelty of a strange culture. This stage is characterized by polite, friendly, and self-effacing behavior by the stranger in a new culture—a working- or middle-class policeman in a lower-class black neighborhood. The second stage consists of a long-run confrontation with the real conditions of life in a strange culture. The individual going through the second stage of culture shock generally manifests hostile and aggressive behavior to the new culture and its people. He seeks out others who are experiencing this phase of culture shock and with them belabors the "shortcomings" of the new locale. This is a critical period for the policeman in a ghetto: "Some never do adjust to the strange culture; they either leave the environment—voluntarily or involuntarily—or suffer debilitating emotional problems and consequently become ineffective in their relations wtih the local population."[21]

The third stage is when there is a genuine beginning of acceptance of the new culture. "He may take a superior attitude to the local people, but he will joke about their behavior rather than bitterly criticize it. He is on his way to recovery."[22] Next comes the phase of almost total adjustment. This is when the individual officer "accepts the customs of the other culture as just another way of living."[23] Finally, even though an individual may have adjusted as completely as he can to a new culture, a phase called "culture fatigue" may ensue. Culture fatigue is a phenomenon experienced by Americans living overseas and takes the form of physical and emotional exhaustion produced by a number of minute adjustments to an alien culture. Culture fatigue may induce a return of a negative attitude toward a foreign culture, and for policemen, as for American business and government personnel in a foreign country, it means a depreciation of all aspects of the foreign culture.

> There is nothing quite so disruptive as a set of experiences which challenge one's working assumptions about the nature of the world and the people in it. Nor does the personal difficulty caused by the initial sub-cultural contact end the officer's problems of adjustment if he weathers the attack of cultural shock. Recent experience indicates that later, more enduring inter-cultural tensions often follow the strains of early adjustment.[24]

Strecher believes that cultural dissonance is at the root of police-minority tensions. And the psychological incapacity to adjust to an alien culture is a vexing problem and one that is not easily solved.

Minority Groups' Perceptions of Police

Although blacks are the most outspoken about discrimination, other minority groups have experienced prejudice in American society as well. Immigrants from southern and eastern Europe encountered hostility from the dominant group during America's rapid industrial growth, when many immigrants were hired instead of native American workers, because of their willingness to work for lower wages. Also, near the beginning of the twentieth century, friction arose over religious differences between Protestant Americans and immigrants from southern and eastern Europe, who were largely Catholic.[25]

But the problems of white minority groups have been substantially different from those still facing nonwhite minorities. The barrier between the dominant group and the immigrant groups was founded on differences in language and life styles, making communication difficult. After a period of time, immigrant groups were able to learn the English language and adopt the dominant-group life style, and were, to a large extent, assimilated into the American mainstream.[26] This has not been the case with the nonwhite minorities, whose skin color has retained their identifiability as a distinct group. Moreover, the inability of large segments of the nonwhite minorities to escape lower-class status has perpetuated a life style in their environment found unacceptable by the dominant group and the police who enforce its laws.

The negative contact with police experienced by nonwhite minority citizens seems to be related to the extent of their density in a community. For this reason, some Chicanos have left the southwestern United States, where they are highly concentrated, for other sections of the country. They have relocated in such cities as Chicago, Detroit, and St. Paul, Minnesota, where they have encountered less discrimination, apparently because of the sparseness of Chicanos in these localities.[27]

Because many nonwhite minorities tend to live in fairly segregated areas and become "ghettoized," police have developed stereotypes about the characteristics of each individual group to provide them with clues about their potential unlawful behavior. For example, police seem to be suspicious of American Indians concerning crimes involving alcohol and sex, and are likely to label the high Indian crime rate as directly related to their need to support their drug and alcohol usage. Oriental Americans are sometimes stereotyped as chronic gamblers, although their overall crime rate is low. Spanish-speaking Americans are perceived as sneaky, dishonest, immoral, heavy drinkers, and heavy drug users.[28]

However, most policemen hold a higher personal opinion of most other minority groups than they do of blacks. A Denver survey asked police officers for their personal feelings about blacks, Jews, and Spanish-named citizens. The results of the survey revealed that the officers indicated the least amount of prejudice against Jews and the most prejudice against blacks; however, some of them felt that the demands for equality by Spanish-named people were more unreasonable than those by the black community.[29] The findings of the Denver study support the contention that the amount of prejudice that an individual encounters is directly related to the darkness of one's skin. For instance, a white, cultured Chicano with a fluent command of the English language will likely meet with very little, if any, prejudiced treatment in America.[30]

Oddly enough, the Denver study also revealed that Chicanos seemed to hold more negative attitudes toward police than did blacks in the survey, even though the police indicated that they were less prejudiced toward Chicanos. In Denver, 24 percent of the Spanish-named people interviewed claimed to have experienced bad police treatment, and 15 percent stated that they had experienced brutality. Of the black respondents, only 10 percent said that they had encountered improper treatment from the police, while 9 percent claimed to have experienced police brutality. When asked to rate police efficiency in their respective neighborhoods, 12 percent of the black respondents and 11 percent of the Spanish-named respondents gave the police an "excellent" rating, but nearly twice as many Spanish-named respondents rated police efficiency poorly, 13 percent of them as compared to 7 percent of the black respondents.[31]

For purposes of this discussion, four minority groups will be singled out and examined for their complaints against the police and their relationship with law-enforcement officials: American Indians, Orientals, Spanish-speaking Americans, and blacks.

American Indian complaints against the police generally include the indifference of law-enforcement officials in maintaining order in the towns and cities where Indians live; the tendency of officials to be harsher with Indian violators than with white offenders; the lack of concern when Indians commit crimes against other Indians, but a severe response to Indian violations against whites; the application of excessive force in making arrests; and the "rolling" of intoxicated Indians by law-enforcement officials.

Oriental-Americans have enjoyed a low crime rate, and the police do not consider them a law-enforcement problem. Police officials attribute the social control mechanisms of the Oriental family as the major reason for their low crime rate. In recent years, however, there has been an increase in criminality among young Chinese-Americans living in the crowded Chinatown of San Francisco. There has been a rising incidence of youth gangs, and these gangs have committed crimes of violence and extortion against rival gangs and Chinese merchants in that section of San Francisco. The reason for the growing crime rate among young Chinese in the major Chinatowns of the West Coast may be the influx of large numbers of legal and illegal Chinese immigrants from Hong Kong and Taiwan. The sudden growth of population in already crowded ghettos may have led to a "behavioral sink" among a number of Chinese-Americans living there, and this may have influenced the rising tendency of antisocial behavior in Chinese-American neighborhoods.

The Americanization of Chinese youths has created some social disorganization and breakdown in the traditional family structures in Oriental-American community life. Young Chinese boys and girls are now more likely to challenge the authority of their elders and to model their behavior on peer-group patterns. This may account for the rising tendency among some Chinese-American youths to participate in unlawful or unacceptable behavior either by the standards of the dominant white culture or by traditional Chinese cultural standards. In the course of their unlawful or disorderly activities, these youths have come in negative contact with the police. It is too soon to assess whether police practices in handling law violations by Chinese-American youths have been anything but an impartial observance of law enforcement.

The only other way that Chinese-Americans have had negative contacts with the police has been through their cultural interest in gambling. The sole complaint by adult Chinese-Americans against the police has been founded on their arrests for a gambling game that is peculiar to their culture. Japanese Americans, as a group, have not voiced any dissatisfaction with the police. They have felt little, if any, discrimination against them in recent years.

Chicanos and Puerto Ricans make up the group called Spanish-speaking Americans. A prevalent cultural pattern among Spanish-speaking Americans is street-corner congregating for recreational and social activities. This pattern of gathering on the street is, to some extent, caused by inadequate housing, lack of recreational facilities, and perhaps a high incidence of unemployment. Police view Spanish-speaking ghettos as a law-enforcement problem. These segregated areas suffer from the typical problems of the disadvantaged, and the associated pathological behavior that this produces makes them a dangerous environment for police officers, who often view these areas as enemy territory.

The complaints of Spanish-speaking Americans against the police concern verbal harassment and the use of such ethnic terms as "Pancho," "*muchacho*," and "*amigo*"; the saturation patrolling of their neighborhoods; the application of excessive force; and the use of unnecessary field interrogation and interactions leading to what they perceive as the violation of their constitutional rights. The landmark Supreme Court cases dealing with police interrogation of suspects, *Escobedo* v. *Illinois* and *Mirando* v. *Arizona*, arose out of incidents of police treatment of Spanish-speaking citizens.

Blacks constitute the largest single nonwhite minority in the country. Approximately 70 percent of all blacks reside in urban areas. The almost universal belief among police, collectively and individually, is that blacks represent a serious law-enforcement problem.

> Black ghettoes are the most dangerous areas to work in, and civil disturbances have, at times, led to open "warfare." Police resources are usually assigned on the basis of criminal incidents and potentially disorderly areas. From the police perspective, these traits characterize black communities.[32]

Blacks pose a serious challenge to dominant-group power by their militant, sometimes violent organized tactics designed to change their status. Their use of pressure to achieve a redistribution of power has ranged from the legalistic strategies of the National Association for the Advancement of Colored People to the nonviolent approach of the Southern Christian Leadership Conference to the aggressive and violent methods employed by such militant groups as the Black Panthers. In all this, white society and the police sense a demand for self-determination, for black power.

The cultural patterns of the black lower class are the most repugnant and feared by the dominant group. A telling example of the dissonance between the white and black cultures in America is suggested by the almost total avoidance of black ghettos by many white citizens. Most white citizens do not venture into black neighborhoods unless there is absolute necessity. This is not the case with other minority-group neighborhoods, where large numbers of white middle-class "tourists" frequently visit to enjoy a "foreign" culture. Oriental-American and Chicano areas have financially profited from majority-group tourists, who spend a great deal of time and money in their restaurants, curio shops, and other trade facilities catering to outsiders.

Black culture, on the other hand, characterized by personal and social disorganization, is generally anathema to the dominant group and police.

> Black ghettoes typically have high crime rates that are disproportionate to white, lower socioeconomic areas. Unemployment, lack of adequate recreational facilities, inadequate housing, and masculine gang activities frequently place blacks on the streets. There exists among black Americans a sub-culture that has high aspirations but limited available opportunities, sees the "power structure" as remote and impersonal, and that sanctions violence. These factors create potentially challenging and disruptive situations for the police.[33]

The black community has a number of grievances against police treatment. The Kerner Commission cited a number of the factors that are the root causes of the hostility between police and the black minority and believed them to be the sources for the disorders that plagued America in the 1960s.[34] However, the commission noted that it would be unfair to point to the police as the single source of the problem. In many ways, the commission noted, the policeman only symbolizes much deeper problems. The policeman in a ghetto has become a symbol not only of the law, but of the entire system of law enforcement and criminal justice.

> As such, he becomes the tangible target for grievances against shortcomings throughout that system: against assembly-line justice in teeming lower courts; against wide disparities in sentences; against antiquated corrections facilities; against the basic inequities imposed by the system on the poor— to whom, for example, the option of bail means only jail.

The commission also identified the policeman in the ghetto as a symbol of the bitter social debate over law enforcement.

> One side, disturbed and perplexed by sharp rises in crime and urban violence, exerts extreme pressure on police for tougher law enforcement.

Another group, inflamed against police as agents of repression, tends toward defiance of what it regards as order maintained at the expense of justice.

Finally, the policeman in the ghetto is victimized for being the most visible symbol of a society from which many ghetto blacks are increasingly alienated. Even though policemen perform tasks that have been made necessary by the incapacities of the schools, the churches, and the family, they are resented for their presence and for the measures that these efforts require.

But the police are not blameless. The Kerner Commission also noted that widespread complaint among ghetto residents has been directed toward police conduct. Many blacks firmly believe that police harassment and brutality occur frequently in their neighborhoods. This belief is responsible for a great deal of the intense resentment that blacks bear against the police. A recurring complaint centers on the practice of aggressive-preventive patrol in ghetto neighborhoods. Ghetto residents consider this practice an irritant that is in violation of their constitutional rights. There is a feeling that aggressive patrol is used less as a crime-control device than as a new method of racial harassment.

Blacks also complain about less rigorous law enforcement in their areas. They believe that police have a tolerance for such illegal activities as drug addiction, prostitution, and street violence that they would not tolerate in other neighborhoods. Moreover, they feel that policemen respond to calls for help from black neighborhoods with much less urgency than they do to complaints and calls from other areas. However, the commission took exception to the complaint by blacks about what they perceive as less rigorous law enforcement in their neighborhoods.

> There is evidence to suggest that the lack of protection does not necessarily result from different basic police attitudes but rather from a relative lack of police personnel for ghetto areas, considering the volume of calls for police. As a consequence, the police work according to priorities. Because of the need for attention to major crimes little, if any, attention can be accorded to reports of a suspicious person, for example, or a noisy party, or a drunk. And attention even to major crimes may sometimes be routine or skeptical.

Another source of hostility to policemen as voiced by ghetto residents was "the almost total lack of effective channels for redress of complaints against police conduct." After reviewing suggestions about external grievance procedures attempted in this country and abroad, the commission was reluctant to recommend a specific procedure but stated that "police departments should be subject to external review." But, the report added, an external review agency is insufficient. Police departments should also develop internal procedures "which will gain the respect and confidence of the entire community. This need can, in the end, be met only by sustained direction through the line of command, through investigation of complaints, and prompt, visible disciplinary action where justified." Finally there have been complaints referring to perceived harassment of blacks in white neighborhoods, and harassment of black men found in the company of white women.

Significantly, the commission found that "how a policeman handles day-to-day contacts with citizens will, to a large extent, shape the relationship between police and the community." The realization that these contacts involve a great amount of discretion led the commission to conclude that how police discretion is exercised will determine the relations between the police and the community. From their survey and supporting studies they discovered that guidance for the exercise of discretion in many situations is not available to the police officer.

> There are guidelines for the wearing of uniforms—but not for how to intervene in a domestic dispute; for the cleaning of a revolver—but not for when to fire it; for use of departmental property—but not for whether to break up a sidewalk gathering; for handling stray dogs—but not for handling field interrogations.

Their recommendation was for police departments to have firm policy guidelines on how to handle contacts between citizens and the police in the ghetto and for these guidelines to be strictly enforced. This requires command supervision and commitment to the guidelines, strong internal investigative units to enforce compliance, and fair and effective means to handle citizen complaints.

Other suggested remedies included the recruitment, assignment, and promotion of black policemen, and the need for police forces to provide better community service functions such as a family crisis intervention program and neighborhood service centers employing civilians and policemen. Finally, the commission concluded that community-relations programs and training can become assets in increasing communication and decreasing hostility between the police and minority groups. However, for community-relations programs to be truly effective, they will require command and rank-and-file interest and participation. "Improving community relations is a full-time assignment for every commander and every officer—an assignment that must include the development of an attitude, a tone, throughout the force that conforms with the ultimate responsibility of every policeman: public service."

Breaking the Chain of Negative Contacts

Negative contacts between police and minority groups in our society have occurred with disproportionate frequency. Although racial bias cannot be absolved as the cause for this phenomenon, there are a number of other factors in police-minority group relationships that have significantly influenced the nature of these relationships. The very fact that there is more contact between police and minority-group citizens than with any other group of citizens adds to the probability of a higher incidence of negative contact with minorities. Minority-group areas have required a larger police presence and more police attention to their needs. Because there is statistical evidence that the poor, the black, and the young are more highly involved in criminal activities and breaches of the peace than other groups, it is inevitable that the police, by the very nature of their job, will focus their attention on them. Moreover, even law-abiding minority citizens are more likely to have frequent contact with police officers than do their white counterparts. This is due to the large number of minority-group persons who are poor and are not self-sufficient in caring for their needs. Consequently, they require assistance from the police, the most available public agency, for a variety of non–law-enforcement situations. Police officers routinely perform service tasks in minority-group areas, such as dealing with family quarrels, that they are not called upon to do elsewhere.

The troubling aspect of police-minority relations is the predetermined nature of negative contacts, which create "a vicious circle perpetuating negative reinforcement of each group by the other."[35] When these contact situations provide cues to what one group believes of the other, the likelihood of a perpetuating negativism in future contact is assured. This diminishes the possibilities for harmonious relations in future police-minorities contacts.

Kuykendall has advanced a theory of negative contacts which focuses on the behavioral and environmental factors that have caused the negative attitudes that police and minority groups hold toward each other. His framework of causalities can be summarized as follows:[36]

I. Minority groups negative perceptions of police are a function of:
   1. perceived and actual verbal and physical abuse and harassment by police;
   2. nonresponsiveness of police to minority needs and grievances; and
   3. the power maintenance function of police.

II. Police negative perceptions of minority groups are a function of:
   1. the extent of personal and social disorganization of the minority culture;
   2. the pressure tactics utilized by minority groups for achieving change in their status; and
   3. occupational influences on the police work personality, in particular:
      (a) productivity stress in the police bureaucracy (productivity as a measure of apprehension rates), and
      (b) socialization in the use of stereotyping as a skill requisite.

If the circle of negative perceptions held by police and minorities is to be broken, then remedies must be found to deal with the root causes of negative contacts between these groups. Some of the perceptions appear to be soluble by police organizational means; others are beyond the control of the police.

Two of the three functions influencing negative perceptions of the police by minority groups are potentially subject to resolution by the police. The actual or perceived abuse and harassment of minorities by police officers can be corrected by closer screening of police recruits, training methods that emphasize decency as well as efficiency in law enforcement, closer supervision of beat patrolmen, and strictly enforced directives dealing with contacts between policemen and citizens. Police departments can also correct the perception that they are not responsive to minority problems by having effective mechanisms for processing citizen complaints, investigating them, and then disciplining the officers who are found guilty of misconduct.

The availability of access channels to police departments is highly advantageous to the police. These channels provide a means for a two-way flow of communication between the police and the citizens. They serve a function that is more than just public relations; they enable the police and the community to explain themselves to each other and to set mutually acceptable ground rules for cooperation. Open lines of communication are extremely useful for gaining the confidence of groups whose cooperation in law enforcement is necessary.

The perception held by minority groups that police are "power maintenance" organizations and the police's negative perception of minority groups for their pressure strategies in effecting change in their status are reciprocating attitudes that presently defy resolution. Bayley and Mendelsohn provide their analysis of the implications of the contest of power that places the police and minority groups in adversarial positions:

> The police are important for minority people not just because of what they do but because of what they are. Minority people recognize that other problems must be solved if substantial improvements are to be made in the quality of their lives. Yet what they experience at the hands of the police is of enormous emotional significance. It symbolizes for them the backhanded treatment they receive from society as a whole. The police are the ubiquitous, public, authority-laden symbols of their own second-class citizenship. Upon them is vented the accumulated frustrations of lifetimes of inequality and subservience. . . . As one commentator [Niederhoffer] has trenchantly put it: "The policeman is a 'Rorschach' in uniform as he patrols his beat." Minority people project upon him their emotional reactions to deprivation at the hands of the majority.[37]

It is up to society and its political institutions to find solutions to the problems in the relationships between majority and minority groups. Unless this is done, the police will continue to symbolize the power attributes of the dominant groups, and thus will serve as lightning rods of minority-group discontent.

The police can address themselves institutionally to developing work personalities among their personnel that will not cause negative tensions or at least will minimize them. The stress on apprehensions should be considered in the light of the tactics employed by police officers who have sought to meet departmental production expectations by means that sometimes violate due process and other constitutional guarantees. For the sake of improved community relations, departments should emphasize crime prevention instead of apprehensions. Although suspicion is a valuable law-enforcement attribute, it should be applied judiciously. It seems that many officers fail to differentiate between law-abiding ghetto residents and ghetto criminals, and in so doing violate the rights of decent citizens. Suspicion triggers the criminal justice process; stereotyping triggers negative contacts.

The most difficult perception to alter is the one that concerns the personal and social disorganization of the minority culture. Police officers form this perception on the basis of (1) prevalence of perceived minority criminal deviance, and (2) prevalence of perceived threatening and challenging situations in minority areas. The problem with overcoming this perception is that by conventional standards and society's laws there is more deviant behavior in ghettos than in other areas. More crime is committed in black ghettos and police work there is more dangerous. As long as minority neighborhoods reflect the pathologies of the lower-class subculture, it is difficult to envision a cessation of the current police-minority discord. While race may play a part in the conflict, Wilson believes that social-class dissonance is decisive:

> [If] all Negroes were turned white tomorrow, this hostility—only slightly abated—would continue. Throughout history the urban poor have disliked and distrusted the police, and the feeling has been reciprocated; the situation will not change until the poor become middle class, or at least working class, or until society decides to abandon the effort to maintain a common legal code and a level of public order acceptable to middle-class persons.[38]

The idea that social-class dissonance is the determining factor in police-minority tensions is enlivened by the problems black policemen encounter in the ghetto. These policemen do not receive a warmer welcome in these neighborhoods than do their white counterparts. Instead, they are likely to be the targets of even greater hostility and are often charged with being Uncle Toms. Lower-class blacks are likely to resent the intrusion of another black who by virtue of the uniform he wears and the authority he displays has chosen to join the dominant "oppressors" and who has, by his chosen occupation, embraced their values and is sworn to uphold them.

A number of studies have revealed that there is considerable racial prejudice among police officers.[39] However, according to the policemen studied, their racial prejudice is not acted out in their job. The surveyed policemen contended that their racial bias is irrelevant; as professionals their occupational behavior is not governed by personal attitudes. Though the police respondents perceived their relationship in predominantly black neighborhoods as warfare, they insisted racial prejudice had nothing to do with it. In effect, what each officer was stating was "I may be prejudiced, but when I'm on duty, I'm fair—I treat 'em all alike, no matter what color they are."[40]

If the key factor in the police-minority embattlement is social-class dissonance, then the statistics provided by *Time* that show a rise of a black middle class is a hopeful sign of ameliorating relations with at least a segment of the black community. *Time*'s data revealed a steady growth of American blacks earning $10,000 or more a year; an increase in the median income of black families across the board; the growth in the number of blacks enrolled in college; and a rise in the number of blacks in professional and technical positions as well as in the number of black managers, officials, and proprietors. However, the magazine also scored the enduring dilemma of the black underclass:

Anybody who looks at a slum knows that not all blacks have made impressive economic and social advances, that huge numbers are weighed down by weariness and desolation. Indeed, the nation's 24 million blacks are split into three groups of roughly equal size. Almost one-third have family incomes of $10,000 or more and enjoy many of the amenities of middle-class status. Another one-third, earning between $4,500 and $10,000, are either on the lower edges of the middle class or stand a bare chance of lifting themselves into it. Beneath them lie still another group: the one-third of black America that struggles by on less than $4,500 a year and makes up the troubled underclass. In recent years the underclass has made some economic and social gains, but its progress has been fitful.[41]

The perpetuation of an underclass in American society continues to be an enduring phenomenon. Poverty culture with its attendant personal and social disorganization will remain a problem for all government institutions, including the police, who have the most face-to-face contact with the poor. Since many of the poor are also black, this places the police and blacks in ready-made adversarial roles.

Banfield is pessimistic about improving the condition of poverty even with the noblest of intentions among members of the dominant group and public officials. He suggests that it is the inherent nature of some persons to remain in the lower class because of a psychological incapacity to improve themselves. This means that the subculture of poverty with all of its pathologies is one with which the police will continue to deal. Consequently, the future of police-minority relations is problematical, insofar as minorities are persistently linked with lower-class cultural traits and their behavior justifies this association. Wilson feels that "[so] long as crime and disorder are disproportionately to be found among young lower-class males, and so long as blacks remain overrepresented in (though by no means identical with) such groups, blacks—especially young ones—and the police are going to be adversaries."[42]

NOTES

1. Victor G. Strecher, *The Environment of Law Enforcement: A Community Relations Guide* (Englewood Cliffs, N.J.: Prentice-Hall, 1971), pp. 70–71.

2. Louis A. Radelet, *The Police and the Community* (Beverly Hills, Calif.: Glencoe Press, 1973), pp. 258–259; emphasis in the original.

3. Jack L. Kuykendall, "Police and Minority Groups: Toward a Theory of Negative Contacts," *Police*, 15, no. 1 (September–October 1970):47. Charles C Thomas, Publisher.

4. Ibid., p. 52.

5. Ibid., p. 53.

6. Ibid.; emphasis in the original.

7. Edward C. Banfield, *The Unheavenly City: The Nature and Future of Our Urban Crisis* (Boston: Little, Brown, 1970), p. 217.

8. Boone E. Hammond, "The Contest System: A Survival Technique" (unpublished essay, Department of Sociology, Washington University, St. Louis, 1965), p. 1, quoted in Strecher, *The Environment of Law Enforcement*, p. 76.

9. Hammond, "Contest System," pp. 11–13, in Strecher, *The Environment of Law Enforcement*, pp. 76–77.

10. Strecher, *The Environment of Law Enforcement*, p. 90.

11. James Q. Wilson, "The Police in the Ghetto," in *The Police and the Community*, ed. Robert F. Steadman (Baltimore: Johns Hopkins University Press, 1972), p. 63.

12. Jerome H. Skolnick, "The Police and the Urban Ghetto," in *Police-Community Relations*, eds. Paul F. Cromwell, Jr., and George Keefer (St. Paul, Minn.: West, 1973), p. 183.

13. Radelet, *Police and the Community*, p. 272; Skolnick, "Police and the Urban Ghetto," pp. 183, 187–188.

14. Wilson, "Police in the Ghetto," p. 52.

15. David H. Bayley and Harold Mendelsohn, *Minorities and the Police: Confrontation in America* (New York: Free Press, 1969), pp. 164–165. Copyright © 1969 by The Free Press, a division of The Macmillan Company.

16. Algernon D. Black, *The People and the Police* (New York: McGraw-Hill, 1969), pp. 130–131.

17. Kuykendall, "Police and Minority Groups," p. 49.

18. Peter H. Rossi, ed., *Ghetto Revolts* (Chicago: Adline, 1970), p. 10.

19. Strecher, *The Environment of Law Enforcement*, p. 85.

20. Ibid., p. 84.

21. Ibid., p. 86.

22. Ibid., p. 86

23. Ibid., p. 86.

24. Ibid., p. 87.

25. Alan Coffey, Edward Eldefonso, and Walter Hartinger, *Human Relations: Law Enforcement in a Changing Community* (Englewood Cliffs, N.J.: Prentice-Hall, 1971), p. 109.

26. Black, *People and Police*, p. 18.

27. Leonard Dinnerstein and Frederic C. Jaher, *The Aliens* (New York: Meredith, 1970), p. 317.

28. Kuykendall, "Police and Minority Groups," p. 51.

29. Bayley and Mendelsohn, *Minorities and the Police*, pp. 145–150.

30. John R. Howard, *Awakening Minorities* (Chicago: Aldine, 1970), p. 90.

31. Bayley and Mendelsohn, *Minorities and the Police*, pp. 111, 129.

32. Kuykendall, "Police and Minority Groups," p. 52.

33. Ibid., p. 51.

34. *Report of the National Advisory Commission on Civil Disorders* (Washington, D.C.: U.S. Government Printing Office, 1968), pp. 299–322.

35. Kuykendall, "Police and Minority Groups," p. 53.

36. Ibid., pp. 228–229.

37. Bayley and Mendelsohn, *Minorities and the Police*, p. 141.

38. James Q. Wilson, *Varieties of Police Behavior* (New York: Atheneum, 1973), p. 297.

39. Radelet, *Police and the Community*, p. 272.

40. Ibid., p. 272.

41. *Time,* June 17, 1974, pp. 26, 19–20. Reprinted by permission from TIME, The Weekly Newsmagazine; Copyright Time Inc.

42. Wilson, "Police in the Ghetto," p. 69.

BIBLIOGRAPHY

BANFIELD, EDWARD C. *The Unheavenly City: The Nature and Future of Our Urban Crisis.* Boston: Little, Brown, 1970.

BANTON, MICHAEL. *The Policeman in the Community.* New York: Basic Books, 1964.

BAYLEY, DAVID H., and MENDELSOHN, HAROLD. *Minorities and the Police.* New York: Macmillan, 1969.

BLACK, ALGERNON D. *The People and the Police.* New York: McGraw-Hill, 1969.

BORDUA, DAVID J., ed. *The Police: Six Sociological Essays.* New York: Wiley, 1967.

COFFEY, ALAN; ELDEFONSO, EDWARD; and HARTINGER, WALTER. *Human Relations: Law Enforcement in a Changing Community.* Englewood Cliffs, N.J.: Prentice-Hall, 1971.

CROMWELL, PAUL F., JR., and KEEFER, GEORGE, eds. *Police-Community Relations.* St. Paul, Minn.: West, 1973.

DINNERSTEIN, LEONARD, and JAHER, FREDERIC C. *The Aliens.* New York: Meredith, 1970.

EARLE, HOWARD H. *Police-Community Relations: Crisis in Our Time.* Springfield, Ill.: C. C Thomas, 1970.

HOWARD, JOHN R. *Awakening Minorities.* Chicago: Aldine, 1970.

RADELET, LOUIS A. *The Police and the Community.* Beverly Hills, Calif.: Glencoe Press, 1973.

Report on the National Advisory Commission on Civil Disorders. Washington, D.C.: U.S. Government Printing Office, 1968.

ROSSI, PETER H., ed. *Ghetto Revolts.* Chicago: Aldine, 1970.

STEADMAN, ROBERT F., ed. *Police and the Community.* Baltimore: Johns Hopkins University Press, 1972.

WESTLEY, WILLIAM A. *Violence and the Police: A Sociological Study of Law, Custom, and Morality.* Cambridge: M.I.T. Press, 1970.

X, MALCOLM. *The Autobiography of Malcolm X.* New York: Random House, 1964.

8

||||||||||||||||||||||||||||||||||||||||||||||||||||||||||||||||||||||||||||||||||||||||||||||||||||||||||||||||||||||

POLICE AND
PROTEST GROUPS

Chapter 7 explored the police and racial tensions and examined how forces of change in the black community exacerbate the problems of police-community relations and jeopardize the balance between majority rule and minority rights. This chapter expands the scope of this exploration and considers the effects that other forces of change in the society, including civil-rights activists, student militants, and youthful revolutionaries, have on the police and more generally on the government. These groups have in varying degrees challenged the fundamental legitimacy of the government of the United States and thereby pose a threat not only to the success of police-community relations but also to the very efficacy and security of police departments altogether.

As has been stated repeatedly throughout this book, the American regime is based on the principle that to prevent either the majority or the minority from oppressing and tyrannizing the other, each must be given power to balance or check the excesses of the other. In that way, only those policies that are in the best interests of all the society—both the majority and the minority—can be enacted, and, as a result, the majority rule principle is itself improved in that the quality of the policy to which consent is given becomes of as great importance as the quantity of the consent received. Thus, this balancing of power promotes "qualitative majority rule," wherein good and decent majorities are encouraged, capable of uniting around policies good for the whole society. This same balance of power and these same beneficial consequences also extend into the criminal justice system, where the police for the most part represent the majority and where courts and corrections represent the minority.

Recently, however, a substantial and growing portion of the society has come to question and even to reject the legitimacy not only of the policies of this qualitative majority rule, but also of the very principles by which they are adopted. This chapter explores the question of governmental legitimacy in the American context, the reasons for its loss of legitimacy, and the ideologies and tactics of those who have come to regard the United States government as illegitimate. Since the police are the most visible representatives of this government, it also assesses the impact this loss of legitimacy has on police forces and their relations with the public.

Objects of Democratic Legitimacy

Legitimacy is a difficult word to define. Generally, however, it refers to rather diffuse support for the regime. Roger Canfield has identified six analytically distinct objects of diffuse support in a democratic regime: ideologies, norms or rules of the game, institutions, authorities, policies, and the effectiveness of the regime.[1] Let us examine each of these objects briefly.

Ideology is perhaps the most important object of citizen support for the regime. If the public believes that those principles that constitute or make up the written and/or living constitution of a nation are acceptable as standards of political justice, then it has a standard for judging the operation of the country's institutions. The legitimating ideology of the American government is that of "liberal democracy" based on the principles of liberty and equality. Even those who would seek its destruction or radical transformation often do so on the basis of these same standards of government. Ideology not only provides a standard for judging the legitimacy of the country's institutions; it also contributes to that legitimacy. As long as the citizens believe that these same principles are actually being applied to, or implemented in, the regime's operating procedures, rules, norms, institutions, and policies, they are likely to develop greater affection or diffuse support for the political system.

Ideology is closely related to the regime's second object of diffuse support— its norms, practical procedures, and rules of the game. As Canfield observes: "A legitimating ideology can sanctify or ritualize various instruments, tools, or procedures for its application to empirical conditions or situations. When widely accepted, these formal procedures and processes become relatively recurring and stable habits, patterns, structures, and institutions."[2] The Constitution of the United States is a good example of this. It represents an effort to transform the more abstract principles of the Declaration of Independence into functioning legal and political institutions. In so doing, it has established, or provided a framework for, the development of particular rules and norms for political activity. Citizens have both deplored and praised these procedures. Some have attacked certain rules of the game—such as qualifications for voting, the seniority system, the Electoral College, political convention procedures, legislative apportionment, or court procedures—because, in their estimation, these procedures fail to coincide with the higher principles of liberal democracy or the

Declaration of Independence. On the other hand, others are aware that support for constitutional procedures or rules of the game may encourage, at least temporarily, support for the system in the actual absence of widespread acceptance of abstract democratic principles, such as minority rights or the right to peaceful dissent.

Once the principles of the regime have been established and the rules of the game consistent with these principles have been worked out, formal institutions to advance these rules and promote these principles become the next matter of concern, and so it is that institutions are the third object of diffuse support for democratic legitimacy. Certain institutional arrangements, such as separation of powers, bicameralism, and federalism, may be regarded as more or less legitimate according to abstract ideological principles. For example, some critics condemn the accretion of presidential power as undemocratic. Similarly, some believe that intervention by the national government in the states and in the economy constitutes a threat to individual liberty. Others, however, see such interventions as necessary for the protection of equality and liberty. The debate over court-ordered busing to achieve racially integrated schools is a more specific example. Both sides of the busing issue claim that individual liberties and opportunities are at stake.

Authorities constitute the fourth object of diffuse support. As with other objects, their legitimacy is affected by, and in turn affects, the legitimacy of the other objects. Thus, for example, the political scandals surrounding Watergate have contributed to a noticeable decline in overall governmental legitimacy in the United States. Reciprocally, this loss of legitimacy has undermined the legitimacy of other authorities of the government, including perhaps most importantly the police. *Time* reports that partially because of the Watergate scandal and any number of police scandals, police testimony in the courtroom is received by juries with increasing skepticism. "Until a few years ago, a cop who testified with assurance was a prosecutor's best asset. Today, the badge is sometimes a downright liability."[3] This same reciprocal effect between the legitimacy of its authorities is also present in, and the cause of considerable concern among, those black radicals who regard the American regime as inherently racist and who see the police as one of the most significant tools of that injustice.

Finally, policies and effectiveness constitute the fifth and sixth objects of legitimacy. Policies that efficiently and effectively respond to the perceived interests of the public are likely to receive diffuse support. Conversely, policies that appear to be nonresponsive to the perceived interests of the public—as the Vietnam war and the draft certainly did to many students—are likely to erode diffuse support. As Canfield generalizes:

> The ineffectiveness of government activities, policies, and outputs; the inability to resolve political issues, to manage crises, to respond to citizens' needs, to provide citizen participation and security, and to reflect contemporary consensus . . . result in diminishing degrees of legitimacy.[4]

These six objects of diffuse support for the government of the United States have recently come under increased attack, especially by blacks and students. Although this attack reached its peak in the late 1960s and early 1970s, and has since moderated considerably, it does continue and must be considered closely. This attack extends even to America's ideological commitment to liberty and equality. It is true that James Prothro and Charles Griggs found that the five following abstract democratic principles receive nearly unanimous consent: "Democracy is the best form of government"; "public officials should be chosen by majority rule"; "every citizen should have an equal chance to influence government policy"; "the minority should be free to criticize majority decisions"; "people in the minority should be free to try to win majority support for their positions."[5] Yet these principles, when applied to concrete situations, generate considerable controversy. A state of tension exists between liberty and equality. Thus, the more liberty a society provides, the greater the opportunity for the natural distinctions that exist among men to emerge and the greater the inequality that results; conversely, the greater the equality of condition that society imposes among men, the less the liberty that it can permit. As Alexis de Tocqueville pointed out, in a democratic society this tension is ultimately and inevitably resolved in favor of equality:

> I think that democratic communities have a natural taste for freedom; left to themselves, they will seek it, cherish it, and view any privation of it with regret. But for equality their passion is ardent, insatiable, incessant, invincible; they call for equality in freedom; and if they cannot obtain that, they still call for equality in slavery. They will endure poverty, servitude, barbarism, but they will not endure aristocracy.[6]

Below this level of ideology, the attack on the legitimacy of the government of the United States becomes all the more intense. A recent study of student opinions at ten elite or large public universities indicates that 41 percent of the students regard American society as "sick" and "repressive," while 46 percent consider it racist.[7] A survey at the prestigious University of Chicago showed over 66 percent of the students there rated the present condition of American society as bad or very bad and as offending many of their ideals.[8] Canfield summarizes this student sentiment:

> A large majority of students (70 percent to 80 percent) are concerned with unspecified social inadequacies but have not rejected the system. Probably only 10 percent to 20 percent have rejected the whole political system. Thirty percent may have rejected the economic system. For examples of more specific student disillusionment, a large minority (40 percent) believe this system is repressive of free speech (twice the rate of such national opinions). A comparable minority also believes the social system is racist. Thus, although most students do not reject the system, probably a majority, perhaps as large as 70 percent, seek major reform of the system.[9]

Blacks are in general agreement with students on this issue. Edward Muller found in his study of Waterloo, Iowa, that among blacks, 41 percent agree and only 36 percent disagree with the statement "The Constitution of the United States is in need of major change."[10]

Belief among blacks and students in the legitimacy of the institutions, authorities, policies, and effectiveness of the American government is even lower. Thus, David Sears, in his study of the Watts riot, found that 45 percent of blacks said that "elected officials cannot generally be trusted."[11] Likewise, Tom Tomlinson's research revealed that 60 percent of blacks as compared with 27 percent of whites agreed that public officials "don't care."[12] Student attitudes are also extremely critical. A recent Gallup poll found that 79 percent of students believe that the American political system "does not respond quickly enough to meet the needs of the people."[13]

This decline in diffuse support for the government has eventuated in more than a general loss of legitimacy; it has led to actual violence. Although active participation in urban and campus disorders is not high and includes only about 2 percent to 20 percent of those living in the vicinity, support for political violence runs much higher.[14] Thus, in the black community, William Brink and Louis Harris found that blanket disapproval of violence is very low. Their Bedford-Stuyvesant survey indicated that only 27 percent would say that violence is wrong.[15] Angus Campbell and Howard Schuman, in their survey of racial attitudes in fifteen American cities, found that "the small proportion of Negroes who participate in a riot are able, at least for the present, to count on a much wider context of moral and perhaps more tangible support from the black community. The rioter does not stand alone."[16] On campus, Allen Barton found that 42 percent of Columbia University students in 1968 felt that the tactics of the SDS (Students for a Democratic Society) were justified.[17] A 1970 Gallup survey of the nation's students revealed that 44 percent felt violence was sometimes justified to initiate change in American society.[18] Finally, Bill Aron found that 69 percent of the students of the University of Chicago felt generally sympathetic toward urban rioters and that only 32 percent disapproved of "the use of violence to bring about changes in society."[19]

Causes for the Decline of Governmental Legitimacy

A variety of factors account for this loss in governmental legitimacy and explain this support for and willingness to engage in political violence. Perhaps the principal explanation is to be found in the way in which the United States has attempted to answer the question: *Quis custodiet ipsos custodes?*—Who governs the governors? Who regulates the regulators? America's answer to this question has been what Theodore J. Lowi calls interest-group liberalism—"an amalgam of capitalism, statism, and pluralism."[20] For the most part, America has recognized market competition or capitalism as the only legitimate form of social regulation or control. Capitalism provides an automatic, mechanistic, self-regulating control. Adam Smith's "invisible hand" is trusted to regulate the society and to do so in such a manner as to provide maximum freedom and benefit to all. With each person selfishly pursuing his own self-interest and thereby contributing automatically and unintentionally to the public interest, capitalism denies the need for rational, conscious social control.

Interest-group liberalism adapts capitalism and the attractiveness of its automatic self-regulation to group (as opposed to market) competition for control over positive and expanding government. Since the New Deal, the American government has been continuously called upon by its citizens to do more and more in the areas of social welfare, economic regulation, and civil rights. As a result, its responsibilities and power commensurate with these responsibilities have expanded tremendously. Interest-group liberalism contends that this increasingly powerful government can be properly controlled only if all groups interested in the government's policies have access to or representation in the government, so that they can compete and bargain with each other and the government itself over what policies are to be formulated and executed. Thus, interest-group liberalism promotes decentralization and broad delegation of power; decentralization allows access to all groups at all levels, and delegation of power assures that decisions reached by administrative agencies as well as legislative assemblies are the result of pluralistic bargaining. On the other hand, it depreciates formalism and procedure; they tend to restrict access and preclude certain bargains. Interest-group liberalism wants nothing to interfere with the automatic, self-regulating control over government which group competition provides. *Quis custodiet ipsos custodes?* Interest-group liberalism's answer and the answer of America is clear: The regulated regulate themselves through group competition.

Interest-group liberalism has a certain attractiveness. To begin with, the emphasis it places on groups is wholly consistent with the "American experience" in three important respects.[21] First, it is consistent with "the federal structure of the American system."[22] As Robert Paul Wolff observes in his perceptive essay, "Beyond Tolerance":

> [F]rom the birth of the nation, a hierarchy of local governments, formally sovereign and autonomous, interposed itself between the individual and the supreme power of the state. The United States, as its name implied, was an association of political communities rather than of individuals. The natural ties of tradition and emotion binding each citizen to his native colony were reinforced by a division of powers which left many of the functions of sovereign authority to the several states. Hence, the relation of the individual to the federal government was from the beginning and even in theory indirect and mediated by intervening bodies.[23]

Second, it is consistent with America's "oft-chronicled penchant for dealing with social problems by means of voluntary associations."[24] Tocqueville made much of this phenomenon in *Democracy in America*. He observed that

> in no country in the world has the principle of association been more successfully used or applied to a greater multitude of objects than in

America. . . . The citizen of the United States is taught from infancy to rely upon his own exertions in order to resist the evils and the difficulties of life; he looks upon the social authority with an eye of mistrust and anxiety, and he claims its assistance only when he is unable to do without it. . . . In the United States associations are established to promote the public safety, commerce, industry, morality, and religion. There is no end which the human will despairs of attaining through the combined power of individuals united into a society.[25]

The advantages that accrue from this penchant for associations and this mistrust of government is made all the more manifest when Tocqueville's reflections on America are contrasted with his observations on the French Revolution:

[U]nder the old order the government had long since deprived Frenchmen of the possibility, and even the desire, of coming to each other's aid. When the Revolution started, it would have been impossible to find, in most parts of France, even ten men used to acting in concert and defending their interests without appealing to the central power for aid. Thus once that central power passed from the hands of the royal administration into those of irresponsible sovereign assemblies and a benevolent government had given place to a ruthless one, the latter found nothing to impede it or hold up its activities even momentarily.[26]

Third, interest-group liberalism's emphasis on groups is also consistent with America's religious, ethnic, and racial heterogeneity. It is perfectly adapted to America's "complex interlocking of ethnic, religious, racial, regional, and economic groups, whose members pursue their diverse interests through the medium of private associations, which in turn are coordinated, regulated, contained, encouraged, and guided by a federal system of representative democracy."[27]

The attractiveness of interest-group liberalism is not limited to its consistency with "the American experience." It also extends to interest-group liberalism's capacity to moderate the stridency of politics. Interest-group liberalism is characterized by tolerance, an ungrudging acknowledgment of the right of opposed interests to exist and be pursued. It regards all human action as motivated by interests rather than principles or norms. Since compromise between competing interests is easier than between opposed principles that purport to be objectively valid, interest-group liberalism assures that politics is conducted in a less strident and ideological manner. The benefits that this more moderate politics provides are immediately apparent when one contrasts the stability of the American regime, with its willingness to treat even matters of principle as though they were conflicts of interest, with the instability of the French regime, with its penchant to regard conflicts of interest as matters of principle.[28]

However, along with these advantages, the practice of attempting to regulate the regulators through the politics of interest-group liberalism is also open to serious criticism. Grant McConnell has observed that

a politics of interest groups and small-constituent units is unlikely to develop its own checks. Government offers the best means of limiting both the conflicts between such groups and the agreements by which conflicts are ended or avoided. To give this service, however, government must be formal and distinct. It cannot be either if it is broken into units corresponding to the interests which have developed the power.[29]

Yet this is precisely what interest-group liberalism has accomplished. It has fragmented the government into units dominated by particular interests and has thereby deprived the government of the ability to check these interests. In so doing, it has provided what Lowi terms "carte blanche for the vested interests."[30]

Anxious to allow individual groups to determine what problems are to be addressed and how, interest-group liberals have been reluctant to formulate laws or define programs with much detail or specificity. They have preferred delegation of power to definition by law. But, in so doing, they have parceled out the sovereignty of policy-making power of the state to those governmental agencies and interest groups close to and most affected by the problems. This practice has led to five untoward consequences.[31] Let us examine each of them briefly, as these consequences in large part explain the increasing loss of the legitimacy of the American government today.

First, interest-group liberalism has atrophied institutions of popular control. "Parcelling out policy-making power to the most interested parties destroys political responsibility."[32] Second, it has maintained and created new structures of privilege. The greater the role a group plays in policy making, the more powerful that group becomes and the more important membership in and loyalty to the group becomes. To partake of the benefits the group can provide, members find that they must often submit to the caprice and dictates of the group's leadership—a new privileged class typically immune to effective or democratic control by the membership. As Robert Michels declares in his iron law of oligarchy: "Who says organization, say oligarchy."[33]

A third consequence of interest-group liberalism is directly related to the above and is of special importance in terms of its effect on governmental legitimacy and its potential for political violence; accordingly, it will receive greater attention. Government by and through interest groups tends to be conservative in almost every sense of the term. This arrangement "systematically favors the interests of the stronger against the weaker parties in interest-group conflicts and tends to solidify the power of those who already hold it. The government, therefore, plays a conservative, rather than a neutral, role in the society."[34]

Wolff has pointed out that according to the tenets of interest-group liberalism, every genuine and legitimate social group has a right to a voice in policy making and to its share of the benefits. Any policy proposed by a group in the system must be tolerated, no matter how potentially destructive it may be. However, a policy or program that lacks legitimate representation has no place in society, regardless of how reasonable or right it might be. The line between acceptable and unacceptable alternatives in American interest-group politics is very sharp indeed. In fact, the territory of American politics may be likened to a plateau with steep cliffs on all sides. On the plateau are all the legitimate interest groups, which compete and bargain with one another. Below, in the deep valley that surrounds the plateau, are the outsiders, the fringe groups, the "extremists." "The most important battle waged by any group in American politics is the struggle to climb onto the plateau."[35] Once on the plateau—once formally recognized as legitimate—it can count on some measure of what it seeks. Of course, no group ever gets all its wants in the bargaining process, but no legitimate group is ever completely frustrated, either. Thus, getting on the plateau becomes extremely critical. To get there, groups will often engage in actions—including violent actions—which they will subsequently repudiate once their legitimacy is recognized. American history is filled with examples of this; American labor history is a case in point.

According to Philip Taft and Philip Ross, "The United States has had the bloodiest and most violent labor history of any industrial nation in the world."[36] The period from January 1, 1902, to September 30, 1904, was particularly bloody. During that time, an estimated 198 persons were killed and 1966 were injured in strikes and walkouts. Altogether, well over seven hundred deaths and several thousand serious injuries have resulted from labor disputes. The principal cause of this violence has been labor's attempt to get on the plateau of American politics. As Taft and Ross write:

> The most common cause of past violent labor disputes was the denial of the right to organize through refusal to recognize the union, frequently associated with the discharge of union leaders. . . . Labor violence was caused by the attitudes taken by labor and management in response to unresolved disputes. The virtual absence at present of violence in the coal and copper mines, breeding grounds for the more dramatic and tragic episodes, are eloquent testimony that labor violence from the 1870's to the 1930's was essentially shaped by prevailing attitudes on the relations between employer and employee. Once these were changed, a change accomplished partly by legal compulsion, violence was sharply reduced.[37]

Once unions got on the plateau—once they were recognized by the government and by industry for purposes of collective bargaining—labor violence subsided, and unions repudiated their erstwhile tactics. Today it is difficult to imagine any interest more committed than labor to the legitimacy of American society and more hostile to its critics, such as those who opposed the Vietnam war. Nevertheless, it is interesting to reflect upon the fact that had many of today's policemen been on the force a generation or two ago, they might have been forced to fight their own fathers as labor struggled to gain a foothold on the plateau.

A fourth consequence of interest-group liberalism is that it makes conflict of interest a principle of government rather than a criminal act.[38] It has wrapped the government in shrouds of illegitimacy. Lowi provides the following scenario: Suppose that everyone in a city knew that traffic tickets could be fixed. Not everyone could get his ticket fixed, and, as a consequence, those individuals who could not were forced to suffer a dual loss; not only did they have to pay the fine, but they were made acutely aware of their lack of access. A mayor is elected who has pledged to end the present traffic ticket fixing situation, where some have access and others do not. However, rather than reforming the system by universalizing enforcement, he universalizes the privilege of ticket fixing. This policy would be a solution of sorts; everyone would have an equal opportunity to bargain with the ticket administrators. However, this solution would come at an extremely high price. Not only would it destroy the purpose of the ticket, but it would also diminish drastically the legitimacy of the government in the eyes of the public.[39] Yet this is exactly what interest-group liberalism does. As Lowi observes, its operative principle appears to be: "Destroy privilege by universalizing it. Reduce conflict by yielding to it. Redistribute power by the maxim of each according to his claim."[40] In so doing, all the legitimacy—all the coercive power and sanctions—of a government are denied. The government is reduced to a mere participant on the plateau of American politics, and in the bargaining process that occurs there, it has no more authority or legitimacy than any other interest group and no more claim to preeminence. It is not strange that a government put in such a position is not respected or obeyed. Neither is it strange that the police, as the most visible and immediate representatives of that government, should likewise be regarded with contempt and disdain.

Finally, a fifth consequence of interest-group liberalism is its capacity to bring about "ends profoundly different from those intended by their most humanitarian and libertarian framers."[41] All of the good intentions of the interest-group liberals to the contrary notwithstanding, it has failed to provide adequate solutions to the problems that beset urban America. Through its broad delegation of authority, interest-group liberalism declares to administrative agencies and their clientele groups: "We don't know what the problems are; find them and deal with them." But this has led to what Lowi calls "sincere humanitarianism gone cockeyed."[42] Thus, for example, urban renewal has not so much provided decent and adequate housing for all as it has promoted "Negro removal" and *apartheid*.[43] Likewise, the "war on poverty" conducted by the Johnson administration in the mid-1960s probably did more to generate ill will and disaffection among the lower class than "benign neglect." The war on poverty was aimed primarily at those who are "relatively deprived"—that is, at those who lack enough income, status, or whatever else may be valued to cause them to feel poor by comparison with others.[44] Yet, as Edward C. Banfield notes, among the relatively deprived,

> the subjective difference of income differences may increase steadily while the objective side of the differences decreases; this process may continue right up to the point (assuming that there is one in some meaningful sense) of income equality. In other words, it is at least possible that the closer they come to income equality the more acutely dissatisfied people with relatively low incomes may feel on account of such differences as we named.[45]

The answer that interest-group liberalism provides to the question *Quis custodiet ipsos custodes?* has obviously contributed greatly to the loss of legitimacy of the American government. So too have the divisive Vietnam war and the revelations concerning the Watergate scandal. Moreover, this decline in diffuse support for the American regime has been further aided by the general teachings of the social sciences. Political science and sociology both have tended to regard all values, all points of view, as equal. The words of Robert A. Dahl, a former president of the American Political Science Association, are typical. A "rigorous analysis in a positivistic spirit" reveals that such terms as justice or injustice, statesman or tyrant, the common good or the public interest—in brief, all the traditional terms in the vocabulary of politics—are simply the "subjective evaluations of the man who uses them."[46] But if this is so, then rejection of the American regime and acts of violence against it are as acceptable and proper as support for it and acts of reform within the system. With his characteristic wit, Walter Berns declares:

> When giants of the profession on principle eschew any use of the words justice and injustice, no one should be surprised when serious students are attracted by the midgets who rant about "power elites" and the "military-industrial complex." They at least are talking about something that matters. Besides, it will have occurred to the serious student that if all "values" are equal, no one can, without being inconsistent, blame them for attaching no value to the rules of the game. Who, after all, taught them, and who can admonish them for failing to measure up to what?[47]

Public Responses to Governmental Legitimacy

For these reasons, and many others derived from them, the legitimacy of the American government's ideology, rules of the game, institutions, authorities, policies, and effectiveness has been called into question. Of course, not everyone's diffuse support of the regime has been equally affected. Some individuals may be occasionally dissatisfied with particular policies of the United States government (for example, the Vietnam war) or its lack of effectiveness in addressing certain problems (for example, its apparent inability to control inflation), but may be wholly supportive of its authorities, institutions, rules of the game, and ideology. On the other hand, others have come to reject even America's commitment to liberty and equality. Table 8.1 broadly classifies a variety of points of view that the public has taken toward the legitimacy of the American government; it presents eight different political orientations, ranging from total rejection to total acceptance.

It should be emphasized that the public's diffuse support for the American government is not static but is subject to change. As a consequence, representatives of various political orientations may, from time to time, increase or decrease in number and visibility. For example, the numerous anarchists, revolutionaries, and radicals of the late 1960s have now all but disappeared from the political scene. It should also be emphasized that these political orientations are themselves analytical or ideal types. As such, it is likely that any particular individual or group will exhibit characteristics of, and behave in a manner con-

TABLE 8.1 Continuum of governmental legitimacy–degree of regime rejection/acceptance

Subcultural categories	Rejection				Acceptance			
	Anarchists	Revolutionaries	Radicals	Reformers	Establishment	Traditionalists	Deviants	Super-patriots
Students	Hippies; Yippies	Rev. youth mov't I ("Weatherman"); Tom Hayden; Trotskyites; Maoists; Progressive labor	Left activists; S.D.S.; rev. youth mov't II	Pacifists; antiwar mov'ts.; democratic socialists; pot smokers; freedom riders	Professional academics; collegiates	Conservatives; vocationalists; Y.A.F.	Juvenile delinquents; drug pushers	
Blacks		Cleaver; Panthers; Communists	Stokely Carmichael; black power; Malcolm X	NAACP; M. L. King; Southern Christian Leadership Conference; Jesse Jackson; Operation Push	Growing black middle class	Southern Baptists; "Uncle Toms"	Numbers racket; drug pushers; pimps	
General population	19th-C. communes	Symbionese Liberation Army (SLA)	Radical liberals; Norman Thomas; Eugene V. Debs	Populists; Americans for Democratic Action; Northern Calif.; N. East; Feminists; "progressive center"; SILENT MIDDLE	AFL-CIO	Orange County, California	Mafia; homosexuals; Hell's Angels	Reactionaries; John Birch Society; Ku Klux Klan; Minutemen

SILENT MIDDLE, MAJORITY AMERICA

NOTE: This table and the subsequent discussion of it are heavily dependent upon Roger Canfield, *Black Ghetto Riots and Campus Disorders: A Subcultural and Philosophical Study of Democratic Legitimacy and American Political Violence, 1964–1970* (San Francisco: R. & E. Research Associates, 1972), pp. 107–122.

sistent with, any number of these orientations. Nonetheless, classifying the responses of various past and present groups and individuals to the question of governmental legitimacy has merit: it can help to identify those most likely to engage in political violence, their ideological premises, and their tactics.

Anarchists and Nonconformers

The first group consists of those who regard essentially no existing regime as legitimate. This group of individuals has been characterized variously as "anarchists, chiliastics, anarcho-syndicalists, communalists, utopians, nihilists, sect-formers, withdrawn radicals, self-indulgent, or counter-culturalists."[48] This group seeks to destroy or stop the regime from functioning, or, at the very least, to refuse to participate in any regime or social institutions. Most within this group contend that institutions ought to be absolutely voluntary and relatively free of restraints on the individual. They see the individual as possessing a right of liberation from almost any restraining authority. Consequently, they do not accept citizenship in any organized, structured, or institutionalized political community, other than the most primitive and voluntary. This general category consists of such recent and to an extent contemporary groupings as hippies, Yippies, and the Telegraph Avenue, Sunset Strip, and East Village drug cultures.

Lewis Yablonsky has provided one of the few scholarly examinations of the hippie movement.[49] Among the things that impressed him the most was that "the hippie phenomenon, although fetal and relatively powerless, emerges as the first American social movement that totally rejects the American social system."[50] The true hippie is a "complete anarchist."[51] His deviant behavior and posture constitute a much more devastating attack on the basic structure of American society than the traditional delinquent pattern. After all, the traditional American delinquent accepts the goals of the society even if he finds it necessary to pursue them in a deviant way. Thus, the lower-class American delinquent is really "affirming the validity of the goals of American society by striving for them at any cost."[52] Traditional crime and delinquency in this context are a tribute to, not a repudiation of, the goals and values of American society. In contrast, the hippie reaction is a condemnation of the total American system. Their condemnation and rejection are total; they reject the American family, religion, education, government, and the economic and materialistic prizes of American society.[53]

The range of tactics available to various anarchists' groups is quite broad. Many simply drop out, but others, such as Abbie Hoffman, assault the American regime's values on drugs, sex, money, and the family by discrediting them through drama, comedy, and ridicule. According to Hoffman, guerrilla theater and "poet revolutionaries are the most dangerous of all."[54] One must "create art and destroy property."[55] Still others, especially the more politically oriented Yippies so prevalent at the 1968 Democratic Convention in Chicago, engage in such confrontation-creating situations as passive resistance, sit-ins, and mass demonstrations, and such more violent acts as destroying property and assaulting police officers. Finally, a few others, such as Charles Manson and his tribe, commit atrocities and mass murder.

Hippies and other anarchistic types, like other dissidents, are not so prevalent today as they were in the late 1960s. Haight-Ashbury and Telegraph Hill are no longer so kind to "flower children" as they used to be. Yet, just because there are no prominent contemporary exponents of this political orientation active on the political scene today does not mean that the police can ignore them or the lessons they provide. So long as a few continue to reject the government's legitimacy and to engage in tactics consistent with that rejection, they will continue to pose problems of unknown and uncertain proportion for the police as representatives of that government.

The Revolutionaries

The second classification on Table 8.1 includes the revolutionaries. Revolutionaries regard the American regime as corrupt, repressive, imperialistic, and racist—in short, as totally illegitimate and beyond redemption. They seek the planned or unplanned, organized or unorganized, use of violence to overthrow or secede from the regime. Such widely diverse groups as Revolutionary Youth Movement I (the Weatherman faction of SDS), the Black Panthers, and the Symbionese Liberation Army can be classified as revolutionary. The ideology and tactics of each of these groups will be briefly assessed.

To understand Revolutionary Youth Movement I, or the Weatherman, a brief history of Students for a Democratic Society is necessary. For all practical purposes, SDS was born at a convention of students meeting at Port Huron, Michigan, in June of 1962. This was the time of the civil-rights struggle in the South, and many SDS members and sympathizers had been active in voter registration drives, freedom demonstrations, and rallies. Enthusiasm at the convention ran high; SDS appeared to be a militant protest group bent on achieving reforms. The original ideological framework of the SDS was proclaimed in the "Port Huron Statement," prepared by Tom Hayden and adopted at the founding convention. The Port Huron Statement was characterized by two key words, "participatory democracy," meaning, among other things, that the institutions of American society should be more open for individual participation and that citizens should be encouraged to develop a sense of personal responsibility and concern.

> As a social system, we seek the establishment of a democracy of individual participation, governed by two central aims: that the individual share in those social decisions determining the quality and direction of his life; that society be organized to encourage independence in men and provide a media for their common participation.[56]

Following the Port Huron convention, SDS leaders returned to their respective campuses and embarked on an ambitious organizing campaign with the primary objective of "radicalizing" the students. While they seized on the 1964 free-speech movement at the University of California at Berkeley, it was the escalation of the Vietnam war that provided them with their real rallying cry. SDS participated actively in the growing student unrest and demonstrations against the war and against ROTC (Reserve Officer Training Corps) facilities on campus. In so doing, it moved from protest to resistance. By the spring of 1968, SDS was a spearhead in the violent student demonstrations at Columbia University. The 1968–1969 academic year saw SDS violence on many campuses, including the conviction of an SDS member at a Midwestern university under the federal sabotage statute for attempting to bomb an ROTC building on campus. In that same year another SDS student, charged with sabotage in the dynamiting of power transmission towers in Colorado, was placed on the FBI's "Ten Most Wanted" list of criminal fugitives.[57]

As SDS became more militant and resistance-oriented, it also took on an increasingly Marxist revolutionary tone. In December 1968 the SDS's National Council approved a resolution entitled "Toward a Revolutionary Youth Movement." This resolution stated flatly:

> The main task now is to begin moving beyond the limitations of struggle placed upon a student movement. We must realize our potential to reach out to new constituencies both on and off campus and build SDS into a youth movement that is revolutionary.[58]

As it became increasingly revolutionary in character, it also became increasingly factionalized. This factionalism came to a head at the SDS National Convention in Chicago in 1969, where SDS split into two major groups, each claiming to be the true SDS. One group came to be known as the National Office faction, the other the Progressive Labor party (PLP). The National Office group was itself beset by factionalism and differing viewpoints. One such subgroup came to be known as the Weatherman, or Revolutionary Youth Movement I; the other, Revolutionary Youth Movement II. These groups differ appreciably in their viewpoints.

The Weatherman tends to emphasize the leading role of the working class in revolutionary struggle. It views blacks in the United States as a separate colonized nation within an oppressor country. Liberation of blacks cannot be accomplished, it believes, until capitalism is overthrown. On women's liberation, the Weatherman's teaching is that women should be organized around anti-imperialist, antiracist struggles.

In contrast, Revolutionary Youth Movement II sees the proletariat as the main force of the revolution. They consider blacks, women, and students as playing a key role in raising the consciousness of the working class by struggling for their liberation. Like Weatherman, Revolutionary Youth Movement II considers blacks in the United States as a separate nation. For them, however, black workers receive special attention, as they occupy a "dual position"—they are oppressed as blacks and superexploited as workers. Their struggle for liberation, along with the women's struggle for liberation from male supremacy, is seen as a means of developing proletarian unity and revolution.

Finally, the Progressive Labor party considers itself as the vanguard of the proletarian struggle and sees the working class as the key to the revolution. It seeks to give all struggle a class character. It juxtaposes the Black Panther party slogan, "Power to the people," with its own demand for "Power to the workers." The Progressive Labor party urges all student action to be in the objective interests of the working class. Women are seen as superexploited workers and as victims of the ruling class, but not as oppressed by men as well.[59]

These groups generally differ on tactics as well. The Weatherman has come to be the most violent, believing that direct, forcible, in-the-street guerrilla incidents must be pursued. RYM II, although not disavowing violence, has been less militant. It regards violent guerrilla tactics as self-defeating and likely to alienate both potential recruits and public opinion. Thus it has tended to stress study and education with an emphasis on the classic definition of the working class as the correct means to attain revolution. The PLP tended to follow RYM II's tactics more than the Weatherman's. It feels extremist tactics at the present will do the movement more harm than good.

Because of the Weatherman's greater propensity for violence, its members have proved to be the greatest threat to society and the police. They were responsible for the Days of Rage in Chicago in October of 1969, an attempt, as they described it, to "bring the war home." In the September 20, 1969, issue of *New Left Notes*, in an article entitled "The Time is Right for Fighting in the Street," they declared: "It is a war in which we must fight. We must open up another front against U.S. imperialism by waging a thousand struggles in the schools, the streets, the army, and on the job, and in Chicago: October 8–11."[60] They even sought to prepare the demonstrators for the violent confrontations they expected by telling them how to dress: "Wear a motorcycle helmet or surplus army helmet." "Wear protective clothing. Wear hard shoes, never wear sandals! Wear shirts and jackets with tight cuffs and high collars for protection against gas." They also gave advice on how to behave medically: "Don't panic if you see someone with blood streaming from the head." "Never try to remove a bullet that is still in the body." "Get a tetanus shot." "If you do go to a hospital, treat the doctors and nurses there as if they were pigs."[61]

As a result, hundreds of Weatherman activists came to Chicago, prepared for street action. Nearly everyone carried some kind of helmet or gas mask. And the violence for which the Weatherman called flourished. Among other incidents, approximately 250 members of Weatherman ran through Chicago's Gold Coast—one of the wealthiest and most exclusive sections of the city—trashing buildings and automobiles and intermittently battling with police. By the time this skirmish was over, more than seventy-five demonstrators had been arrested and twenty-one policemen had been injured. One policeman who had increduously witnessed this indiscriminate and frenzied violence gasped, "I just don't believe it."[62] Before the Days of Rage were over, hundreds of Weatherman activists had been arrested and major felony indictments, both state and federal, were initiated against the Weatherman's leadership. In large part because of these indictments, and indictments for other acts of violence, the Weatherman faction went underground in early 1970, but they have continued to engage in acts of terrorist violence, including the bombings of the New York City police headquarters and the Pentagon. In fact, as of July 1974, they have claimed credit for a total of nineteen terrorist bombings across the country.[63]

What does the Weatherman expect to accomplish by these sporadic acts of violence? For many revolutionary and radical groups alike, the answer is to be found in the writings of that guru of the New Left, Herbert Marcuse. Marcuse, perhaps most famous as Angela Davis' major graduate professor, argues that in a fundamentally illegitimate regime, any action taken to make life more rewarding or meaningful in it is simply "repressive" in that it helps to perpetuate the regime and its illegitimacy. In other words, acts of reform merely make a bad situation more tolerable and thereby help to dissipate revolutionary zeal.

> [W]ithin a repressive society, even progressive movements threaten to turn into their opposite to the degree to which they accept the rules of the game. To take a most controversial case: the exercise of political rights . . . in a society of total administration serves to strengthen this administration by testifying to the existence of democratic liberties which, in reality, have changed their content and lost their effectiveness. In such a case, freedom (of opinion, of assembly, of speech) becomes an instrument for absolving servitude.[64]

Only violence and other acts of confrontation can heighten contradictions in the illegitimate regime, make a bad situation worse, and thereby hasten the collapse or overthrow of the regime. Revolutionaries like the Weatherman and many radical groups on college campuses have learned this lesson well. Consequently, they frequently engage in actions designed to escalate tensions and invite repression or overreaction by police and other government or college officials in the hopes of thereby politicizing or radicalizing previously uncommitted students or members of the public. The comments of William H. Orrick, Jr., regarding the San Francisco State College strike of 1969 are telling:

> What is important to an understanding of the campus confrontations is that the reservoir of hostility among students provides a ready tool for those who would use it. If a police over-reaction can be provoked (or if through error or lack of proper control or of their own hostility the police should over-react), radical activists win immediate converts among the so-called "silent majority." Previously uncommitted students are "radicalized." The police are the common enemy, and "getting the pigs off campus" becomes the common goal. The appearance of the police on campus may then be enough in itself to turn a calm day into an angry confrontation. The police

themselves recognize this. As one police officer . . . [observed], "It's a victory for those just to have us on that campus."[65]

Revolutionary and radical groups often engage in acts of violence and destruction not in an attempt to help alleviate the difficulties that exist but rather in an effort to escalate tensions and stimulate an overreaction on the part of the police and other public authorities, thereby radicalizing previously uncommitted students or members of the public and increasing the likelihood that the regime will collapse or be overthrown. In so doing, both the students and the police are treated by them as pawns. Leo Rosten has witnessed this manipulation and has found it "tragic to see students rampaging like mindless buffaloes. . . . It is mind-boggling to see yammering young herds lock step to the tyranny of gurus who say, 'Do your own thing,' but mean 'Conform to our eccentricities.' "[66]

Police as well as students should be aware of this manipulation and of the way in which they are being used, so that their actions do not simply play into the hands of those whose ends are not the preservation and improvement of the American regime, but its demise and ultimate destruction.

The Black Panther Party for Self-Defense represents a second revolutionary group recently active in the United States. The Panthers were originally organized after the long hot summers of the 1964–1966 period by two "new ghetto men," Huey Newton and Bobby Seale. It soon became an important organizing force in black ghettos, especially among young black men.[67] The Black Panthers' chief indictment of the American regime or white "mother country" is its essentially colonialist exploitation of people of color, both at home and abroad. As Eldridge Cleaver, the Panthers' most influential theoretician, has argued: "The first thing that has to be realized is that it is a reality when people say that there's a 'black colony' and a 'white mother country.' . . . Black people are a stolen people held in a colonial status on stolen land, and any analysis which does not acknowledge the colonial status of black people cannot hope to deal with the real problem."[68] According to Cleaver, the colonial status that blacks occupy in American society deprives them of equality—intellectually, politically, economically, emotionally, sexually, and spiritually. To achieve that full equality guaranteed by the Declaration of Independence, the black community must be decolonized; it must be free to determine its own destiny, to form a separate nation if it so desires. This decolonization will be inevitably violent. As Frantz Fanon, another source of theoretical support for the Panthers, notes: "National liberation, national renaissance, the restoration of nationhood to the people, commonwealth: whatever may be the headings used or the new formulas introduced, decolonization is always a violent phenomenon. . . . The naked truth of decolonization evokes for us the searing bullets and bloodstained knives which emanate from it."[69] Thus Cleaver invites the black community to prepare to fight against the American regime, Babylon, as he calls it: "Why not die right here in Babylon fighting for a better life, like the Vietcong? If those little cats can do it, what's wrong with big studs like us?"[70]

This fight for revolution and decolonization can take on many forms. For Cleaver, it has even included the rape of a white woman. As Cleaver explains it:

> Rape was an insurrectionary action. It delighted me that I was defying and trampling upon the white man's law, upon his system of values, and that I was defiling his women—and this point, I believe, was the most satisfying to me because I was very resentful over the historical fact of how the white man has used the black woman. I felt I was getting revenge.[71]

Of course, violence for Cleaver and the Black Panthers has also taken more traditional forms as well, including such acts as sniping, rioting, and bombing.

Not all of the actions of the Black Panthers are violent and revolutionary, however. They support free breakfast programs for ghetto children and help to raise money for research into sickle-cell anemia. The more positive aspects of the Black Panther party are perhaps summarized in their ten-point platform and program. In it, they support such goals as (1) self-determination for the black community, (2) full employment or a guaranteed income, (3) the elimination of capitalism from the black community, (4) black housing cooperatives, (5) locally controlled education that includes black studies, (6) exemption of all black men from military service as "the black people should not be forced to fight in the military service to defend a racist government that does not protect us." (7) armed defensive actions by blacks to forestall police brutality, (8) freedom for all black prisoners "because they have not received a fair and impartial trial," (9) trial of black people by black jurors, and (10) a United Nations plebiscite of black people in America to determine "the will of black people as to their national destiny."

The Black Panther party has been decimated by police actions and arrests and torn by internal discord; it now appears to be in decline. Perhaps because of this, it has recently cooled its rhetoric and altered its tactics. Huey Newton now considers the use of violence as counterproductive and advocates instead greater participation in the existing political arena. However, as Feagin and Hahn have warned, the Black Panther party "should not be perceived as an isolated phenomenon which gained no support from the wider black community. In fact, a 1970 *Time* poll found that no less that a quarter of a representative sample of black Americans openly admired the Panthers a great deal."[72]

As the Black Panthers' revolutionary fervor has recently waned, that of other groups, including the Symbionese Liberation Army, has increased and the challenge to the legitimacy of both the government and its chief agents, the police, continues. The SLA is an obscure revolutionary band that came to prominence for the assassination of Oakland, California, Superintendent of Schools Marcus Foster and the "kidnapping" of newspaper heiress Patricia Hearst. The SLA had its genesis in late 1972, among a group of black inmates in the California prison system and white middle-class activists deeply interested in penal reform. Once formed, the SLA patterned itself after such South American revolutionaries as the Tupamaros of Uruguay and drew up a set of goals that included the disappropriation of "the capitalist class," the disbanding of the prison system, and the destruction of "all forms of racism, sexism, ageism, capitalism, fascism, individualism, possessiveness, and competitiveness."[73] At the heart of the organization, however, is a cold determination to act violently against "enemies of the people," and violently they have acted, with assassinations, kidnappings, bank robberies, and a climactic shootout with the police during which six of its leaders were killed.[74] With these deaths, the SLA appears to have fallen back into that obscurity from which it briefly emerged. Nonetheless, that such groups can be formed and can be prompted to such violence is itself significant. It serves as a reminder of the challenges that the police must confront and of the difficulties that exist for police-community relations when from the community itself such revolutionary groups can arise.

Radicals

The radical seeks to gain a position of influence in the regime in order to transform it. Unlike the revolutionary, he does not renounce it, and unlike the reformer, he does not merely seek to change its policies. As Arthur Lothstein writes, radicalism "is not content to be a parliamentary opposition or a countervailing political power. . . . It challenges the vested interests, entrenched institutions, and dominant life-styles endemic to the advanced capitalist societies. . . ."[75] The radical thus sees a need for a fundamental transformation of the existing system. However, while he may reject America's whole economic, social, and political structure, he is likely to remain fully committed to America's ideology and rules of the game. As Kenneth Keniston has observed, most radicals retain allegiance to such

> ancient, traditional, and creedal American values . . . [as] free speech, citizens' participation in decision-making, equal opportunity and justice. Insofar as the activist rejects all or part of "the power structure," it is because current political realities fall so far short of the ideals he sees as essential to the American creed. And insofar as he repudiates careerism and familism, it is because of his implicit allegiance to other human goals he sees, once again, as more crucial to American life. Thus, to emphasize the "alienation" of activists is to neglect their more basic allegiance to creedal ideas.[76]

One of the American ideals is, of course, a belief in the desirability and efficacy of political and social action. But a question arises: What is appropriate action for a radical? Are radicals not ultimately required to choose between the purposes and tactics of the reformers and those of the revolutionaries? Has not Malcolm X properly stated the alternative open to them: "It's the ballot or the bullet"?[77] Because of the tendency for radical groups to become ultimately either reformist or revolutionary in character, few groups or individuals are easily characterized as radical.[78] Two groups of individuals will be briefly considered here: student activists of the New Left and Malcolm X and the Black Muslims.

Radical student activists tend for the most part to be members of the New Left, committed if perhaps less intensely to many of the same goals as their more revolutionary counterparts. Thus, they tend to be anticapitalist, antiauthoritarian, anti-imperialist, antiracist, anti–male chauvinist.[79]

Most radical student activists also tend to be possessed of what psychologist Kenneth Keniston calls a "protest-prone personality."[80] They come from families that are "unusually equalitarian, permissive, 'democratic,' and highly individuated."[81] They have been encouraged to talk back to their parents at the dinner table and to expect that "rational" solutions exist for all family problems and conflicts. As a consequence, they tend to find the problems of politics and government all the more enticing yet frustrating, for they are seemingly so immune to mere "rational" disposition, hence their commitment to a fundamental and radical transformation of the regime into one where rationality alone prevails. The families of protest-prone students are also possessed of a solidarity between the younger and older generations. Many radical student activists appear to be living out the expressed but unimplemented values of their parents; and, as Keniston continues, it is likely that they "receive both covert and overt support from their parents because the latter are secretly proud of their children's eagerness to implement the ideals they as parents have only given lip service to."[82] Keniston has also found that student protesters tend to be "generally outstanding students."[83] His overall summary description is significant; they "are not drawn from disadvantaged, status-anxious, underprivileged, or uneducated groups; on the contrary, they are selectively recruited from among those young Americans who have had the most socially fortunate upbringings."[84]

Because of this "socially fortunate upbringing," the public, by and large, does not know how to respond properly to these radical student activists and their deliberate lawbreaking and occasionally violent behavior. They are inclined to say that "a country that fears its young is sick," and when they see their children arrested for criminal acts, they typically cry out that "those are our children out there"—as if children can do no wrong.[85] But radical student activists obviously can do wrong and have done wrong, as the events surrounding the 1968 Democratic National Convention in Chicago and the disturbances that have marked many college campuses give witness.

There is blame enough for all involved in the violence surrounding the Democratic National Convention in Chicago. In an official report to the National Commission on the Causes and Prevention of Violence, Daniel Walker, vice-president of the Chicago Crime Commission and later elected governor of Illinois, and his staff concluded that a "police riot" erupted in Chicago during the convention.

> [O]n on the part of the police there was enough wild club swinging, enough cries of hatred, enough gratuitous beating to make the conclusion inescapable that individual policemen, and lots of them, committed violent acts far in excess of the requisite force for crowd dispersal or arrest. To read dispassionately the hundreds of statements describing at first hand

the events of Sunday and Monday nights is to become convinced of the presence of what could only be called a police riot.[86]

But the police, of course, were not alone to blame for the violence. Demonstrators were also at fault. The Walker Report, as it came to be called, catalogued some of the weapons employed by demonstrators against the police: rocks, bricks, sticks, empty and filled cans; bags of urine, feces, paint, or ink; golf balls with nails impailed in them; knives, pieces of wood or shoes with embedded razors, oven cleaner, and acid.[87] Demonstrators also attempted to rip off the badges of police officers and stab the officers with them.[88]

The Walker Report was quick to point out that the police violence of convention week was committed by a small minority of the Chicago Police Department. The great majority of policemen had "acted responsibly."[89] The same may be said of radical student demonstrators and protestors. Nevertheless, the frequency and extent of violence and disruptive demonstrations that have occurred on college campuses indicate that the tactics employed by many radical student activists in Chicago were by no means unique.

Many radical students see the university as an institution of the American regime, and hence subject to all of the criticisms and in need of the same transformation as the regime itself. As SDS members Cathy Wilkerson, Mike Spiegel, and Les Coleman exhort, "We must attempt to make clear the historical role of those [middle-class, materialistic] values, and politically attack the university for its role in the perpetuation of those relationships." They also see the university as exploiting surrounding working-class communities and as turning out "corporate morons to take up the task of administering the world." For them, the university is not a place dedicated to human development, but rather a place "dedicated to the perpetuation of class exploitation and class oppression." It catches students in the "stupid chains of individualism" and makes them identify with the exploiters and the oppressors. As a result, they seek to attack the university on every front. Their goal is to shut it down completely. Reform of the university is out of the question, for as long as society exists in its present form, the university can function only as its tool.[90]

Toward this end of shutting down the university, student radicals have employed such tactics as student strikes, class boycotts, sit-ins, destruction of university property, and, on rare occasions, even bombing. The gravity of these actions, not only for the police who are called upon to restore order and ensure safety, but also for society as a whole, is revealed in the following passage from Ernest van den Haag:

> [I]n a democracy the law is ideally the expression of the majority's will. Opponents are allowed opportunity to change the law peacefully—that is, by persuading the majority to their own view. But to give the opponents the right to achieve by violence what the unpersuaded majority rejects is to give the minority the right to impose its will on the majority. The situation can only lead to tyranny by the minority, for the minority cannot

keep itself in power and impose laws that the majority does not want except by oppression and restriction of the majority's freedom.[91]

Malcolm X and his Black Muslim followers comprise a second group of radicals. Malcolm X is especially significant in that he expressed so skillfully and clearly the tension that radicals experience as they are drawn toward the revolutionaries on the one hand and the reformers on the other. Malcolm X perhaps nowhere explored this tension better than in his speech "The Ballot or the Bullet."

Malcolm X expressed much of the outrage of the revolutionary. He declared, "No, I'm not an American. I'm one of the 22 million black people who are the victims of Americanism . . . I am speaking as a victim of this American system. And I see America through the eyes of the victim. I don't see any American dream; I see an American nightmare."[92] Yet, despite these sentiments, he was also fundamentally committed to the legitimacy of the Constitution and the political and economic system of the United States. This is readily apparent in his comment on the courts:

> Anyone who puts forth any effort to deprive you of that which is yours,
> is breaking the law, is a criminal. And this was pointed out by the Supreme
> Court decision. It outlawed segregation. Which means segregation is
> against the law. Which means a segregationist is breaking the law. A
> segregationist is a criminal. You can't label him as anything other than that.
> And when you demonstrate against segregation, the law is on your side.
> The Supreme Court is on your side.[93]

The black "victims" of Americanism presently occupy the deep valley that surrounds the American plateau of politics. How are blacks to ascend to the plateau and participate fully there? Malcolm X's answer is simple and direct: "You've got to control your own. Just like the white man has control of his, you need to control yours."[94] Blacks must fight their way onto the plateau. They cannot wait for the present white participants to invite them on.

> Don't change the white man's mind—you can't change his mind, and that
> whole thing about appealing to the moral conscience of America—
> America's conscience is bankrupt. She lost all conscience a long time ago.
> Uncle Sam has no conscience. They don't know what morals are. They don't
> try and eliminate an evil because it's evil, or because it's illegal, or because
> it's immoral; they eliminate it only when it threatens their existence.[95]

The fight to gain access may be either violent or nonviolent; that will be determined by the tactics of those who may seek to deny them a place on the plateau. But even if violence and death should result, these eventualities would simply reaffirm the validity of America's commitment to equality.

> I'm non-violent with those who are non-violent with me. But when you drop
> that violence on me, then you've made me go insane and I'm not responsible
> for what I do. And that's the way every Negro should get. Anytime you
> know you are within the law, within your legal rights, within your moral

rights, in accordance with justice, then die for what you believe in. But don't die alone. Let your dying be reciprocal. This is what is meant by equality. What's good for the goose is good for the gander.[96]

"What's good for the goose is good for the gander." This captures the sentiments of the radical rather well. All the rights and protections of the regime must be available to all, or they will be available to none.

Reformers

The fourth group is the reformers. Reformers usually give overt support for the regime's ideology, norms, institutions, and authorities, but may oppose particular policies, customs, or laws that they see as inconsistent with the broader meaning and intention of the regime. As Canfield notes: "Reformist groups are usually deeply committed to the fundamental regime principles and accept them as legitimate standards for judging the actions and policies of government. Reformers may find the regime wanting according to its own ideals, but they believe that it is capable of progress and social change."[97] What reformers hope to accomplish is often fairly specific. They often have a single set of well-defined policy grievances, such as civil rights, labor legislation, or peace. An extremely large and varied group of movements and organizations can be labeled reformist. They include labor movements, antiwar movements, the civil-rights movement including the National Association for the Advancement of Colored People (NAACP) and the Southern Christian Leadership Conference, Americans for Democratic Action, Common Cause, the American Civil Liberties Union, and young College Democrats.

The most common tactics of reformist movements and organizations are usually peaceful and include such legal demonstrations and protests as strikes, "teach-ins," and legal picketing, and such illegal acts as civil disobedience. Civil disobedience is usually understood to involve the peaceful, nonviolent disobedience of a law believed to be immoral or unjust and a willingness to accept the resulting punishment.[98] It is a deliberate challenge to civil authority by persons whose consciences compel their loyalty to what they see as a higher order of authority. Louis Radelet observes that "acts of civil disobedience are usually engaged in by relatively few people, a small minority raising its voice against a prevailing and generally accepted norm or practice. Civil disobedience challenges what the majority deems acceptable and puts the social conscience to a test."[99] Thus, civil disobedience constitutes more than mere illegality; it is an open challenge to the legitimacy of the majority. Little wonder, then, that a recent study by the International Association of Chiefs of Police reveals that over 90 percent of police officers, who, after all, typically represent the majority and enforce its laws, are opposed to civil disobedience.

Civil disobedience is not a new tactic. Henry David Thoreau practiced it in the nineteenth century to protest American toleration of slavery and participation in the Mexican-American War. Thoreau argued that "we should be men

©1974 LOS ANGELES TIMES SYNDICATE
THE DENVER POST
OLIPHANT

ACLU

NOW, WHO'S OVER-REACTING?

'SHE WANTS TO KNOW WHY YOU MEN OVER-REACT SO NASTILY TOWARDS TERRORISTS WHO USE CYANIDE BULLETS AND 50-CALIBER MACHINE GUNS!'

Editorial cartoon by Pat Oliphant. Copyright, The Denver Post.
Reprinted with permission Los Angeles Times Syndicate.

first, and subjects afterward."[100] Man is possessed of a conscience that tells him what is right or wrong, just or unjust. When a law requires an act inconsistent with what his conscience dictates, he must disobey the law.

> If the injustice is a part of the necessary friction of the machine of government, let it go, let it go: perchance it will wear smooth,—certainly the machine will wear out. If the injustice has a spring, or a pulley, or a rope, or a crank, exclusively for itself, then perhaps you may consider whether the remedy will not be worse than the evil; but if it is of such a nature that it requires you to be the agent of injustice to another, then, I say, break the law. Let your life be a counter-friction to stop the machine. What I have to do is to see, at any rate, that I do not lend myself to the wrong which I condemn.[101]

Thoreau remains the patron saint of the American tradition of civil disobedience.[102] His teaching is all the more controversial today as the "machine of government" is now employed by the majority in a much more expansive way than Thoreau could ever have imagined. After all, Thoreau began his famous essay by heartily accepting the notion " 'that government is best which governs least'; . . . Carried out, it finally amounts to this, which also I believe,—'that government is best which governs not at all.' "[103] While civil disobedience in recent years has been employed by antiwar demonstrators in efforts to bring about an end to America's military involvement in Southeast Asia, it has been used with much greater effectiveness by civil-rights activists in their efforts to gain full and equal political, legal, economic, and social rights for black Americans. The classic defense for civil disobedience in the context of the contemporary struggle for civil rights was given by Dr. Martin Luther King, Jr., in his "Letter from Birmingham Jail." Jailed along with other members of the Southern Christian Leadership Conference for illegally parading without a permit to protest against the law enforcing segregation in Birmingham, Alabama, King justified his actions by declaring that there are two types of laws: just and unjust. "I would be the first to advocate obeying just laws. One has not only a legal but a moral responsibility to obey just laws. Conversely, one has a moral responsibility to disobey unjust laws. I would agree with St. Augustine that 'an unjust law is no law at all.' "[104] King continued, however, that one who breaks an unjust law must do so "openly, lovingly, and with a willingness to accept the penalty." In so doing, the individual does not depreciate the rule of law but rather elevates it. "I submit that an individual who breaks a law that conscience tells him is unjust and who willingly accepts the penalty of imprisonment in order to arouse the conscience of the community over its injustice, is in reality expressing the highest respect for law."[105] Former Supreme Court Justice Abe Fortas heartily concurs, declaring King's actions to be "in the great tradition of social protest in a democratic society where all citizens, including protestors, are subject to the rule of law."[106]

King's words ring eloquently and his argument has substance. As he reminds his readers, "We should never forget that everything Adolph Hitler did in Germany was 'legal' and everything the Hungarian Freedom Fighters did in Hungary was 'illegal.' "[107] Yet, despite King's defense of civil disobedience, it is, as Professor Herbert J. Storing has perceptively observed, "the resort—always a theoretically and practically weak resort—of the subject of law, exercised because the subject cannot or will not take up the rights and duties of the citizen."[108] Civil disobedience reduces those who practice it to subjects, for whom the important political inquiry is "Shall we obey?" It in no way prepares them to be citizens, for whom the relevant question is "What shall be done?"[109] Thus, "it is inherently subordinate, responsive, dependent, and—for the citizen of a democracy—degrading."[110] Shortly before his tragic assassination in 1968, Martin Luther King had become increasingly aware of this destructive dimension of civil disobedience, and he anxiously sought ways by which to enroll blacks "formerly confined to the school of protest, in the school of citizenship."[111]

> How shall we turn the ghettoes into a vast school? How shall we make
> every street corner a forum, not a lounging place for trivial gossip and petty
> gambling, where life is wasted and human experience withers to trivial
> sensations? How shall we make every houseworker and every laborer a
> demonstrator, a voter, a canvasser, and a student? The dignity their jobs
> may deny them is waiting for them in political social action.[112]

Civil disobedience is not only detrimental to the development of proper citizenship; it is also destructive to government itself, and hence inimical to those individuals who trust in it for their security. As Ernest van den Haag declares, "To recognize the legitimacy of a government is to recognize its authority to make laws; for, to govern is to make laws."[113] Whatever else laws are, they are rules that are to be obeyed. One cannot consent to a government's authority to make laws and at the same time claim the right to disobey them, for the claim would deny the authority to which one has consented. To accept the authority to make rules—that is, to acknowledge the government as legitimate—is to accept the obligation to obey them. Nor can one claim a right to disobey some laws. A law is a law to the extent that it can require obedience; otherwise, it is merely a suggestion and not a law. As Sir William Blackstone put it, "[O]bedience is an empty name, if every individual has a right to decide how far he himself shall obey."[114]

Furthermore, one who claims a right to engage in civil disobedience when the laws are in conflict with the superior obligations of his conscience must, unless he asserts that only his conscience is superior to law, concede this right to others as well.[115] Yet, as Burke Marshall has observed, the law cannot distinguish between the consciences of saints and sinners. "If the decision to break the law really turned on individual conscience, it is hard to see in law how Dr. King is better off than Governor Ross Barnett of Mississippi, who also believed deeply in his cause and was willing to go to jail."[116]

If all obedience is voluntary and dependent upon conscience, then laws lose their binding legal character and are reduced to mere suggestions. But suggestions are simply not enough. Professor van den Haag underscores this when he declares that "without laws to proscribe some acts (e.g., murder, or theft, or driving on the wrong side of the street) and prescribe others (e.g., the payment of taxes needed to enforce laws) there would be no social order and viable society."[117] Without laws, chaos and disorder would prevail. Men would return to a "state of nature" where life is, in Thomas Hobbes's famous language, "solitary, poor, nasty, brutish, and short."

For society to exist and for the protection it provides citizens to continue, obedience to the law must be habitual; as Abraham Lincoln put it in his address before the Young Men's Lyceum in 1838, it must become a political religion.

> The question recurs "how shall we fortify against it [disobedience to the law]?" The answer is simple. Let every American, every lover of liberty, every well wisher to his posterity, swear by the blood of the Revolution, never to violate in the least particular, the laws of the country, and never to tolerate their violation by others. As the patriots of seventy-six did to the support of the Declaration of Independence, so to the support of the Constitution and Laws, let every American pledge his life, his property, and his sacred honor;—let every man remember that to violate the law, is to trample on the blood of his father, and to tear the charter of his own, and his children's liberty. Let reverence for the laws, be breathed by every American mother, to the lisping babe, that prattles on her lap—let it be taught in schools, in seminaries, and in colleges;—let it be written in Primers, spelling books, and in Almanacs;—let it be preached from the pulpit, proclaimed in legislative halls, and enforced in courts of justice. And, in short, let it become the *political religion* of the nation; and let the old and the young, the rich and the poor, the grave and the gay, of all sexes and tongues, and colors and conditions, sacrifice unceasingly upon its altars.[118]

Lincoln appreciated that the power of habit is indispensable in ensuring obedience to law. Civil disobedience, however, helps to undermine this habit of obedience. Because the distinction between civil disobedience and testing the constitutionality of a law is often blurred, individuals often violate a law—which the Court later declares unconstitutional—with apparent immunity, and habitual obedience is thereby even further weakened. Professor Storing has described this consequence all too well: "Disobedience abounds, but it has thrust civility aside."[119]

Civil disobedience is subject to still another criticism, and one that is perhaps the most serious of all: for civil disobedience to have an effect, it must take place in a fundamentally just regime, which it in turn helps to destroy. Martin Luther King declared that those who engage in civil disobedience must break unjust laws "openly, lovingly, and with a willingness to accept the penalty." He also declared that everything done in Hitler's Germany was "legal." Yet, one may ask, should King have violated the laws of Hitler's Germany "openly, lovingly, and with a willingness to accept the penalty"? The mere posing of the question provides its answer. Laws can be broken "openly, lovingly, and with a willingness to accept the penalty" only in a fundamentally just regime. However, if this disobedience itself helps to undermine that habitual obedience so essential for the perpetuation of the regime itself, perhaps other ways—political ways—must be used for the eradication of unjust laws or laws that offend the conscience.

Herbert J. Storing has astutely observed that civil disobedience constitutes an unsuccessful attempt to combine both in principle and in practice revolution and conventional political action.[120] Like Martin Luther King, many who have engaged in it ultimately have realized its deficiencies and have come to embrace orthodox political action. When dealing with individuals who participate in civil disobedience, the police must take every precaution to prevent driving them to revolution instead. The police must understand their basic commitment to the legitimacy of the regime, the limited nature of their grievances, their basic commitment to nonviolence, and their genuine if at times ill-founded trust in the American judicial system to declare the laws they are violating unconstitutional, and deal with them accordingly. With these considerations in mind, the police response is likely to be one that will encourage those who have chosen civil disobedience to come to realize the effectiveness of and potential for conventional political action.[121]

The Establishmentarian

The establishmentarian is likely to give diffuse support to all of the objects of democratic legitimacy: its ideology, rules of the game, institutions, authorities, policies, and effectiveness. He looks askance at any political violence, although he may understand its use by others. He is likely to be a middle-of-the-road

Democrat or a liberal Republican and to belong to a labor union or chamber of commerce.[122] The establishmentarian is genuinely supportive of and committed to the existing regime; but the very nature of his support and commitment places the regime in serious jeopardy. The establishmentarian is the most likely of all to promote interest-group liberalism and the notion that if enough groups get together and bargain and compete with one another over how to deal with a particular problem, the appropriate solution will emerge. He is the most likely to believe that good intentions are sufficient to see America through any crisis or problem. Yet, as Edward C. Banfield appropriately observes, this outlook contributes to "the perversity that characterizes the choices of measures for dealing with the urban 'crisis.' "[123] This outlook tends to employ two simple rules: "First, don't just sit there. Do something! And second, do good!"[124] It believes that any crisis can be solved if the public just works at it hard enough. The result of this, however, is that expectations have been raised unrealistically. When governmental programs have been unable to keep pace with expectations, resentment, frustration, and contempt for the government is common among those who have come to expect more. The result is a decline in governmental legitimacy and a concomitant increase in willingness to resort to political violence.

The Traditionalist

The traditionalist, like the establishmentarian, is a supporter of the regime. His political participation is more limited, however. If he belongs to any organization, it is likely to be a fraternal or veterans' group or perhaps even a church. As Canfield describes him: "On campus he is a conservative or a vocationalist. In the black community, he is an Uncle Tom who still votes Republican. Among the white middle class, he is likely to be prototypically an ordinary citizen of Orange County who does not belong to the super-patriotic John Birch Society."[125] He is a "middle American" who all too frequently regards himself as a forgotten man. As such, he is likely to feel resentment, envy, disappointment, and uncertainty, all of which detract from his support for the regime.[126]

The resentment the traditionalist feels is tied to a perception of a loss of status and power to those who are less well off, especially to black Americans. He sees certain minorities and other out-groups rapidly closing the social distance that previously had them "castes away."[127] The envy he feels is associated with this resentment and relates to the potency and actual success that these power-grabbing out-groups have had in climbing the social ladder. The disappointment he experiences results from his belief that elements of the government have abandoned neutrality and have gone over to support out-group power-grabbers. In fact, he is increasingly likely to regard all large organizations—including government, business, and labor—as "having it in for the little guy," the ordinary citizen who finds himself ever more voiceless, powerless, and friendless. Given these other feelings, his uncertainty is perhaps inevitable. Aware of America's bloody political history, including Shays' Rebellion, the Civil War draft riots, and presidential assassinations, his concern with where the government is heading is perhaps surpassed by his apprehensions that it may all come crashing down. Recent actions by the federal government's Department of Health, Education, and Welfare and the United States Supreme Court have done nothing to allay the fears and apprehensions of the traditionalists. Perhaps no issue has highlighted this as dramatically as affirmative action programs and preferential hiring and admissions policies.

In an effort to eliminate the effect of generations of discrimination and to provide full and equal access to blacks and other minorities on the American plateau of politics, the federal government has vigorously pursued a course of action that many middle-class whites regard as discrimination in reverse. *De Funis* v. *Odegaard* is a case in point.[128] Marco De Funis, a white Phi Beta Kappa undergraduate, was denied admission to the University of Washington's School of Law while minority applicants with lower undergraduate grades and Law School Admission Test (LSAT) scores were admitted. De Funis brought suit, claiming that the law school had violated his right to equal protection of the laws by denying him admission while accepting those less qualified. The Washington State Supreme Court rejected the De Funis claim, noting among other things that

> the "preferential" minority admissions policy administered by the law school is clearly not a form of invidious discrimination. The goal of this policy is not to separate the races, but to bring them together. And, as has been observed, "preferential admissions do not represent a covert attempt to stigmatize the majority race as inferior; nor is it reasonable to expect that a possible effect of the extension of educational preferences to certain disadvantaged racial minorities will be to stigmatize whites."

While this and other preferential admissions and hiring policies may not make traditionalists and other members of the white middle class feel the stigma of inferiority, they have intensified their feelings that they are neglected, powerless, and used. Thus far the rulings of the United States Supreme Court have in no way neutralized these sentiments. Thus, in *De Funis*, the Supreme Court, noting that the petitioner had ultimately gained admission to law school and was in fact soon to graduate, refused to rule on the merits of preferential admissions and dismissed the suit on grounds of mootness. Many whites, rightly or wrongly, have come to interpret this action by the Court as a tacit endorsement of continued efforts to uplift the minority by holding down the majority. To the extent that these views prevail and gain in prominence, the solid support these groups have traditionally given to the American regime will remain in question. Witness, after all, the recent violence in Boston, especially South Boston, as the federal courts have attempted to desegregate the public schools of that city.

Deviants

A seventh category includes those criminal or deviant groups or individuals who generally regard the regime as legitimate but who have few scruples about violating those of its laws or norms that are in conflict with their desires and aspirations. The juvenile delinquent is representative of this category. He accepts the goals of the American society even though he finds it necessary to pursue them in a deviant way. In fact, as Louis Yablonsky has pointed out, he is really affirming the validity of the goals and values of the American society by striving for them at any cost.[129] Organized crime also fits into this category. For example, Gay Talese describes the anger of Mafia leaders at black rebellion and student disruption; they were greatly perplexed at what they saw happening to the country in the late 1960s.[130]

Street-corner gangs and roving bands of hoodlums like the Hell's Angels also may be categorized as deviant. Canfield writes that young street-corner gangs probably employ violence for a variety of reasons, for kicks and fun as well as for profit and some community control. Like all violence, these tactics produce the same consequences: harm, death, destruction, and disorder. However, the purpose for these criminal tactics is important. Street-corner gangs and the criminal element generally can be distinguished from revolutionaries in that they generally accept the regime's fundamental values and lack a radical ideology.[131] Hell's Angels also tend to lack a radical ideology and, for that matter, much awareness of the regime at all. They enjoy and indulge in the advantages and creature comforts that the regime, and the stability and industry that it fosters, allows. However, like parasites, they are not above unthinkingly killing the goose that lays the golden eggs. As Robert Shellow and Derek V. Roemer describe them, they "seem to be people who need and seek the stimulation of collective action, excitement, and violence. Without it they become depressed and demoralized. They have an affinity for the romantic role of outlaw, which is perhaps the only status in which they feel they can stand as individuals."[132]

The Superpatriots

The eighth and final category can appropriately be referred to as the super-patriots. Superpatriots generally are deeply committed to their own perceptions of the meaning and purpose of the regime. They typically seek either to maintain the system or regime as it presently is or to push it back to a "golden era" when its principles and commitment were supposedly more pure.[133] Thus, as Alan F. Westin has noted, their program typically consists of advocating the repeal of things or the removal of the United States from something or somewhere. A partial list of those things superpatriots generally oppose would surely include U.S. membership in the United Nations, the World Health Organization, and UNICEF (the United Nations International Children's Emergency Fund); reciprocal trade agreements and all foreign aid; diplomatic relations with the Soviet Union and all other Communist nations; social security, the REA (Rural Electrification Administration) and the TVA (Tennessee Valley Authority); the graduated income tax; government wage and price controls; "forced integration"; the Federal Reserve system; urban renewal; fluoridation; metro government; federal aid to housing; and all programs regulating farmers.[134]

Superpatriots constitute a "peculiar breed of citizen."[135] Even in the post-Watergate era, most citizens go about their daily activities confident that the government can for the most part be trusted to take care of the most important things competently, albeit with some corruption and graft; superpatriots are less trusting. They are inclined to see a web of conspiracy at work consistently frustrating solutions to the problems America faces and encouraging its ruination.[136] As a result, they feel obliged vigorously to protect the regime and are often willing to go outside the law if necessary to do so.

When these groups resort to violence in an effort to assist the government, most people have categorized them as vigilantes. Examples of such vigilantism include the violence of "hard hats," nativist movements,[137] Know-Nothings, the Ku Klux Klan, the American Nazi party, the Minutemen, the John Birch Society, and, on occasion, even police themselves.[138] Of these groups, the Ku Klux Klan has been "one of the most consistent features in the last hundred years of American violence."[139] As such, it deserves closer consideration.

In fact, there have been three Ku Klux Klans. The first was of Reconstruction times, the second was prominent in the 1920s, and the third is current today. The first Ku Klux Klan employed violence and threats to intimidate Radical Republicans of the Reconstruction era and to force recently freed slaves to accept the renewed rule of Southern whites. The second Klan differed significantly from both its predecessor and its successor. Although it was founded in Atlanta in 1915, it grew far beyond the boundaries of the old Confederacy and during the early 1920s became a truly national organization. Unlike the first or the third Klans, it viewed blacks as only secondary targets, and although its rhetoric was filled with denunciations of Catholics and Jews, recent research has established that most Klan violence—whippings, torture, and murder—was directed less against Catholics, Jews, and blacks than against "ne'er-do-wells and the allegedly immoral of the same background as the Klansmen: white, Anglo-Saxon, Protestant."[140] The third Klan, the Klan of today, has been largely restricted to the South and is all too well known for its acts of violence against the civil-rights movement and desegregation.

According to Richard Hofstadter, the dominant form of violence in American history has been the violence by these conservative vigilante groups.

> [O]ne is impressed that most American violence—and this also illuminates
> its relationship to state power—has been initiated with a "conservative"
> bias. It has been unleashed against abolitionists, Catholics, radicals,
> workers and labor organizers, Negroes, Orientals, and other ethnic or racial
> or ideological minorities, and has been used ostensibly to protect the

American, the Southerner, the white Protestant, or simply the established middle-class way of life and morals.[141]

Some of the contemporary acts of superpatriots suggest that they are willing to continue this use of violence in the future. Among the most frightening of these acts are the clandestine desert maneuvers and the stockpiling of weapons arsenals by some groups, such as the Minutemen. Since these superpatriot groups commonly perceive their violent activity as generally reactive to leftist or black violence, they constitute perhaps one of the greatest threats to the security and peaceful continuation of the regime. After all, they can conceivably mobilize far greater public support through distorted appeals to traditional "American" values than revolutionary or other dissident minorities or subcultures.

The Majority and Governmental Legitimacy

The eight different orientations to the legitimacy of the American regime have now been explored. Representatives of each of these orientations, along with their ideological premises and tactics, have been identified. Although each of these orientations has been presented as if it were of equal weight and significance with any of the others, by far the vast majority of Americans tend to fit into the reformist, establishmentarian, and traditionalist categories. Thus, public opinion research indicates that a substantial majority of 60 to 90 percent of the general public believes that governmental authority is just in terms of doing "what is right."[142] Likewise, they overwhelmingly condemn the use of political violence, so much so that 58 percent of whites are "unwilling to engage in any deviant dissident behavior."[143] When violence does occur, the public as a whole considers it to have a universally negative effect. Thus, one Harris poll found that 94 percent of whites felt blacks had more to lose than to gain by rioting.[144] Rioting, in fact, is so strongly opposed by the public that 58 percent support the shooting of looters.[145]

Most Americans—those classified as reformists, establishmentarians, and traditionalists—are fundamentally committed to the American regime. Some may feel that the government's response to certain problems and difficulties is too slow; others may consider it too fast. As a result, even those fundamentally committed to the legitimacy of the government may occasionally engage in acts of illegality or even violence in an effort to bring their grievances to the government's attention. These actions are likely to bring them into contact with the police. On such occasions, it is essential that the police do nothing that may further or permanently alienate them from the American regime. The police must recall that their behavior is an aberration and that the way in which the police treat them will in large part confirm their basic faith in—or more recent frustration with—the government. The exercise of police-community relations on these occasions is both possible and likely to succeed.

However, when other groups that fundamentally challenge or reject the institutions and rules of the game of the American regime engage in similar or more violent acts, what the police can hope to accomplish in terms of fostering goodwill toward both them and the regime itself is far more limited. In these instances, the police must try to prevent themselves from being manipulated into behaving in a manner most beneficial or useful to these groups. The police must exercise great restraint so as not to confirm their suspicions regarding the corruption and worthlessness of the regime. Of course, the police must realize them to be the threat that they are, but they must also have sufficient confidence in the strength of the American regime and in the probity and discernment of its people to treat them as Thomas Jefferson would: "If there be any among us who would wish to dissolve this Union or to change its Republican form, let them stand undisturbed as monuments of the safety with which error of opinion may be tolerated where reason is left free to combat it."[146]

NOTES

1. Roger B. Canfield, *Black Ghetto Riots and Campus Disorders: A Subcultural and Philosophical Study of Democratic Legitimacy and American Political Violence, 1964–1970* (San Francisco: R. & E. Research Associates, 1972), p. 90.

2. Ibid., p. 92.

3. *Time*, "Cops' Credibility," February 4, 1974, p. 79.

4. Canfield, *Black Ghetto Riots*, p. 96.

5. James W. Prothro and Charles M. Griggs, "Fundamental Principles of Democracy: Bases of Agreement and Disagreement," *Journal of Politics*, 22 (May 1960):282.

6. Alexis de Toqueville, *Democracy in America*, ed. Phillips Bradley, vol. 2 (New York: Random House, 1945), pp. 102–103.

7. The colleges and universities included in this study were Yale, Williams, Sarah Lawrence, Brandeis, Stanford, Reed, Maquette, Indiana, South Carolina, Howard, and Davidson. Phillip R. Ardery, "Special Report: Opinion on the Campus," *National Review*, 23 (June 15, 1971):635–650.

8. Bill Aron, *Radical Ideology on the University of Chicago Campus* (Chicago: University of Chicago Community and Family Study Center, 1970), p. 7.

9. Canfield, *Black Ghetto Riots*, p. 177.

10. Edward N. Muller, "A Test of a Partial Theory of Potential for Political Violence," *American Political Science Review*, 66, no. 3 (September 1972):938.

11. David O. Sears, "Political Attitudes of Los Angeles Negroes," in *The Los Angeles Riots: A Socio-Psychological Study*, ed. Nathan E. Cohen (New York: Praeger, 1970), p. 696.

12. Tom M. Tomlinson, "Ideological Foundations for Negro Action: Militant and Non-Militant Views," in *The Los Angeles Riots*, ed. Cohen, p. 347.

13. Canfield, *Black Ghetto Riots*, p. 191.

14. Ibid., p. 212.

15. William Brink and Louis Harris, *Black and White: A Study of U.S. Racial Attitudes Today* (New York: Simon & Schuster, 1966), p. 264.

16. Angus Campbell and Howard Schuman, "Racial Attitudes in Fifteen American Cities," *Supplemental Studies for the National Advisory Commission on Civil Disorders* (Washington, D.C.: U.S. Government Printing Office, 1968), p. 55.

17. Barton also found that 31 percent of the Columbia faculty gave support for SDS tactics. See Allen H. Barton, "The Columbia Crisis: Campus, Vietnam, and the Ghetto," *Public Opinion Quarterly,* Fall 1968, p. 341.

18. Canfield, *Black Ghetto Riots,* p. 219.

19. Aron, *Radical Ideology,* pp. 7, 16.

20. Theodore J. Lowi, *The End of Liberalism* (New York: Norton, 1969), p. 29.

21. Robert Paul Wolff, "Beyond Tolerance," in *A Critique of Pure Tolerance,* eds. Robert Paul Wolff, Barrington Moore, Jr., and Herbert Marcuse (Boston: Beacon, 1969), pp. 8–12.

22. Ibid., p. 8.

23. Ibid.

24. Ibid., p. 9.

25. Tocqueville, *Democracy in America,* vol. 1, pp. 198–199.

26. Tocqueville, *The Old Regime and the French Revolution,* trans. Stuart Gilbert (Garden City, N.Y.: Doubleday, 1955), p. 206.

27. Wolff, "Beyond Tolerance," p. 14.

28. Ibid., p. 21.

29. Grant McConnell, *Private Power and American Democracy* (New York: Knopf, 1967), p. 363.

30. Lowi, *End of Liberalism,* p. 268.

31. Ibid. See pp. 85–93, 287–293.

32. Ibid., p. 86.

33. Robert Michels, *The Political Parties: A Sociological Study of the Oligarchical Tendencies of Modern Democracy,* trans. Eden and Cedar Paul (New York: Dover, 1959), p. 401.

34. Wolff, "Beyond Tolerance," p. 46.

35. Ibid., p. 45.

36. Philip Taft and Philip Ross, "American Labor Violence: Its Causes, Character, and Outcome," in *Violence in America: Historical and Comparative Perspectives,* eds. Hugh Davis Graham and Ted Robert Gurr. A Staff Report to the National Commission on the Causes and Prevention of Violence (Washington, D.C.: U.S. Government Printing Office, 1969), p. 221.

37. Ibid., p. 289.

38. Lowi, *End of Liberalism,* p. 86.

39. Ibid., p. 292.

40. Ibid.

41. Ibid., p. 263.

42. Ibid., p. 248.

43. Ibid., pp. 250–283.

44. Edward C. Banfield, *The Unheavenly City: The Nature and the Future of Our Urban Crisis* (Boston: Little, Brown, 1970), p. 116.

45. Ibid., p. 24.

46. Robert A. Dahl, "Political Theory: Truth and Consequences," *World Politics,* October 1958, p. 91.

47. Walter Berns, "The New Left and Liberal Democracy," in *How Democratic is America? Responses to the New Left Challenge,* ed. Robert A. Goldwin (Chicago: Rand McNally, 1971), p. 35.

48. Canfield, *Black Ghetto Riots,* p. 108.

49. Lewis Yablonsky, *The Hippie Trip* (New York: Pegasus, 1968).

50. Ibid., p. 320.

51. Ibid., p. 321.

52. Ibid., p. 320.

53. *Newsweek,* July 27, 1970, pp. 22–24.

54. Abbie Hoffman, *Revolution for the Hell of It* (New York: Dial Press, 1968), p. 183.

55. Ibid., p. 161.

56. Students for a Democratic Society, "The Port Huron Statement," in *How Democratic is America?,* ed. Goldwin, p. 7.

57. See John Edgar Hoover, "A Study in Marxist Revolutionary Violence: Students for a Democratic Society, 1962–1969," *Fordham Law Review,* 38, no. 2 (December 1969):6.

58. SDS National Council, "Toward a Revolutionary Youth Movement" (December 1968), in *Guardian (Independent Radical Newsweekly),* January 18, 1969, p. 7.

59. "SDS Ousts PLP," *Guardian (Independent Radical Newsweekly),* June 28, 1969, pp. 3–11.

60. *New Left Notes,* September 20, 1969, p. 6.

61. Ibid., p. 14.

62. Tom Thomas, "The Second Battle of Chicago, 1969," in *Weatherman,* ed. Harold Jacobs (New York: Ramparts, 1970), p. 202.

63. *The Commercial Appeal,* Memphis, July 25, 1974, p. 46.

64. Herbert Marcuse, "Repressive Tolerance," in *A Critique of Pure Tolerance,* eds. Wolff, Moore, and Marcuse, pp. 83–84.

65. William H. Orrick, Jr., *Shut It Down! A College in Crisis: San Francisco State College, October 1968–April 1969.* A Staff Report to the National Commission on the Causes and Prevention of Violence (Washington, D.C.: U.S. Government Printing Office, 1969), p. 154.

66. Leo Rosten, "Who Speaks for the Young?: Some Startling Facts and Fictions," *Look,* May 19, 1970, p. 18.

67. Joe R. Feagin and Harlan Hahn, *Ghetto Riots: The Politics of Violence in American Cities* (New York: Macmillan, 1973), p. 324.

68. Eldridge Cleaver, "The Land Problem," *Ramparts* (May 1968), reprinted in *What Country Have I? Political Writings by Black Americans,* ed. Herbert J. Storing (New York: St. Martin, 1970), pp. 184, 186.

69. Frantz Fanon, *The Wretched of the Earth*, trans. Constance Farrington (New York: Grove, 1963), pp. 35, 37.

70. Eldridge Cleaver, *Soul on Ice* (New York: Dell, 1968), p. 129.

71. Ibid., p. 26.

72. Feagin and Hahn, *Ghetto Riots*, p. 324.

73. "The Hearst Nightmare," *Time*, April 29, 1974, p. 13.

74. "The War for Patty," *Newsweek*, May 27, 1974, p. 18.

75. Arthur Lothstein, "Introduction" to *"All We Are Saying . . .", The Philosophy of the New Left*, ed. A. Lothstein (New York: Capricorn, 1970), p. 13.

76. Kenneth Keniston, *Young Radicals: Notes on Committed Youth* (New York: Harcourt, 1968), p. 301.

77. Malcolm X, "The Ballot or the Bullet," in *Malcolm X Speaks* (New York: Grove, 1965), p. 44.

78. Canfield, *Black Ghetto Riots*, p. 115.

79. For a good description of the principal attitudes and beliefs of the New Left, see Arthur Lothstein's "Introduction" to *"All We Are Saying . . .", The Philosophy of the New Left*, pp. 11–23.

80. Keniston, *Young Radicals*, p. 306.

81. Ibid., p. 310.

82. Ibid., p. 308.

83. Ibid., p. 306.

84. Ibid., p. 307.

85. See Berns, "New Left and Liberal Democracy," p. 38.

86. *Rights in Conflict*. A Report Submitted to the National Commission on the Causes and Prevention of Violence (New York: New American Library, 1968), p. xxii.

87. Ibid., p. 317. See also pp. 171, 183, and 199.

88. Ibid., p. 124.

89. Ibid., p. 28.

90. Cathy Wilkerson, Mike Spiegel, and Les Coleman, "The False Privilege," *New Left Notes*, October 7, 1968.

91. Ernest van den Haag, "America's No. 1 Dilemma," quoted in Louis A. Radelet, *The Police and the Community* (Beverly Hills, Calif.: Glencoe Press), pp. 332–333.

92. Malcolm X, "The Ballot or the Bullet," p. 26.

93. Ibid., p. 33.

94. Ibid., p. 42.

95. Ibid., p. 40.

96. Ibid., p. 34.

97. Canfield, *Black Ghetto Riots*, p. 117.

98. See Abe Fortas, *Concerning Dissent and Civil Disobedience* (New York: New American Library, 1968), pp. 67–68. Not everyone agrees with this definition of civil disobedience. Noted constitutional authority C. Herman Pritchett declares that civil disobedience "involves deliberate violation of law, but the violation is not necessarily limited to laws protestors regard as unjust. Rather, practitioners of civil disobedience will violate admittedly valid laws, such as traffic regulations, in order to dramatize their grievances by creating a maximum of confusion, trouble, and danger for the community. Actual or threatened tactics of civil disobedience have included sitting down in busy street intersections or on major bridges, concerted turning on of water faucets to reduce water pressure, stalling automobiles on expressways, occupying offices of government officials, blocking entrances to construction sites, and the like" (C. Herman Pritchett, *The American Constitution,* 2nd ed. [New York: McGraw-Hill, 1968], p. 486).

99. Radelet, *Police and the Community,* p. 296.

100. Henry David Thoreau, "Civil Disobedience," in *On Civil Disobedience: American Essays, Old and New,* ed. Robert A. Goldwin (Chicago: Rand McNally, 1969), p. 12.

101. Ibid., p. 19.

102. See Harry V. Jaffa, "Reflections on Thoreau and Lincoln: Civil Disobedience and the American Tradition," in *On Civil Disobedience,* ed. Goldwin, pp. 33–60.

103. Thoreau, "Civil Disobedience," p. 11.

104. Martin Luther King, Jr., "Letter from Birmingham Jail," in *What Country Have I? Political Writings by Black Americans,* ed. Hedbert J. Storing (New York: St. Martin, 1970), p. 121.

105. Ibid., p. 122.

106. Fortas, *Concerning Dissent,* p. 68.

107. King, "Letter from Birmingham Jail," p. 123.

108. Herbert J. Storing, "The Case Against Civil Disobedience," in *On Civil Disobedience,* ed. Goldwin, p. 96.

109. Ibid., p. 117.

110. Ibid.

111. Ibid., p. 118.

112. Martin Luther King, Jr., *Where Do We Go from Here, Chaos or Community?* (Boston: Beacon, 1967), pp. 138, 156.

113. Ernest van den Haag, *Political Violence and Civil Disobedience* (New York: Harper & Row, 1972), p. 13.

114. Sir William Blackstone, *Commentaries on the Laws of England,* vol. 1, p. 251.

115. van den Haag, *Political Violence,* p. 13.

116. Burke Marshall, "The Protest Movement and the Law," *University of Virginia Law Review,* 51 (1965):800, quoted in *To Establish Justice, To Insure Domestic Tranquility: Final Report of the National Commission on the Causes and Prevention of Violence* (New York: Award Books, 1969), p. 101.

117. van den Haag, *Political Violence,* p. 14.

118. Abraham Lincoln, "The Perpetuation of Our Political Institutions," in *On Civil Disobedience,* ed. Goldwin, p. 5, emphasis in the original.

119. Storing, "The Case Against Civil Disobedience," p. 95.

120. Ibid., p. 96.

121. See Nelson A. Watson, "Group Behavior and Civil Disobedience," in *Police and Community Relations: A Source Book*, eds. A. F. Brendstatter and Louis A. Radelet (Beverly Hills, Calif.: Glencoe Press, 1968), p. 112.

122. Canfield, *Black Ghetto Riots*, p. 118.

123. Edward C. Banfield, *The Unheavenly City: The Nature and the Future of Our Urban Crisis* (Boston: Little, Brown, 1970), p. 249. See also Banfield, *The Unheavenly City Revisited: A Revision of The Unheavenly City* (Boston: Little, Brown, 1974), p. 274.

124. Banfield, *The Unheavenly City*, p. 249.

125. Canfield, *Black Ghetto Riots*, p. 119.

126. James S. Campbell, Joseph R. Sahid, and David P. Stang, *Law and Order Reconsidered: A Staff Report to the National Commission on the Causes and Prevention of Violence* (Washington, D.C.: U.S. Government Printing Office, 1969), pp. 56–57.

127. Ibid.

128. 94 Sup. Ct. 1704 (1974). See Robert M. O'Neil, "Preferential Admissions: Equalizing the Access of Minority Groups to Higher Education," *Yale Law Journal*, 80, no. 4 (March 1971):699–767.

129. Yablonsky, *Hippie Trip*, p. 315.

130. Gay Talese, *Honor Thy Father: The Inside Book on the Mafia* (New York: World, 1971).

131. Canfield, *Black Ghetto Riots,* p. 120.

132. Robert Shellow and Derek V. Roemer, "No Heaven for Hell's Angels," in *Law and Order: Police Encounters*, ed. Michael Lipsky (Chicago: Aldine, 1970), p. 142.

133. Canfield, *Black Ghetto Riots*, p. 120.

134. Alan F. Westin, "The John Birch Society: 'Radical Right' and 'Extreme Left' in the Political Context of Post World War II," in *The Radical Right*, ed. Daniel Bell (New York: Doubleday, 1963), pp. 246–247.

135. Canfield, *Black Ghetto Riots,* p. 120.

136. Westin, "John Birch Society," p. 141.

137. See John Higham, *Strangers in the Land* (New Brunswick, N.J.: Rutgers University Press, 1955), for a superb discussion of nativistic movements in the United States in the nineteenth and twentieth centuries.

138. The execution squad depicted in Clint Eastwood's *Magnum Force* is more than a cinematic fiction, as the discovery within the Chicago Police Department of a death squad dedicated to the assassination of drug pushers on Chicago's South and West Sides has made abundantly clear.

139. Richard Maxwell Brown, "Historical Patterns of Violence in America," in *Violence in America: Historical and Comparative Perspectives*, eds. Hugh Davis Graham and Ted Robert Gurr (Washington, D.C.: U.S. Government Printing Office, 1969), p. 39.

140. Ibid.

141. Richard Hofstadter, "Reflections on Violence in the United States," in *American Violence*, eds. Richard Hofstadter and Michael Wallace (New York: Random House, 1971), p. 12.

142. Canfield, *Black Ghetto Riots*, p. 180.

143. Muller, "Test of a Partial Theory," pp. 934–935.

144. Louis Harris, "After the Riots: A Survey," *Newsweek,* August 21, 1967, pp. 18–19.

145. Canfield, *Black Ghetto Riots,* p. 215.

146. Thomas Jefferson, "Inauguration Address," March 4, 1801, in *The Life and Selected Writings of Thomas Jefferson,* eds. Adrienne Koch and William Peden (New York: Random House, 1944), p. 322.

BIBLIOGRAPHY

ADELSON, ALAN. *SDS.* New York: Scribner, 1972.

ARON, BILL. *Radical Ideology on the University of Chicago Campus.* Chicago: University of Chicago Community and Family Study Center, 1970.

BANFIELD, EDWARD C. *The Unheavenly City: The Nature and Future of Our Urban Crisis.* Boston: Little, Brown, 1970.

———. *The Unheavenly City Revisited: A Revision of The Unheavenly City.* Boston: Little, Brown, 1974.

BELL, DANIEL, ed. *The Radical Right.* Garden City, N.Y.: Doubleday, 1963.

BLACKSTONE, SIR WILLIAM. *Commentaries on the Laws of England,* vol. 1.

BRANDSTADTER, A. F., and RADELET, LOUIS A., eds. *Police and Community Relations: A Sourcebook.* Beverly Hills, Calif.: Glencoe Press, 1968.

BRINK, WILLIAM, and HARRIS, LOUIS. *Black and White: A Study of U.S. Racial Attitudes Today.* New York: Simon & Schuster, 1966.

CAMPBELL, JAMES S.; SAHID, JOSEPH R.; and STANG, DAVID P. *Law and Order Reconsidered:* A Staff Report to the National Commission on the Causes and Prevention of Violence. Washington, D.C.: U.S. Government Printing Office, 1969.

CANFIELD, ROGER B. *Black Ghetto Riots and Campus Disorders: A Subcultural and Philosophical Study of Democratic Legitimacy and American Political Violence, 1964–1970.* San Francisco: R. & E. Research Associates, 1973.

CLEAVER, ELDREDGE. *Soul on Ice.* New York: Dell, 1968.

COHEN, NATHAN E., ed. *The Los Angeles Riots: A Socio-Psychological Study.* New York: Praeger, 1970.

FANON, FRANTZ. *The Wretched of the Earth,* trans. Constance Farrington. New York: Grove Press, 1963.

FEAGIN, JOE R., and HAHN, HARLAN. *Ghetto Riots: The Politics of Violence in American Cities.* New York: Macmillan, 1973.

FORTAS, ABE. *Concerning Dissent and Civil Disobedience.* New York: New American Library, 1968.

GERBERDING, WILLIAM P., and SMITH, DUANE E., eds. *The Radical Left: The Abuse of Discontent.* Boston: Houghton Mifflin, 1970.

GOLDWIN, ROBERT A., ed. *How Democratic Is America? Responses to the New Left Challenge.* Chicago: Rand McNally, 1971.

———. *On Civil Disobedience: American Essays, Old and New.* Chicago: Rand McNally, 1969.

GRAHAM, HUGH DAVIS, and GURR, TED ROBERT, eds. *Violence in America: Historical and Comparative Perspectives:* A Staff Report to the National Commission on the Causes and Prevention of Violence. Washington, D.C.: U.S. Government Printing Office, 1969.

HIGHAM, JOHN. *Strangers in the Land.* New Brunswick, N.J.: Rutgers University Press, 1955.

HOFFMAN, ABBIE. *Revolution for the Hell of It.* New York: Dial Press, 1968.

JACOBS, HAROLD, ed. *Weatherman.* New York: Ramparts, 1970.

KENISTON, KENNETH. *Young Radicals: Notes on Committed Youth.* New York: Harcourt, 1968.

KING, MARTIN LUTHER, JR. *Where Do We Go from Here? Chaos or Community?* Boston: Beacon, 1967.

―――. *Why We Can't Wait.* New York: New American Library, 1964.

KOCH, ADRIENNE, and PEDEN, WILLIAM, eds. *The Life and Selected Writings of Thomas Jefferson.* New York: Random House, 1944.

LIPSKY, MICHAEL, ed. *Law and Order: Police Encounters.* Chicago: Aldine, 1970.

LOTHSTEIN, ARTHUR, ed. *"All We Are Saying . . ." The Philosophy of the New Left.* New York: Capricorn, 1970.

LOWI, THEODORE J. *The End of Liberalism: Ideology, Policy, and the Crisis of Public Authority.* New York: Norton, 1969.

MCCONNELL, GRANT. *Private Power and American Democracy.* New York: Knopf, 1967.

NATIONAL COMMISSION ON THE CAUSES AND PREVENTION OF VIOLENCE. *To Establish Justice. To Insure Domestic Tranquility.* New York: Award Books, 1969.

ORRICK, WILLIAM H., JR. *Shut It Down! A College in Crisis: San Francisco State College, October 1968–April 1969:* A Staff Report to the National Commission on the Causes and Prevention of Violence. Washington, D.C.: U.S. Government Printing Office, 1969.

RADELET, LOUIS A. *The Police and the Community.* Beverly Hills. Calif.: Glencoe Press 1973.

Report of the National Advisory Commission on Civil Disorders. New York: Bantam, 1968.

Rights in Conflict. A Staff Report to the National Commission of the Causes and Prevention of Violence. New York: New American Library, 1968.

SEARS, DAVID O., and MCCONAHAY, JOHN B. *The Politics of Violence: The New Urban Blacks and the Watts Riot.* Boston: Houghton Mifflin, 1973.

STORING, HERBERT J., ed. *What Country Have I? Political Writings by Black Americans.* New York: St. Martin, 1970.

TALESE, GAY. *Honor Thy Father: The Inside Book of the Mafia.* New York: World, 1971.

TOCQUEVILLE, ALEXIS DE. *Democracy in America,* ed. Phillips Bradley, vol. 2. New York: Random House, 1945.

―――. *The Old Regime and the French Revolution,* trans. Stuart Gilbert. Garden City, N.Y.: Doubleday, 1955.

VAN DEN HAAG, ERNEST. *Political Violence and Civil Disobedience.* New York: Harper & Row, 1972.

WOLFF, ROBERT PAUL; MOORE, BARRINGTON, JR.; and MARCUSE, HERBERT. *A Critique of Pure Tolerance.* Boston: Beacon, 1969.

X, MALCOLM. *The Autobiography of Malcolm X.* New York: Grove, 1964.

YABLONSKY, LOUIS. *The Hippie Trip.* New York: Pegasus, 1968.

IV

COMMUNITY RELATIONS:
THE STATE OF THE ART

9

||||||||||||||||||||||||||||||||||||||||||||||||||||||||||||||||||||||||||||||||||||||||||||||||||||||||||||||||||||||||||

POLICE-COMMUNITY
RELATIONS PROGRAMS

The turbulent 1960s witnessed a number of challenges to governmental legitimacy in this country. Citizens, especially the young, the poor, and the black, violently protested against a variety of rules and decisions of the political realm. In
particular, the protest centered around society's resource and power allocation,
perceived as unfair by the nonwhites and poor, and the war in southeast Asia,
perceived as immoral by the young. Riots spread across the ghettos and college
campuses of the nation. Police forces assigned to enforce the law and maintain
the peace were the first to come in conflict with the dissidents—conflict that
often turned into war. With the immediacy of modern communication, the nation was able to witness the battles fought between police and citizens depicted
on television screens.

These were times of hardship for governmental authority, and especially for
law enforcement. The decade of conflict, rebellion, burning, and destruction
saw a great many police departments initiate programs in police-community relations as a preventive treatment for civil disorders. At first these programs were
designed as public relations for the police. Later the concept was expanded to
provide more far-reaching effects. Police-community relations have now evolved
as a means to develop "dialogue and discussion which involves 'two-way' communication with all individuals and groups in the community (popular, cooperative, supportive, and . . . unpopular, negative, and rebellious), in order to develop meaningful public participation (at beat and precinct level) in police policy
formulation, decision making, administration and operations."[1]

Fundamentally, police-community relations programs seek to obtain law observance through respect rather than enforcement.[2] The police employ these
programs in an attempt to gain public support and confidence. If they succeed,
then police work will be held as legitimate by segments of the population that

heretofore have withheld their support of law enforcement or of the men who enforce the law. How the police are regarded by these groups has a bearing on whether governmental authority and legitimacy will have meaning in some neighborhoods in America. In effect, if the nation is to avoid a permanent division of diverse life-style factions, it must have political institutions mediating among the contending groups. The task of mediation begins at the street level, where the police, as the most visible symbols of governmental authority, have their close contact with the public.

Presently there are approximately three hundred departments with police-community relations programs.[3] A 1973 study of these programs found that the typical police-community relations unit is between four and five years old. On the average, police departments have assigned fourteen commissioned officers and eleven civilian employees to their special police-community relations units. Additionally, the average unit spends 57 percent of its man-hours delivering such community services as counseling and job placement, servicing store-front centers, sponsoring athletic leagues, and providing youth activities and other social welfare services.[4] The remainder of the time is spent in administrative functions that include press relations, recruiting, and preservice and in-service training in police human relations techniques and police-minority relations designed to provide beat patrolmen with some awareness of the environment in which they practice their occupation.[5]

Nature of Police-Community Relations Programs

Although, in theory, police-community relations programs are supposed to be directed toward every segment of the community, in practice they have been essentially directed toward the black community. Louis Radelet states that "at the practical level, police-community relations programs are still defined today largely in the sense of police and minority groups, police and racial tensions, police and the disaffected, etc."[6] A high-ranking police official supports this contention: "You're fooling yourself to think that these community relations programs are aimed at anyone else but the black community."

The emphasis of these programs is understandable, if simply for the reason that it was the rioting in black ghettos that prompted their creation. Because law-enforcement problems are most acute in lower-class black neighborhoods, and because it is there that police receive the most hostility and face the greatest danger, it is practical to make a special effort to improve their relations with the citizens of these areas. However, by limiting their community relations efforts to minority citizens, the police are in danger of slighting other citizens, many of whom already perceive a neglect of their needs by governmental authorities. While the police presently enjoy the support and confidence of majority-group citizens, this condition could change if there were a widespread feeling that the police were paying too much attention to the problems of minority groups and if this new focus in police work were perceived as potentially detrimental to public safety. Furthermore, the effectiveness of these programs requires their support by law-enforcement officers throughout a department's hierarchy. Should the programs be seen as solely concerned with black citizens, then support for them by the officers of a department is not likely to be forthcoming.

The success of these programs crucially depends on the commitment of every individual officer to the practice of good police-community relations. It is not enough simply to have command support and a specialized unit dispensing police cheer among the citizens. The beat patrolman will make or break a police-community relations program; he is the one who has an ongoing contact with citizens at the street level, and his attitudes and behavior will determine the fate of police-community relations. In a real sense, the effectiveness of community relations relies on a total orientation of a police organization.

> It is an attitude and an emphasis for all phases of police work, not merely for a specialized unit in a department. It is a way for a police officer to view his work in dealing with citizens. For citizens, it is a way of viewing the police officer: what he does and how he does it. Ideally, it is a matter of striving to achieve mutual understanding and trust, as with any human relationship. Every problem in police work today is in some way a problem of police-community relations. Its solution depends in some sense upon police and community cooperation, indeed *partnership.*[7]

Properly understood, police-community relations programs have a *preventive* thrust. They serve to bring the police and the community together, to work on preventing problems, to provide correctives for problems before a crisis takes place. "Police-community relations programs should operate on the premise that the best way to control a riot is to prevent it; the best way to control a crime is to prevent it. When the police are in the streets armed with shotguns, volleying tear gas, and crouched behind protective shields, it is too late for police-community relations."[8]

Components of Community Relations Programs

Community relations programs are generally based on three components: public relations, community service, and advocacy policing. Police departments vary in the emphasis they place on the various components of their community relations program. Some departments offer one or two of the components while others provide all three.[9] The public relations approach to community relations is a planned channel of communication designed to create favorable public opinion about a police department. In this approach the emphasis is on fostering harmonious relations with the communications media and with "responsible" citizens, including responsible minority-group leaders. It does not seek to establish street-level police contact with minority citizens on a personal basis.

The community service approach attempts to combine good public relations with some services that would be of benefit to the community. Community service programs concern a wide variety of activities, including such youth-related activities as sports, skilled games, camping, and so on.

The advocacy policing component of community relations programs is the most ambitious and controversial of the approaches. It seeks to bring the police and the community, along with other interested agencies, to work as a team for coordinated, cooperative problem solving. The problem to be solved in this manner could be one of crime prevention. However, it could also relate to housing conditions in a neighborhood, the inattention of governmental agencies to citizen needs in an area, or any other problem deemed to be of social consequence and community interest. In this approach, the police, through its specialized police-community relations unit, or any other departmental agency for that matter, seeks to provide aid to the community in any way it can. In essence, this approach is founded on having a police agency instrumental in the development of the social work concept of community organization. Fundamentally, to gain the confidence of groups it seeks to reach, the specialized police unit acts as an advocate for the needs and demands of the groups vis-à-vis other governmental agencies, including the police department.

The chief problem with the advocacy approach is that while it professes to apply to the whole community, it in fact focuses mainly on the minority community. Moreover, this approach is generally performed by a specialized unit without the involvement of the rest of the officers in the department. This has tended to isolate community relations officers from the mainstream of policemen, thus making community relations a specialized endeavor wholly unrelated to actual relations between "real" policemen and citizens.

The following sections will provide examples of programs within each of the three components of community relations. The examples were chosen to illustrate how public relations, community service, and advocacy policing are performed functionally.[10]

Public Relations

Police departments employ the communications media and personal contacts to influence public opinion favorably. Goodwill promoted through the media is done by news releases, radio and television promotional activities, and newspaper articles. Under the policies of the Federal Communications Commission, free time is made available by radio and television for public service broadcasts. This has included police public relations messages and police recruiting spot announcements. Additionally, some police departments have sponsored children's shows—or have had police officers as program regulars—and radio programs directed toward minority groups, usually to black and Chicano audiences. Other police departments have put on personal safety programs on local educational television. The Los Angeles department gained goodwill and visibility through its association and consultantship with network programs such as "Adam Twelve" and "Dragnet." A regular question-and-answer column in a newspaper, minority group or otherwise, has been utilized by departments in smaller communities.

Public relations involving personal contact include police speakers' bureaus, guided tours of police facilities, and "cruiser tours." A police speakers' bureau is generally coordinated through a department's community relations unit and consists of individual officers giving talks to civic and church groups on request. Guided tours of police facilities for various adult and youth groups is another approach designed to increase public support. "Cruiser tours" is a public relations technique that has citizens riding in patrol cars or in police-community relations cars for a firsthand observation of police field operations.

There are a number of other public relations programs that have been practiced by police departments across the nation. The Los Angeles Police Department devised a "Lock Your Car" campaign, which has educational features in addition to being good public relations. The campaign brought out the department's interest in the protection of property. The program was conducted as an advertising campaign and enlisted the aid of the media, citizens' groups, the clergy, educational facilities, and business firms.

The police departments of St. Louis, Missouri, and Fort Worth, Texas, welcome conventioneers to their cities by placing an informational packet and a letter of welcome in each hotel room for the visitors. The police of Kingsville, Texas, have a "Welcome to Our City" program that sends each newcomer an informational packet from the chief of police. Kingsville and St. Louis also have informational packets that are distributed to business firms. This literature gives information on crime prevention affecting businesses and serves to help businessmen avoid being victims of crime.

New York City has a unique program of public art shows in police station houses. Neighborhood residents are urged to display their art in police stations, and the art show is publicized by the community relations unit throughout the station's neighborhood. The residents of the neighborhood are invited to visit their local police station to view the artistic creations of their neighbors. The Des Moines, Iowa, police department has a "freeway aid" program. The department equips each car assigned to patrol freeways within the city limits with a jack, lug wrench, screwdriver, pliers, a gas suction hose, and a can of gasoline. This is a service designed to aid drivers stranded on the freeway.

Community Service

STORE-FRONT AND MOBILE CENTERS. These are police-community relations centers located in the neighborhoods to provide the police with the opportunity to help citizens on a personal, man-to-man basis. The centers are manned by police-community relations officers or by patrolmen who are able to deal with the problems brought to them by residents of the neighborhood. Most centers have a service commitment only, and, unlike police substations, generally do not participate in law-enforcement activities.

The community service work of the centers—or "store fronts"—include such tasks as driver education and training, English-language training for foreign residents, sponsorship of neighborhood citizen-police meetings, coaching athletic teams, speaking in schools, helping citizens find jobs, explaining laws to citizens who do not understand the laws or do not speak English, teaching citizens how to fill out accident and insurance claim reports, and teaching patrol officers how to communicate with residents of the neighborhood. "Store fronts" may occupy space in a permanent structure or be mobile. Fixed centers are found in shopping centers, office buildings, church basements, reconverted city buses, house trailers, tool sheds on construction sites, and housing projects.

There are a number of other programs that provide the police with a positive visibility as well as perform valuable service to the community. The following programs are a representative sample of police-community relations programs that try to fulfill the criteria of public relations and public service:

CITIZEN CRIME-PREVENTION PROGRAMS.   Citizen crime-prevention programs are ways of enlisting the public to cooperate with the police in combating alarming increases in the crime rate. These programs provide the extra eyes and ears that alert the police about suspicious persons or acts.

There are basically two program approaches to citizen crime prevention, although there may be several ways to describe them. The first approach is named "Operation Crime Stop," but is also known as "Crime Spot," "Operation Observer," "Operation Citizen Alert," "Community Radio Watch," "Citizens Observer Corps," and "Project Alert." The program is relatively simple to implement: the police department establishes a special telephone number for incoming calls, briefs its personnel, prints wallet-size cards with "Operation Crime Stop" instructions and distributes these to the citizens, and coordinates an advertising campaign to convey the program to the public. When the program is operational, citizen-participants report their observations of suspicious activities through the police department's special telephone number.

The benefits of the citizen crime-prevention program are twofold: The program serves a community relations function because of the large number of citizens it reaches and because it helps in the development of citizen self-help; and it gives the citizens a chance to help the police department with encouraging results. The Chicago Police Department has over a million citizens enrolled in the program since its creation in 1964. The program has been credited with aiding the Chicago police in reducing the crime rate.

A second approach to citizen crime prevention is the "Citizen Block Watch" program. The St. Louis police-community relations unit initiated an action project that enables a community's residents to watch each other's homes during the day. The program was created in one of the city's police districts to help cut down daytime burglaries. The success of the program has led to its expansion to all nine police districts. The program's operation is as follows:

Each block in a district is under continuing surveillance during the daytime. Every block resident has his neighbor's phone number and, between them all, they maintain a front and rear surveillance team from their homes, reporting any suspicious persons or acts to the police immediately. The block watchers are briefed to take down auto license numbers and physical descriptions of suspects and are cautioned that well-dressed persons on the block need not be legitimate businessmen but could conceivably be burglers or confidence men. The block watchers hold monthly meetings to discuss problems occurring in their districts.

OPERATION LONE WOMAN. This is a Fort Worth, Texas, police-community relations program designed to aid women motorists in distress, and to make the streets safer at night. The program's first stage consists of an educational campaign aimed at women to help prevent them from being victims of crime. Lectures are given at the locations of organizations that employ large numbers of women, such as hospitals, telephone offices, and restaurants; in addition presentations are also given to women's groups, PTAs, and church societies. Next, police-community relations officers organize twenty-four-hour service stations and garages by districts and obtain their promise of cooperation in the program. Finally, all police patrols are ordered to be observant of women motorists—and senior citizen motorists—requiring assistance. In the eventuality that assistance is needed, police officers are to notify the police dispatcher of the location of the distress and the type of aid required. The police officer then stands by until assistance arrives, or, in the case of a flat tire, the officer may change the tire himself. In the event that the officer standing by receives an emergency call, he responds to the call but first assures the stranded motorist that he will return, and does.

SCOOTER PATROLS. The rationale for scooter patrols is that they combine the advantage of wider territorial coverage of squad cars and the personalized community contact of foot patrolmen. These patrols are operational in Detroit; New York City; Nassau County, New York; and Cleveland. In Detroit the technique is called Community Oriented Patrol (COP), although it is geared primarily to crime prevention, and only secondarily to community relations. Scooter patrolmen in each patrol district are linked to squad cars via radio contact. Each patrol is responsible for an area of eight to ten city blocks. All scooter patrol officers undergo two weeks of specialized training covering curriculum in police methods as well as community relations.

OPERATION HANDSHAKE. A fundamental of the community relations program in the Philadelphia Police Department is to have newly graduated police rookies taken on a tour of the city's high-crime areas, where they visit stores, recreation centers, and homes and meet the residents, shake hands, and smile. The purpose of the program is to acquaint the new officers with the many decent law-abiding citizens who live in high-crime neighborhoods before negative conditioning sets in from their daily encounters with lawlessness in these same districts.

RUMOR CONTROL CENTERS. These primarily function to quell rumors and hearsay during crisis situations, but they may prevent trouble from occurring in the first place if they are operational prior to the development of a crisis. Chicago, which established the country's first such center in July 1967, operates a twenty-four-hours-a-day telephone hookup with the mayor's office, the police department, and welfare agencies. Chicago's telephone network is also supplemented by fieldworkers. Rumor control centers are often manned by staff workers and volunteers and are established by an agency other than the police.

BICYCLE PATROL. The Long Beach, California, Police Department organized a bicycle patrol in 1964 in an effort to curtail many downtown crimes, which had given the police a bad rating in public opinion polls. The bicycle patrol has been instrumental in the reduction of crimes against citizens in the downtown area.

The patrol uses English-style bicycles with speed shifts and no lights. The bicycle patrol officers are volunteers and work in pairs patrolling one block apart, crisscrossing periodically. Each officer is equipped with a gun, badge, flashlight, handcuffs, blackjack, and small transistor radio equipped with a convertor for monitoring police calls. The bicycles afford the police department with a transportation device that is quiet, lightweight, inexpensive, and with speed enough to overtake suspects fleeing on foot.

COMMUNITY RELATIONS KAFFEEKLATSCH. This program has the officer on the beat meet socially with the residents of the neighborhood he patrols, thereby involving patrolmen in community relations. The police department of Covina, California, sponsors a "social" once a month in the home of a district resident. Members of the women's clubs arrange for a host home. The officer, in uniform, is the host of the event and the police department supplies and delivers coffee, cookies, a movie projector, and a short film on home burglaries. All beat officers participate in the program and receive several hours of community relations training prior to hosting their first kaffeeklatsch.

ALCOHOL AND NARCOTICS EDUCATION PROJECTS. In communities where racial problems are minimal or nonexistent, but large numbers of adolescents are experimenting with drugs, a police-community relations unit may be primarily concerned with drug education programs. This may involve having mobile narcotics education exhibits of programs encouraging parents and teachers to take the initiative in narcotics and alcohol education at home and in the schools.

Safety education programs, featuring the dangers of drinking and driving, are sponsored by numerous police-community relations units or, as in New Orleans, offered by the police traffic unit.

REASSURANCE FOR THE ELDERLY. There is a North Miami Beach, Florida, community relations program that builds the image of the police department as a protector of citizens. Elderly residents of the community who live by themselves are enrolled in the program. The police department maintains files that include health records and vital statistics to aid in giving emergency treatment, if required. Each morning the participants telephone a special police department number and report in. If a participant fails to call by a prearranged time, then the police dispatcher calls him, and should there be no answer, an emergency vehicle is sent immediately to the participant's address.

POLICE RESERVES.   This is a program that seeks to involve citizens in police work. The Los Angeles Police Reserves program has as its slogan "Get Involved." In Los Angeles, police reserve officers receive 282 hours of training over a period of seven months at the Police Academy. Reserve officers are required to work two eight-hour shifts a month. There are approximately two thousand men and women police reserves in the Los Angeles Police Department.

PROGRAMS FOR MINORITY GROUPS

While the previously discussed programs have been germane to the minority groups, they have been considered in the context of total community application with the option of selectivity for appropriate community groups. The following experiences, however, have been uniquely directed to minorities.

SPECIAL PATROLS. There are a number of programs involving the cooperation of a police department and residents of a low-income area for expanded patrols aided by citizen volunteers to deter lawlessness in the high-crime neighborhood. Three of these arrangements are "Mothers on Patrol" (MOPS) in Hartford, Connecticut; "Create a Healthy Atmosphere in Newark" (CHAIN) in Newark, New Jersey; and "Tension Area Patrol" in Washington, D.C.

"Mothers on Patrol" consists of women employed to patrol playgrounds, recreation rooms, laundries, and parking lots in low-income housing projects. The women, usually residents of the housing projects, patrol in pairs; they wear uniforms but have no police power. They primarily function as the eyes and ears of the police department by providing oral and written reports to police supervisors concerning suspicious activities and persons, unsafe conditions, and other latent hazards.

"Create a Healthy Atmosphere in Newark" was founded in 1969 by central city blacks with the cooperation of the Newark Police Department. The program involves approximately one hundred men, district residents who voluntarily patrol their high-crime neighborhoods as auxiliary policemen. Members of Create a Healthy Atmosphere in Newark obtain training at the Newark Police Academy.

"Tension Area Patrol" involves the constant patrolling of high-crime areas by Washington's Police-Community Relations Unit. The basis for the program is that high-crime neighborhoods are high-tension areas that would benefit from a continued presence of community relations officers. The officers also maintain open lines of communication with the residents of the patrolled areas and try to spot quickly situations that are potentially explosive.

EMPLOYMENT AIDS.   Several police-community relations units are helping unemployed minority-group citizens find work or, in concert with federal anti-poverty agencies, are making available civil service jobs and training. The Dallas, Texas, police-community relations store-front operation includes aid for the unemployed in obtaining jobs. The Los Angeles police-community relations unit, in cooperation with the federal New Careers Program, has sponsored a Concentrated Employment Program for unemployed and underemployed young adults in east and south Los Angeles.

Some cities with a large number of non–English-speaking residents have provided driver training programs in a foreign language. For example, the police-community relations store-front centers in Fort Worth, Dallas, and Houston offer driver training programs in Spanish for their Chicano population, thereby enhancing their employment opportunities.

YOUTH EMPLOYMENT WITH THE POLICE.   Several police departments employ minority young men and women from low-income neighborhoods and provide them with a career development potential within the department, or with job training useful in other employment. The Community Service Officer (CSO) is one of the employment programs.

CSO's are generally men and women between seventeen and twenty-one who do not meet all the educational or physical requirements for the Police Academy, but are interested in police work and have contact with minority groups in the city. CSOs are usually assigned to a police-community relations unit and serve as liaisons between the unit and the hard-to-reach minority citizens. CSOs wear police uniforms, or reasonable facsimiles, but do not have law-enforcement powers and do not carry weapons. CSOs serve to bridge the gap between the police and the ghetto community, and therefore are often recruited from the neighborhood in which they will function. Los Angeles has also had some success in enlisting ex-convicts as Community Service Officers.

The President's Commission on Law Enforcement and the Administration of Justice cited the following justifications for the Community Service Officer position:

1. To improve police service in high crime areas.
2. To enable police to hire persons who can provide a greater understanding of minority group problems.
3. To relieve police officers of lesser police duties.
4. To increase the opportunity for minority-group members to serve in law-enforcement careers.
5. To tap a new reservoir of manpower by helping talented young men who have not as yet been able to complete their education to qualify for police work.[11]

RECREATIONAL ACTIVITIES.   The Los Angeles and New Orleans police-community relations units provide police-sponsored entertainment to their minority-group communities. It is an approach that seeks to gain minority approval for the police department through movies and music.

The Los Angeles unit sponsors drives to obtain equipment for black and Chicano musical groups. Community relations officers publicize the need for the instruments through the media. The New Orleans police-community relations unit shows free outdoor movies to residents of low-income housing projects during the summer months. The unit has also provided police band concerts in minority neighborhoods in the summer.

REACHING THE YOUTH

Police-community relations units have sponsored numerous youth activities including teenage traffic safety programs, teen clubs, athletic programs, and police "mod squads"—police cadet programs, police-sponsored boys' clubs, police drum and bugle corps, summer camps, talent shows, and Boy Scout Explorer posts.

One of the oldest police-community relations programs in the country has been the Police Athletic Leagues (PAL), which have existed in many Northeast and Midwest cities for years. The thrust of the PAL program has been to come to grips with juvenile delinquency and crime. PAL attempts to fulfill these goals by providing supervised recreation programs to channel youthful exuberance and restlessness away from antisocial interests and activities. Furthermore, it seeks to bring teenagers, who are in a critical period of character development, under the guidance of police officers and influence them to perceive the police in a positive light.

Another program that has proliferated across the nation is the "mod squad" approach. The mod squad is called by several different names. In Rochester, New York, it is "Teen on Patrol"; in Eau Gallie, Florida, it is known as "Junior Police League"; the Jacksonville, Florida, program is termed "Police Youth Patrol"; and in Los Angeles, California, it is called "Community-Police Service Corps."

Some of the mod squad programs are solely directed to minority youths; others cut across the socioeconomic spectrum. Most of the programs provide formal training in police basics. Uniform allocations range from a complete official uniform issuance for the Charleston, West Virginia, Police Cadet Corps—paid for by grants and donations from civic groups and local businesses—to arm patches and badges for the Police-School Cadet Program of Flint Michigan. In addition to their training, cadets may ride in patrol cars and, in general, receive a thorough understanding of police operations.

The mod squad programs provide teenagers with "constructive roaming" by assigning them to aid beat policemen in some cities or by having them patrol playgrounds, parks, vacant recreational lots, and school grounds during the summer months in other communities. Ultimately, this approach serves to increase the teenagers' knowledge of police services and policemen, and encourages the cadets to make the police department a career in the future.

Finally, there are several programs promoting a positive police image at the elementary school level. These consist of policemen visiting the school and talking and showing films to the children about the role of police officers. One of the programs is "Officer Friendly," financed by the Sears, Roebuck Corporation, which consists of programmed and outlined visits to public and parochial elementary school classrooms by members of a police-community relations unit. Officer Friendly comes into a school, introduces himself, shows a short film, and tells the children about the police as a public helper. Before leaving, Officer Friendly may give each child a copy of the Police Department coloring book, which stresses the idea of the policeman as a friend and protector.

Advocacy Policing

Police departments have employed the social work concept of community organization for a teamwork approach to problem solving. Furthermore, some community relations units are advocates on behalf of citizens in order to gain for them benefits that they are unable to obtain on their own. The objectives of this approach in police-community relations is to develop better two-way communication between the public and the police and to bring together all the resources needed to cope with the complex problems of the urban environment that have proved so difficult for law-enforcement agencies to handle alone. Generally there are four types of arrangements for this approach to community relations: (1) meetings with city-wide advisory committees; (2) meetings with neighborhood advisory committees; (3) meetings with committees of minority-group leaders; and (4) police-community workshops.

CITY-WIDE ADVISORY COMMUNITY

This is a vehicle by which the high officials of a police department (possibly including city government officials) and the city's leading citizens can meet and exchange ideas about problems and policies and, it is hoped, provide solutions to police-community friction. In large cities, city-wide advisory committees coordinate the functions of small-scale councils, such as neighborhood councils. These committees function as a liaison between the police and the community; they do not operate as civilian review boards.

MEETINGS WITH NEIGHBORHOOD ADVISORY COMMITTEES

The St. Louis Police Department, the first in the nation, in 1957, to form a community relations unit, employs this type of community organization, and its format has been adopted by other departments. St. Louis has nine neighborhood councils that are called district committees. The district committees resemble city-wide councils, but they operate in limited geographical areas, high-crime areas, or in sections of the city where there are police-community tensions.

The membership of the St. Louis neighborhood advisory councils is drawn from neighborhood residents who volunteer to serve. Each council holds a monthly general meeting at a district store-front police-community relations center or in a district police station. The police district commander or his representative is present at each meeting. Meetings are conducted by the council district chairman, who is elected each year by the membership. Councils have four operating subcommittees: law enforcement, juvenile, sanitation, and business. Chairmen of the four subcommittees are appointed by the council chairman. Complaints to the police district representatives are presented in written form and are reported on at the meeting.

The St. Louis police-community relations unit also recruits neighborhood leaders from each of the city's patrol districts to belong to crime-prevention committees. This program is named the Patrol Area Leader Plan (PAL). PALs involve citizen volunteers who are drawn from the membership of police-community relations district committees. This relationship strengthens the program because it obtains the cooperation of established neighborhood organizations. All district police sergeants are assigned to this program and their job is to serve as the PAL's contacts and to develop a closer alliance between the residents of their districts and the patrolmen assigned to the area.

Each district's PAL meets with its district sergeant contact once a week. The group has coffee and discusses the district's problems and offers ways to eliminate them. The St. Louis Police Department considers the contributions of PALs to be very valuable because they live or work in the involved districts and therefore know their neighborhoods well.

PAL committee members have meetings as often as they wish. All of their meetings are attended by police officers selected by their supervising officers or by the chief of police. District sergeants are expected to attend at least three of these meetings a year. The main function of PAL committees is to deal with crime-prevention matters. Specifically, these committees discover and discuss crime problems in the neighborhood; determine areas where police patrol resources can be most effectively used; evaluate patrol capabilities in the neighborhood; and determine ways for citizen cooperation with the police in the neighborhood. A representative of the police-community relations unit is always in attendance at the meetings in the event community relations questions are raised, even though the main orientation of the committee is to deal with crime problems.

MEETINGS WITH COMMITTEES OF MINORITY-GROUP LEADERS

These take place where community relations problems exist, mainly in high-crime, minority neighborhoods. The emphasis of this approach is to maintain open lines of communication with minority and militant organizations, covering the spectrum of political persuasion. For example, San Antonio's police-community relations unit has an ongoing dialogue with white, black, and Chicano militant organizations.

POLICE-COMMUNITY WORKSHOPS

These workshops range from informal exchanges to highly structured meetings. Workshops usually take the form of "controlled verbal confrontation" —group sensitivity sessions. The objective of these meetings is to bring a number of policemen and citizens together for a period of time so that each group can be made aware of the damaging stereotypes that they have of each other and learn how these stereotypes affect their attitudes and behavior. The highlight of each session comes when both groups agree to form a basis for cooperation so that future problem solving can be done constructively. This form of controlled verbal confrontation is complex and delicate and requires the guidance of trained professionals. Houston's highly structured workshops are sponsored under the auspices of the Cooperative Crime Prevention program and employ psychologists to conduct the sessions. Workshops in other cities generally involve professionals from local universities.

Examples of Police Department Programs

It is difficult to evaluate the quality of community relations programs. For example, when the head of Atlanta's Crime Prevention Bureau (the name for that city's police-community relations unit) was asked what the unit's most essential contribution has been, his reply was that "the bureau is instrumental in crime prevention in the areas it serves." However, he was not able to come up with crime-rate statistics to substantiate his contention. He suggested that crime statistics are not a true index of a police-community relations unit's effectiveness. He concluded that the measure of a community relations unit's contribution is in the improved attitudes of the residents of the ghetto toward the police —an intangible index.[12] In a separate survey conducted in Atlanta, respondents living in a Model Neighborhood area where the Atlanta police-community relations unit is quite active were asked questions pertaining to their awareness of and reactions to the police-community relations program in their neighborhood. The results of the survey, as provided in Tables 9.1 and 9.2, offer some surprises. Most of the respondents did not show any reaction to the police-community relations program. None of the white males indicated an awareness of the existence of the program, and only one white female knew of its existence. Significantly, 56 of the 86 black respondents were unaware of ongoing programs in their neighborhoods. This indicates that police efforts to initiate contact with the community in this area of Atlanta have been token. If this survey is representative of citizen attitudes toward police-community relations programs in the rest of the country, then there is reason to suspect that the programs are far more promising in promotional pamphlets issued by police departments than they are in reality.

The examples of departmental community relations programs included in this chapter were not chosen because they are paradigms. Selection was based solely on the comprehensiveness of program offerings. The Baltimore and Chicago models of police-community relations programs are illustrations of departmental commitment to all three components of community relations: public relations, community service, and advocacy policing. The selection of these particular programs as illustrations was made randomly. Their description relies for the most part on what the departments say their community relations effort is.[13]

TABLE 9.1 Awareness of race-sex groups of police community service

	Yes	No	Totals
White male	0	10	10
White female	1	23	24
Negro male	13	17	30
Negro female	17	39	56
TOTALS	31	89	120

Source: William J. Mathias, "Perceptions of Police Relations with Ghetto Citizens," *Police Chief,* March 1971, p. 49.

TABLE 9.2 Reactions by race-sex groups to police community service

	For	Against	Undecided	Totals
White male	0	0	0	0
White female	0	1	0	1
Negro male	9	0	0	9
Negro female	15	0	0	15
TOTALS	24	1	0	25

Source: William J. Mathias, "Perceptions of Police Relations with Ghetto Citizens," *Police Chief,* March 1971, p. 49.

Baltimore. The Baltimore Police Department underwent a major reorganization as a result of a 1965 study of the department by the International Association of Chiefs of Police. Several sections and divisions were altered or abolished, and new ones were created. The study recommended that a community relations division be instituted to deal with the conflicts that had developed between the police department and some of the citizens of Baltimore.

In 1966 the police commissioner established a community relations division under the Administrative Bureau. The Community Relations Division was structurally changed in the fall of 1971 and redesignated the Community Services Division. The new division was placed under the command of the deputy commissioner of operations, along with the Traffic Division, Patrol Division, and Criminal Investigation Division. The deputy commissioner of operations reports directly to the police commissioner, as do the deputy commissioners of administrative and service bureaus.

The Community Services Division is headed by a chief (lieutenant colonel in rank) who has under his command two sections, Community Relations and Youth. Each of these sections is headed by a director (major in rank). The Community Relations section consists of a headquarters complement and a patrol district complement. Within each of the nine police patrol districts of the city is one police-community relations officer (sergeant in rank), who is responsible and reports directly to his respective district commander.

In an appendix to their *Police-Community Relations Handbook,* the Baltimore Police Department explains the nature of their community relations endeavor:

> . . . [To] create understanding and cooperation between the police and the citizens. The ultimate goal of this broad objective is to hopefully reduce crime in Baltimore.
>
> We sincerely feel that crime is a social problem caused by society itself and if good police-community relations can motivate the public as well as the police to participate as a cooperative concerned community in the "war against crime," then the objectives, efforts and intent of the Community Relations section will be achieved.
>
> We emphasize that even though there are only 31 people assigned on a full-time basis to Community Relations, there are approximately 3500 community relations specialists in the Department—meaning that every person employed in the Police Department can increase or decrease the police-community relations objective.
>
> Therefore, we insist that no matter where the police officer works geographically within the City of Baltimore, community relations concepts must be practiced everywhere.
>
> Being realistic, however, we must set priorities to specific areas and clientele of the city where current social conflict is paramount. In Baltimore City the "target area" would particularly include the black and poor white areas of the city.

The objectives and duties of Baltimore's Community Services Division are outlined in the division's brochure:

To create understanding and cooperation between the police and the citizens, through communication.

To provide opportunities for citizens to suggest improvements in police service.

To acquaint police officers with the citizens they protect and to consider the ideas of these citizens in police matters.

To acquaint citizens with the professional operation of police activities.

To promote increased cooperation between the police department and other agencies.

To assist in crime prevention by distributing information on crime deterrence.

To consult with Police Department District personnel on problems of law enforcement in the District.

To refer to the Police Department all questions requiring clarification on departmental policy.

Baltimore's Community Services Division undertakes a number of programs. The Officer Friendly program was initiated in city schools in 1970. This program was designed to provide a comprehension and appreciation of the police officer's role vis-à-vis the child, the family, and the community. Additionally, the program seeks to enlighten the primary grade child about his rights, responsibilities, and obligations as a junior citizen of the city of Baltimore. The objectives of each officer assigned to the program are: (1) establish a rapport between himself and the child; (2) develop a wholesome image of the Baltimore Police Department in the child; and (3) reinforce basic rules and regulations that govern experiences and activities within the child's environment.

The Community Services Division also sponsors a drug abuse program that is designed to provide an awareness about dangerous drugs. Presentations have been made to elementary, junior, and senior high school classes and to adult groups. Officers involved in this program have attended the narcotics and dangerous drugs seminar at the Bureau of Narcotics and Dangerous Drugs Training School in Washington, D.C. In response to requests by teachers of elementary schools and junior and senior high schools, the department implemented police headquarters tours.

Members of the Community Relations Section address church groups, civic organizations, and business and professional groups. Following a speech or lecture, the participating police officer conducts a question-and-answer session as a way of encouraging a two-way exchange between the citizens and the police.

Another aspect of the speakers' program involves the appearance of officers from the section on radio and television talk shows, where problems of interest to the community are discussed. Concomitant to this activity is a weekly scheduled radio program entitled "Police and the Community." This radio show was designed to inform the public about the many services available to them from the police department as well as from other community agencies. Members of the general public are invited to participate on the talk program and to pose questions for immediate on-the-air discussion.

A crime-prevention program was developed by policewomen assigned to the Community Relations Section. The objective of the program is to demonstrate inexpensive means of crime protection. The program's emphasis has been upon the protection of women and burglary prevention. Talks, films, and publications have been presented to college campuses, citizens' groups, and business and professional organizations. An underprivileged children's program was initiated by a policewoman assigned to the section with the assistance of four officers from the section. The program consists of providing tours and swimming trips for underprivileged children.

As a part of its activities the Community Relations Section maintains a "tension area" patrol. These patrols operate in areas within the city where there is a likelihood of disruptive behavior or racial tension. The objective of these patrols is to develop closer lines of communication with residents of the districts involved and to be able to identify quickly any potentially difficult situation.

The Community Relations Section operates four store-front centers located in the inner city. These centers are located in convenient neighborhood locations and encourage informal interchanges between the citizens and representatives of the police department.

During the year, officers from the center work with other agencies, such as the Department of Social Services, Legal Aid, Consumer Protection, YMCA, and community schools. The officers also serve as coaches of Little League baseball, basketball, softball, and football teams. They organize boys and girls, serve as club counselors, and assist young people in obtaining employment. Additionally, the officers transport neighborhood children on planned excursions, sponsor bands, gather clothing for destitute families, and distribute Christmas baskets to the needy.

A police officer is assigned full-time as community relations officer in each of the city's nine districts. The officer's duties are to work with the District Council on its projects; serve as the district commander's community relations representative; encourage citizens and businessmen to join the District Council; and conduct special projects assigned by the Community Relations Section and the district commander. The officer's role is to provide assistance and guidance to the District Council. The link between the District Council and the Community Relations Section is not replaced by the district community relations officer.

Membership in District Councils, with whom district community relations officers interact, is open to all citizens who live or work within the district boundaries. Application for membership is made to the individual council chairman or to the district community relations officer.

Baltimore's District Councils are patterned after the neighborhood advisory committees in St. Louis. Elected officers of each district council are the chairman, vice-chairman, and secretary-treasurer. The latter position may be divided into two offices. The chairman conducts executive and District Council meetings, maintains liaison with the Community Relations Section, and is responsible for the operation of the council. The chairman also appoints all subcommittee chairmen. The vice-chairman is in charge of the law-enforcement subcommittee, and may substitute for the chairman when necessary. The secretary-treasurer is responsible for the minutes of the meetings, publicity, membership rosters and drives, and financial accounts. The Community Relations Section assists with all of these activities when requested.

Each district council has four subcommittees: law enforcement, juvenile, sanitation, and businessmen's. Subcommittee chairman and elected officers constitute the council's executive committee. The subcommittees meet at least monthly and present a report at the regular monthly general meeting of the District Council, usually held at the district police station. The district commander or his representative is present at the meeting whenever possible, and reports on the crime situation in his district. Complaints from the council are submitted to the police representative in writing for response at the following general meeting.

The chairman or his representative is expected to meet monthly with all other district chairmen and the director of the Community Relations Section for the coordination and dissemination of information regarding the improving of District Council functions.

Chicago. The Chicago Police Department responded to the violent disturbances of the 1960s by establishing, in late 1970, the Bureau of Community Services. According to a department brochure, the bureau was established to provide urgently needed programs "that would more actively promote mutual understanding and respect between police and citizens. The program should reach as many as possible of those alienated on issues such as race, poverty, and the generation gap." The bureau, headed by a deputy superintendent reporting directly to the police superintendent—the highest ranking officer in the department—has three divisions, each headed by a director: the Neighborhood Relations Division, the Preventive Programs Division, and the Public and Internal Information Division. It also has a program development and evaluation unit. This unit, commanded by a police lieutenant, assists the deputy superintendent, the bureau's commanding officer, in the formulation and development of community service policies and programs.

The Neighborhood Relations Division is broken up into three sections: the Human Relations Section, the School Visitation Section, and the Staff Assistance Section. The Human Relations Section, a unit originally created in 1948, is concerned with maintaining community stability in an environment of potential strife between groups of different racial, religious, and ethnic background. Officers in this section work in five geographic areas of the city: the South Side, largely black; the southwest, almost all white; the west, increasingly black; the Near North, predominantly Chicano; and the remaining north, mostly white. The officers keep close watch on potentially explosive situations such as may arise out of picketing and demonstrations or out of members of minority groups' moving into white residential neighborhoods. They also investigate reported violations of laws and ordinances pertaining to human rights.

Human relations officers have regular contact with formal and informal community leaders. The former group includes officers of recognized community organizations. The latter group are often made up of young persons without official status but who are quite active in the community and provide the human relations officers with a valuable source of information. Contacts such as these enable the officers to keep abreast of impending difficulties, and when needed, to involve other agencies such as the Commission on Human Relations, the Department of Human Resources, the National Association for the Advancement of Colored People (NAACP), the Urban League, and the Anti-Defamation League.

These community contacts also enable officers to learn about and deal with individual citizens who, rightly or wrongly, feel that police service has been inadequate. For example, an officer may reassure a citizen whose home has been burglarized that the house will be under close though unobtrusive surveillance. Or he may suggest to the beat officer that he more clearly demonstrate the department's sincere concern by visiting the citizen in his home. When certain aspects of minority life style prove vexing to district police personnel, a human relations officer can offer valuable assistance in distinguishing between law-abiding and criminal elements. Finally, officers of the section make regular contact with youths through biweekly rap sessions conducted at the city's Center for Continuing Education. The groups are quite small, usually no more than twenty high school boys and girls, and they are chosen by school administrators.

The School Visitation Section develops and implements a number of programs for school-age youngsters. Best known is the Officer Friendly program, addressed to some 570,000 children in public, parochial, and private elementary schools. The Officer Friendly program is directed to lower and upper grades in the elementary schools. The lower grades consist of kindergarten through fourth grade, and the upper grades run from the fifth through the eighth grades. Officers Friendly serving the lower grades are also responsible for Junior Police activities, conducted during the summer months and during school holidays. Officers Friendly for the upper grades are the advisers for Explorers' groups. District Explorer programs are police-oriented. They include tours of police headquarters and observation of police procedures. The youngsters usually meet biweekly for sports and other recreational activities. A 4-H pilot program for upper-grade youngsters is also under way at several districts. Although they are responsible to the commanding officer of the School Visitation Section, Officers Friendly work in close cooperation with district personnel. During the summer months and holidays they assist neighborhood relations sergeants on various programs. Four policewomen, together with the Officers Friendly, conduct classroom sessions for high school students. Among the subjects discussed are drug abuse, arrest procedures, and self-protection.

The third section subsumed under the Neighborhood Relations Division is the Staff Assistance Section, which provides supervision and coordination of activities conducted by neighborhood community relations sergeants in each of the police districts with the exception of the nonresidential central district.

Among the district programs is the Police-Community Workshop, which makes it possible for citizens and police to work together toward solving problems of mutual concern. Workshop meetings are scheduled at least once a month and are usually held at a district police station. The meetings are planned by a steering committee that includes residents of the neighborhood, the police district commander, and other police personnel. A wide variety of topics are discussed, including such things as how to prevent burglary, the role of parents in the community, traffic safety, vice, gambling, and drugs. One of the aspects of the workshop program is that citizens may articulate problems that are unrelated to police service. Police personnel at the workshop then intercede on behalf of the citizens and present their complaints to appropriate public agencies. For example, if a citizen complains about a broken sidewalk or a fallen tree, a neighborhood relations officer makes note of the complaint and subsequently refers it to the appropriate agency. Such referrals are valuable in neighborhoods where the police are the only visible presence of government officialdom.

Throughout the year district-based neighborhood relations personnel conduct many kinds of educational and recreational activities for young people. Among these are team sports, drill teams, and band and choral programs. In some districts, too, youngsters participate in discussion groups and youth community workshops sponsored by the districts. During the summer, neighborhood relations personnel in the districts provide additional programs that attempt to reach out to young people, such as field trips to museums and zoos, day camps, fishing trips, and sports competition. Finally, a major effort is made to aid young people over sixteen in obtaining employment during the summer.

Another division within the Bureau of Community Services is the Preventive Programs Division. The purpose of this division is to promote crime prevention as a joint responsibility of the public and the police. To this end the division has three sections whose efforts are directed to various groups of citizens. The Business Crime Prevention Section coordinates efforts in providing guidance in crime prevention for management and security personnel of both commercial and noncommercial establishments such as stores, banks, factories, service and repair shops, apartment buildings, hospitals, and colleges. To effect an ongoing dialogue with their clientele groups, the section arranges and conducts conferences where invited citizens meet with police department representatives qualified to discuss relevant topics. For example, if the topic is shoplifting, a specialist from the Criminal Investigation Division is invited. If the subject is robbery, a police artist may be asked to explain the details about making a composite drawing at one of these conferences. Citizens invited to a conference are restricted to a small group of persons sharing common interests that are scheduled topics of discussion for the meeting.

Another section of the Preventive Programs Division, the Youth Crime Prevention Section, regularly conducts meetings of young people in their early teens. The meetings usually follow a workshop format, with the group broken into small discussion groups, each attended by an officer or a policewoman. Subjects of the discussions are self-initiated and reflect wide-ranging problems,

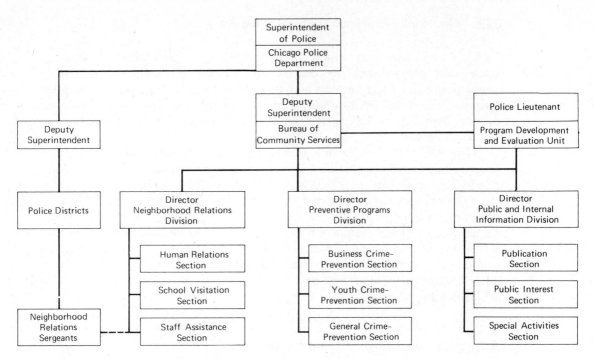

FIGURE 9.1   Chicago Police Department Bureau of Community Services.

among them forcible gang recruitment and conflict between younger and older young persons. Additionally, police personnel of the section maintain contact with a number of social agencies and, whenever possible, urge the promotion of concerned citizen groups to provide guidance for young people.

A third component of the Preventive Programs Division, the General Crime Prevention Section, conducts the Community Services Aides Project. This project is part of a federally financed, five-year Model Cities Program. Approximately 320,000 citizens in four police districts are served by the program. Under the program, 422 men and women, residents of the target areas, serve as community service aides. Working out of six store-front community service centers, the aides assist commissioned personnel in the patrol of their neighborhoods. Patrolling as teams under the supervision of police officers, the aides perform a number of tasks such a looking for and reporting abandoned and stolen cars, following up on missing persons and dog-bite reports, and alerting other citizens to the problems of crime. In rendering these and other services, the aides help the police to understand better the needs of the community and, in turn, explain police practices and objectives to the community.

The third division subsumed under the Bureau of Community Services is the Public and Internal Information Division. This division provides services that benefit both citizens and police department members. The Publication Section of this division prepares a variety of publications addressed to citizens. Among these are the police department's annual reports, the monthly *Community Workshop Reporter,* and pocket-sized brochures entitled *Out After Dark, Traffic*

Tickets Save Lives, Protect Your Family, and *Young People Within the Law.* The section also prepares exhibits, posters, and other displays that are helpful in publicizing police programs and activities. The section also prepares a monthly magazine called the *Chicago Police Star.* This publication informs officers about new developments in the department and the activities of individual policemen and policewomen.

The Public Interest Section within the division conducts visitors on tours of department facilities such as the communications center and the criminalistics division. It also arranges for speakers to address citizen groups and responds to citizen requests for information by distributing folders and lending films for use by citizen groups. Finally, the Special Activities Section focuses on services for police department members that are publicized to the community. The section arranges and conducts promotional awards and public recognition ceremonies. It implements intradepartmental athletic and other activities; it conducts a blood donor program; and it provides aid and counsel to families of deceased police officers.

Attitudes About Police-Community Relations Programs

Although police-community relations programs have become increasingly popular, they have not made all police-community relations amicable. To some members of the community, police-community relations is "preaching to the converted." While these programs have facilitated contact between police and black leaders, who now meet to discuss large-scale problems, "the individual police officer and the individual black man on the street find little improvement —more often a worsening—in their encounters."[14]

Police-community relations programs have succeeded in making inroads with some segments of the community traditionally hostile to the police. However, the rapprochement has been mainly gained with persons potentially assimilable into the dominant culture: minority citizens who are either already middle class or who aspire to the middle class. The hard-to-reach—poor blacks, youths, and the disaffected—remain intransigent to the idea of the policeman as social worker. To them the policeman is still an adversary. And even if they respond favorably to police-community relations personnel, they distinguish between these and what they perceive to be the "real police force." A young black officer assigned to Atlanta's Crime Prevention Bureau—a police-community relations unit—expressed this opinion: "The Bureau is achieving rapport with the black community. But unless every police officer practices community relations, we [bureau officers] are the illusion and reality rides in the squad cars."[15]

Within departments, police-community relations personnel and programs have met with resistance and hostility from other officers. For example, in a study of the police-community relations division in the New Orleans Police

Department it was found that its black officers were proud that their unit was "run by blacks for blacks." White officers assigned to other areas in the police department concurred with this assertion—with some derision.[16]

Fundamentally, police-community relations units and programs conflict with basic institutional cultural traits. First, the creation of a new unit specialized in dealing with minority groups appears to be an acknowledgment that other police units have been incapable of handling the problems of these groups. "No governmental agency is easily responsive to an innovation based upon a charge of failure by a portion of the community."[17] Second, police-community relations suffers from the stigma of departing from traditional police practices. A major obstacle in gaining police acceptance of the community relations concept attaches to the prevalent feeling that the work of community relations units is not "real" police work. An officer formerly assigned to the Memphis Police-Community Relations Department provides an example of this kind of attitude: "Most men I have previously worked with ignored me while I was working for the PCR department. Later, when I was transferred to the Theft Bureau, I got reactions like, 'How does it feel to be a policeman again? How does it feel to be back in the fold?' " Many policemen view the role of police-community relations as social work. The idea of social work activities for policemen violates the basic police perceptions of their role. "Police like to see themselves as strong, aggressive, masculine hunters protecting the weak. They are the good guys who beat up the bad guys who threaten the littler people."[18] It is difficult for policemen to reconceptualize their identities for an acceptance of the notion that social work may be a part of their function.

Finally, one of the greatest causes of police hostility to police-community relations units is that in order to gain the confidence of minorities, these units often serve as their informal ombudsmen. In this capacity, the units respond to the concerns of minority citizens by encouraging and channeling complaints against a number of public agencies including the welfare department, the fire department, and the schools, and even the police. This kind of police-community relations service presents a major source of intradepartmental hostility and distrust. It tends to encourage a perception among other police officers in a department that the police-community relations unit is another internal security force.

Police-community relations is also a political issue. The political climate of a community has a decisive influence on community relations programs. Because the concept of police-community relations is generally associated with the bettering of police-minority relations—and the emphasis of programs in many departments validates this perception—popular support for innovations in this area is predicated upon a community's attitude toward race relations. For this reason public and political support for police-community relations provides a measure of race relations in a community. In effect, since community relations units often focus their efforts on dealing with problems of minorities, the success or failure of their endeavor is closely linked with the politics of race.

The history of the rise and fall of San Francisco's Police-Community Relations Unit and its commanding officer, Lieutenant Dante Andreotti, provides a microcosm of the kind of politics that surround a police-community relations unit.[19] The unit's troubled history reflects the ongoing struggle between opposing views of the role of the policeman and his relationship to the community. What happened in San Francisco depicts the antagonism of factions representing differing views about the police and their inability to find a basis for accommodation. The conflict had each side securing a political power base with the purpose of undermining the other side's position. The zeal with which the battle was joined underlines the ideological nature of the split over the police roles.

San Francisco's Police-Community Relations Unit was formed in May 1962, over the objection of the police force, with Dante Andreotti as commanding officer. According to Jerome Skolnick, the unit's establishment was made possible by a general political climate that was supportive of innovations aimed at improving race relations.[20] The Kennedy administration was now in power, and new victories were being recorded by blacks in the area of civil rights. In general, the San Francisco political climate was receptive to minorities, even if most of the police were not. The unit was founded out of an optimism that the assumption of new police roles would help to foster better conditions throughout society. Skolnick writes:

> Implicit in the creation of this Unit was a recognition that changing social needs required a more expansive concept of police work. The idea was that police work was no longer simply a matter of apprehension, that police work also should include the prevention of crime. More explicitly, the police-community relations idea gave organizational meaning to the notion that police prevent crime not only by the threat of deterrence but also by a sympathetic understanding of the problems of people residing in high-crime areas. Crime was not, in this view, simply an act of perverted will but was a phenomenon arising out of frustrations and degradations felt by disadvantaged people; thus, the police would help to reduce crime by reducing despair—by acting as a social service agency to ameliorate some of the difficulties encountered by minority group persons.[21]

At first Lieutenant Andreotti benefited from favorable media publicity and public praise by the chief of police. The unit quickly grew to a complement of thirteen officers, all of whom prided themselves on being specialists in the field of community relations. But from the start the unit was faced with a persisting problem: How could it maintain its identity as a police organization and at the same time win the confidence of the minority-group population, which included not only blacks, but also "prostitutes, homosexuals, and hippies, each an identifiable minority group ordinarily considered a police problem."[22] Meanwhile, members of the unit went about their tasks of working with racial minorities—blacks, Chicanos, and Chinese—and drug addicts, alcoholics, male and female homosexuals, and prostitutes. The services performed for persons in these groups included aiding them in getting jobs and informing them of their rights. The result of these efforts was that the unit gained the confidence of minority groups in San Francisco. However, as their duties and responsibilities increased, the men of the Police-Community Relations Unit incurred a growing hostility from the rest of the police department. The hostility of the other men in the police force arose out of the avowed sympathy of police-community relations officers toward minority groups, a departmental stigmatization of community relations as social work, and the unit's practice of serving as an informal bureau for minority complaints against police practices, as well as against other public agencies in the city. Additionally, because members of the Police-Community Relations Unit had little contact with the rest of the department, the unit came to be "regarded as a suspicious, aloof, mysterious, and probably subversive branch of the Police Department."[23] By Andreotti's own estimate, more than 90 percent of the San Francisco police force were opposed to the unit.

With hostility growing within the department, San Francisco's police chief, Thomas Cahill, came under increasing pressure to disband the unit. In December 1966 a committee of the grand jury of San Francisco issued a recommendation for the breaking up of the central Police-Community Relations Unit, with its personnel assigned to perform the same work under district police captains. Although Chief Cahill initially refused to comply with this recommendation, at the end of December he proposed details of a plan that bore a great deal of similarity with that of the grand jury.

Andreotti reacted to the proposed dismemberment of his unit by mobilizing his constituency, largely derived from the minority-group community. Meetings in support of the Police-Community Relations Unit and Andreotti took place in local churches and neighborhood organizations. With a growing political support for Andreotti, the chief of police was reluctant to appear publicly to condemn him. Although Andreotti did not openly challenge the police chief, his ability to gain a personal political following constituted a threat to the chief's authority. This led to a deterioration of personal relations between Andreotti and the chief of police. Moreover, conservative pressures within the department were mounted in support of Andreotti's ouster.

Skolnick reports that Cahill, like any other administrator, was subjected to a variety of counterpressures. He was under fire from a majority of his own men to put an end to the "elusive, 'minority-coddling' PCR Unit." However, he was also under considerable pressure from an increasingly restless minority population to continue with police-community relations work. Had the PCR Unit not obtained the support of a number of influential organizations, such as the National Conference of Christians and Jews, the NAACP, several members of the Board of Supervisors, and the *San Francisco Examiner,* and the backing of a number of large companies such as Standard Oil, the Pacific Telephone Company, and Sears, Roebuck, it is quite possible that he could have quietly and slowly phased the program out. As it was, however, "there was a ruckus."[24]

The sides were clearly drawn. "Cahill, who had been a 'consensus' police chief in a pluralist, liberal city, was pushed increasingly into a more conservative position partly by the general political atmosphere, and more specifically by explicit demands of his men, coupled with his identification and sympathy with them."[25] Andreotti, too, was subjected to cross-pressures. He could have defined his job as primarily one of public relations and remained on good terms with members of his department. However, he saw the social condition of urban blacks and chose to represent them. He became what Skolnick calls a "black man living in a white skin. As such, he came to share black frustration and despair, became more and more militant, and increasingly offensive to his fellow policemen."[26]

The outcome was that Andreotti was eased out of the San Francisco Police Department, to join subsequently the Department of Justice. He was given a farewell dinner, well attended by minority-group persons and by the mayor, where he was praised. However, the chief of police, the deputy chief, and the captains of the police force were not present at the dinner. Chief Cahill's plan of having district captains primarily responsible for community relations within their jurisdictions was implemented shortly thereafter.

Skolnick attributes the outcome of the conflict over San Francisco's police-community relations unit to more than just a personality clash between Cahill and Andreotti; the outcome was principally shaped by the political climate. According to Skolnick, there occurred a significant change in the political mood of California signaled by "the rise to power of a conservative political philosophy, dominated . . . by indignation against violations of conventional middle-class morality." This emergent political influence came from those directly opposed to the sort of people whose interests police-community relations was intended to serve—"the poor, hippies, urban Negroes, homosexuals."[27]

The San Francisco example serves to demonstrate the difficulties surrounding certain aspects of the police-community relations concept. The "public relations" and "community service" approaches are not likely to offend the police rank and file. However, the "advocacy policing" approach, exemplified by Andreotti and the San Francisco Police Department Community Relations Unit, poses the problem of alienating officers of the rest of the department as well as large segments of the majority community, even though it is probably the most successful approach insofar as relations between minority groups and a police-community relations unit are concerned. The social work attitude that this approach carries out, coupled with its avowed emphasis on helping minority-group citizens, are strategies that are, in the main, not consistent with the prevailing attitudes in police departments. If the police-community relations concept is to take hold in police forces around the country, then departments will probably need to choose among the following options: (1) they can stop practicing the "advocacy policing" approach altogether; (2) they can modify this approach so that police-community relations units service a wider community than just the minorities; or (3) they can seek to alter the existing socialization processes existing within the police, so that officers are more in sympathy with the direction of the advocacy policing approach.

Despite the negative sentiment or indifference to police-community relations, there is some evidence that the concept of community relations has some support among police as well. Tables 9.3 and 9.4 provide the results of a survey of police officers in the cities of Augusta, Georgia; Ocala, Florida; St. Petersburg, Florida; Birmingham, Alabama; Charlotte, North Carolina; and De Kalk County, Georgia. The survey, with 444 usable responses, found that these officers felt that police-community relations programs are important. However, interestingly, a far larger percentage of black officers than white officers indicated that these programs were "very important."

There appears to be a contradiction between the results of the survey in Table 9.3 and Table 9.4 and police attitudes toward community relations as obtained from case studies and interviews. This may arise from either a misconception of what police-community relations entails or may be a matter of professing a positive attitude while in fact harboring a negative one. In any event, even if police-community relations programs are considered important by policemen, there is little indication that many of them want to be involved in the actual operations of the program. Moreover, there is a widespread antipathy and distrust of officers who do take an active role in police-community relations activities by the other members of a department. These are critical obstacles for police-community relations units to overcome if their practices are to be successful. In a very real sense, the first target group of these units should be other policemen. Improved community relations can occur only with the par-

TABLE 9.3   Police attitudes toward community relations

Police-community relations programs are:	Percentage
Very important	57.0
Fairly important	19.0
Slightly important	8.3
Not important	7.9
Undecided	7.2

Source: Richard C. Huseman and Stephen H. McCurley, "Police Attitudes Toward Police-Community Relations Programs," *Police Chief,* December 1972, p. 72.

TABLE 9.4   Racial breakdown of community relations attitudes

Police-community relations programs are:	Black officers	White officers
	Percentage	
Very important	90.9	55.3
Fairly important	4.5	20.3
Slightly important	4.5	8.6
Not important	0.0	8.1
Undecided	0.0	7.1

Source: Richard C. Huseman and Stephen H. McCurley, "Police Attitudes Toward Police-Community Relations Programs," *Police Chief,* December 1972, p. 72.

ticipation of every police officer. This will require the conversion of many officers to the values of providing a service to the public in addition to their commitment to the imperatives of law and order.

NOTES

1. Fred I. Klyman, Floyd B. Hannon, and Max L. Armstrong, *Police Roles in a Changing Society* (Wichita: Kansas Criminal Justice Community Relations Training Institute, 1973), pp. 306–307.

2. Alan Coffey, Edward Eldefonso, and Walter Hartinger, *Human Relations: Law Enforcement in a Changing Community* (Englewood Cliffs, N.J.: Prentice-Hall, 1971), p. 8.

3. U.S. Advisory Commission on Intergovernmental Relations, *State-Local Relations in the Criminal Justice System* (Washington, D.C.: U.S. Government Printing Office, 1971), p. 265.

4. Klyman, Hannon, and Armstrong, *Police Roles,* p. 86.

5. Ibid., p. 3.

6. Louis A. Radelet, "Police-Community Relations: At This Point in Time . . ." *Police Chief,* March 1974, p. 25.

7. Louis A. Radelet, *The Police and the Community* (Beverly Hills, Calif.: Glencoe Press, 1973), p. 24. Emphasis in the original.

8. Ibid.

9. See Jerome H. Skolnick, "The Police and the Urban Ghetto," in *Police-Community Relations,* eds. Paul F. Cromwell, Jr., and George Keefer (St. Paul, Minn.: West, 1973), p. 201; and Radelet, *Police and the Community,* pp. 24–25.

10. The discussion about specific police-community relations programs relies heavily on Betty Bertothy, *Police-Community Relations: A Practical Guide for Texas Police Officers* (Austin: Texas Commission on Law Enforcement Officers' Standards and Education, 1970); Alan Edward Bent, *Toward Improving the Police Image: A Survey of Urban Police-Community Relations Program* (Memphis: Memphis State University, Institute of Governmental Studies and Research, June 1972); Alan Edward Bent, *The Politics of Law Enforcement: Conflict and Power in Urban Communities* (Lexington, Mass.: Heath, 1974); and promotional brochures from police-community relations units of a number of police departments in the United States.

11. The President's Commission on Law Enforcement and Administration of Justice, *Task Force Report: The Police* (Washington, D.C.: U.S. Government Printing Office, 1967), p. 123.

12. Bent, *Politics of Law Enforcement,* p. 53.

13. The information describing the Baltimore and Chicago police-community relations programs was primarily obtained from these departments' community relations brochures.

14. Victor G. Strecher, *The Environment of Law Enforcement: A Community Relations Guide* (Englewood Cliffs, N.J.: Prentice-Hall, 1971), pp. 69–70.

15. Bent, *Politics of Law Enforcement,* pp. 54–55.

16. Ibid., p. 56.

17. Jerome H. Skolnick, "The Police and the Urban Ghetto," in *Police-Community Relations,* eds. Paul F. Cromwell, Jr., and George Keefer (St. Paul, Minn.: 1973), p. 194.

18. Ibid., p. 196.

19. The account of the history of the San Francisco Police-Community Relations Unit is obtained from Skolnick, "Police and the Urban Ghetto," pp. 180–210.

20. Ibid., p. 194.

21. Ibid., p. 192.

22. Ibid., p. 195.

23. Ibid., p. 197.

24. Ibid., p. 199.

25. Ibid., p. 200.

26. Ibid.

27. Ibid., p. 199.

BIBLIOGRAPHY

BENT, ALAN EDWARD. *The Politics of Law Enforcement: Conflict and Power in Urban Communities.* Lexington, Mass.: Heath, 1974.

————. *Toward Improving the Police Image: A Survey of Urban Police-Community Relations Programs.* Memphis: Memphis State University, Institute of Governmental Studies and Research, June 1972.

BERTOTHY, BETTY. *Police-Community Relations: A Practical Guide for Texas Police Officers.* Auston: Texas Commission on Law Enforcement Officers' Standards and Education, 1970.

COFFEY, ALAN; ELDEFONSO, EDWARD; and HARTINGER, WALTER. *Human Relations: Law Enforcement in a Changing Community.* Englewood Cliffs, N.J.: Prentice-Hall, 1971.

CROMWELL, PAUL F., JR., and KEEFER, GEORGE, eds. *Police-Community Relations.* St. ·Paul, Minn.: West, 1973.

KLYMAN, FRED I.; HANNON, FLOYD B.; and ARMSTRONG, MAX L. *Police Roles in A Changing Society.* Wichita: Kansas Criminal Justice Community Relations Training Institute, 1973.

PRESIDENT'S COMMISSION ON LAW ENFORCEMENT AND ADMINISTRATION OF JUSTICE. *Task Force Report: The Police.* Washington, D.C.: U.S. Government Printing Office, 1967.

RADELET, LOUIS A. *The Police and Community.* Beverly Hills, Calif.: Glencoe Press, 1973.

STRECHER, VICTOR G. *The Environment of Law Enforcement: A Community Relations Guide.* Englewood Cliffs, N.J.: Prentice-Hall, 1971.

U.S. ADVISORY COMMISSION ON INTERGOVERNMENTAL RELATIONS. *State-Local Relations in the Criminal Justice System.* Washington, D.C.: U.S. Government Printing Office, 1971.

10

||||||||||||||||||||||||||||||||||||||||||||||||||||||||||||||||||||||||||||||||||||||||||||||||||||||||||||||||||||||||||||||||||||||||||

POLICE
IN DEMOCRATIC SOCIETY

Chapter 9 emphasized the great importance of communication for better police-community relations. This theme deserves additional consideration. As William R. Carmack writes, police represent that component of the criminal justice system called upon to enforce the laws that the majority, through their elected representatives, make and claim to want enforced. Yet as police go about their work, they are frequently aware that, although strict law enforcement may be desired in the abstract, it is not likely to be valued by the particular individual whose behavior is checked by the police. And, as Carmack further notes, "in many instances, the mass of people tend to identify with the lawbreaker."[1]

On the basis of Carmack's statement, it becomes necessary for the police to understand the role they are called upon to play in the community, and, in turn, for the community to understand fully the nature and function of the police. The image of the police is frequently negative. They are seen as interfering with or abridging the freedom of movement of the community. Their positive role or function is less apparent, in large part because the performance of that function seldom involves "news." Thus, as Carmack continues, "collectively and individually, one of the most important tasks of the police is to interact or communicate with the community more fully."[2]

This chapter will explore the nature of communication and the way it can be used more effectively by the police. It will also take up some of the problem areas in communication which must be understood and astutely handled if relations between the police and the public are not to suffer: the problems of police-media and criminal-justice–media relations will receive special consideration. Finally, this chapter will argue that for police-community relations to be truly successful, communication, important as it is, is not enough. The concept of police-community relations will have to be internalized institutionally within police departments, and this will require organizational and operational changes as well as increased communication.

The Process of Communication

The process of communication consists of four essential components: source, receiver, message, and channel.[3] Obviously, communication must begin with a source—the person who places the message in the channel. He is the communicator, the one who utters the words that the receiver hears. In turn, the receiver is the individual who perceives a message in the channel. The receiver brings the same resources to the communication situation as the source: his own experiences, biases, needs, wants, desires, and communicative abilities. These resources help to determine the meaning he derives from the message and any response he may make to it. In police-community relations programs that constitute authentic efforts at two-way communications, both the police and the community must reciprocate as the source and receiver of messages.

Far too often, police-community relations consists of one-way communication through public relations programs, with the police doing all the talking and the community doing all the listening. This one-way communication is most unfortunate for two critical reasons. First, the police are thereby effectively denied valuable information concerning the apprehensions and anxieties of the community; as a consequence, they are denied the opportunity to bring their talents, energies, and resources to bear so as to address and perhaps even resolve these concerns. Second, with the police doing all of the talking and none of the listening, the police have no way of knowing whether the message they are communicating is being properly received and understood by the community. After all, the third component of the communications process, the message, is not always as apparent as the police may believe.

Kenneth Andersen defines the message as

the constellation of stimuli that the source actually places in the channel(s). The message is not what the source intended to say; nor is it what the receivers think was said. It is only a set of physical stimuli which exist in the channel.

While this way of defining a message may seem difficult or even arbitrary, it becomes very useful, once understood. For one thing, it makes it easier to remember that potential messages exist separate from and regardless of people's responses to them. Second, it stresses that meanings do not exist in messages. Instead, they exist in the minds of people. The meaning one person assigns to a message may differ greatly from those others assign to it. Further, the meanings assigned to the message today may not be the same as those assigned tomorrow. The source may think the message "says" one thing; the receiver may think it "says" something different.[4]

With the message so defined, three areas related to messages must be kept continually in mind: (1) what the source intends the message to mean; (2)

what the receiver interprets the message to be; and (3) what third persons make of the message in relation to these and other possible meanings. The relevance to police-community relations programs of these three areas within which communication breakdowns can occur is immediately apparent. For example, the police should be aware that when they use the phrase "law and order," although it may have positive connotations to them and refer to the fair and even-handed yet firm enforcement of the law, it may have distinctly negative connotations in the ghetto, where it might be interpreted as a code term for racism and harassment. Likewise, the community should also be aware that certain street language, used freely and harmlessly, may, if directed toward police, be regarded by them as both insulting and demeaning; offense may be taken when none was intended.

The fourth component of the process of communication is equally important to police-community relations: the channel. The channel may be defined as the medium in which the message exists. Anything that can affect the five senses—sight, hearing, touch, taste, smell—can be used as a communication medium. However, the channels most often used affect the senses of sight and hearing, either singly or in combination.[5]

These channels are generally associated with verbal communication; that is, the transmission of a message through the spoken or written word. However, they are also capable of sustaining a great deal of nonverbal communication, perhaps equally important in the overall communication process. The term "nonverbal communication" amounts to a sophisticated way of saying that actions frequently speak louder than words.[6] The nonverbal dimensions of human communication are many. They include:

1. Body motion or kinesic behavior. These nonverbal cues include gestures, facial expressions, eye behavior (blinking, direction and length of gaze, and pupil dilation), movements of the body, limbs, hands, head, feet, and legs, and posture.
2. Physical characteristics. These influential nonverbal cues are not movement-bound; instead, they include such things as physique or body shape, general attractiveness, body or breath odors, height, weight, hair, and skin tone or color.
3. Touching behavior. Of particular concern here are handshakes, greetings and farewells, and actions designed to guide another's movements.
4. Paralanguage. Paralanguage is concerned with how something is said, not with what is said. As such, it deals with the range of nonverbal vocal cues surrounding common speech behavior, including pitch range, pitch control, rhythm control, tempo, articulation control, resonance, pitch height, intensity, and accent.
5. Proxemics. Proxemics deals with the study of man's use and perception of his social and personal space. It is especially concerned with "territoriality," the human tendency to stake out personal territory—or un-

touchable space—in much the same manner as wild animals and birds do.[7]

6. Artifacts. Nonverbal cues may also be obtained from artifact, which include the manipulation of objects in contact with the interacting persons. These artifacts may include perfume, clothes, lipstick, eyeglasses, wigs, false eyelashes, and a whole repertoire of "beauty" aids.

7. Environmental factors. Much can be learned about an individual from the conditions of his surroundings—neat or squalid, tasteful or garish, simple or cluttered. The same can be said of groups and organizations.[8]

The uses of nonverbal communication are as varied as its dimensions. It can be employed to repeat what was said verbally, contradict verbal behavior, serve as a substitute for verbal messages, modify or elaborate on verbal messages, emphasize the spoken word, or regulate the communicative flow between those engaged in interaction.[9] The use of an example with which everyone is familiar, the classroom situation, can bring the significance of the dimensions and uses of nonverbal communication into proper perspective. The classroom is a "veritable goldmine of nonverbal behavior."[10] Consider the following variety of classroom nonverbal cues: (1) the frantic hand-waving of one who is sure he has the correct answer; (2) the student who is sure he does not know the answer and therefore attempts to avoid any eye contact with the teacher; (3) the effects that student dress and hair length can have on teacher-student interaction; (4) facial expressions, threatening gestures, and tone of voice, all of which are frequently employed for discipline in elementary schools; (5) the teacher who requests student questioning and criticism, but whose nonverbal actions make it apparent that he will not be receptive; (6) the message communicated by absence from class; (7) a teacher's trust of his students, which may sometimes be indicated by his arrangement of seating and his monitoring behavior during examinations; (8) the variety of techniques employed by students to make sleeping appear to be studying or listening; (9) the professor who insists that he has plenty of time for student conferences, but who by fidgeting and continually glancing at his watch suggests otherwise; (10) teachers who attempt to assess facial expressions and other visual feedback to determine student comprehension; and (11) even classroom design (the presence or absence of windows and the arrangement of desks into rows or circles), which may have an influence on student participation in the classroom.[11]

The subtle influence of nonverbal communication in the classroom can occasionally have dramatic results. Thus, in a study conducted in a primarily lower- and working-class public school, Robert Rosenthal and Lenore Jacobson chose 20 percent of the student population at random and described them as high scorers on an "intellectual blooming test" that ostensibly indicated that they would show unusual intellectual development soon. Teachers were given this information. When these "bloomers" were tested at the end of the year, they showed a sharp rise on IQ tests, with some gaining as much as twelve IQ points.

Rosenthal and Jacobson attributed this increase to teacher expectations and the way these special students were treated.

> To summarize our speculations, we may say that by what she said, by how and when she said it, by facial expressions, postures, and perhaps by her touch, the teacher may have communicated to the children of the experimental group that she expected improved intellectual performance. Such communications together with possible changing in teaching techniques may have helped the child learn by changing his self-concept, his expectations of his own behavior, and his motivation, as well as his cognitive style and skills.[12]

The use of the classroom example is altogether fitting in a book on police-community relations. After all, like teachers and social workers, police are street-level bureaucrats. As Michael Lipsky observes, they represent the American government to its citizens. "They are the people citizens encounter when they seek help from, or are controlled by, the American political system."[13] As such, police and teachers have much in common, including the need to appreciate the significance of nonverbal communication. Police are, of course, not totally unaware of the uses and importance of nonverbal communication. Thus, for example, in police interrogations police officers are often encouraged to sit very close to the suspect, thereby invading his personal territory and communicating to the suspect their ability to dominate and control both him and his environment. However, police sensitivity to the pervasiveness and impact of nonverbal communication must be heightened. As teachers communicate their expectations to students, so police communicate their expectations to the community, and these expectations can in turn profoundly effect both student and community performance, for good or ill.

Police should also understand that these expectations are communicated not only by kinesic behavior (body motions such as gestures and facial expressions) but also by the environmental setting. With this in mind, the all-too-common outmoded and decrepit precinct station becomes an obvious liability; it communicates contempt for the police who work there and disdain for the community they serve. Police and their organizational representatives should strongly encourage the provision of adequate and attractive physical facilities. The President's Commission on Law Enforcement and Administration of Justice addressed itself to this need, although its focus was different. "All too often, police precinct stations are old, cramped and badly maintained; equipment is deficient; and clerical help is limited. These conditions adversely affect police morale and detract from the professional nature of police work."[14] Improved working conditions will certainly add to the attractiveness of careers in law enforcement, and it will also create a favorable community impression and thereby enhance the message communicated by the police environment.

Finally, police should also be aware that nonverbal communications can contradict verbal communication, and when this occurs, the community is inclined to trust and believe the nonverbal message. The community is likely to assume that nonverbal signals are more spontaneous, harder to fake, and less apt to be manipulated—in brief, more likely to reveal the source's true feelings and emotions. If this is true, it has obvious implications for community relations. If the police say one thing—that they are totally nondiscriminatory and non-racist—but communicate through their actions that they are far more suspicious of blacks than of other groups, the community is likely to consider what they do as reflecting the police's true intentions much more than what they say, and to hold them in even greater contempt for being not only racist, but also hypo-critical.

Police are, of course, not the only component of the criminal justice system which would benefit from an increased appreciation of the impact of nonverbal communication. The physical facilities of the courts, like the police, are in al-most every state inadequate. "The judicial system is characterized by a physical deterioration, design and space inadequacies, and inappropriate location of existing facilities."[15] As Leonard Downie, Jr., complains, in too many metro-politan areas the criminal courts occupy old, dreary, makeshift courtrooms in police stations located in deteriorating neighborhoods. The courtrooms are often badly lit, acoustically impossible, and poorly maintained. Halls and entrances are often blocked with sleeping vagrants. In stark contrast, civil trial courts often are located in downtown areas; their courthouses are well designed, and their courtrooms are bright and well furnished.[16] The message communicated by this contrast is not lost on the public. Neither is the criminal court's emphasis on efficiency and assembly-line production, Both clash openly with the United States Supreme Court's declaration that these courts are "palladiums of liberty" and "citadels of justice."[17] Corrections is likewise affected by nonverbal com-munication that conflicts openly with verbal assurances. Many inmates become increasingly cynical and their successful reintegration into society is further jeopardized as they witness purely punitive behavior flatly contradict rehabilata-tive rhetoric.

Perhaps the chief determinant of communicative success, be the com-munication verbal or nonverbal, is "source credibility"—the receiver's estima-tion of the character and trustworthiness of the source.[18] The same speech will have a much greater impact if the public believes that it has been given by Billy Graham than if it believes that it has been given by Abbie Hoffman. All one has to do is look at newspaper and magazine advertisements or television commer-cials to see this. Advertisers have learned that the public, although aware that an athlete may know nothing about automobiles, nevertheless is likely to be profoundly influenced to accept his communication as the result of its prior attitude toward the source in a general way.

The relevance of this for police-community communication is easy to see. As Carmack writes: "The acceptance of any given message from the police is, in a sense, filtered through all previous experiences and attitudes relating to the police."[19] As a consequence, as long as the press insists upon playing up negative incidents involving the police and as long as the public continues to regard law enforcement as the police's primary function, subsequent messages from the police will suffer from low source credibility. Stories of graft in police departments in New York and Chicago and the telecast of the shooting of a black man in Atlanta will make it more difficult for police anywhere else to communicate effectively with the public.

Source credibility is determined by the receiver's prior attitudes toward the source, which in turn are affected by the norms of his reference groups. Receivers do not exist in isolation, but as parts of groups, and it is as parts of social groups that they must be studied. Efforts to understand and improve communication must take account of this. As Carmack says: "[I]t is clear that any account of the changes in opinion that an individual group member undergoes must recognize, not only the communication directed to him, but the norms his groups share, and the communication that takes place within the groups about the new idea."[20] This is especially true when dealing with juvenile groups and other subcultural groups in society. In order to communicate effectively with them, the police must understand more fully the norms by which these groups behave. Thus, for police-community communication to be effective, the police must keep in mind a number of considerations. To begin with, they must focus on the receiver of the messages, not just on the messages themselves. Moreover, they must emphasize the things that interest and motivate the receiver. They must also recall that the meaning of the message is not so much determined by the languages and codes they employ as it is by the personal background, experiences, and reference groups of the receiver. Finally, the police must recognize that they will remain relatively unsuccessful until they consciously adapt their messages to the intended receiver.

Police-Media Relations

For police-community communication to be effective, the police must appreciate the promise of, as well as the problems involved in, communicating with the community not only directly through face-to-face interactions, but also indirectly through the use of the media. The relationship between the police and the news media can be characterized as potentially complementary. As the National Advisory Commission on Criminal Justice Standards and Goals notes: "The news media have a legitimate need for more information about police activities; they offer an excellent channel for informing the public about the nature of police tasks and problems."[21] However, they are often far more appropriately characterized by hostility, suspicion, and conflict. As Louis Radelet has pointed out:

> Relationship problems between governmental bodies and the media of public information are endemic in democratic societies. Conflict of interest is embedded in this relationship, and it is perfectly normal and generally healthy in terms of the common good. If the newspapers and other media

were not "policing the police" and other governing factions; if they were not channelling information and interpreting the communication between criminal justice agencies and the public, they would be shirking a vital responsibility and would be open to serious criticism.[22]

A number of factors explain this conflict of interest between the police and the media. To begin with, there is the problem of disclosure of information. Police often deem it necessary to withhold certain information from the media. They may consider such basic police objectives as a manhunt, a criminal investigation, or a crackdown to be threatened by their release. It is not always in the best interests of either the police or the public for the police to disclose all they may know about a given case. This judgment on withholding information, however, is likely to be questioned by the media, and their questions transmitted to the public, to the possible disadvantage of the police. Since the police cannot explain their decision without disclosing information that they believe is best withheld, their "No comment" is often translated as pugnacity or evasiveness.

The controversy surrounding disclosure of information is often exacerbated by the deadline pressures under which the media operate. Newspapers work under the deadline of editions; radio and television reporters work under even harsher deadlines. Thus, as former New York City Police Commissioner Patrick V. Murphy writes, "The area of possible friction with police doubles because of the constant demand for speed in getting the story."[23] The police, on the other hand, are concerned about matters other than deadlines; they are concerned with the orderly and systematic gathering of facts and other evidence necessary for arrest and future court presentation. This is often a slow and deliberate process, likely to frustrate and exasperate the deadline-conscious reporters. While this roadblock to smooth police-media relations perhaps can never be completely removed, Murphy nonetheless does admonish the police to "realize the time element under which the press operates and do their best within legal means to provide information as soon as it may be used."[24]

Still another factor that has contributed to police-media problems is the stormy social turbulence of the past two decades. As William Bopp writes:

> During the civil rights demonstrations of the early 1960s, police-media relations began to deteriorate as the electronic and print media representatives took a sympathetic view toward Negro demonstrators and a not-so-sympathetic view toward the police. Urban rioting exacerbated the conflict, rank-and-file police militancy escalated it, and the violence at the 1968 Democratic National Convention in Chicago, in which policemen and journalists came into physical confrontation, increased the break to an abyss.[25]

These problems have been made all the more severe by the advent of television news. The nature of this medium is cited by many newsmen and law-enforcement officials as contributing significantly to the animosity that exists between the police and the press. Since television news programs are constantly competing with other media for the attention of the public, they must use their natural ability to dramatize a situation. To accomplish this end, they emphasize "action" news film that often conveys a distorted image of the situation being reported. The viewer is psychologically drawn into the action shown on the film. This tends to divorce his attention from other equally important but unfilmed aspects of the story. For example, in the 1967 Detroit riots, camera crews did not film the cooperative effort of the Detroit police, members of the United Automobile Workers Union, and groups of young blacks who joined forces in an attempt to cool things down in the riot area.[26]

The use of action film also results in an unintentional emphasis on police action in civil disturbances. Camera crews that are filming riots are frequently advised, warned, or ordered by police to stay behind police lines, which the crews are often glad to do for their own safety. However, from their positions behind the lines, the violence they witness and film will most likely be what police do to rioters. Even if the police do nothing, most of the people filmed are likely to be policemen. As a result, the lasting impression of a tense, angry riot is likely to be that of tense, angry policemen.[27] Moreover, protest groups that engage in civil disturbances are often quick to make use of the emotional impact of television. More than once, television stations have received calls informing them that particular groups intend to engage in certain acts of protest or civil disobedience. When they have asked when these demonstrations are to occur, the answer is often, "As soon as you get here." This practice was frequently employed with explosive results during the 1968 Democratic National Convention in Chicago, where crowds of noisy protesters often remained relatively orderly and restrained until network television cameras were turned on, at which time they became frenzied, riotous, and altogether irresponsible. Obviously, the nature of their protest changed once the cameras were on. As David L. Lange and his associates unemotionally declared in their report on violence and the mass media to the National Commission on the Causes and Prevention of Violence: "Sometimes the grievances of demonstrators include police brutality. To bring the excesses of the police into public view, they may seek to provoke them when television cameras are present."[28]

Police-media relations have also suffered from the news media's stress on spot reporting, which is usually confined to the unexpected or the unusual. They too often neglect what may be called "perspective" reporting. For example, the 5 percent of students who rioted on a college campus are reported; the perspective provided by the fact that 95 percent did not is often overlooked. Likewise, seldom does the public hear about the police officer who has carried out his assignment with a devotion to duty. This is not news; dereliction of duty or corruption is, and that makes the headlines. This, of course, distorts the image of the police in the eyes of the public and heightens police-media relationship problems.[29]

This media emphasis on tragedy, conflict, disorder, and the bizarre is often joined in the minds of many policemen and even a substantial portion of the public with the charge that the media are guilty of biased reporting. Newsmen are often accused of being dogmatic liberals with a strong leftist bias, and hence out of touch with the American mainstream. Former Vice-President Spiro T. Agnew articulated these suspicions when he characterized the Eastern establishment press as "an effete corps of impudent snobs." The media, however, are quick to deny this. They point out that there are in the United States today approximately 1750 daily, 578 Sunday, and 8000 weekly newspapers; 150 general editorial magazines; 6400 radio stations; and 840 television outlets.[30] Among these media, there is intense competition. For every reporter who may slant a story one way, there is another who sees an advantage both for himself and his paper or station in exposing this bias and reporting the whole story. Moreover, the media continue, most of the criticism they receive today results from a conscious or unconscious willingness on the part of public officials, including the police and even the public, to be more upset with the bearer of bad news than with the bad news itself. The ancient Greeks used to kill the messengers who brought news of defeat in battle. Many spokesmen of the media believe much of the present criticism to which they are subjected is simply a more restrained version of the same response.

All of these issues have been brought into sharper focus by the recent debate surrounding the rights of reporters. The case of Earl Caldwell, a black reporter for the *New York Times,* can help set the stage for this discussion. Caldwell was assigned to cover the Black Panthers and other black militant groups. He had written articles about the Black Panthers and had interviewed their leaders. He was subpoenaed by a federal grand jury for "all notes and tape recordings" of his interviews with Black Panther leaders, particularly for an interview with David Hilliard, who was charged with threatening President Nixon's life. Caldwell refused. He and other newsmen were outraged at the catch-all nature of the subpoenas: they termed them nothing less than "fishing expeditions." But, more importantly, they feared that if every legitimate source of information knew that he or his journalist friend could be subpoenaed at will and hauled into court for questioning or even jailing, not many headlines would be written or broadcast except for cut-and-dried events covered in routine fashion. They were apprehensive that the traditional investigative role of the press would fade forever.[31] They also warned that "lazy law-enforcement types" might come to rely on the use of subpoenas to force the press to do their investigating, and thereby turn the free press into an arm of governmental surveillance.

However, the issue of freedom of the press, resting on the protection of confidential information and sources, was not the only issue involved in the *Caldwell* case. It was joined with the obligation of every citizen to serve as a witness in support of law and judicial process. For his refusal to obey the subpoena and fulfill his obligation as a citizen, Caldwell was held in contempt of court. However, the matter did not end there. *United States* v. *Caldwell* ultimately worked its way up to the United States Supreme Court, where it was considered in conjunction with two other cases: In *re Pappas* and *Branzburg* v.

Hayes.[32] In a five-to-four decision, the Court ruled against Caldwell. Justice Byron White wrote for the majority:

> We are asked to [interpret] the First Amendment to grant newsmen a testimonial privilege that other citizens do not enjoy. This we decline to do. . . . On the record now before us, we perceive no basis for holding that the public interest in law enforcement and in insuring effective grand jury proceedings is insufficient to override the consequential but uncertain burden on news gathering which is said to result from insisting that reporters, like other citizens, respond to relevant questions put to them in the course of a valid grand jury investigation or criminal trial.

For all of these reasons, the relations between the police and the media have often been marked with acrimony and suspicion. The police are not the only component of the criminal justice system to experience these problems, however. Both the courts and corrections have likewise experienced problems with the media that interfere with communication and jeopardize successful criminal justice–community relations. Thus, the courts are faced with the classic dilemma posed by the rights of a fair trial versus a free press. In his concurring opinion in *Irvin* v. *Dowd* in 1961, Justice Felix Frankfurter posed the problem involved:

> Not a term passes without this Court being importuned to review convictions, heard in States throughout the country, in which substantial claims are made that a jury trial has been distorted because of inflammatory newspaper accounts—too often, as in this case, with the prosecutor's collaboration—exerting pressures on potential jurors before trial and even during the course of the trial, thereby making it extremely difficult if not impossible to secure a jury capable of taking in, free of prepossessions, evidence submitted in open court. Indeed such extraneous influences, in violation of the decencies guaranteed by our Constitution, are sometimes so powerful that an accused is forced, as a practical matter, to forgo trial by jury.[33]

In Great Britain, the issue of a fair trial versus a free press does not arouse the controversy that it does in this country. The right of every man to a free and impartial trial simply takes precedence over the right of a free press. Thus, the general rule in Great Britain is that nothing that might conceivably affect the attitude of a potential juror may be published unless and until it is formally disclosed in court.[34] Large fines are meted out to newspapers that violate this general rule. The *Daily Record* of Edinburgh was fined £7,500 ($21,000) for using on its front page a picture of a soccer star charged with indecent exposure. In addition, the editor who was in charge when the issue went to press was fined £500 ($1,400), and the only reason no individual was jailed for contempt was that the editor responsible had been at home sick that night. As the presiding judge in the case queried, "How is a judge or a jury to know that the witness is identifying the man seen on the occasion of the crime and not the man whose photograph has been blazoned on the front page of a newspaper?"[35]

In the United States, however, the way in which the Constitution's First

Amendment guarantees of free speech and a free press have been interpreted has precluded this solution to the problem. As a result, the Supreme Court of the United States, on a number of occasions, has had to reverse the criminal convictions of defendants because of adverse pretrial or trial publicity.[36] In an effort to obviate this necessity and to promote more harmonious relationships between the media and the judiciary, a number of cities and states throughout the country have formed panels of journalists, judges, and lawyers to consider their respective responsibilities. The results of some of these panels has been the adoption of guidelines for disclosure and reporting of information in criminal proceedings, commonly referred to as bar-media codes. In some forty-two states, voluntary codes have been endorsed or are now under consideration. The Oregon bar-media code is typical. According to its provisions, it is generally appropriate to disclose or report the following:

1. The arrested person's name, age, residence, employment, marital status, and similar biographical information.
2. The substance or text of the charge, such as would be contained in a complaint, indictment, or information.
3. The amount of bail.
4. The identity of and biographical information concerning either the complaining party or victim.
5. The identity of the investigating and arresting agency and the length of the investigation.
6. The circumstances of arrest, including time, place, resistance, pursuit, and weapons used.

However, it is generally not appropriate to disclose for publication or to report prior to the trial the following:

1. The contents of any admission or confession, or the fact that an admission or confession has been made.
2. Opinions about the arrested person's character, guilt, or innocence.
3. Statements concerning the evidence or arguments in the case.
4. Statements concerning anticipated testimony or the truthfulness of prospective witnesses.
5. The results of fingerprints, polygraph examinations, ballistics tests, or laboratory witnesses.
6. The precise descriptions of items seized or discovered during an investigation.
7. Prior criminal charges and convictions of the defendant.[37]

Problems in corrections-media relations have also occurred. In their efforts to bring to the public's attention the colossal failure of correctional endeavors, many newsmen have sought to gain interviews with prison inmates and to report their impressions and experiences. Correctional authorities have typically promulgated regulations that bar such face-to-face communication with newsmen, both because of the deleterious effects they have on prison security and discipline and, quite understandably, because of their reluctance to have these failures and shortcomings publicized. As a result, conflict has ensued, resolved for the moment at least by the Supreme Court's decisions in *Pell* v. *Procunier*[38] and *Saxbe* v. *Washington Post.*[39] In these June 1974 decisions, the Supreme Court rejected the argument of the news media that these regulations are violative of their right of access to information. As in *Caldwell* v. *United States,* it refused to single out the press for special treatment. After all, the Court noted, the general public is not entitled to enter prisons and interview at will. The Supreme Court also rejected the contention of the inmates that these regulations deprived them of their rights of free speech. The court observed that in light of *Procunier* v. *Martinez,*[40] which effectively ended all censorship of inmate mail, sufficient alternative channels of communication were available to justify, in balance, these restrictions.

Internalizing Police-Community Relations

Even when the police have come to appreciate fully the problems and the promise of communication and have come to improve their communicative abilities, both directly through face-to-face interactions and indirectly through the use of the media, the success of police-community relations programs will by no means be assured. As the experience of police-community relations in San Francisco reveals, communication between the police and the public is not enough; there must also be communication within police departments themselves between police-community relations units and the rest of the force. Thus, police-community relations are and remain problematic not only because of the difficulty of persuading the public that they are serious, but also because of the difficulty of convincing the police rank and file that they have merit. The difficulties police have experienced in gaining community acceptance of police-community relations programs have already been discussed in previous chapters. The remainder of this chapter will explore the difficulties involved in convincing police personnel—especially the officer on the street—of their importance and the institutional and organizational changes that may be needed to gain acceptance of them.

Three major obstacles stand in the way of acceptance by police rank and file of the need for police-community relations. First, police-community relations are an admission of the failure of police professionalism. As James F. Ahern puts it, "The creation of a police-relations squad says that a police department cannot relate to a community through decent and fair responses to that community's problems as a whole and that it must create a gimmick to gloss over its deficiencies."[41] Second, police-community relations are derogated by the police, for they see them as little more than social service and hence as a departure from such main-line police work as law enforcement and order maintenance. And third, they are viewed with suspicion by the police, for police-community relations units, as they seek to ingratiate themselves with the community, will often accept and even invite complaints that the community may have about the police. The rest of the department is likely to resent these actions and to regard the police-community relations unit as simply another internal investigation unit. This leads to obvious tension within police departments between the police-community relations unit and the rest of the force.

In a sense, this is what police-community relations is supposed to accomplish; it is to bring the tension between majority rule and minority rights—inadequately preserved in the criminal justice system as a whole—into the police departments themselves, with the police-community relations units representing and promoting the interests of the minority and the rest of the department articulating the aspirations and apprehensions of the majority. But, as the experiences of the San Francisco Police Department suggest, the infusion of the majority rule–minority rights tension into police departments themselves cannot stop at the level of the police-community relations units versus the rest of the department. At this level, the rest of the force is still so powerful that it can simply prevail and force the abandonment of police-community relations efforts. Rather, the tension between majority rule and minority rights must be brought down to, and introduced at, the level of the individual police officer. He must come to internalize the concept of police-community relations. For this to occur, communication between the police-community relations unit and the rest of the department is essential but insufficient. It will also require a change in police culture, with police-community relations becoming the prevailing cultural mode. For this change to take place, substantial institutional and organizational changes will be necessary.

Establishment of Adequate Selection Standards

To begin with, the establishment of adequate standards for selection of police personnel is imperative. The President's Commission on Law Enforcement and Administration of Justice stated bluntly:

> Existing selection requirements and procedures in the majority of departments, aside from physical requirements, do not screen out the unfit. Hence, it is not surprising that far too many of those charged with protecting life and property and rationally enforcing our laws are not respected by their fellow officers and are incompetent, corrupt, or abusive. One incompetent officer can trigger a riot, permanently damage the reputation of a citizen, or alienate a community against a police department. It is essential, therefore, that the requirements to serve in law enforcement reflect the awesome responsibility facing the personnel that is selected.[42]

For those requirements to be met, selection standards should surely include sound character, emotional stability, and above-average intelligence.

The President's Commission recommended that all police departments use thorough background investigations and personal interviews as an absolute minimum in determining the moral character and the intellectual and emotional fitness of police candidates.[43] Few departments, however, use these techniques systematically.[44] Some conduct no background investigations; others make merely routine checks of local police records, FBI files, and references supplied by the applicant. These are generally extremely limited in scope, and investigators seldom probe deeply enough to uncover information needed for a professional evaluation. That such background investigations should be taken more seriously is apparent from the fact that those departments that do make thorough background checks find that they produce high rates of rejection.

Emotional stability to withstand the stresses of police work must also be a primary requisite of police personnel. Officers must be able to cope rationally with violence, verbal abuse, resentment, and emergencies.[45] The emotionally unfit cannot meet these stresses. For this reason, several police departments conduct psychological and psychiatric examinations, such as the Minnesota Multiphasic Personality Inventory (MMPI) and the Group Rorschach. Departments that administer these tests report that they are useful in weeding out the mentally unfit.[46] However, a recent survey by the International Association of Chiefs of Police reveals that only about 25 percent of all departments administer these psychiatric examinations.

Above-average intelligence is also an essential requirement for effective police performance. Charles Saunders, Jr., in his influential *Upgrading the American Police,* considers an IQ of 110–120, the high-average range for the general population, to be the minimum acceptable score for admission into a police department.[47]

Most departments do not administer IQ tests; however, educational qualifications provide a rough but important index of intelligence, competence, and capacity for professional training. In keeping with this emphasis on educational qualifications, the President's Commission on Law Enforcement and Administration of Justice recommended as an ultimate goal that "all personnel with general enforcement powers have baccalaureate degrees."[48] The subsequent standards of the National Advisory Commission on Criminal Justice Standards and Goals are marked by considerably more urgency and specificity. They would require, as a condition of initial employment, by 1975, the completion of at least two years of college; by 1978, the completion of at least three years of college; and by 1982, the possession of a baccalaureate degree or its equivalent.[49]

This emphasis on educational requirements can be justified on a number of grounds. To begin with, as Charles Saunders notes, "The most compelling argument for higher educational standards for police is the steadily rising educational level of the general population."[50] During the decade of the 1960s, the proportion of high school graduates who enrolled in college rose from 50.1 percent to 59.8 percent, and it is anticipated that it will reach 65 percent by 1979.[51] As educational attainments rise, so do entry standards in other occupations, intensifying competition for the talented manpower that is so desperately needed in law enforcement. After all, many prospective applicants with college education will be unwilling to associate themselves with police educational standards that are presently so low.

There are also other reasons for higher educational standards for police. As more and more police departments employ college graduates, the evidence mounts that college-educated persons are better suited for police work. Thus, Ventura, California, which instituted a four-year college degree requirement in 1966, has found fewer personnel complaints against college-educated police officers, a lower rate of personnel turnover, and an overall reduction of 3 percent in the crime rate.[52] Likewise, a 1972 study of the New York Police Department revealed that men with at least one year of college were very good performers and had fewer citizen complaints than those with no college-level education. Men with college degrees performed even better, had a lower incidence of misconduct, and took less sick leave.[53] The findings of a 1968 Chicago study also disclosed that the highest rated group of tenured officers were those with significantly higher levels of education.[54] Finally, Alexander Smith and his colleagues report in the *Journal of Criminal Law, Criminology, and Police Science* that college-educated police officers are not only significantly less authoritarian than non–college-educated police officers, but also less authoritarian than college graduates in other fields.[55]

Along with the requirements of good moral character, emotional stability, above-average intelligence, and advanced education, minimum standards concerning the physical health, strength, stature, and ability of the potential police officer are also important. These standards should provide some flexibility, however. Any police officer working in the field must possess a modicum of strength, stature, and agility. As the National Advisory Commission appropriately points out, "Cops still have to slug it out in back alleys, chase fleet-footed burglars, and physically disarm dangerous persons."[56] However, many police department requirements are unduly restrictive, and many otherwise exceptional applicants are summarily rejected because of their height, weight, or vision. For this reason, the President's Commission on Law Enforcement and Administration of Justice recommended that police administrators be given the discretion to establish flexible standards that would allow physical requirements to be assessed on an individual basis.[57] The 1973 National Advisory Commission concurred. It proposed the establishment of "minimum standards that incorporate compensating factors such as education, language skills, or experience in excess of that required if such factors can overcome minor deficiencies in physical requirements such as age, height, or weight."[58]

Individuals who can meet all of these selection standards are an exceptional lot, as well they should be. A question then arises, however: How will police departments be able successfully to recruit these men? The answer is simple yet far-reaching: Only through major reforms in their present institutional arrangements and operations. To begin with, police departments should implement the recommendation of the President's Commission on Law Enforcement and Administration of Justice to divide police functions more rationally among their personnel.

> At present a patrolman is equally responsible for the most complex and the most menial of police tasks. The wide range of skills required in performing all of these tasks seems possible of attainment for only limited numbers of personnel. This being so, these tasks should be divided according to the skills required to perform them. For example, instead of having all patrol officers respond to all demands placed upon a department, the most competent officers should devote their time to the police work that requires the greatest degree of ability, education, and judgment.[59]

To bring this about, the President's Commission recommended the establishment of three classes of officers: the police agent, the police officer, and the community service officer (CSO). Tasks would be assigned to these officers on the basis of the skills, the intelligence, and the education necessary to perform these tasks well.

Police agents would receive those tasks that require the highest degree of judgment, intelligence, education, initiative, and understanding of community and human behavior. Thus, they would be assigned such complicated, sensitive, and demanding tasks as serving as uniformed patrol officers in high-crime and high-tension areas, investigating major crimes in a plain-clothes capacity, making difficult arrests, enforcing gambling, vice, and narcotics statutes, and maintaining contact with citizens in the community to ascertain potential signs of strife. The responsibilities of these tasks, along with status and compensation commensurate with these responsibilities, would help to make police work an attractive career for highly qualified individuals.

Police officers would perform those police duties such as enforcing laws and investigating those crimes that can be solved by immediate follow-up investigations or that are most likely to have suspects close to the crime scene. They would also perform routine patrol, render emergency services, and enforce traffic regulations and investigate traffic accidents. Since their duties are less demanding, selection standards for police officers could be lower, in terms of both their intellectual and physical qualifications and their level of completed education. Of course, police officers would be encouraged and assisted to qualify for the position of police agent.[60]

Finally, community service officers could be used to improve police service in high-crime-rate areas: enable police to hire members who can provide a greater understanding of minority-group problems; relieve police agents and police officers of lesser police duties; increase the opportunity for minority-group members to serve in law enforcement; and tap a new reservoir of manpower by helping talented young men who have not yet been able to complete their education to qualify for police work. As such, the position of community service officer would serve a valuable recruitment function presently only inadequately met by traditional cadet programs. The idea behind cadet programs is a good one. It ear-

marks potential recruits in the eighteen-to-twenty-one-year age bracket and retains their interest in law enforcement, as it prepares them for their chosen occupation by subsidizing their academic preparation. In so doing, it cuts down on
the loss of potential recruits who may have found other career opportunities,
despite a primary preference for police work, by the time they reach the normal
age minimum (twenty or twenty-one years of age) required by most police departments for entry.

Most police cadet programs have not worked out in practice. Only a limited
number of persons have been attracted to the program, and the work done by
recruits typically has not justified the expenditures. Moreover, most recruits
simply perform clerical functions and therefore learn little about police work or
the rewards of a police career. The community service officer, however, would
be "an entirely new type of police cadet working on the street under close supervision, and in close cooperation with the police officer and police agent."[61] He
would be an apprentice policeman. Through the extensive educational opportunities and police training they would be provided, and through the assistance
they could give police officers and police agents, "CSO programs could serve as a
valuable recruiting device and a method of upgrading the quality of personnel."[62]

This more rational division of police functions will not by itself be sufficient
to attract better personnel. To begin with, salaries are presently so low in many
departments that they are interpreted by the police as palpable evidence of the
contempt in which they are held by both the public and its elected respresenta-
tives. For successful recruitment, salaries must be competitive. Police departments must meet or exceed the salaries offered by other employers seeking individuals with similar qualifications. In 1972, for the first time in the nation's
history, the median income for an average family of four exceed $10,000. How-
ever, during that same year, 87.5 percent of police officers in cities of over
100,000 population were employed by departments with starting salaries lower
than $10,000. In fact, 24 percent of these officers were employed by depart-
ments with a maximum basic rank salary lower than $10,000.[63] If police de-
partments are serious about improving the quality of their personnel and the
success of their police-community relations programs, they simply must provide
salaries that keep pace. They must also provide working conditions that are com-
parable. Too many precinct stations are antiquated; inadequate in area, lighting,
and ventilation; poorly laid out; unsanitary; and unattractive. Competent officers
cannot easily be attracted or retained if forced to work under such conditions.

Finally, if qualified personnel are to be recruited and retained, police departments must establish precedures that assure that only the best qualified personnel are promoted or advanced to positions of greater authority and responsibility in higher pay grades and ranks. Likewise, they must provide for the
recruitment of personnel through the means of lateral entry.[64] Under existing
police structures, recruitment takes place only at the lowest levels, and recruits
are expected to work their way up the bureaucratic hierarchy. In contrast, within
the private sector and in most public agencies, lateral entry is common. Thus,

major corporations do not start all their employees on the production line and expect their future executives to emerge from among the most efficient of their workers. Rather, they produce management talent by hiring college graduates and starting them out in lower management ranks and by locating and attracting the most capable persons from other agencies and putting them in positions of responsibility commensurate with their proven abilities. Likewise in the military, top-level executives, with rare exceptions, do not rise from the enlisted ranks. Its officer corps comes from the service academies or from civilian colleges and universities. In the police, however, the entire organizational hierarchy is composed of men who are, or at one time were, patrolmen. Police administrators simply "fish ladder" their way up through the ranks without being prepared in anything more than a "by chance" manner for the difficult and demanding roles they are required to play in the complex enterprise that is the hallmark of contemporary police work.[65] The police department directed by such promoted policemen is the sad equivalent of an army commanded by noncommissioned officers.

Preservice and In-Service Training

No recruit, regardless of his individual qualifications, is prepared to perform police work on native ability alone. Even if police departments succeed in attracting men with sound character, emotional stability, high intelligence, and considerable education, they must still provide them with extensive vocational training.[66] Presently, however, most police departments are not providing the training they should. A 1967 study by the International Association of Chiefs of Police revealed that the average policeman receives less than 200 hours of formal training.[67] In striking contrast, physicians receive more than 11,000 hours, lawyers more than 9,000 hours, teachers more than 7,000 hours, embalmers more than 5,000 hours, and barbers more than 4,000.[68] No one would reasonably argue that the responsibility of a barber is twenty times greater than the responsibility of a police officer.

Police training must be upgraded. The National Advisory Commission recommends that every police recruit should successfully complete a minimum of 400 hours of basic police training. In addition to traditional and basic police subjects such as patrol, traffic training, criminal law, evidence, and investigation, this training should include (1) instruction in law, psychology, and sociology, especially as they relate to interpersonal communication, the police role, and the community the police recruit will serve; (2) assigned activities away from the training academy to enable the recruit to gain specific insight into the community, criminal justice system, and local government; and (3) remedial training for individuals who are deficient in their training performance but who demonstrate potential for satisfactory performance.

As with any skilled occupation, the maintenance of effective performance in law enforcement requires continual training.[69] The National Advisory Commission recommends that every police officer up through and including the rank of captain should receive at least forty hours of in-service training a year.[70] This training should be designed to maintain, update, and improve the officer's necessary knowledge and skills. The subject matter of in-service programs will, of course, vary with the specific needs of the individual department and officer, but common subject areas include law and legal changes, field procedures (particularly civil-disorder control), evidence collection, weapons use, law-enforcement innovations, and interpersonal communications.

In addition to in-service vocational training, police departments should adopt formal programs of educational incentives to encourage police officers to achieve college-level education. There are a number of educational incentives police departments can provide for their officers. They include scheduling an officer's work shift to accommodate attendance at a local college; financial assistance to defer the expenses of books, materials, tuition, and other reasonable expenses; and incentive pay for the attainment of specified levels of academic achievement. Table 10.1 lists the minimum educational requirements necessary for entry into, and the educational incentive programs provided by, the police departments of nineteen selected cities. It also indicates the college credit that officers can earn from police training programs.

Effectiveness as Well as Efficiency

For police-community relations to become the prevailing cultural norm in police departments, more than improved personnel through improved selection processes and training programs is required. These officers are likely to make departments more efficient, but it is not enough for departments to be efficient; they must also be effective. They must be as concerned with crime prevention as with crime apprehension; they must be as interested in citizen satisfaction with police service as they are with high productivity as measured by low crime rates or high clearance rates.

Police efficiency is extremely important. Police departments are continuously seeking ways by which to make more efficient use of their personnel. Toward this end, the President's Commission on Law Enforcement and Administration of Justice spelled out seven steps that police departments should take to derive maximum utilization from field personnel.

1. Distribute available field officers according to need for their services. This can be accomplished by either of two methods: proportional distribution, which schedules police patrols at the time which, and at the places where, crimes are most likely to occur; or saturation techniques, which assign additional men to patrol areas that, according to available statistics, require greater-than-usual patrol coverage.
2. Improve supervision of the field force.
3. Improve coordination of effort among field personnel.
4. Improve patrol techniques by critically evaluating the need for foot patrol

TABLE 10.1 Educational incentives for police officers

Police Department	Required entry-level education	College incentive program	Work shifts for college attendance	Promotional education requirement	College credit for police training
Boise, Idaho	Associate degree	$135 monthly, bachelor degree	Shifts rotate with college semesters	Assumed to give some advantage for college	None
Chicago, Illinois	High school	Suggested only	Shift adjustments when necessary	No college required	12 hours credit
Denver, Colorado	High school	Suggested only	On-duty attendance permitted	No college required	None given
Detroit, Michigan	High school	Tuition paid	None provided	Degree for supervisory ranks	6 hours credit
Evansville, Indiana	High school	None	None provided	No college required	None given
Jackson, Mississippi	High school	Incentive pay plan pending	Fixed shifts	No college required	14 hours credit
Joliet, Illinois	High school	5% salary increase, bachelor degree	Special shifts on request	No college required	None given
Long Beach, California	High school	$88 monthly maximum	Transfers, shift changes, twice-daily classes	No college required	9 hours credit
Los Angeles, California	High school	$238 per month maximum (city, $150; state, $88)	Shift adjustments when necessary	No college required	16 hours credit
Louisville, Kentucky	High school	Paid tuition; incentive pay	Arrangements when necessary	No college required	15 hours credit
Memphis, Tennessee	Two years college	$30 per month for bachelor's, $50 for master's degree	None provided	No college required	3 hours credit
Miami, Florida	High school	$130 per month maximum (state funds)	Fixed shifts	Early test eligibility	18 hours credit
New Orleans, Louisiana	High school	Suggested only	Special shifts (early or late)	No college required	25 hours credit
New York, New York	High school	Honorary citations	Special shifts, twice-daily classes, leaves of absence	No college required	16 hours credit
San Francisco, California	High school	None	None provided	No college provided	6 hours credit
Seattle, Washington	High school	Suggested only	Arrangements when necessary	No college provided	Based on police experience
Tallahassee, Florida	High school	$130 per month maximum (state funds)	None provided	No college required	None
Tucson, Arizona	High school	None	None provided	No college required	None
Wilmington, Delaware	Must enter college while in police training	Cash grants; $500 for associate, $600 for bachelor's degree; net $1100 cash maximum grant	On-duty attendance permitted	Degree for promotion recommended; new officers must enter college studies to retain job	21 hours credit

and two-man motor patrols. As a rule, uniformed personnel should be deployed singly unless there are found to be personnel hazards of an extraordinary nature.

5. Deploy investigators singly unless there is an unusual series of cases which requires that two or more men be assigned jointly.
6. Modernize report preparation and duplicating techniques.
7. Relieve police officers of certain routine menial tasks.[71]

More efficient utilization of field personnel is certainly one step toward greater overall police efficiency. There are others as well, including the coordination or consolidation of all police service on a metropolitan-wide or regional basis. As James F. Ahern argues:

One of the most important ways in which a department can increase its efficiency and the quality of its service is to cooperate with other departments and to move towards regionalization. This is the only way in which small and medium-sized departments will be able to gain the resources for proper support services like training, and for effective elimination of complex crime problems.[72]

In addition to seeking ways by which to increase police efficiency, departments have also been striving to develop techniques by which to measure this efficiency. Standard measures involve the crime rate and the clearance rate. These indicators are readily available, but are so general that they tell one little about the efficiency of a particular department. Moreover, since recent studies indicate that the actual rates of victimization in America's major cities run anywhere from two to five times the number of crimes reported to police, crime-rate statistics become virtually meaningless and reliance on them as a measure of police efficiency becomes altogether inappropriate.

Arrest per police department employee or per $1000 expenditure is another readily available measure of police efficiency, measuring in this case police apprehension productivity. Like the clearance rate, however, it tells one nothing about the "quality of arrest." Lack of uniformity in the quality of arrest biases efficiency measurement in favor of a department with a large number of poor-quality arrests. The percent of arrests that lead to conviction would measure the effectiveness of arrests and to an extent the quality of arrests. However, this measure is heavily dependent upon the adjudicative phase of the criminal justice system—that is, the court, the prosecutor's office, and the grand jury. As such, the measure evaluates more the efficiency of the criminal justice system than of the police. The percent of arrests surviving initial review in courts of limited jurisdiction is perhaps a better measure. It focuses on that stage in the judicial process where the police role is predominant. Such a measure, however, requires considerable additional data-gathering before it can be used for the purposes of comparative evaluation. Still another available measure of police service is the population served per police employee or per dollar expenditure, but again, this measure tells one nothing directly about the quality of that service. Average response time for calls of service would indicate how quickly police respond, and thereby provide some measure of police efficiency and perhaps even police quality. Again, however, before this measure can be employed, additional data-gathering is necessary.[73]

While efficiency as measured on some cost-per-unit basis is important, so too is effectiveness as measured by citizen satisfaction. If police-community relations programs are ever to be successful, this concern for effectiveness and citizen satisfaction must also come to dominate the thinking in police departments. High rates of criminal apprehension are not enough; they must be accompanied by high rates of crime prevention, and this requires citizen satisfaction. As George Barbour and Stanley Wolfson declare: "The percent of population expressing satisfaction with police services is a basic objective of a police force and of concern to the community. Public acceptance and cooperation enable the police to be more effective in deterring crime and in apprehending criminals."[74]

Police effectiveness is hard to measure. The National Advisory Commission on Criminal Justice Standards and Goals points out that:

> Perhaps the major problem related to measuring police effectiveness lies in identifying the relationship between police activity and crime prevention or deterrence. It is difficult, if not impossible, to estimate the amount of crime that does not occur because of police prevention. It is obvious, however, that the relative success of a police agency in preventing the occurrence of crime or in deterring criminal behavior will make its crime control more effective. At best, police agencies can only hope to devise optimum measures of deterrence effectiveness by using victimization surveys to obtain better indices of actual criminal occurrences.[75]

Police effectiveness is not only difficult to measure; it is also difficult to know how to achieve. Moreover, since the present rewards systems of most police departments do not recognize efforts in this direction, there are few incentives for individual officers to direct their attention and talents to this end. Nevertheless, more and more research suggests that a number of methods that police departments presently employ to increase efficiency serves to undermine effectiveness as measured by citizen satisfaction. Thus, foot patrols have been abandoned by most departments because they are a highly expensive form of coverage, geographically restrictive in nature, and wasteful of manpower; in short, because they are inefficient. However, they provide an intimate, personal police-citizen contact and police presence that contributes to citizen satisfaction, assists in deterring crime, brings existing but otherwise unreported crime to the attention of the police, and helps in the apprehension of criminals.

The movement toward police coordination and consolidation can also be harmful to improved police effectiveness. Elinor Ostrom and her associates found that citizens of three independent communities bordering on Indianapolis, Indiana, and served by small-scale locally controlled police departments rated the quality of their police service more highly than citizens of adjacent and socioeconomically identical Indianapolis neighborhoods who were served by the central city's large-scale department.[76] Of the citizens of the three independent communities, a higher proportion rated the police as responding very rapidly, rated police-citizen relations as good, and rated the job being done by the police in their neighborhood as good or outstanding, and a lower proportion indicated that they thought crime was increasing than did the citizens of Indianapolis.[77] The difference is probably explained by the higher level of formal and informal communication present between citizens and their police in the three independent communities, a communication likely to be adversely affected by consolidation and regionalism.

A number of police departments have become increasingly aware of the deleterious effects that the preoccupation with efficiency has had on police effectiveness and citizen satisfaction, and are taking steps to ensure that neither criterion is hereafter disregarded. Other departments should do likewise. One step that a number of departments are taking is the introduction of team policing systems. Basically, team policing involves the assignment of police responsibility for a certain area to a team of officers.

> Total team policing can be defined as: 1) combining all line operations of patrol, traffic, and investigation into a single group under common supervision; 2) forming teams with a mixture of generalists and specialists; 3) permanently assigning the teams to geographic areas; and 4) charging the teams with responsibility for all police services within their respective areas.[78]

Most team policing systems have not taken the total approach; rather they have limited operation to a small area within the department or have focused only on reorganizing the patrol function without including in the team investigative personnel or other specialists. Nonetheless, despite these varied and often limited approaches, there are certain structures and goals common to all policing programs. Structurally, they all assemble officers who have previously functioned alone or in two-man teams and assign them shared responsibility for policing a relatively small geographic area. Their common goal is improved crime control through better community relations and more efficient organization of manpower.[79]

Team policing has proved to be successful in a number of cities. One example is Detroit's Beat Commander System, inaugurated with the help of the Ford Foundation in Detroit's Tenth Police Precinct in the spring of 1970. Each beat commander team is permanently assigned a beat, consisting of approximately 15,000 citizens. It is comprised of a beat commander, a sergeant, and twenty-three other men, including three detectives who investigate only cases originating in the beat command area. Consistent with team policing programs elsewhere, its goals are improved police-community understanding, cooperation in crime control, and police efficiency and job satisfaction. According to a preliminary assessment of the beat commander system by the Urban Institute, a federally funded urban "think tank," it is achieving these goals.[80]

New York City's Neighborhood Police Team is similar to the Detroit system, except that patrolmen in New York take greater investigative initiative, as no detectives are directly involved in the program. It, too, has proved to be successful. In addition to greater crime control and better community relations, improved supervision and motivation and increased productivity and efficiency have resulted. It has also contributed to a substantial reduction in response time to calls.[81]

Perhaps the experiences of the New Orleans Urban Squad are the most encouraging of all. The Urban Squad was formed in February 1971 to patrol with specially selected, racially integrated two-man teams the Desire Housing Project. At that time, the area had a notorious reputation as the site of a nationally reported battle with the Black Panthers, along with the dubious distinction of having the highest crime rate in the city. Remarkably, today it has the lowest crime rate in New Orleans. This achievement is entirely attributable to the Urban Squad.[82]

The Urban Squad, consisting of a total of six sergeants, thirty-three patrolmen, and four civilians, is currently assigned to patrol four housing projects containing approximately 40,000 residents. The patrol is handled by "salt-and-pepper" teams of white and black patrolmen. Urban Squad officers usually wear casual civilian dress on duty as a means of establishing rapport with the community. However, they are armed and carry handcuffs and police badges.

The Urban Squad's success can be attributed to careful screening of applicants for the squad, quality investigation, and positive supervision. Every applicant is carefully screened to determine his temperament, awareness of social problems, and overall suitability for the squad. With these high-quality officers, the squad conducts quality investigations aimed at getting to the roots of crime. Thus the squad goes after narcotics pushers, not users. When the squad uncovers the causes of crime, it seeks to provide correctives. For example, one of the housing projects was plagued by a series of daylight burglaries committed by a group of teenagers. When the Urban Squad discovered that the youths were free to roam the neighborhood because of a New Orleans school system rule that suspended students for the day if they were late to school, it persuaded the school board authorities to revoke this rule and allow students to remain in school, despite their tardiness.

In this example, the Urban Squad went far beyond routine police activity, but for the Urban Squad, there are few routine activities. It seeks to gain the goodwill and cooperation of the community in whatever way it can so that it may more fully accomplish its primary function of protecting life and property. The Urban Squad will often seek to solicit better public services for the residents of the project. For example, when the Desire Project was overrun by rats, the Urban Squad requested the Sanitation Department to clear the rats out.

Finally, positive supervision has contributed to the Urban Squad's considerable success. Its supervisors do not stress high arrest rates as the criterion of police excellence. Quite the contrary, they emphasize community support and cooperation, believing this to be the only way to ensure a diminishing crime rate and hence lower arrest rates. To that end, they seek a close working relationship with their patrolmen to ensure that these values remain at the forefront during all field operations.

The Urban Squad has proved to be a remarkable success. Shortly after its personnel began to patrol the Desire Project, residents of another New Orleans housing project asked for the same kind of team policing. They wanted an Urban Squad, "just like the one at Desire." Without question, the residents of other cities would, too.

Police Integrity

Along with more stringent selection standards, better training, and a combined emphasis on effectiveness as well as efficiency, if police-community relations are to be fully institutionalized in police departments, there must also be a renewed commitment to total and unquestioned police integrity. Exacting ethical standards and complete honesty are simply imperative for police. Because they are entrusted with the enforcement of the fundamental rules that guide society's conduct, violation of the law by the police or corrupt failure on their part to enforce it dishonors the law and the authority they represent. Moreover, "[d]ishonesty within a police agency can, almost overnight, destroy respect and trust that has been built up over a period of years by honest local government and police officials."[83] Nothing can destroy public confidence in the police and the process of criminal justice faster than the illegal acts of officers.

While the police have a greater need for complete honesty and integrity than most of the rest of society, the police are also subjected to far greater temptations to succumb to dishonesty and corruption than most. To begin with, the low salaries they receive contribute to police dishonesty both by making it more difficult to recruit and retain men of higher character and by providing a convenient rationale for illegal enrichment. The climate of isolation between the police and the community that exists in some places—especially in slum neighborhoods—also encourages police misconduct.

> In such neighborhoods a policeman tends to see only the bad and to have contact with residents only when they have committed an offense. He may come to feel that the problems he has to deal with are insoluble and that he has no support or cooperation from the community. It is easy for a man who feels himself to be an outcast to react by disregarding standards of ethics and law.[84]

The public also promotes this corruption. One West Coast police officer related to the President's Commission on Law Enforcement and Administration of Justice how a bookie once attempted to influence him:

> These people really work on you. They make it seem so logical—like you are the one that is out of step. This bookie gave me this kind of line: "It's legal at the tracks, isn't it? So why isn't it legal here? It's because of those crooks at the Capitol. They're getting plenty—all drivin' Cads. Look at my

customers, some of the biggest guys in town—they don't want you to close me down. If you do they'll just transfer you. Like that last jerk. Even the Judge, what did he do?; fined me 100 and suspended 50. Hell, he knows Joe Citizen wants me here, so get smart, be one of the boys, be part of the system. It's a way of life in this town and you're not gonna change it. Tell you what I'll do. I won't give you a nickel; just call in a free bet in the first race everyday and you can win or lose, how about it?"[85]

It is not merely the bookie who offers the patrolman a free bet who promotes corruption. It is also the motorist who offers a traffic officer $5 to avoid a traffic ticket and the businessman who presses gifts and gratuities on police in return for indulgences or other favors. These practices may seem relatively harmless, in and of themselves, but taken together, they help to establish an atmosphere wherein it become extremely difficult, if not impossible, to resist more serious bribery.

All of these inducements to police corruption and dishonesty are accompanied by the seemingly limitless opportunities police have to succumb. New York City's Commission to Investigate Alleged Police Corruption, more commonly known as the Knapp Commission after its chairman, Federal District Judge Whitman Knapp, provides in its final report a distressing litany of the areas of police work wherein corruption can take place.[86] Thus, the most common form of police corruption involves the acceptance of bribes in exchange for nonenforcement of laws, particularly those relating to gambling, narcotics, liquor, and prostitution offenses. Corruption in narcotics law enforcement has grown to the point where the Knapp Commission considers it the "most serious problem" facing urban police departments today.[87] Because of this importance, it deserves additional consideration.

Commander Donald F. Cawley of the New York Police Department's Inspections Division testified before the New York State Commission of Investigation:

> Police officers have been involved in activities such as extortion of money and/or narcotics from narcotics violators in order to avoid arrest; they have accepted bribes; they have sold narcotics. They have known of narcotics violations and have failed to take proper enforcement action. They have entered into personal associations with narcotics criminals and in some cases have used narcotics. They have given false testimony in court in order to obtain dismissal of the charges against a defendant.[88]

The Knapp Commission, in the course of its investigation, became familiar with each of these practices as detailed by Commander Cawley, as well as many other corrupt patterns, including:

> keeping money and/or narcotics confiscated at the time of an arrest or a raid
> selling narcotics to addict-informants in exchange for stolen goods
> passing on confiscated drugs to police informants for sale to addicts
> "flaking," or planting narcotics on an arrested person in order to have evidence of a law violation

"padding," or adding to the quantity of narcotics found on an arrested person in order to upgrade an arrest

illegally tapping the telephone of suspects in order to obtain incriminating
  evidence to be used either in making cases against the suspects or in
  blackmailing them

purporting to guarantee freedom from police wire taps for a monthly service
  charge

introducing potential customers to narcotics pushers

revealing the identity of a government informant to narcotics criminals

kidnapping critical witnesses at the time of trial to prevent them from testifying

offering to obtain "hit men" to kill potential witnesses.

In the past, there has been an unwritten rule among policemen that narcotics graft is "dirty" money, not acceptable even to those who take "clean"
money from gamblers, bar owners, and the like. However, with today's more
relaxed attitude toward drugs and the tremendous profits to be realized from drug
traffic, narcotics-related payoffs have become more acceptable, and the problems they pose for fair and respected law enforcement have multiplied.

Gambling, narcotics, liquor, and prostitution are not the only areas in which
police corruption can occur. The Knapp Commission also chronicles incidents
of corrupt nonenforcement of laws regulating construction, traffic, parking, and
the Sabbath, as well as kickbacks from tow-truck companies. Intradepartmental
bribery is also a problem, with individual officers buying temporary or permanent assignments or medical discharges. And the list of areas of police corruption continues: the commission notes instances where police have shaken down
loan sharks, robbed DOAs (dead on arrivals) of their valuables, served as guards
for truck hijackings and auto-theft rings, stolen property from burgled premises,
and sold information. Court-related payoffs are also common: police may be paid
to alter their testimony or may pay others to have their cases called quickly,
thereby sparing them the need to spend hours awaiting for trial.[89]

Of course, most officers do not engage in such police corruption or dishonesty, and, even among those officers who do, a distinction should be made between what the Knapp Commission calls the "grass eaters" and the "meat eaters."
"Grass eaters" are those who may accept gratuities and solicit $5 to $20 payments
from contractors, tow-truck operators, gamblers, and the like, but who do not
aggressively pursue corruption payments. "Meat-eaters," on the other hand, are
those who spend a good deal of their working hours aggressively seeking out
situations that they can exploit for financial gain, including gambling, narcotics,
and other serious offenses that can yield payments of thousands of dollars; they
consist of a much smaller percentage of the force.[90] Nonetheless, to the extent
that police corruption and dishonesty occur at all, they adversely affect all policemen. They undermine the morale of all those thousands of honest policemen who
suffer from popular identification with those involved in corruption and miscon-

duct. Moreover, they make the prospect for improved relations between the police and the community all the more remote.

In order to cut down on the opportunity for police corruption, a number of people propose the decriminalization of all victimless crimes.[91] If this were done, their argument continues, the police could no longer be corrupted through bribery payments for nonenforcement. However, as a cursory glance at the Knapp Commission's report makes painfully apparent, plenty of opportunities for police corruption and misconduct would still exist. Rather than attempt to reduce the opportunities for police corruption, the Knapp Commission proposes instead to reduce the susceptibility to corruption among police officers. It proposes to do so through improved screening and selection methods and standards, through lateral entry to supervisory ranks, through the establishment of a national police academy at the college level, and through improved training for all ranks in dealing with the hazards of corruption and the proper response to them.[92]

The solutions proposed by the Knapp Commission to promote and establish police integrity are fundamentally the same as those proposed earlier in this chapter to encourage and ensure better police-community relations. This is as it should be, for the institutionalization of both police integrity and police-community relations requires the police to internalize new values and concerns—to adopt a new culture. Just as an internal investigation unit is not enough to guarantee police integrity, neither is a police-community relations unit sufficient to ensure harmonious relationships between the police and the community. Only when exacting ethical conduct is reflected in the behavior of every patrolman will the problem surrounding police integrity pass from the scene. And only when the tension of majority rule and minority rights is reduced to the level of the individual patrolman so that his concern is as much with crime prevention as with crime apprehension will the prospects for police-community relations be enhanced. Even then, however, problems will remain. Even when the police, through better selection standards, improved training, a combined emphasis on effectiveness as well as efficiency, and a renewed concern for police integrity, come to internalize the concept of police-community relations, it may still not be accepted by the community. Police-community relations are, after all, two-way communications. Whether the police, having once internalized the concept of police-community relations, will find themselves involved in a monologue or a dialogue will then depend altogether upon the community.

NOTES

1. William R. Carmack, "Communication Within the Community," in *Police and Community Relations: A Source Book,* eds. A. F. Brandstatter and Louis A. Radelet (Beverly Hills, Calif.: Glencoe Press, 1968), p. 441.

2. Ibid.

3. See Kenneth B. Andersen, *Introduction to Communication Theory and Practice* (Menlo Park, Calif.: Cummings, 1972), pp. 8–20; David K. Berlo, *The Process of Communication* (New York: Holt, Rinehart & Winston, 1960), chaps. 1 and 2; and Kathleen M. Galvin and Cassandra L. Book, *Speech/Communication* (Skokie, Ill.: National Textbook Co., 1972), chap. 1, for a sound introduction to the communication process.

4. Andersen, *Introduction to Communication*, p. 10.

5. Ibid., p. 11.

6. See Judy Carter, "Cross Cultural Communications," in *Police Roles in a Changing Community: A Community Relations Planning Guide for Law Enforcement Agencies*, eds. Fred I. Klyman, Floyd B. Hannon, and Max L. Armstrong (Wichita: Wichita State University, Kansas Criminal Justice Community Relations Training Institute, 1973), pp. 181–184.

7. See especially Robert Ardrey, *The Territorial Imperative* (New York: Atheneum, 1966), and Desmond Morris, *The Naked Ape* (New York: McGraw-Hill, 1967), for a fuller discussion of the concept of territoriality in human behavior.

8. See Mark L. Knapp, *Nonverbal Communication in Human Interaction* (New York: Holt, Rinehart & Winston, 1972), pp. 5–8.

9. Ibid., pp. 9–12.

10. Ibid., p. 14.

11. Ibid., pp. 14–15.

12. Robert Rosenthal and Lenore Jacobson, *Pygmalion in the Classroom* (New York: Holt, Rinehart & Winston, 1968), p. 180.

13. Michael Lipsky, "Street-Level Bureaucracy and the Analysis of Urban Reform," *Urban Affairs Quarterly*, 6, no. 4 (June 1971):392.

14. The President's Commission on Law Enforcement and Administration of Justice, *Task Force Report: The Police* (Washington, D.C.: U.S. Government Printing Office, 1967), p. 135.

15. National Advisory Commission on Criminal Justice Standards and Goals, *Report on Courts* (Washington, D.C.: U.S. Government Printing Office, 1973), p. 192.

16. Leonard Downie, Jr., *Justice Denied: The Case for Reform of the Courts* (Baltimore: Penguin, 1972), pp. 36–37.

17. *Illinois v. Allen,* 397 U.S. 337 (1970). See Michael E. Tigar, "Foreword: Waiver of Constitutional Rights: Disquiet in the Citadel," *Harvard Law Review*, 84, no. 1 (November 1970):1–28.

18. Carmack, "Communication Within the Community," p. 442.

19. Ibid., p. 443.

20. Ibid., p. 444.

21. National Advisory Commission on Criminal Justice Standards and Goals, *Report on Police* (Washington, D.C.: U.S. Government Printing Office, 1973), p. 44.

22. Louis A. Radelet, *The Police and the Community* (Beverly Hills, Calif.: Glencoe Press, 1973), p. 469.

23. Patrick V. Murphy, "Police-Press Relations," in *Police and Community Relations: A Source Book*, eds. A. F. Brandstatter and Louis A. Radelet (Beverly Hills, Calif.: Glencoe Press, 1968), p. 437.

24. Ibid.

25. William J. Bopp, ed., *Police-Community Relationships* (Springfield, Ill.: C. C Thomas, 1972), p. 197.

26. Loyal Gould, "Is There a Gap Between Police, Press, and Community?" in *Police Roles in a Changing Community*, eds. Klyman, Hannon, and Armstrong, p. 135.

27. Irving E. Fang, *Television News* (New York: Hastings, 1972), p. 24.

28. David L. Lange, Robert A. Baker, and Sandra J. Ball, *Mass Media and Violence*. A Report to the National Commission on the Causes and Prevention of Violence (Washington, D.C.: U.S. Government Printing Office, 1969), p. 92.

29. See Raymond M. Momboisse, *Community Relations and Riot Prevention* (Springfield, Ill.: C. C Thomas, 1967), pp. 230–235.

30. Radelet, *Police and the Community*, p. 474.

31. Richard L. Topin, "Reporters, Subpoenas, Immunity, and the Court," *Saturday Review*, December 11, 1971, pp. 63–64.

32. 408 U.S. 665 (1972).

33. 366 U.S. 717, 730 (1961).

34. Alfred Friendly and Ronald Goldfarb, *Crime and Publicity* (New York: Twentieth Century Fund, 1967), p. 141.

35. Quoted in Henry J. Abraham, *Freedom and the Court: Civil Rights and Liberties in the United States*, 2nd ed. (New York: Oxford University Press, Inc., 1972), pp. 152–153.

36. See *Estes* v. *Texas*, 381 U.S. 532 (1965), and *Sheppard* v. *Maxwell*, 384 U.S. 333 (1966).

37. *The Right of a Fair Trial and a Free Press* (Chicago: American Bar Association, 1969), p. 26.

38. 15 CrL 3202 (1974).

39. 15 CrL 3210 (1974).

40. 15 CrL 3009 (1974).

41. James F. Ahern, *Police in Trouble: Our Frightening Crisis in Law Enforcement* (New York: Hawthorn, 1972), p. 221.

42. *Task Force Report: The Police*, pp. 125–126.

43. President's Commission on Law Enforcement and Administration of Justice, *The Challenge of Crime in a Free Society* (Washington, D.C.: U.S. Government Printing Office, 1967), p. 110.

44. Charles B. Saunders, Jr., *Upgrading the American Police: Education and Training for Better Law Enforcement* (Washington, D.C.: Brookings, 1970), p. 41.

45. *Task Force Report: The Police*, p. 129.

46. Saunders, *Upgrading the American Police*, p. 42.

47. Ibid., p. 42.

48. *Task Force Report: The Police*, p. 126.

49. *Report on Police*, p. 369.

50. Saunders, *Upgrading the American Police*, p. 89.

51. *Report on Police*, p. 370.

52. Ibid.

53. Ibid., p. 371.

54. Saunders, *Upgrading the American Police*, p. 88.

55. Alexander B. Smith, Bernard Locke, and William F. Walker, "Authoritarianism in College and Non-College Oriented Police," *Journal of Criminal Law, Criminology, and Police Science*, vol. 58 (March 1967); and "Authoritarianism in Police College Students and Non-Police College Students," *Journal of Criminal Law, Criminology, and Police Science*, vol. 59 (September 1968).

56. *Report on Police*, p. 335.

57. *Task Force Report: The Police*, p. 130.

58. *Report on Police*, p. 334.

59. *Task Force Report: The Police*, p. 122.

60. See Alan Edward Bent, *The Politics of Law Enforcement: Conflict and Power in Urban Communities* (Lexington, Mass.: Heath, 1974), pp. 163–164. See also *Task Force Report: The Police*, pp. 122–123.

61. *Task Force Report: The Police*, p. 123.

62. Ibid., p. 131.

63. *Report on Police*, p. 357.

64. See Committee for Economic Development, *Reducing Crime and Assuring Justice* (New York: Committee for Economic Development, 1972), pp. 32–33. See also *Report on Courts*, pp. 437–439, and Bent, *Politics of Law Enforcement*, pp. 158–160.

65. Samuel G. Chapman, "Developing Personnel Leadership," *Police Chief*, vol. 33 (March 1966), p. 24.

66. Saunders, *Upgrading the American Police*, p. 119.

67. Not all police officers are poorly or inadequately trained. Chicago and Los Angeles provide 1,040 hours of training; Dayton, Ohio, 960 hours; Dade County, Florida, 949 hours; and Seattle, 880 hours. See *Report on Police*, p. 393.

68. *Report on Police*, p. 380.

69. Saunders, *Upgrading the American Police*, p. 133.

70. *Report on Police*, p. 404.

71. *Task Force Report: The Police*, pp. 52–56.

72. Ahern, *Police in Trouble*, p. 225. See also *Task Force Report: The Police*, chap. 4, "Coordination and Consolidation of Police Service," pp. 68–119.

73. See George P. Barbour and Stanley M. Wolfson, "Productivity Measurement in Police Crime Control," *Public Management* (April 1973), pp. 16–19. See also *Report on Police*, pp. 151–153.

74. Barbour and Wolfson, *Productivity Measurement*, p. 19.

75. *Report on Police*, pp. 151–152.

76. Elinor Ostrom, Roger B. Parks, and Gordon P. Whitaker, "Do We Really Want to Consoli-

date Urban Police Forces? A Reappraisal of Some Old Assertions," *Public Administration Review*, 33, no. 5 (September/October 1973):423–432.

77. Ibid., p. 425.

78. *Report on Police*, p. 156.

79. Ibid., p. 157.

80. Joseph F. Zimmerman, *The Federated City: Community Control in Large Cities* (New York: St. Martin, 1972), p. 61.

81. *Report on Police*, p. 157. See also Zimmerman, *Federated City*, pp. 61–62.

82. See Bent, *Politics of Law Enforcement*, pp. 57–59.

83. *Task Force Report: The Police*, p. 208.

84. Ibid., p. 212.

85. Ibid., p. 209.

86. *The Knapp Commission Report on Police Corruption* (New York: Braziller, 1972), pp. 71–192.

87. Ibid., p. 91.

88. Ibid.

89. Ibid., pp. 183–192.

90. Ibid., pp. 4, 65

91. See Norval Morris and Gordon Hawkins, *The Honest Politician's Guide to Crime Control* (Chicago: University of Chicago Press, 1970), pp. 108–109.

92. Ibid., pp. 31–33.

BIBLIOGRAPHY

ADAMS, THOMAS F. *Law Enforcement: An Introduction to the Police Role in the Criminal Justice System*, 2d ed. Englewood Cliffs, N.J.: Prentice-Hall, 1973.
———. *Police Patrol: Tactics and Techniques.* Englewood Cliffs, N.J.: Prentice-Hall, 1971.

AHERN, JAMES F. *Police in Trouble: Our Frightening Crisis in Law Enforcement.* New York: Hawthorn, 1972.

AMERICAN BAR ASSOCIATION. *The Rights of Fair Trial and Free Press.* Chicago: American Bar Association, 1969.

ANDERSEN, KENNETH E. *Introduction to Communication Theory and Practice.* Menlo Park, Calif.: Cummings, 1972.

BENT, ALAN EDWARD. *The Politics of Law Enforcement: Conflict and Power in Urban Communities.* Lexington, Mass.: Heath, 1974.

BISH, ROBERT L., and OSTROM, VINCENT. *Understanding Urban Government: Metropolitan Reform Reconsidered.* Washington, D.C.: American Enterprise Institute for Public Policy Research, 1973.

BOPP, WILLIAM J., ed. *Police-Community Relationships.* Springfield, Ill.: C. C Thomas, 1972.

———— and SCHULTZ, DONALD O. *Principles of American Law Enforcement and Criminal Justice.* Springfield, Ill.: C. C Thomas, 1972.

BRANDSTATTER, A. F., and RADELET, LOUIS A., eds. *Police and Community Relations: A Source Book.* Beverly Hills, Calif.: Glencoe Press, 1968.

COMMITTEE FOR ECONOMIC DEVELOPMENT. *Reducing Crime and Assuring Justice.* New York: Committee for Economic Development, 1972.

DOWNIE, LEONARD, JR. *Justice Denied: The Case for Reform of the Courts.* Baltimore: Penguin, 1971.

FOLLEY, VERN L. *American Law Enforcement.* Boston: Holbrook, 1973.

GALVIN, KATHLEEN M., and BOOK, CASSANDRA L. *Speech/Communication.* Skokie, Ill.: National Textbook Co., 1972.

KLYMAN, FRED I.; HANNON, FLOYD B.; and ARMSTRONG, MAX L. *Police Roles in a Changing Community: A Community Relations Planning Guide for Law Enforcement Agencies.* Wichita: Kansas State University, Kansas Criminal Justice Community Relations Training Institute, 1973.

The Knapp Commission Report on Police Corruption. New York: Braziller, 1972.

KNAPP, MARK L. *Non-Verbal Communication in Human Interaction.* New York: Holt, Rinehart & Winston, 1972.

LANGE, DAVID L.; BAKER, ROBERT K.; and BALL, SANDRA J. *Mass Media and Violence: A Staff Report to the National Commission on the Causes and Prevention of Violence.* Washington, D.C.: U.S. Government Printing Office, 1969.

MORRIS, NORVAL, and HAWKINS, GORDON. *The Honest Politician's Guide to Crime Control.* Chicago: University of Chicago Press, 1970.

NATIONAL ADVISORY COMMISSION ON CRIMINAL JUSTICE STANDARDS AND GOALS. *Report on Police.* Washington, D.C.: U.S. Government Printing Office, 1973.

PRESIDENT'S COMMISSION ON LAW ENFORCEMENT AND ADMINISTRATION OF JUSTICE. *The Challenge of Crime in a Free Society.* Washington, D.C.: U.S. Government Printing Office, 1967.

————. *Task Force Report: The Police.* Washington, D.C.: U.S. Government Printing Office, 1967.

SAUNDERS, CHARLES B., JR. *Upgrading the American Police: Education and Training for Better Law Enforcement.* Washington, D.C.: Brookings, 1970.

WESTON, PAUL D., and WELLS, KENNETH M. *Law Enforcement and Criminal Justice: An Introduction.* Pacific Palisades, Calif.: Goodyear, 1972.

ZIMMERMAN, JOSEPH F. *The Federated City: Community Control in Large Cities.* New York: St. Martin, 1972.

11

IIIIIIIIIIIIIIIIIIIIIIIIIIIIIIIIIIIIIIIIIIIIIIIIIIIIIIIIIIIIIIIIIIIIIIIIIIIIIIIIIIIIIIIIIIIIIIIIIIIIIIIIIIIIIIIIIIIIIIIIIIIIIIIIIIIIIIIII

IMPROVING COMMUNITY RELATIONS

The Art of Policing

Police work is an art, not a science. No doubt the scientific method can be used with effectiveness in some aspects of police work. Crimes have been solved in police labs, even if more crimes are solved through the use of police informants. Computer technology is an aid in determining when and where crimes are committed in a city. It allows a department to deploy its manpower in the most useful and economical way. But the essence of police work concerns the daily street-level encounters between policemen and citizens. And the unpredictability of human beings and human behavior does not lend itself to scientifically ordered rules governing each police-citizen encounter. A set of rules, no matter how rationally derived, has little or no applicability in situations where there is a low predictability of outcome. Police work on the street level, with its human interactions in all possible situations, defies standard rules.

This is not to say that police departments, especially those governed by concepts of professionalism, have not attempted to provide policies or rules suggesting applicability in every possible law-enforcement situation. The concept of police professionalism strives for efficiency in police operations. In departments where crime fighting is emphasized, professionalism is seen as a set of attributes that are believed to contribute to this function; for example, courage, respect for superiors, obedience, and reliability.[1] Along with relying on such management techniques as centralized discipline and command, professional departments strive for universality in every police activity. Policemen are admonished to go "by the book" and limit their exercise of street-level discretion.

Idle conversation with residents of the community is discouraged as a waste of time. Instead, policemen should engage in "aggressive patrol" and be on the lookout for suspicious persons, especially in high crime areas. Citizens should be treated civilly, but policemen should never show sympathy or other emotion toward a "mere civilian."[2]

In effect, police professionalism, when it emphasizes mechanistic efficiency in law enforcement, can be so professional that it seeks efficiency without concern for citizen satisfaction, which is another way of saying good community relations. The fundamental weakness of this kind of professionalism is that operating efficiency is gained at the cost of isolating the police from the community, especially in high-crime areas. This is antithetical to the concept that policing in democratic society is facilitated by a cooperative public.

This does not mean that police professionalism is to be avoided. Police departments can and should be professional. However, it must be understood that professionalism is not just a matter of management efficiency; it is also a matter of citizen satisfaction. This requires knowing when rules and guidelines are applicable and when and where they are not. It means recognizing that street-level policing is an art that requires police officers who are possessed of the necessary attributes to handle those conflict management functions that so often play a part in police-citizen encounters. An appreciation for the conflict-management role in policing means that the attributes of professionalism should also include intelligence, common sense, friendliness, courtesy, patience, and a sense of humor.[3]

It bears repeating that policing, insofar as the term applies to police-citizen encounters, is an art. Thus, a good policeman is aware of the environment; he has knowledge of the local culture and social structure. He has a sophisticated, humane understanding of life, of human needs and behavior. He does not represent simply dominant culture values and judge everyone and everything according to these standards. Instead, he strives to understand and deal with highly varied life styles in a nation fast becoming characterized by "a *social, hyper* pluralism of bewildering diversity."[4] Recruiting policemen from particular subcultures and having them police citizens of their own extraction is not a substitute for humanizing police forces. Such a practice would balkanize the American city, for law-enforcement purposes, according to the racial and cultural groups found within it. It would also suggest that the United States does not constitute a nation, with a common government for all the citizens. It would admit that some communities are not governable by the whole; that they require their own laws and their own police. What is needed in contemporary policemen, according to David Bordua, is "trainability and flexibility, the capacity to work in and run small teams with little direct supervision, and the capacity to absorb and expand organizational goals in rapidly changing circumstances."[5] Fundamentally, it is not enough to professionalize police organizations through improvements in training, selection, command and control, planning, manpower allocation, and so on; it is also imperative to professionalize policemen.

Police forces around the country have discovered that management efficiency has done little to help community relations, particularly with minority groups. This was vividly shown in the 1960s, a period marked by riots, civil disorder, violent protest, increasing street crime, a dramatic growth in narcotics addiction, political assassination, and other manifestations of a troubled society. Although the unrest centered in densely populated minority-group neighborhoods and on college campuses, few areas of the nation escaped its effects. In view of these occurrences, the police were forced to consider the subject of public relations or community relations in a new way.[6] The "new way" was an active police attitude toward community relations.

Police departments in the United States have realized that in the interest of law enforcement they must seize the initiative in improving community relations. The term "police-community relations" has meant the development of a relationship with the community that serves as the basis of cooperation for the police and the public in fighting crime and disorder. The need for this kind of relationship has stimulated an active effort to obtain public support for police activities. Thus effective community relations has become a professed major objective in a great number of urban police departments.

Interestingly, the creation of new institutional mechanisms by police bureaucracies designed to secure links with the community has been made necessary by fundamental changes in police operations. In the past, links between the police force and the community were provided by foot patrolmen. Today, large city departments dismiss foot patrol as an inefficient use of personnel resources. But the patrolman walking his beat had an advantage of at least knowing the social and cultural patterns in his patrol area.[7] In the absence of this personal one-to-one relationship that foot patrol afforded, police forces are seeking to find new means of forming relationships with the public, for they have discovered that poor community relations have made the law-enforcement task that much more difficult.

While the public is obviously dependent upon the police for protection and maintenance of order, the police are also dependent upon public cooperation and assistance in performing the functions expected of them. "Even a well-equipped, well-staffed department cannot patrol all parts of a city at all times. The police must also rely upon the citizens for 'eyes and ears' in assisting them to do their jobs better."[8]

Despite the need for effective police-community relations, police departments have provided less than wholehearted support for police-community relations programs. The lack of interest by high police officials and rank-and-file policemen is partially responsible for this, but so is apathy on the part of community leaders. The way in which police-community relations programs are organized and the emphasis which they are given may account for the attitudes toward them. Some departments have community relations units that stress communication—discussions, meetings, the hearing of complaints, the explanation of police actions. Other departments' community relations units stress service and even act as advocates on behalf of certain groups, helping to solve community problems, acting on grievances, and handling complaints. In the first instance, the police try to obtain the cooperation of citizens by explaining themselves to the public. This generally involves the police with middle-class or working-class families and organizations. In the second, police actively represent the community—most likely lower-class and minority-group persons—vis-à-vis the police department and other public agencies in the city. When communication is emphasized, police-community programs are likely to have the support of officers in other units of the department and the public to whom the programs are addressed. When service and advocacy are stressed, however, police-community relations programs are likely to obtain the support of lower-class and minority persons but also to antagonize the other officers of the department and possibly segments of the dominant group.[9] Employing either strategy is likely to result in a zero-sum matrix of support: in each instance, the support gained from one group or groups is likely to be matched by the dissatisfaction of another group or groups. This is a product of majority-minority group competition and tension in American society.

This thought is important and deserves additional stress. A competition, a tension, a balance between the powers of the majority and the rights of the minority is an essential feature of the American political system. Neither must be allowed simply to prevail, and neither must be allowed to feel that the other has prevailed. This becomes a major problem area for police-community relations. Police-community relations programs have been directed primarily toward members of minority groups. However, while this is necessary and altogether appropriate, these programs must never appear simply to submit the wishes of the majority to the interests of the minority.

This point is perhaps best explored through the following analogy. Imagine a body of water and a dock extending into it. Imagine three men standing on the dock: one representing the state, a second representing the minority, and a third representing the majority. Most members of American society, including most of those who have earlier been labeled as establishmentarians and traditionalists, would acknowledge that it would be wrong for the man representing the state to push the man representing the minority into the water. That would be an altogether inappropriate discrimination by the state against the minority. Most Americans would also concede that it would be wrong for the man representing the state not to throw an available life preserver to the man representing the minority if he were thrashing about in the water and unable to keep his head above the surface. Generations of discrimination against America's minorities, especially its black citizens, have made it all but impossible for them to learn to swim in American society and difficult for them even to keep afloat. Most Americans, however, would think that the man representing the state would be going too far if he were to push the man representing the majority into the water to save the floundering man representing the minority. The man representing the majority knows how to swim in American society, but such an action by the state could easily end up sacrificing the majority for the minority.

Many members of American society, especially the establishmentarians and the traditionalists, see increasing instances of what they regard to be such action, in the form, for example, of preferential admissions and hiring policies. For the most part, however, their complaints have fallen on deaf ears. They are likely to view advocacy-oriented police-community relations programs in much the same way. They are likely to dismiss them as just another example of how the members of America's silent majority—its "forgotten men"—are being sacrificed to an unappreciative and undeserving minority. Police-community relations units must be aware of these apprehensions and do everything in their power to minimize these fears. If they proceed apace, with no effort to consult with or accommodate their programs to the wishes of the majority, they are likely to invite a profound negative reaction or backlash. The consequences of such a reaction on police-community relations, and in fact on the overall relationship between the majority and the minority, could be devastating, After all, as John Locke has advised, a society will ultimately "move that way whither the greater force carries it."[10]

Police-community relations programs have also suffered from the way they have been developed and implemented in a community. Bruce Olson states that

> [T]here are at least three conventional ways of starting police-community relations programs. One way is to find a program which seems to be successful in another community and "transplant" it and hope it works. Another is to adopt a program which a local interest group is demanding. A third is to organize a new program around the skills, personal interest, and perhaps political ties of a police official. All three methods, it will be noticed, pay little attention to the actual needs of the community as a whole, although, for better or worse, they do get some kind of program started.[11]

Despite these problems, for greater effectiveness, large police departments should have a central police-community relations unit. This unit should have the responsibility of coordinating the overall community relations program of the department. It should be headed by a director who reports to the highest administrative authority in the department, the chief of police or police commissioner.[12] This would enable the community relations unit to become incorporated in the hierarchical structure of the department and thus be more likely to become acceptable within the department. In addition, as an integral element in the hierarchy responsible to the chain of command, it is more likely to gain administrative support.

Once the decision is made to establish a police-community relations program, it must have the genuine support of the highest administrative authority in the department. If the chief of police or police commissioner is not truly committed to the concept of police-community relations and to the community relations program, and is only expressing support because it is the expedient thing to do, the concept is not likely to take hold within a department. Even with command support of police-community relations, it will require a selling job to the rest of the department to persuade other police officers that community relations are efficacious as well as essential to police work. Without command support, the task is hopeless. When the program has achieved support in the department, if indeed it does, the job of gaining and maintaining public support begins.

Relations between police and the community, and especially between police and minority groups, are complex and multifaceted. The diversity of opinion and culture found in American society presents the most difficult problem for community relations. It involves trying to satisfy often conflicting needs and demands among a variety of groups. Yet each of the groups must be handled separately and satisfied if there is to be a wide acceptance of police by the citizenry.[13] Thus, community relations becomes a task of satisfying divergent interest-group demands.

Realistically, satisfying all segments of society is clearly impossible. The police must walk a careful tightrope between majority and minority demands. This is a tenuous situation, because real success in community relations programming depends on general community support. But the police are faced with the dilemma that by receiving the support of one segment of society, they are likely to lose the support of another. This may cause the police to make a choice: (1) they can select a target group for their community relations programs and continue to service this group even if it alienates other groups, or (2) they can make a judgment about the relative political power of interest groups in a community and direct their efforts at the group with the most power. Unfortunately, both options have serious drawbacks. The first choice is politically unwise; the second one may result in having to ignore the very persons to whom community relations programming is essentially addressed. Consequently, prudence may dictate a balanced approach that alienates as few groups as possible.

Thomas Adams notes that a spirit of democratic application must pervade the atmosphere of community relations.[14] Police officials should be mindful of equal protection and justice for all people in accordance with constitutional and legal guarantees. It is not enough for a department to have a community relations unit that espouses these principles, if the behavior of beat patrolmen is influenced by other considerations. If a community relations program is to be a valid exercise, then a police force cannot have two departments, one made up of men who like to knock heads and another of men providing Band-Aids for the cuts and bruises. Community relations should not be the sole responsibility of a specialized unit within a department; it must be the responsibility of every man and woman on the police force.

Community relations training for police officers should be considered a basic and continuous program. It should be comprehensive in scope and method and made a part of recruit and in-service training. The training of officers, especially new recruits, for community relations is important if this concept is to be internalized within police departments. In addition, ongoing training in the values of community relations should provide a countervailing influence to current socialization influences in police departments.[15] This kind of training could lend itself to the development of a new police culture, one that is community relations oriented.

A community relations program should avail itself of every means to communicate with the public. The press, motion pictures, and television have a dominant influence in shaping public opinion in America. A police-community relations program that skillfully employs the mass media contributes to the furthering of communications. Fundamentally, contact with the media is essential for the improvement of police service. The media have a capability to publicize widely police desires and ideas to the general public. This has the potential to gain a greater public understanding of police needs and problems and with it to engender the kind of public cooperation needed for the functioning of law enforcement. Moreover, the media can assist in improving the quality of police service by pointing out the need for improved personnel practices—including exposures of police malpractices—as well as informing the public about the need for better equipment and adequate manpower.

Police departments must be open and honest with members of the media if they are to expect a positive relationship with them. The media, on their side, must be fair and honest with the police if they expect this valuable news source to remain open. Good press relations have not always existed in police forces, possibly because the police have often failed to appreciate the power of the press. In fact, in a democratic polity, public opinion and reaction are made possible by the enlightenment of a free and outspoken press. Thus, cooperation with the press is essential to good police-community relations, and police departments should wisely maintain good relations with the media to their advantage. The comprehensive nature of police-community relations is summed up by Raymond Momboisse:

> Police-community relations means exactly what the term implies—the relationship between members of the police force and the community as a whole. This includes human, race, public, and press relations. This relationship can be bad, indifferent, or good, depending upon the action, attitude, and demeanor of every member of the force, both individually and collectively.[16]

Even the best police-community relations program, however, has its limitations. As James Q. Wilson teaches, there is a fundamental conflict between the basic police mission of reducing crime and the community relations mission of reducing tensions. The conflict is based in the strategies employed to achieve each respective mission. Crime reduction necessitates such techniques as saturation patrol, close surveillance, and widespread use of field interrogation; those designed to minimize tensions stress an avoidance of "street stops" and excessive surveillance.[17] The tension is inescapable so long as law enforcement and the maintenance of peace and order are primary functions of the police, and so long as there are members of society who break the laws and violate the peace.

Freedom and Responsibility

The laws of society, especially of democratic society, guarantee certain individual freedoms. But they are also concerned with responsibilities so that one man's freedom does not endanger another's right to life, liberty, and the pursuit of happiness. So it is in civilized society that personal freedom must be balanced by personal responsibility. And the police are the designated agents of the political system authorized to enforce laws of freedom and responsibility. Essentially, the police are there to see to it that persons are not free to come and go as they please, nor to do what their whims dictate. In light of this, it is difficult to improve relations between police and persons whose sense of freedom violates the laws of society. This has a bearing on police-ghetto relations. The adversarial role of the police vis-à-vis young lower-class males, especially young, lower-class black males, will likely persist so long as crime and disorder continue to be disproportionately committed by persons in this category.

The best way to reduce police-community tensions is through an emphasis on crime prevention, effectiveness, and citizen satisfaction. The use of team policing systems such as New Orleans' Urban Squad is a step in that direction. However, the solution also requires the mobilization of a wide range of nonpolice agencies and methods. The police are only one component—albeit the most visible component—of a complex and interrelated criminal justice system. If crime prevention and citizen satisfaction are to be improved, the cooperation and commitment of the courts and corrections are simply imperative.

There is a great deal that these other components of the criminal justice system can and should do. To begin with, courts can play a part in crime prevention and deterrence by providing speedier trials and more effective decisions. This is only the beginning, however. Like the police, courts also operate in a context that subjects them to public scrutiny, and hence the courts must also become increasingly concerned with community relations. "The quality of these relations has an important impact upon courts' ability to perform their function effectively."[18]

Favorable court-community relations must be developed if the courts are to contribute to a law-abiding atmosphere. After all, the perceptions the community has of the courts will have a direct effect on the willingness of the members of the community to appear as witnesses, serve as jurors, and support efforts to provide the courts with sufficient resources. Presently, however, there are several areas where court-community relations are deficient. First, court facilities in almost every state are inadequate. They are far too often marked by physical deterioration, design and space inadequacies, and inappropriate locations. For example, in the New York Criminal Court, "former robing rooms for judges are now being used as courtrooms. These rooms have no front entrance. Public space, such as hallways and elevator foyers, has been partitioned off to serve as office space for the prosecutor's office."[19] These inadequate facilities not only impede the effective mechanical operation of the courts, they also effect the courts' relationship with the community. Thus, a study of the New York City civil courts, conducted by the National College of the State Judiciary, found that a court's public image in the community is directly related to its physical facilities.[20]

The lack of information services in the courthouse itself constitutes a second major deficiency in court-community relations. Participation in the criminal justice process is often a confusing and traumatic experience. It leaves the participants, be they witnesses, jurors, or defendants, with an unfavorable impression of the system. They often experience difficulty in locating the courtroom in which their appearance is scheduled. Typically, there is no provision made for answering their basic questions concerning their rights and responsibilities or the meaning of various parts of the process. As a result, they often fail to exercise rights they otherwise would or come away from contact with a criminal case with an erroneous impression of the system. In either case, their respect for the courts is lowered.

This lack of information services also leads to another unfortunate consequence: the public may resort to requesting information from busy and harried court personnel, only to have them respond abruptly or even rudely. This sort of thing is deplorable, not only because of the effect it has on those individuals, but also because of its impact on the general attitude of the community toward the judicial process.

The lack of public information and education concerning the role of the courts in the criminal justice system is a third deficiency. There are many reasons for this. Legal proceedings, with their specialized terminology and procedures, are often difficult for the public to understand. Sources of information are typically informal; as a result, the flow of information is uneven. No one office or position in the criminal process is assigned the responsibility for the dissemination of information, and this surely contributes to the problem. Finally, many courts are reluctant to engage in public relations work, considering it an inappropriate function and not in keeping with the dignity and serenity of the judicial process.

Finally, a fourth deficiency in court-community relations involves the methods and procedures by which witnesses are used. Witnesses are often required to make appearances that serve no function. Moreover, they are often not compensated for the time they spend testifying and traveling, or they are compensated at inadequate rates. For example, in Connecticut and South Carolina, witnesses are reimbursed at a rate of fifty cents per court appearance. In Alabama, they receive seventy-five cents. In Texas, witnesses other than those called as experts receive no compensation at all. In California, witnesses must show need before they are reimbursed. In fact, in only nineteen states are witnesses compensated at the rate of $5 a day or more, and in only six are they paid more than $9.[21] Mileage compensation is equally inadequate, generally ranging from three cents to ten cents a mile with no compensation allowed for travel wholly within a city. Such inadequate compensation cannot help but generate in the witness feelings of contempt for the criminal justice system.

The financial burden that the combination of repeated court appearances and inadequate or nonexistent compensation imposes on witnesses is serious, especially for those of limited economic means who are paid on an hourly or daily basis. Yet it is precisely on these people that the burden has been placed. Most victims of crime, like most defendants, are from the lower to middle income stratum. In a survey of 131 victims of aggravated assault conducted by the President's Commission on Crime in the District of Columbia, fifty-one were laborers, twenty were unemployed, eleven were office workers, nine were house-wives, six were students, five were professionals, and twenty-nine held other jobs.[22] These major deficiencies must be acknowledged and corrected if court-community relations are to be upgraded.

There is also a great deal that corrections can do to promote crime prevention and citizen satisfaction. Most importantly, of course, they can help to reduce the horrendously high rates of recidivism that presently plague the criminal justice system. Community-based correction programs such as probation, parole, and pretrial diversion seem to be the most promising in this respect. However, these programs are fundamentally dependent upon citizen involvement for success.[23] And, as the National Advisory Commission on Criminal Justice Standards and Goals notes: "The correctional system is one of the few public services left today that is characterized by almost total isolation from the public is serves."[24] They have "hidden themselves and their problems behind walls, legal procedures, and fear tactics for many years. To the maximum possible extent citizens have been systematically excluded."[25]

Where correctional agencies have actively sought citizen action and involvement in the rehabilitation process, the results have been most gratifying. The Royal Oaks Probation Program is a case in point. Judge Keith J. Leenhouts sought to reduce crime in Royal Oaks, Michigan, by combining the services of both citizen volunteers and correctional professionals to provide a more intensive probationary supervision of youthful misdemeanants than could be otherwise provided. Since this bellwether program was initiated in 1959, is has met with unequivocal success. When probationers from the Royal Oaks program are compared with probationers from nonvolunteer courts, they have recidivism rates that are drastically lower, averaging anywhere from 7 to 15 percent, as compared with nearly 50 percent of the other group.[26] Of perhaps equal importance, they are far less hostile toward themselves and society. This has been the experience elsewhere as well. In Denver County, Colorado, thirteen probationers with volunteers were compared with thirteen probationers without volunteers. They were tested on a sociometric self-evaluation at the beginning of probation and again one year later. Those probationers with volunteers improved in twelve out of thirteen of these self-evaluated characteristics, while those probationers without volunteers improved in only three of the thirteen and, in fact, retrogressed in ten of the thirteen.[27]

There is, therefore, a great need for citizen involvement in the correctional process. The National Advisory Commission notes that citizens are needed as volunteers to fill such essential positions as:

Advisory council member
Arts and crafts teacher
Home skills teacher
Recreation leader

Coordinator or administrator of programs
Employment counselor
Information officer
Foster parent (group or individual)
Group guidance counselor
Miscellaneous court support services worker
Neighborhood worker
Office worker (clerical, secretarial, etc.)
Volunteer for one-to-one assignment to probationers
Professional skills volunteer
Public relations worker
Community education counselor
Record keeping volunteer
Religious guidance counselor
Tutor, educational aide[28]

Correctional agencies and their personnel must do everything in their power to encourage citizens to participate in these volunteer programs. By so doing, not only will they contribute to the criminal justice system's overall goals of crime prevention, but they will also promote improved citizen understanding of the problems involved in the correctional process and thereby foster more harmonious and effective corrections-community relations.

To date, however, wide-scale citizen involvement in these programs has been limited. The public has not supported the idea of sharing the burden of crime prevention and law enforcement with the criminal justice system. It has tended to think of the "crime problem" as primarily a matter for the police, the most visible and significant component of the criminal justice system. This proclivity has been reinforced in recent years by the great progress that has been made in social conditions in the United States. This has encouraged a feeling that the gains achieved in reducing poverty and unemployment "may both reduce crime rates and ease tension between the police and those persons who, because of their class position, are the natural objects of police suspicion."[29] But there are those who believe that this kind of optimism may be premature. Wilson, for one, feels that in the short run, "progress may well produce even higher crime rates (social change, by offering expectations and weakening traditional controls, always seems to have an unstabilizing effect, at least initially) and even greater mutual resentment between young men and patrolmen."[30]

Moreover, there is also the danger that the rhetoric of social progress will promise far more than is realizable. For example, in the 1960s, rising expectations fed by promises of progress led to widespread disorders when it became apparent to some members of society that their expectations far exceeded their actual gains. In a perverse sort of way, social reformers contributed to the unrest of the previous decade. Their outspoken commitment to power redistribution and equality in resource allocation awakened the aspirations and hopes of the underclass in urban ghettos. And when these objectives were slowly or not at all realized, rage and frustration swept the inner cities of the land.

Even more perverse, however, was the tendency to lay the entire blame for disparate social conditions on the political system and its agencies. Crime and disorder became excusable; it was not the criminal's fault, it was society's. Other determinist rationalizations held constant to this theme: poverty was always a condition beyond the control of the poor; deviancy was not unlawful, it was simply a matter of cultural relativity; if the law did not suit you, break it. Given this kind of encouragement, the underclasses rebelled against their perceived conditions, and, in some circles, their actions were condoned, even championed. Consider, for instance, the time's paradigm of "radical chic": Leonard Bernstein, then conductor of the New York Philharmonic, hosting a fund-raising party for the Black Panthers in his Park Avenue apartment, attended by a large number of the city's socialites who eagerly brought out their checkbooks after hearing a talk by a Panther about how their money was going to be used to buy guns to help put an end to the "capitalist pig establishment." The event was such a success that the presence of Black Panthers at a party was considered a must by every stylish East Side hostess during the social season. This was the atmosphere of the 1960s in which the police were expected to maintain control.

Today, many of the conditions that led to the disorders are still with us. Poverty, unemployment, and social disparity have not been eradicated. Crime, perhaps even more than ever, remains a critical urban problem. There is little to indicate that the central police mission of law enforcement and order maintenance will be changed. Men have not turned into angels, and until they do there will always be need for police.

How, then, will the police be able to deal with the tension between the need to reduce street crime and the need to minimize tensions between themselves and citizens? The role of police-community relations programs is central to this issue. In view of the inescapable realities of the human condition, total reconciliation may be an illusory aspiration. Nonetheless, the community relations effort can serve a twofold purpose: it can ensure that guaranteed freedoms are observed under the law, and it can teach democratic responsibility to persons unfamiliar with this concept. Fundamentally, this means that police-community relations must straddle the imperatives of "law" and "order." On the one hand, police departments must have their personnel behave in a manner consistent with the law; on the other, they must inculcate the value of order—that is, decency and responsibility—in the community. The latter now becomes a police responsibility because of the failings of other social agencies.

This task, however, is made difficult by the attraction of other teachings that emphasize the value of personal freedom without regard to personal responsibility, and in the future it will become increasingly more difficult. Police departments and other public agencies are coming under increasing pressure to accommodate a diversity of life styles. Public institutions, the argument goes, can no longer operate on the assumption of a predominant life style in society and within the organization. The urban environment is experiencing the phenomenon of cultural pluralism, which is affecting the social and political spheres. As a result, organizations such as the police must adapt to these social imperatives. They must provide institutional strategies and structures that are capable of mediating between contending social groups. To do so, they are obligated to adopt a bifurcated approach: "accommodation between diverse groups in the environment and between diverse groups in the organizations themselves."[31] Police-community relations, in the context of this, is the kind of organizational innovation that can provide this mediational response. It is the police's adaptation to cultural tensions within society and the organization.

This argument is rapidly gaining in currency, but it is fatally flawed. Because it is flawed, it will make the efforts of the police to teach responsibility to the community all the more fraught with difficulties. This argument stresses diversity and freedom. However, it is sorely lacking in any concern for continuity or community. The word "community" suggests a commonness, a oneness, a unity, a sharing of standards and values. Community implies that men will live responsible lives consistent with commonly held principles. Police can help teach men to live responsibly according to these shared values and standards. However, a question arises: How well will they be able to teach this responsibility if they are themselves organized around and reflective of the principles of diversity and freedom?

For police-community relations to succeed, freedom must be protected and responsibility must be taught; both values must be emphasized. This requires the active involvement and participation of both the police and the community. After all, police-community relations is more than a one-sided proposition. It requires no less a receptivity on the part of citizens to whom community relations efforts are directed than it does a receptivity and sensitivity on the part of the police toward the community. In essence, community relations is a reciprocating affair. It can succeed only when there is mutual accommodation, understanding, and effort. The police must learn more about the public they serve; but, in turn, the community must learn more about the police. Even more fundamentally, they must learn responsibility as well as freedom. If they are to do so, the contemporary police officer must master yet another role: that of street-level teacher. To succeed as a teacher, he must set the example in the ideals he is empowered to personify. This is what police-community relations is about. But even then, it must be said, successful police-community relations remains problematic. The best teacher in the world will fail if the pupil refuses to learn.

NOTES

1. Louis A. Radelet, *The Police and the Community* (Beverly Hills, Calif: Glencoe Press, 1973), p. 55.

2. Ibid., pp. 69–70.

3. Ibid., p. 55.

4. Orion White, Jr., "Organization and Administration for New Technological and Social Imperatives," in *Public Administration in a Time of Turbulence,* ed. Dwight Waldo (Scranton: Chandler, 1971), p. 165; emphasis in the original.

5. David J. Bordua, "Comments on Police-Community Relations," in *Police-Community Relations,* eds. Paul F. Cromwell, Jr., and George Keefer (St. Paul, Minn.: West, 1973), p. 59.

6. O. W. Wilson and Roy Clinton McLaren, *Police Administration* (New York: McGraw-Hill, 1972), p. 216.

7. Raymond M. Momboisse, *Community Relations and Riot Prevention.* (Springfield, Ill.: C. C Thomas, 1967), p. 92.

8. Raymond M. Hill, III, "The Novato Police Department and Police-Community Relations," in *Police,* January/February 1970, p. 34.

9. James Q. Wilson, "The Police in the Ghetto," in *The Police and the Community,* ed. Robert F. Steadman. A supplementary paper of the Committee for Economic Development. (Baltimore: Johns Hopkins University Press, 1972), p. 76.

10. John Locke, "An Essay Concerning the True Origin, Extent, and End of Civil Government," sec. 96, in *Two Treatises of Government,* ed. Peter Laslett (New York: New American Library, 1965), p. 375.

11. Bruce T. Olson, "Public Preferences for Police-Community Relations Programs," *Police Chief,* September 1972, p. 64.

12. Lee P. Brown, "Establishing a Police-Community Relations Program," *Police,* April 1972, p. 63.

13. Raymond E. Clift, *A Guide to Modern Police Thinking* (Cincinnati: W. H. Anderson, 1956), p. 303.

14. Thomas F. Adams, *Law Enforcement: An Introduction to the Police Role in the Community* (Englewood Cliffs, N.J.: Prentice-Hall, 1968), p. 221.

15. Kenneth N. Fortier, "The Political Culture: Its Effects on Sound Police-Community Relations," *Police Chief,* February 1972, p. 33.

16. Momboisse, *Community Relations,* p. 97.

17. Wilson, "Police in the Ghetto," pp. 89–90.

18. National Advisory Commission on Criminal Justice Standards and Goals, *Report on Courts* (Washington, D.C.: U.S. Government Printing Office, 1973), p. 192.

19. Ibid., p. 193.

20. Ibid.

21. Ibid., p. 194.

22. Ibid., p. 195.

23. National Advisory Commission on Criminal Justice Standards and Goals, *Community Crime Prevention* (Washington, D.C.: U.S. Government Printing Office, 1973), p. 7.

24. National Advisory Commission on Criminal Justice Standards and Goals, *Report on Corrections* (Washington, D.C.: U.S. Government Printing Office, 1973), p. 600.

25. Ibid., pp. 242–243.

26. See Joe Alex Morris, *First Offender: A Volunteer Program for Youth in Trouble with the Law* (New York: Funk & Wagnalls, 1970), pp. 115–130.

27. Law Enforcement Assistance Administration, U.S. Department of Justice, *Volunteers in Law Enforcement Programs* (Washington, D.C.: U.S. Government Printing Office, 1972), p. 25.

28. *Community Crime Prevention*, p. 15.

29. Wilson, "Police in the Ghetto," pp. 89–90.

30. Ibid.

31. White, "Organization and Administration," p. 165.

BIBLIOGRAPHY

ADAMS, THOMAS F. *Law Enforcement: An Introduction to the Police Role in the Community*. Englewood Cliffs, N.J.: Prentice-Hall, 1968.

CLIFT, RAYMOND E. *A Guide to Modern Police Thinking*. Cincinnati: W. H. Anderson, 1956.

CROMWELL, PAUL F., JR., and KEEFER, GEORGE, eds. *Police-Community Relations*. St. Paul, Minn.: West, 1973.

LOCKE, JOHN. *Two Treatises of Government*, ed. Peter Laslett. New York: New American Library, 1965.

MOMBOISSE, RAYMOND M. *Community Relations and Riot Prevention*. Springfield, Ill.: C. C Thomas, 1967.

MORRIS, JOE ALEX. *First Offender: A Volunteer Program for Youth in Trouble with the Law*. New York: Funk & Wagnalls, 1970.

NATIONAL ADVISORY COMMISSION ON CRIMINAL JUSTICE STANDARDS AND GOALS. *Community Crime Prevention*. Washington, D.C.: U.S. Government Printing Office, 1973.

————. *Report on Corrections*. Washington, D.C.: U.S. Government Printing Office, 1973.

————. *Report on Courts*. Washington, D.C.: U.S. Government Printing Office, 1973.

RADELET, LOUIS A. *The Police and the Community*. Beverly Hills, Calif.: Glencoe Press, 1973.

WALDO, DWIGHT, ed. *Public Administration in a Time of Turbulence*. Scranton: Chandler, 1971.

WILSON, O. W., and MCLAREN, ROY CLINTON. *Police Administration*. New York: McGraw-Hill, 1972.

INDEX

75 76 77 78 79 9 8 7 6 5 4 3 2 1